D0403517

THE AMERICAN
INQUISITION

THE AMERICAN INQUISITION

Justice and Injustice in the Cold War

STANLEY I. KUTLER

HILL AND WANG • NEW YORK
A division of Farrar, Straus and Giroux

Library of Congress Cataloging in Publication Data
Kutler, Stanley I.
The American inquisition.
Includes bibliographical references and index.
1. Internal security—United States. 2. Trials (Political crimes and offenses)—United States.
3. Communist trials—United States. 41. Loyalty—security program, 1947–   5. United States
—Politics and government—1945–1953. I. Title.
KF4850.K87   1982   345.73'0231   82–11976
347.305231

For WILLARD HURST
and the memory of
FOSTER RHEA DULLES

ACKNOWLEDGMENTS

ABOUT four years ago, Charles Maier encouraged me to write this book. It would be, he said, easy, fast, and fun. One out of three is not bad. And some of the special joy lies in the opportunity to publicly acknowledge the kindness and support of many friends and some institutions. None of the following persons or agencies, of course, is responsible for this book; but to a considerable extent they are responsible for whatever merits it may have.

Writing contemporary history has its pitfalls, but there is the special pleasure of meeting and learning from some of the players. Beatrice Braude, George Crockett, Caroline and the late Richard Gladstein, Abraham Isserman, Owen Lattimore, John William and Sylvia Powell, and Julian Schuman graciously allowed me access to their lives and materials. All were most open and generous; none interfered with my judgments. In addition, many people who were involved in the particular episodes offered their materials and insights. Wayne Collins, Jr., shared his father's and his own Tokyo Rose case file; Maxwell Mehlman of Arnold and Porter, who represented Beatrice Braude and Owen Lattimore, offered useful advice; Dr. Jerome Kavka shared his long-standing interest in Ezra Pound; Dr. Walter Briehl, whose suit against John Foster Dulles and the Passport Office was joined with Rockwell Kent's, related his experiences; Carole Schwartz, librarian at the Longshoremen's Union in San Francisco, provided invaluable assistance with her meticulous organization of the Bridges case files; Harry Sacher's daughter, Susan Philipson, filled in some details of her father's career; Benjamin Dreyfus and Norman Leonard in San Francisco described their roles in defending Richard Gladstein; and Professor Robert Newman graciously culled out the relevant materials in Owen Lattimore's files.

These essays simply would be incomplete were it not for the authors, supporters, and executors of the Freedom of Information Act. I have a feeling that current (and forthcoming) changes in the administration of the law would have made the writing of this book almost impossible. In my encounters with FOIA administrators, I was ably seconded by Stuart Applebaum, administrative aide to my congressman, Robert Kastenmeier. He cut through much of the proverbial red tape and suggested several fruitful inquiries.

Numerous research assistants, including Kevin Cronin, John Hollitz, and Lynn Malchow, traced and analyzed various materials. Steven Kelly was nearly indispensable, organizing voluminous papers, discovering important data, and continually sharpening (and correcting) my ideas. Susan Bissegger first listened to much of this as a student; since then she has been a devoted, enthusiastic helper, critic, and friend.

Generous support from the Rockefeller Foundation, as well as the University of Wisconsin Foundation, administrators of the E. Gordon Fox Professorship, which I am honored to hold, facilitated my research and provided precious freedom.

Various colleagues and friends graciously offered some important research assistance and criticism, among them John Dower, Susan Grigg, Joel F. Handler, J. Woodford Howard, Leonard Kaplan, Miriam Feingold Stein, Fuller Torrey, and, uniquely, Philip Dibble. I must note the special pleasure in working with Arthur Wang, editor, publisher, and *mensch*. But three extraordinary people worked overtime to make sense of my ideas and prose. Herbert Hill's firsthand, intimate knowledge of many of the events described in this book significantly enlarged my perspective; Richard H. Sewell's command of the language, his sense of style, and just good sense simply have been priceless; and, as always, Willard Hurst's criticism and encouragement enriched and enhanced my efforts.

My deepest gratitude is for my family, as always.

Madison, Wisconsin
February 1982

CONTENTS

ix

PREFACE

Perhaps it is a universal truth that the loss of
liberty at home is to be charged to the provisions
against dangers, real or pretended, from abroad.
—JAMES MADISON, 1776

L IBERTY is a constant, familiar theme in American history, yet the counter-
point of official repression is part of the reality. All governments, including our
own, have limits to their tolerance as they seek to repress or punish foes, real or
imagined. Their action serves to satisfy political needs and reinforce their power.
Consequently, a regime will seek to punish those who directly challenge its
security or symbolically threaten it. The victim may be a person or group directly
challenging the stability of the regime, or he may be simply a scapegoat selected
to serve a higher purpose or explain a failure of the regime.

Political demands invariably distort any equation of law to justice. In the
United States, within the framework of constitutionalism, the government legitimately claims authority to defend itself against direct assaults on its integrity and
security. But when power holders use the system repressively to pursue their own
political and social goals, they risk—and often do—violence to the constitutional
recognition of political diversity and due process.

Political repression reflects the particular attitudes and will of power holders,
often supported by popular consent. Liberty is never absolute. Government may
legitimately restrict individual liberty in pursuit of social stability and for the
protection of some interests essential to humane society. Law and public policy
are designed to restrain the potentially disruptive tendencies of personal passions
and pursuits. Yet law presupposes a system of equal protection and equal restraint,
with a known, readily observed content of policy. Government certainly may
punish citizens who offer aid and comfort to its enemies during wartime; it may
require passports for travel abroad; it may deport aliens who violate their lawful
obligations; it may extract a measure of loyalty (other than partisan) from its
employees; and it may even punish the expressions of opinions designed to raise
a substantive evil the government may prohibit. But when such policies are

implemented in a vindictive, capricious, haphazard, secret, or illegal manner by legislators, administrators, or judges largely to serve the purposes of power holders, then official action becomes repression and violates whatever legitimacy or high purpose may have been intended. There is nothing inevitable about the process. The operation of a legal system is largely a story of rendered choices. The system is not some vast, impersonal *deus ex machina;* instead it operates through discretionary judgments reflecting political and personal needs of power holders. Yet in the American system, the machinery is so vast and complex that it is difficult to manipulate—as long as the process is in open view—and its various parts can negate and check abuses in other parts.

The formula for political repression follows a classic pattern, reflecting a wider state of affairs. Internal stress and external threats, sometimes in combination, heighten tensions in a society and stimulate demands for conformity. Such developments have periodically plagued the United States. The controversy over the Alien and Sedition Acts in the 1790s, the conflicts between slaveholders and advocates of abolition in the pre-Civil War years, the confrontation between capital and labor in the late nineteenth and early twentieth centuries, the Red Scare of the World War I era, and, in our own time, Cold War concerns for loyalty and national security have generated bitter, divisive uses of official power. We can view these experiences optimistically as contributions to the evolution of liberty; yet they also left permanent scars, both for the victims and for society.

The essays in this book depict events largely dictated by the loyalty and security demands of the post-World War II period. The Cold War of the late 1940s and 1950s evoked official repression on an unprecedented scale. The outline of that repression is familiar, as well as its expression through a variety of laws, legislative inquiries, executive orders and policies, judicial opinions, and surveillance. Sometimes the repression operated within the law, sometimes not. The focus usually is on broad, often abstract concerns, such as anti-Communism, loyalty, and security. Our understanding of how and why events and incidents occurred largely involves the consideration of vague trends and movements. Curiously, this often results in a simplistic, overarching interpretation, such as notions of conspiracy or a paranoid style, or, on a more personal level, the cynical opportunism of Senator Joseph McCarthy or the ineptness of President Harry Truman.

While I have acknowledged the traditionally understood causes, incidents, and references in this study of political repression in the Cold War period, I have sought to portray this history through the prism of in-depth case studies. The essays do not necessarily fit the mold of the Great Political Trial, such as those of Socrates, Thomas More, Galileo, Warren Hastings, Alfred Dreyfus, or Stalin's purge trials, where prominent but isolated persons confront the massed resources of the state in often contrived show trials, laden with symbolic and ulterior purposes. My essays seek to illustrate the whole process of legal repression—a process that involves the interaction between law and politics, public and private power alike, and the covert, as well as the overt, operations of power. These essays, although focusing on individuals or particular groups of persons, nevertheless project a symbolic and larger meaning for the incidents.

I am, of course, interested in the individual versus the government. While the actions and motives of the persecuted are relatively easy to discover, the "government" is another matter altogether. We often use the term in a focused way when in fact we are dealing with a vague, inchoate, amorphous apparatus—and an entity that has its own inherent conflicts and contradictions.

In the American process, power is fragmented; the sources of authority are divided, so that power is in a measure both independent and countervailing. The system, while certainly capable of abuse, lacks the terror of a Stalinist scheme where the only check on power was a dictator's self-restraint. In short, there *is* a Rule of Law, whatever its periodic lapses. Certainly the American institutional device of separation of powers is not foolproof. That system requires some continuing conflict and tension to function properly, to check and balance rampaging power. Indeed, Justice Louis Brandeis praised the separation-of-powers design, for he believed it produced "inevitable friction," thereby limiting power "to save the people from autocracy." The most prominent periods of anti-libertarian drives—the late 1790s and the Red Scare periods following each of the two world wars in our century—largely witnessed concerted, coordinated activities by the executive, legislative, and judicial branches, with melancholy, often tragic results.

Governmental functions in the post-World War II period are particularly complicated. The scale of governmental activities in the twentieth century stimulated the rise of the administrative state, with a subsequent growth and sprawl of governmental agencies, with their own drives, biases, and interests. Modern Presidents have expended enormous energies prodding or combating the independent, often self-fulfilling will of what in formal organization are their departments. The fact is that the various agencies—bureaucracies, as we may call them for convenience—are also power holders. The situation is not so new. A century ago, the sociologist William Graham Sumner suggested that "the State" is not just the known and accredited high officials, but rather often is "some obscure clerk, hidden in the recesses of a Government bureau, into whose power the chance has fallen for the moment to pull one of the stops which control the Government function."

My essays offer some attention to the activities of such power holders, who often operated with their own agendas reflecting their parochial interests. Operating backstage, as it were, this supporting cast of relatively anonymous players constituted another important source of authority and sometimes even another check on the powers of others. The process of checking bureaucratic power, however, is not as neat and overt as, for example, a presidential veto or a judicial ruling. Bureaucracies perform their tasks largely hidden from public view. Furthermore, their jurisdictions and duties overlap. The FBI, for example, may be restrained or uninterested in a particular case, but that same case may stimulate determined drives from a Senate subcommittee staff or concerned sections in the State, Defense, or Justice departments. The consequence is delay, as each separate entity demands deference and its own accounting. Thus the government took nearly four years to try Tokyo Rose for treason, despite opposition from numerous agencies. For twenty-five years, the government groped for a means to deport and punish labor leader Harry Bridges, again despite internal opposition and despite its being rebuked in repeated trials, hearings, and investigations. For decades, Presidents and Secretaries of State tolerated the virtual autonomy of the Passport Office.

Some of the persons discussed in these essays are familiar, others less so. Their stories are intrinsically interesting, but more importantly, I am interested in who did what to whom in the name of the law and what happened to the victims. I have sought to explain how the political demands of the state, often coupled with the drives and interests of bureaucracies, distorted the relationship between law and justice. I have tried to locate the role of political interests both in and out of government, and the operation of discretionary power to repress persons and groups regarded as threatening and dangerous. In one case I have considered how such interests and power thwarted the government's legitimate pursuit of retribution.

Such explanations would be impossible without the extraordinarily rich documents of the bureaucracies, made available through the Freedom of Information Act. These documents provide an opportunity to penetrate the façade of official, public pronouncements and enable us to explore the subterranean recesses of governmental authority and comprehend their complexity. Bureaucrats leave footprints, almost compulsively, it seems, and their traces take us to more informed levels of reality, largely unseen when they occurred. However obscure and undramatic, those bureaucratic roles and actions were significant and often decisive. Ideology certainly forms an important component of official behavior and drives; but the whole panorama reveals the diverse range of motives—personal ambitions or pique, institutional aggrandizement or rivalry, and accidental or unintended actions. The victims were real; their antagonists too had substance. The recognition of both heightens our sense of the human tragedies and realities and enlarges our understanding of the sad, troubled times of the American Inquisition.

Crimes against the state! and against the officers of the state! History informs us that more wrong may be done on this subject than on any other whatsoever.

—JAMES WILSON, 1788

THE AMERICAN
INQUISITION

1

FORGING A LEGEND
The Treason of "Tokyo Rose"

> Treason against the United States, shall consist
> only in levying War against them, or in adhering
> to their enemies, giving them Aid and Comfort.
> No Person shall be convicted of Treason unless on
> the Testimony of two Witnesses to the same overt
> Act, or on Confession in open Court.
> —UNITED STATES CONSTITUTION,
> ARTICLE III, SECTION 3

> *Se non è vero è ben trovato.*
> [If it is not true it is very well invented.]
> —GIORDANO BRUNO

i

As victorious American military forces poured into Japan at the close of the war in late August 1945, they were inevitably accompanied by war correspondents eager for hard news, a scoop, or unusual features for a curious home audience. Clark Lee, a correspondent for International News Service, and Harry T. Brundidge, who worked for *Cosmopolitan* magazine, both part of the Hearst publishing empire, were in the first wave of American reporters. Both saw themselves in the swashbuckling Richard Harding Davis journalistic tradition—intrepid, daring, and arrogant—and both wrote in the same racy manner.

The arriving American correspondents had a particular interest in finding the mysterious "Tokyo Rose," an English-speaking woman who had broadcast from Radio Tokyo to Allied troops in the Pacific throughout much of the war. Some imagined her a beautiful Eurasian Mata Hari, others thought of her as an American turncoat. According to Lee, because of the intense curiosity about her, there was a "race" to find her—a race that Lee described in dramatic tones, resembling, as one observer noted, "a movie script, right out of M-G-M and [the part] could have been played by Clark Gable instead of Clark Lee."

Lee and Brundidge won the race and found a twenty-nine-year-old Nisei—"a pleasant-looking girl, but by no stretch of the imagination a siren," as Lee admitted—who identified herself as Iva Ikuko Toguri d'Aquino. Eager for an exclusive story, Lee and Brundidge hid Mrs. d'Aquino and her husband in the Imperial Hotel while they obtained her confession that she was the "one and only Tokyo Rose."

The two reporters claimed they had found Mrs. d'Aquino largely as a result of tips from her Radio Tokyo associates. While she indicated that other women broadcasters could just as well be "Tokyo Rose"—a name never actually used in the broadcasts—she apparently was eager enough to give Lee and Brundidge the exclusive story they wanted. Lee carried a holstered gun during the interview. The reporters gave her a contract promising $2,000 upon publication of her story in *Cosmopolitan*, no insignificant amount in war-ravaged Tokyo in September 1945. The contract stated that Mrs. d'Aquino was "the one and original 'Tokyo Rose' " and that she had no female assistants or substitutes. Ironically, these are the only clearly provable lies d'Aquino told throughout her experience; as early investigations would demonstrate, d'Aquino was only one of several female broadcasters for Radio Tokyo who were collectively labeled "Tokyo Rose" by Americans.

A few days later, however, d'Aquino refused the money and broke the contract, giving her story to *Yank* magazine instead. But Lee and Brundidge persisted with subsequent stories. Ignoring evidence to the contrary, they certified the legend of the "one and only 'Tokyo Rose' "—a legend that, like many, blossomed from silly to dangerously exaggerated. Hollywood embellished the story with an instant movie in 1946, appropriately entitled *Tokyo Rose* and described as "the story of the notorious Japanese Mata Hari," "the slinky female propagandist."[1]

Lee lost interest in the matter after 1947. Harry Brundidge, however, spent the next four years trying to give credence to that legend. Ultimately, he succeeded, with the aid of some fellow journalists, intimidated bureaucrats, and his own suborning of perjury. In September 1949, four years after the end of the war, Mrs. d'Aquino was convicted on one count of treason and sentenced to ten years in prison and a $10,000 fine.

ii

Several days after the news stories of "Tokyo Rose" first appeared, General MacArthur's Tokyo headquarters announced the impending arrest of American citizens suspected of treasonous activity during the war. First questioned on September 6, 1945, d'Aquino was arrested on October 16, five weeks after the warrant had been issued. She was held in Yokohama Prison until November 16, then transferred to Sugamo, near Tokyo, where she would remain for nearly a year. Until Christmas 1945, she was held incommunicado; after that, she was granted twenty-minute monthly visits from her husband. D'Aquino and an American military policeman later testified that prison authorities treated her as a Japanese national rather than as an American. Most important, she was denied counsel and forbidden to write or receive letters.[2]

From October until April 1946, army intelligence officers steadily interrogated d'Aquino. They readily elicited from her the basic story of her involvement, a story which never materially changed and which regularly received substantial corroboration. The basic facts concerned her trip to Japan in 1941; her entrapment by the war; her need for work; her recruitment for broadcasting; her admission of broadcasting essentially as a "disc jockey"; the names of other English-speaking women who had appeared on her program and on others; her denial that there was any such person as "Tokyo Rose"; her outspoken criticism of the war and support for the United States; her assistance to Allied prisoners of war; and her steadfast determination to retain her American citizenship despite numerous opportunities to renounce it and assume either Japanese nationality or the Portuguese citizenship available to her as a result of her marriage in April 1945 to Felipe J. d'Aquino, a Japanese-Portuguese.[3]

The suspect identified two Allied prisoners of war who had recruited her for broadcasting: Major Charles Hughes Cousens, an Australian captured at Singapore, and Major Wallace E. (Ted) Ince, an American captured at Corregidor. Both had prior radio experience. In affidavits given to army investigators in late 1945 and early 1946, both men testified that the Japanese Army had ordered them to work for Radio Tokyo, that the Army had ultimate command at the station, that they had enlisted d'Aquino, and that they had done so largely to undermine the effectiveness of the propaganda broadcasts. Cousens specifically stated that d'Aquino's lack of broadcasting knowledge, "combined with her masculine style and deep aggressive voice, . . . preclude[d] any possibility of her creating the homesick feeling which the Japanese Army were trying to foster." He denied that certain incriminating statements allegedly broadcast by "Tokyo Rose" had ever been given on d'Aquino's program. Both Cousens and Ince testified that d'Aquino had smuggled gifts of food and supplies to Allied prisoners, along with truthful war news which she learned from her husband, who was employed at the Domei News Agency. Most important in explaining why d'Aquino was singled out from all the women employed as broadcasters was that Cousens and Ince kept d'Aquino alone informed of their tactics and real purposes, thus arousing the antagonism of other broadcasters.[4]

D'Aquino's statements were meticulously pursued and checked by army investigators. In comparing her own affidavit of December 21, 1945, with the final report from the legal section of army counterintelligence, no significant factual discrepancies appear. The army investigators even turned up additional evidence that buttressed d'Aquino's claims. The Foreign Broadcast Intelligence Service of the Federal Communications Commission had monitored Radio Tokyo broadcasts and had determined that despite widespread rumors and legends of a charming entertainer named "Tokyo Rose" who allegedly had access to top secret American military plans, the name had been coined by Allied servicemen and referred to at least two other women on different programs.

The final army recommendations were somewhat ambiguous, yet it is clear the army investigators and legal advisers no longer desired jurisdiction. They found that the facts of the case fell within the definition of treason. Then followed a seemingly rare bureaucratic judgment: another agency (obviously, the Justice Department) would have to determine "whether the case should, as distinguished from could, be prosecuted." Finally, the report concluded that since there were no offenses against military law, there was no need for the military to hold d'Aquino. The matter now belonged to civilian authorities. A recommendation followed a few days later that d'Aquino be released immediately.[5] Nevertheless, she remained in Sugamo for six more months as the civilian bureaucracy insisted on an independent accounting.

The Criminal Division of the Justice Department had requested investigative assistance from the Federal Bureau of Investigation as early as October 1945. At that time, FBI Director J. Edgar Hoover assigned Special Agent Frederick G. Tillman, then in Manila, to the case.[6] Tillman appeared in Japan in early 1946 and secured access to the army materials. From this initial trip to Tokyo, through d'Aquino's trial in 1949, Tillman had an intimate connection with the case as investigator, witness, and, most important, as confidant and participant in Justice Department machinations. In April 1946, d'Aquino gave Tillman a remarkably restrained twelve-page statement of her experiences. In it she matter-of-factly related her activities, offering neither an emotional confession of collaboration nor a heated defense of mitigating circumstances. This document, together with the army materials, provided a thorough record; subsequent investigators could not hide behind a veil of ignorance.

After relating the basic facts of her life to 1941, d'Aquino described for Tillman the events surrounding her departure to Japan. Shortly after she graduated from UCLA in June 1941, her family received word that her mother's sister in Tokyo was ill and wanted Mrs. Toguri to visit her. Because of her own mother's illness, her lack of employment, and her desire to see Japan, the family dispatched the oldest daughter as its representative. Her father made the travel arrangements, but, d'Aquino told Tillman, he was unable to get a passport. She made no effort herself to obtain one. (Earlier, she stated to army interrogators that passports were not being issued at the time.) She did, however, secure a notarized identification certification.

On July 1, 1941, identifying herself as Ikuko Toguri, she signed a statement entitled "Certificate of Identification to Facilitate Return to the United States of America." Prepared by a Japanese-American notary public in Los Angeles, the certificate actually was a deposition to the effect that Miss Toguri was born in Los Angeles on the Fourth of July 1916, that she currently resided in the city, that she was temporarily leaving the United States on July 5 on the *Arabia Maru* for Yokohama, that she intended to visit her aunt, who was eagerly awaiting her, and that she expected to return to the United States in six months. The document was duly signed by Miss Toguri, witnessed and sealed by the notary public, and embellished with Toguri's photograph and fingerprints.[7]

This simple, typewritten document produced in 1941 played havoc with the young woman's fate. To subsequent generations of Americans who have traveled abroad, such a piece of paper hardly would be useful; it strains credulity to imagine trying either to leave or to re-enter the United States today under such circumstances. But when Miss Toguri left the country, the certificate had substantial validity. Proof of citizenship was adequate for either leaving or re-entering at that time. A 1918 law provided that citizens would need passports only in time of war or national emergency.

President Franklin D. Roosevelt's proclamation of November 14, 1941—several months after Miss Toguri's departure—declared the existence of a national emergency and specifically required the use of passports. Even if Miss Toguri had managed to get passage on a ship back to the United States between November 14 and the bombing of Pearl Harbor on December 7, there is no assurance she would have been admitted without a passport. And with nothing more than this paper in hand, Toguri's fate, as of December 7, 1941, was for all purposes sealed for the duration of the war. Ostensibly a lifeline for a return to the United States, the certificate served instead as a hawser mooring her to Japan.

Toguri sailed from San Pedro on July 5 and arrived in Yokohama on July 24. She immediately went to her uncle's house in Tokyo, where she lived until June 1942. She paid room and board and attended the Japanese Language and Culture School. In 1946, she claimed that she had moved out in 1942 because transportation to the school had become too expensive; at her trial in 1949, she contended that her family's fears of the secret police *(kempeitai)* prompted the move.

In August 1941, Toguri received her residence permit from the Japanese police. The police instructed her to register at the American Consulate office in the Embassy. On the advice of a consular official, she submitted an application for a passport, along with her birth certificate. Again according to her 1946 recollection, she made periodic inquiries about the passport until October 1941. She then was told that the office would contact her when it received word from Washington.

It is not clear whether she understood the implications of the President's November 14 proclamation of national emergency as it related to her request for a passport. In any event, she "became nervous" upon hearing of the Hull-Nomura-Kurusu negotiations, which reflected the worsening relations between the United States and Japan. She called her father in Los Angeles in late November, but he could not estimate the danger for his daughter, advising her simply to see as much of Japan as she could. Mr. Toguri soon afterward perceived the danger, for on December 1 he cabled her to hurry home. She learned a ship was scheduled to depart for the United States on December 2 and immediately went to the American Embassy for clearance. She as yet had no passport and her birth certificate had been sent to Washington. The Embassy gave her a letter confirming the passport application and the accompanying birth certificate. For some reason, she was told to secure a certificate of attendance from the language school in order to facilitate re-entry into the United States. But when her uncle attempted to buy a ship ticket, he was told his niece would also need clearance from the Finance Ministry in order to take back any money she had brought with her. That would take three or four days—alas, no clearance, no ticket, no passage. Less than a week later, the war came and with it her bureaucratic tangles increased by geometric bounds.

On December 8, Toguri appeared at the U.S. Embassy to advise the vice-consul that she did not possess dual citizenship and offered a certified copy of her family's census register *(koseki)* recognizing her renunciation of Japanese nationality. In the meantime, she worked as a part-time typist at the language school. In March 1942, she appeared at the Swiss Legation and filed an application for evacuation. But she was advised that without a passport it was unlikely she could be sent home on the first repatriation ship. By April, the American consul in Yokohama determined that Toguri's citizenship had not been proven. In September, the Swiss notified her of a second ship, which would provide free passage to Goa, Portuguese India; passage from there to New York, however, required $425, payable in advance or upon arrival.

By then, her own resources were exhausted, her uncle had no funds, and there was no way to contact her parents, who (unknown to her) already had been evacuated from Los Angeles to Arizona. She owned real estate worth $2,000 in Los Angeles, but apparently was uncertain whether her holdings could be converted to cash. Her uncle, she claimed, advised her to stay. Accordingly, on September 2, she filed a document with the Swiss Legation stating: "I hereby wish to express my wish to remain in Japan for the present and hereby withdraw my request to be evacuated." The following day, she notified the Japanese police of her decision. According to her recollections, the police notified her she would be treated as a foreigner and she would have to renew her residence permit every six months. She could not travel outside Tokyo without a permit. The police, she recalled in 1946, visited her at irregular intervals, suggesting she become a Japanese citizen. She was never jailed or otherwise ill-treated by the police.

In July 1942, Toguri had begun to work at the Domei News Agency, monitoring English-language broadcasts. She did not take verbatim notes but prepared rough translations of the news broadcasts into Japanese. Apparently her training at the language school had been successful. She worked approximately five hours per day for 130 yen per month. In 1946, she stated she did "not know what disposition was made of my work and I made no comment upon, or evaluation of, the news I received." She worked in this capacity until December 1943.

In August 1943, Toguri also found typing work in the business office of Radio Tokyo through contacts with Ed Kuroishi, a Nisei employed there. For this she received 100 yen per month. Her duties largely consisted of typing material for broadcast—"lists of Allied army personnel and the like"—in English.

In November 1943, George Nakamoto Mitsushio asked Toguri to audition for a planned "entertainment" program to be directed at Allied soldiers in the South Pacific. Mitsushio in turn introduced her to Cousens and Ince, the two Allied prisoners of war already working at the station. Cousens described the projected program as consisting of messages from prisoners of war, recorded music, and news from the American home front as well as the war areas. He added that he would write the scripts and she would only introduce the music. In 1946, she claimed that Cousens chose her because he thought she had "a Yankee personality." After the voice test, Cousens said he would coach her in using a "cheerful voice."

In d'Aquino's 1946 statement to Tillman, she said she accepted the position because she thought she could entertain American soldiers. She offered no hint of coercion or duress: "No pressure was put on me by Cousens, Ince, the Japanese or other persons to force me to take the job and no one threatened me if I did not take the job or continue in it." But during her trial in 1949, she and other defense witnesses testified that the Mitsushio and Cousens "requests" were tantamount to army orders which one did not disobey. She also emphasized that she feared the Army and the secret police and therefore continued to broadcast. Her work began in mid-November 1943. Cousens wrote her scripts until he became ill in the summer of 1944; after that, she wrote scripts herself, using Cousens' "as a guide," with the help of Norman Reyes, a captured Philippine Army officer and fellow broadcaster.

The program, entitled *Zero Hour*, was broadcast daily except Sunday from 6 to 7:15 P.M. The typical format consisted of prisoner-of-war messages, music, with an introduction by Toguri, American home front news read by Reyes or Ince, more music, general news (usually read by Ince), music again, and news commentaries by Charles Yoshii, a Nisei. Around Christmas 1943, Cousens and Ince told Toguri that they were trying to make the program "as entertaining as possible rather than propaganda." They also said that there was "a double meaning" in their scripts and that they wanted to increase the POW messages.

Although they never directly or positively told her that they were trying to defeat the Japanese purpose of the program, Toguri stated that Cousens instructed her to laugh when she referred to herself as "the enemy."

Throughout the broadcasts, Toguri was introduced as "Orphan Ann," "Orphan Annie," "your favorite enemy, Ann," and "your favorite playmate and enemy, Ann." The names had evolved from "Ann," which was shorthand for "Announcer" on the scripts. She identified for Tillman at least three other women who appeared on *Zero Hour:* Ruth Hayakawa, whom Toguri believed had once lived in Los Angeles; Mary Ishii, a Eurasian; and Miyeko Furuya, the wife of fellow employee Ken Oki. She admitted she never heard them broadcast and was not familiar with their scripts.

Life in wartime Japan apparently continued to be difficult. Toguri received no extra salary for broadcasting, although every employee at the station received a raise to 150 yen per month in August 1944 because of increased living costs. In December 1943, however, she resigned her Domei job to work for Danish minister Lars Tillitse as a clerk-typist. She worked for him until his departure in July 1945 and received 150 yen per month, 20 more than she had earned with Domei. At the same time, however, she further complicated her life by marrying Felipe Jairus d'Aquino, a Japanese-Portuguese with Portuguese citizenship. He was a fellow employee at Radio Tokyo and also was a linotype operator. They were married in the Jesuit church at Sofia University in Tokyo and registered the marriage with the Portuguese consul. She later claimed that the consul gave her a certificate of Portuguese citizenship, but she continued to register as an American citizen with Japanese officials.

Toguri admitted to Tillman that her program was "propaganda" designed to lower Allied troop morale and at the same time demonstrate Japanese "sportsmanship" by sending POW messages. But her purpose in participating, she insisted, "was to give the program a double meaning and thus reduce its effectiveness as a propaganda medium." Cousens' remarks about his ulterior aims "almost convinced" her she was defeating the Japanese purposes. Finally, she acknowledged "all of their programs were propaganda," but maintained she did not believe she was working "against the interests of the United States."[8] The conclusion of the statement to Tillman in 1946 is heavily laden with contradiction and ambiguity, perhaps reflecting the tension between an interrogator anxious to establish some culpability and a suspect equally determined to proclaim her innocence.

The statement was forwarded to Washington, where Theron L. Caudle, Assistant Attorney General, Criminal Division, turned it over to Nathan T. Elliff, Chief of the Internal Security Section, for evaluation and recommendation. Elliff's response in May 1946 was prompt and straightforward: prosecution for treason was "not warranted."

Elliff's memorandum at the outset attempted to destroy an important misconception. There was no "Tokyo Rose," he said. The name never had been used by Radio Tokyo or by the Japanese; rather it had been popularized by American soldiers and applied to numerous female radio announcers. Subsequent investigations and depositions identified ten English-speaking broadcasters at Radio Tokyo. There were still others in Manila, Batavia, and Bangkok. Elliff then reviewed the peculiar circumstances that trapped Toguri in Japan after Pearl Harbor and her need for work. Although she admitted broadcasting, Elliff found decisive the unanimous claims of Cousens, Ince, and Reyes that she merely introduced music. In his report to Caudle, Elliff attached script portions that substantiated her simple role. Yet while he recommended that the case be dropped, he suggested the Department await a report from James Carter, the United States Attorney in Los Angeles, who had been considering the case for possible prosecution.[9]

Throughout the summer of 1946, Caudle prodded Carter for an opinion on prosecution. By then, the War Department was pressing Justice as to the future of the occupation army's now famous prisoner. Carter finally replied on September 13 with a terse telegram: further investigations, he said, had "not strengthen[ed]" the case; he and his staff found the "evidence inadequate"; and finally, he recommended that a "treason prosecution be declined."[10]

Following Carter's recommendation, Elliff wrote again to Caudle on September 19, agreeing with the California prosecutor. He suggested the matter be closed and the suspect released. Although Elliff acknowledged that d'Aquino was an American citizen who had broadcast for the enemy, presumptive treason was not for him: "[T]he available scripts and the testimony of the majority of witnesses indicate that her broadcasts were innocuous, and could not be considered giving aid and comfort to the enemy." Elliff qualified his conclusion by adding that additional information might offer cause for reconsideration. Perhaps that was a typical bureaucratic hedge; in this case, however, it was prophetic. Caudle agreed with Elliff's report and asked him to prepare a separate memorandum for the Attorney General regarding the findings and recommended "that the file be closed."[11]

Caudle relayed the formal recommendation to Attorney General Tom Clark on September 24, 1946. He reiterated the decision as he had given it to Elliff, but in two brief paragraphs he summed up the evidence—the weight of which never substantially changed during the next two years, although interpretations did. Caudle acknowledged that Radio Tokyo never identified a "Tokyo Rose"; there were several women announcers who were indiscriminately given that name by American troops and publications; Toguri's activity "consisted of nothing more than the announcing of musical selections"; her co-workers corroborated this, except for "two or three" who vaguely charged she had made anti-United

States remarks; recording cylinders, scripts, and transcripts from monitoring by the Federal Communications Commission substantiated her basic role as a disc jockey; and finally, there apparently was a so-called "Tokyo Rose" broadcast which occurred prior to Toguri's employment by the station in November 1943. On September 26, Clark's assistant acknowledged receipt of Caudle's report and replied: "We agree with you—no prosecution unless more facts."[12]

FBI Director Hoover had to have his separate accounting. Three days after Caudle sent his "final" report to Clark, the Director queried him "for an opinion as to prosecution." By the time Caudle replied, the War Department had been advised on October 1 to release Mrs. d'Aquino. But bureaucratic delays held up the release order from the War Department to MacArthur's headquarters and thence to the Sugamo Prison commander until October 23. Two days later, d'Aquino left Sugamo a free woman—for the moment, at least. The decision not to prosecute was played in a low key, for the Department allowed Carter to make the announcement in Los Angeles and it merited little more than a brief news item in the New York *Times* on October 22.[13]

Upon her release from Sugamo, d'Aquino chose not to return immediately to the United States. The reasons are not clear; her subsequent pregnancy or simple fear of a hostile reception may have played a part in her remaining in Japan. But one year later, she initiated efforts to come home. Possibly a desire to have her child on American soil motivated her. In any event, her passport application in the fall of 1947 triggered renewed—and hostile—interest in her case. On October 20, 1947, the State Department's Passport Office queried the Justice Department regarding d'Aquino's status. Four days later, T. Vincent Quinn, Assistant Attorney General, offered no objection to the passport request, replying that the evidence in the case had not warranted prosecution. The case truly seemed closed. But word leaked that "Tokyo Rose" had applied for a passport, bringing a swift and predictable response from veterans' organizations and West Coast nativist groups, which vociferously criticized issuing a passport and called instead for prosecution.

In November, the national commander of the American Legion demanded a treason trial. A few months later, the Legion's Executive Committee joined in protesting "the lack of interest [in] and the lenient treatment of war criminals." The chairman of the Native Sons of the Golden West Americanism Committee protested to the Justice Department, J. Edgar Hoover, and Secretary of State George C. Marshall, among others. His letter noted that "from all reports, her mission was one of lower and vicious propaganda," and indicated that the decision to drop the case had not been accompanied by adequate public explanation.[14] Had the Justice Department made clear the insufficiency of evidence and, more important, the flimsiness of the charges, such protests might have been easily countered. But it was a day for timid, placating men in the bureaucratic chain of command—with a touch of pettiness and an inner drive to "get" the infamous "Tokyo Rose." And these men marshaled the awesome investigative and legal resources of the state against an isolated individual.

iii

Within a month, the correspondent representing the Native Sons of the Golden West was informed that d'Aquino would not receive a passport and that the investigation had been renewed. Attorney General Clark's assistant, Peyton Ford, replied more elaborately to a congressman who had passed on a local Legion protest. Ford pointed out that at least six women had been identified on the Radio Tokyo broadcasts, but only d'Aquino was American-born. He also noted she had been investigated for two years, but the Department had not been able to secure the required two witnesses to obtain a treason conviction. Ford had all flanks secured: the investigation would continue and the government would present the case to a grand jury as soon as the "necessary proof" could be obtained. In other words, legal technicalities, it now appeared, rather than the lack of evidence and the insignificance of d'Aquino's action, prevented prosecution. In the meantime, Ford noted that she was not permitted to return to the United States.[15]

In a press release dated December 3, 1947, the Justice Department indicated its sensitivity to the growing pressures. The Department mentioned its ongoing investigation, although admitting difficulty in securing evidence to fulfill the two-witness requirement for a treason conviction. The Department promised, however, that if such evidence could be obtained, the case would be promptly presented to a grand jury. Accordingly, there was an appeal for persons who witnessed the broadcasts or recognized her voice to inform the FBI. The release also noted that d'Aquino's passport would not be issued while the investigation progressed.[16]

Patriotic and veterans' protests continued to bombard Justice. But apparently Attorney General Clark was decisively impressed by Walter Winchell's public demands for action. Winchell was then at the peak of his power and influence. Millions read his daily column and heard his weekly radio newscasts. His appeal was seductive. Blending petty gossip of celebrities with a political primitivism befitting the style of a neighborhood saloon, Winchell both satiated mass desires and articulated a simple grass-roots political mood of cynicism toward government. Before and during World War II, Winchell had been militantly anti-Fascist and pro-Roosevelt. In the postwar period, he swung sharply to the right, probably not much differently from many ordinary citizens, the mainstay of his constituency. A monumental dose of vanity and a swollen ego animated Winchell. His column periodically chided or maligned public officials who failed to respond to his concerns.

Sometime after d'Aquino applied for her passport in late 1947, Winchell lent his public support to the opposition. His sentiments were clear, and presented in his usual breathless, staccato style: "If 'Tokyo Rose' can be brought to this country and tried for treason, o.k.," Winchell said in one column. "Otherwise," he continued, "we're for letting her stay forever in Japan. And if protests are what the State Department needs to keep her there, here's one. We imagine plenty more will be forthcoming."[17] Winchell had the wrong agency in mind, but the message was clear: if enough protests could be made, such pressure would keep d'Aquino in Japan or force the Justice Department to prosecute.

A protest Winchell received from a Gold Star mother in early 1948 regarding Mrs. d'Aquino's request for a passport probably sparked his involvement. He broadcast the complaint and called for Tom Clark to consider the matter carefully. Shortly thereafter Winchell heard from Harry Brundidge or possibly from J. Edgar Hoover (who had been in touch with Brundidge) that the former war correspondent had d'Aquino's "confession" which she had given to him and Lee. The so-called confession, however, consisted of Brundidge's story as developed from Lee's notes and, being unsigned, had little validity. According to Brundidge, Winchell and other columnists were giving him "a kicking around" and a "shaming"—which only made Brundidge more determined to bring d'Aquino to trial.[18]

Attorney General Clark was sensitive enough to Winchell's activity so that he dispatched Los Angeles U.S. Attorney James Carter as an emissary to explain the facts to the columnist. Carter, of course, was no stranger in the matter, for he had recommended in 1946 that prosecution be dropped. He still held that opinion in late 1947, but his report to Clark of his visit to Winchell (at the Twentieth Century–Fox film studios) has the obsequious flavor of the temporal lord's retainer trying to appease the spiritual lord of the realm.

Notwithstanding the flat, narrative, diplomatic tones of Carter's report, there is a surrealistic quality to the account. Carter claimed that he had persistently adhered to the facts of the case during the interview with Winchell to demonstrate the weaknesses of a potential prosecution. Winchell, on the other hand, recited a litany of comments and charges as to the Department's duties and obligations, berated Clark for his personal ingratitude toward him, and complained about the failure to mention his role in rekindling interest in the case. In particular, Winchell expressed considerable pique that he "had been plugging" Clark for Attorney General and "had never received proper thanks." Moreover, he was annoyed because Clark had not told him in advance he would receive the appointment—in other words, Winchell missed a "scoop," a not inconsiderable event in his special world. While Winchell admitted that many of d'Aquino's broadcasts were innocuous, he characteristically added that ex-soldiers who offered to testify that she was a morale builder "were probably communists."

Carter told Winchell he would not recommend prosecution unless there was a stronger case. He believed a trial probably would result in a dismissal or an acquittal; Winchell agreed that that would be worse than no prosecution. As a final observation, Carter perceptively reported to Clark that "somewhere along the line [Winchell's] pride had been injured," and that a personal conversation between Clark and Winchell "could go a long way towards smoothing things out." There is no record of a reply from Clark to Carter, but there is a notation that Clark's assistant, Peyton Ford, sent a personal and confidential note to the U.S. Attorney.[19]

It is tempting to dismiss Carter's report and its subject as trivial—save for the fact that such pressure and his fear of public opprobrium apparently drove Clark enthusiastically to endorse subordinate recommendations for prosecution and explicitly countermand every opinion that recommended dropping the case. Winchell was indeed a powerful figure and could not be treated lightly. Furthermore, harassing the Attorney General and the Department to "do something about" people such as d'Aquino fit into a larger movement decrying the Administration's "softness" and lack of concern toward disloyalty. In short, Clark's and the Administration's need for political credibility made prosecution expedient—and d'Aquino expendable.

Carter's efforts to appease Winchell ultimately proved fruitless; so too did a similar attempt by one of Winchell's friends, Hollywood producer and nightclub operator Earl Carroll. Carroll visited Tokyo in March 1948 to prepare a film and he arranged to meet d'Aquino at Army G-2 headquarters. He asked if she had ever called herself "Tokyo Rose"; predictably, she denied the canard. Carroll thereupon informed her that Major General Charles A. Willoughby, MacArthur's intelligence chief, had told him d'Aquino's "trial days are over," and as far as the Army was concerned, her case was closed. Carroll had very close contact with Willoughby. After Carroll returned home in April, Willoughby sent him a summary of the dossier on d'Aquino, adding that he could attribute the information to an "authoritative" source. Carroll was aware of Winchell's role in delaying her passport clearance and he told d'Aquino to write a personal letter to the columnist explaining her case. Clearly persuaded that the affair was frivolous, Carroll mailed the letter upon his return, but he received an enigmatic reply. "I have confidence in the administration of United States justice," Winchell wrote, "and she will get a fair trial in court." At the end of May, Carroll passed the message to d'Aquino, adding that he was bewildered by Winchell's response in the light of Willoughby's statements. He promised to meet personally with Winchell in New York in June. On his way East to attend the Republican National Convention, however, Carroll was killed in a plane crash.[20]

Concurrently with Carter's "negotiations" with Winchell, the Criminal Division of the Justice Department was preparing its first report of the reopened investigation. Caudle's successor as head of the Criminal Division, T. Vincent Quinn, forwarded the first lengthy evaluation to Peyton Ford, Attorney General Clark's assistant, on December 12, 1947. The document apparently was written by John B. Hogan, an attorney in the Department's Internal Security Section. It summarized the suspect's background and her activities in Tokyo, offered excerpts from her broadcasts, and mentioned possible witnesses against her in both Japan and the United States.

Despite firm evidence on the matter, d'Aquino's recruitment by Radio Tokyo was handled a bit gingerly. The Criminal Division's account merely stated that Cousens and Ince wanted "a person who would not report them to the Japanese authorities and who would not give the program a sentimental touch." The memorandum then summarizes the basic evidence—which consisted simply of portions of two scripts and had "Ann" of Radio Tokyo introducing music to Allied soldiers. The script dialogue blended idle chatter with the introductions. The following samples as reconstructed from the scripts (with no intended ellipses) are characteristic:

FEB. 22 . . .
ANN: Hello there, Enemies . . . how's tricks? This is Ann of Radio Tokyo, and we're just going to begin our regular programme of music . . . news and the zero hours for our Friends . . . I mean, our enemies! . . . in Australia and the South Pacific . . . so be on your guard, and mind the children don't hear! . . . All set? . . . O.K. here's the first blow at your morale . . . the Boston Pops . . . playing "Strike Up the Band" . . .

"STRIKE UP THE BAND"

ANN: How's that for a start? . . . well now listen to me make a subtle attack on the Orphans of the South Pacific. Sergeant! . . . where the Hell's that Orphan Choir? . . . Oh, there you are Boys . . . this is Ann here! . . . How about singing for me to-night? . . . You won't alright you thankless wretches, I'll entertain myself and you go play with the mosquitoes . . . thank you, Mr. Payne . . . when you're ready!
. . .

"THE LOVE PARADE"

APRIL 10 . . .
ANN: Thank you kindly, Sir, she said! . . . Hello, Everybody, this is Ann of Radio Tokyo with our regular programme for our Friends in Australia and the South Pacific. It's pretty music to-night, guaranteed to take your mind off the present, and to make you forget for a while "the haunting spectres of the might-have-been"! . . . Yes, it's a quotation, but I don't know who wrote it, do You? . . . think it over, and here's some music to oil the wheels . . . Franz Lehar's "Gipsy Love" . . . played as a Concert Waltz by Nat Shilkret and Orch. . . .

"GIPSY LOVE" . . . CONCERT WALTZ . . .

ANN: Like that? well be good and we'll have an even better one directly, in the meanwhile here's an old smoothy for you, Savino's "A Study in Blue" . . . please to listening!

"A STUDY IN BLUE" . . .

ANN: This is Radio Tokyo's special programme for listeners in Australia and my Boneheads in the South Pacific. Right now I'm lulling their senses before I creep up and annihilate them with my nail file . . . but don't tell anybody! . . . Now here's the next waltz I promised you, Victor Herbert's "Kiss Me Again" . . . you heard me!
. . .

"KISS ME AGAIN" . . .

The other evidence cited was d'Aquino's own admission to army investigators and to FBI agent Tillman that she had worked as a broadcaster. The memorandum also noted the contract between d'Aquino and the Hearst reporters, Lee and Brundidge, for an exclusive *Cosmopolitan* story detailing her activities as the "one and original 'Tokyo Rose.' " The memorandum, however, acknowledged she never used that name and that there were other female broadcasters on Radio Tokyo. Yet citation of the contract implied that it constituted reliable evidence of an admission of culpability. The fact that the contract was a nullity was ignored.

In conclusion, the memorandum stated that d'Aquino's voluntary acceptance of the position, her performance, and the Japanese military's approval of her duties demonstrated an adherence to the enemy. Moreover, her broadcasting lent "aid and comfort" to the enemy to such an extent that prosecution could be considered. The basic recommendation, though, was that the various witnesses, largely employees and technicians at Radio Tokyo, be extensively "reinterviewed" to determine whether they heard or saw d'Aquino on the programs. Until this was accomplished, the case should not go to the grand jury; moreover, if the new interviews still failed to produce the necessary witnesses, "then further consideration can be given as to the advisability of presenting the case to a grand jury on the evidence that is or may become available in the United States." Ford did not receive this document until January 9, 1948; apparently, the holiday season delayed things. In any event, Ford told Quinn to proceed with the case: "All available lead[s] should, of course, be developed," he wrote. "There are several loose ends."[21]

The "loose ends" had to be tied up in Japan. Accordingly, on March 11, 1948, Clark directed that John Hogan go to Tokyo—with none other than Harry T. Brundidge, the reporter with a long-standing stake in the story. From his initial meeting with d'Aquino in September 1945, through the trial in 1949, Brundidge had a consuming passion for her case. But from his trip in March 1948 until the trial began, he is particularly omnipresent. Not only did he travel in 1948 to Japan, but he returned a year later to join FBI agent Tillman in further investigations. Significantly, the Japanese he talked to believed he was serving in an official capacity—an impression he rather easily conveyed. Whatever his role, Brundidge carried on his peculiar crusade. And whether it was the crusade of a true-believing zealot or an ambitious man is perhaps immaterial. No doubt his personal involvement brought him close to Attorney General Clark, and the articles he published after he returned with Hogan pushed the decision ever closer to prosecution. The oddity that someone so familiar with the case never appeared at the trial as a witness is probably owing to the government's reluctance to call a man who had by all indications suborned perjury.

On March 20, 1948, Brundidge located a prospective witness, Hiromi Yagi, who was employed by the Japan Travel Bureau. Yagi not only was willing to cooperate himself but offered to find other witnesses. For example, Hogan later claimed that Yagi located Leslie Nakashima, a wartime Domei News Agency employee who, in 1948, worked for the Associated Press in Tokyo. Nakashima, however, denied ever having seen or heard d'Aquino broadcast and stuck to his story despite "prolonged cross-examination" by both Hogan and Brundidge; the latter were convinced he was lying. Nakashima certainly was no surprise find for Brundidge, for Nakashima had brought d'Aquino to Brundidge and Lee in 1945 and witnessed the abortive contract.

Another witness, identifying himself only as a friend of Yagi's, offered exactly the same story as Yagi but refused to testify publicly. Brundidge and Yagi surmised that the friend feared reprisals from American military authorities. Yagi promised to "persuade" his friend to testify in the future. Because of Brundidge's own fear—imaginary or real—of the army people, he insisted that prospective witnesses be interviewed in his hotel room rather than in the office provided by the Civilian Intelligence Service of Army G-2. Actually, General Willoughby's aide in G-2 provided Hogan with complete cooperation, including access to army files, although he denied Brundidge the same privilege. Hogan accommodated his friend's fears by refusing to identify any of the witnesses to army authorities.[22] Nine months later, the murkiness surrounding Yagi and his friend would be clarified.

Hogan and Brundidge interviewed d'Aquino on March 26, 1948. Confronted with Clark Lee's notes of their September 1945 interview, she stated that they were accurate to the best of her recollection, but she refused to sign a statement that a story Brundidge had prepared from those notes was correct, insisting there were too many discrepancies. She also was unable to identify any scripts shown to her as ones she actually had broadcast. Most important, she refused to admit she had broadcast any intelligence material.

Hogan and Brundidge returned to Washington on April 5 and met with the Attorney General the next day. Clark asked for another review of the case and a recommendation. In his initial summary dated April 12, 1948, Hogan attached Yagi's statement to his own. Hogan did not prepare his recommendations until April 20. But the April 12 memorandum, sent to Quinn, had been promptly forwarded to Ford and the Attorney General. Clark did not need a final report, for on the covering page, carrying a date of April 15, Clark noted: "Let[']s expedite consideration. Do we need anything further?"[23]

Clark's views only reinforced Hogan's apparent eagerness. Hogan's April 20 recommendations flatly asserted that the case should be brought to a grand jury. His only concession was that the name "Tokyo Rose" never should be mentioned in the indictment or in court. He acknowledged the name had not been used by Radio Tokyo and added there was "an unanswered question" as to whether any other English-speaking women had broadcast. For a man who supposedly had carefully reviewed the files, he had conveniently overlooked some well-established evidence.

In his recommendations, Hogan dealt primarily with the problem of locating two witnesses to the overt act of broadcasting, and the extent of harm of d'Aquino's broadcasts. He admitted that thus far he had not turned up two people who had observed or heard a single broadcast. At this time, Hogan had hopes that two people in Los Angeles who knew the suspect before the war, and who recognized her voice on radio, might have heard the same broadcasts. He remained optimistic, moreover, that Yagi and his still unnamed friend would come forth. But Hogan's primary resources were Cousens, Ince, and Reyes, d'Aquino's former colleagues at Radio Tokyo. Obviously, he was not interested in any mitigating or ulterior purposes that the Allied prisoners may have had; he simply wanted their testimony that d'Aquino had broadcast for the enemy. Hogan suggested the number of Japanese witnesses be kept to a minimum to avoid appearances that the prosecution had resulted from Japanese nationals' hatred of Nisei.

As to the extent of harm, Hogan believed a sufficient number of ex-soldiers would testify that their morale had been lowered by the broadcasts. If not, he still insisted the government was duty-bound to prosecute on the theory "that the mere act of broadcasting popular music and indulging in friendly chatter was intended to and did hold an audience to which the Japanese could broadcast propaganda." This conduct, he concluded, met the constitutional requirement of "aid and comfort" to the enemy. He nowhere intimated that d'Aquino herself had broadcast propaganda. Finally, Hogan recommended that she be brought to the United States in custody. Fearful that anti-Japanese sentiment would preclude a fair trial on the West Coast, he suggested she be flown to the United States via the Atlantic and be tried somewhere in the East.

Once again, there was prompt action on Hogan's recommendation. Quinn sent it to Clark on April 26, concurring in the suggestion that "Tokyo Rose" (ignoring Hogan's injunction against that label) be brought to the East Coast. Two days later, Clark pushed a bit more, telling Quinn: "OK—let[']s expedite prosecution if it[']s decided to proceed." In turn, Quinn told one of the lawyers in his division to "go to work."[24]

While Hogan was writing his reports, Brundidge had his own enterprise going. Upon his return he prepared a ten-part series on "Tokyo Rose" for the *Nashville Tennessean*, which was published in May. The articles largely covered familiar material, but from Brundidge's point of view, d'Aquino's recent remarks in her interview with Brundidge and Hogan amounted to a "confession." One article was headlined "Rose Confesses Tokyo Broadcasts." The stories even had an advance "tip" in Drew Pearson's radio broadcast of April 22 in which he explicitly congratulated Tom Clark and Silliman Evans, publisher of the *Tennessean*, for "co-operating in getting this confession."

Understandably, Brundidge's Justice Department friends were not pleased. Indeed, they betrayed a tentativeness and uncertainty quite contrary to their internal recommendations. Quinn sent Clark a copy of the Pearson story and complained that Brundidge was "going pretty far" in his stories. "We don't think too much of this case from a prosecution standpoint, but Harry is blowing it up," he added. Clark responded it might be best to "ask him to hold up as it would affect [the] case." Soon afterward, J. Edgar Hoover sent Clark and Quinn some copies of the Brundidge stories. Clearly, Brundidge's articles unnerved high officials in the Department. Peyton Ford wanted "to put a clamp on Harry's mouth or typewriter." But he feared calling him, knowing Brundidge would "blow it into a story thus giving him a leg . . . of credence." Clark personally wrote to publisher Evans, an old political friend: "The boys are a little disturbed on the Tokyo Rose matter. It would be helpful if no publicity came out until after action was taken. I will let you know."[25]

Despite the Department's apparent wholehearted endorsement of Hogan's recommendations, nagging doubts persisted. Stacked against earlier investigations and recommendations, Hogan's letter indeed seemed a flimsy reed. MacArthur's army investigators, no strangers to political decision making under the color of law, already had favored d'Aquino's release; Carter's supplemental investigation in behalf of the Justice Department had concurred in that finding; and the Department's higher bureaucracy had supported both decisions. Therefore, following Hogan's memorandum, Quinn turned to the Department's resident treason expert in May 1948 for further examination of the files and of Hogan's recommendation.

Tom DeWolfe had been with the Justice Department since 1927. Most important, he had spent considerable time as a member of the prosecution team in the treason trials of Douglas Chandler and Robert H. Best, both of whom were convicted for giving aid and comfort to the German government by broadcasting propaganda during World War II.

DeWolfe prepared a six-page report for Raymond P. Whearty, Quinn's top assistant in the Criminal Division. It is best read as a master's dissection of a novice's (i.e., Hogan's) brief. DeWolfe's report was about evenly divided between a statement of known facts and his own recommendations. After reciting the familiar story of d'Aquino's trip to Japan in 1941 and her entrapment by the war, DeWolfe concentrated on her work as a broadcaster from November 1943 until the end of the war. He noted that three prisoners of war—the Australian, Cousens; the American, Ince; and the Filipino, Reyes—had charge of the radio program *Zero Hour*. All had been extensively investigated but their respective governments declined to press treason charges. Because of their connection to the program and to d'Aquino, the three obviously had to be prime witnesses. But for whose benefit? DeWolfe knew they would testify that d'Aquino's broadcasts had neither military nor propaganda value. They also would testify that d'Aquino personally endeavored to see that no propagandistic material was inserted in the scripts. Furthermore, these witnesses would testify that they selected her because she was the only available woman, "white or Nisei, whom they could trust not to betray" their efforts to sabotage any Japanese attempts to use the program for propaganda. (This, incidentally, offers some light on the animosity between d'Aquino and the other Nisei at Radio Tokyo, who rather eagerly identified her as "Tokyo Rose" and later testified against her at the trial.) DeWolfe also knew Cousens and Ince would claim they selected her because her "masculine voice" would not have much appeal to Allied soldiers.

DeWolfe's argument was simple: with such prosecution witnesses, the defense would need none. The three Allied military men, he noted, lived in a rather luxurious Japanese hotel during the war and had no more police surveillance than the suspect. "They," DeWolfe argued, "seem just as much, or more, culpable than she"—and they, including the American, Ince, had been cleared. Finally, as to the overt acts of broadcasting certain scripts, DeWolfe gave the evidence short shrift: "The scripts of her programs seem totally innocuous and might be said to have little, if any, entertainment value." Incidentally, DeWolfe contemptuously dismissed the "evidence" garnered by correspondents Lee and Brundidge. Their methods, including the offer of a cash payment for the statement, made the "confession" of doubtful propriety and a jury would have to determine whether it was given of her own free will.

DeWolfe's summary of the case was damning enough; his recommendations were equally forthright: *"There is insufficient evidence to make out a prima facie case."* He grounded his opinion on the Supreme Court's recent decision in *Cramer* v. *United States* (1945), ruling that to support a treason conviction the accused's overt acts must be accompanied by an *intention* to betray. DeWolfe flatly stated that the government could not make a case able to withstand a motion for an instructed verdict for acquittal. In the Boston trials of Chandler and Best, which he handled, DeWolfe contended that the evidence had clearly demonstrated the pro-German and anti-American sentiments of the defendants, that their scripts clearly intended to dissuade Americans from supporting the war, and that they broadcast military information on Allied losses clearly to impede the American war effort by lowering morale. By comparison, the evidence in the present case, DeWolfe declared, "is the direct antithesis of that available and utilized in the Boston litigation." DeWolfe clearly favored dropping the case; if, however, the Department found it expedient to present the evidence to a grand jury, then he recommended that a no true bill be sought.

On May 27, Quinn passed DeWolfe's memo directly to Tom Clark. The covering form had a notation to the effect that the Attorney General might want to see the document "in the light of all the publicity" recently given to the case. Clark's response was almost immediate and must have jolted the bureaucracy from Quinn to Whearty to DeWolfe: "Prosecute it vigorously," Clark instructed.[26]

In retrospect, Clark's decision was more than a veto of DeWolfe's memorandum. In fact, it reaffirmed a policy decision he had been fostering over the previous five months. From that standpoint, it seems clear that DeWolfe had been brought in as a final reviewer, probably anticipating his role as prosecutor. His negative recommendation, however, was too late to stop the policy-making process that ground inexorably toward a decision to prosecute.

Yet Quinn (and apparently Clark) needed something to counter DeWolfe's devastating critique. Quinn suggested they turn to Frederick Bernays Wiener, then in the Solicitor General's office, who, like DeWolfe, had participated in the German broadcasting cases. In July 1948, Wiener recommended that d'Aquino and Major Ince both should be presented to a grand jury. He admitted that the cases were "not open and shut . . . in which conviction can be guaranteed," but their innocence was not clear enough to justify dropping their cases.

Wiener believed d'Aquino's defense would be based on lack of treasonable intent, while Ince's would rely on duress. He considered both insubstantial. The subjects had assisted an enemy in furthering war aims, the very essence of "aid and comfort." However innocuous their broadcasts appeared, the fact that the Japanese continued to use them indicated the enemy believed they advanced their war aims. Wiener said that the Cramer case's question of treasonous intent could be met instead by the objective standard of the defendant's awareness of the "natural and probable consequences" of their actions. Significantly, Wiener adamantly insisted that if d'Aquino were tried, then Ince certainly had to be prosecuted, for he had recruited her. Wiener was disinclined to believe Ince had acted under duress (his claim, Wiener said, had "a fishy smell"), but that was a jury's task to determine. Long-standing treason precedents recognized mitigating circumstances if the subject acted "for fear of Death, and while the Party is under Actual Force."

Wiener believed there had been too much concern to prove individual, "segmented" overt acts. The fact that d'Aquino admittedly had broadcast for a continuous period was sufficient, a fact corroborated by ample witnesses. He suggested adding a few Japanese policy officials as witnesses to establish the importance of the radio program in the larger scheme of psychological warfare. Wiener believed the Supreme Court's most recent decision in the *Haupt* v. *United States* treason case unduly created an "artificiality" to the segmented theory. "That sort of thing is legal hocus-pocus at its sorriest," he stated, "and I am far from convinced that even the law of treason requires it."

Finally, Wiener thought it best not to return d'Aquino to the East Coast. He feared the "possibly adverse overtones" resulting from the government's discretionary power to pick the venue. A trial in a district distant from her home and family would create hardships that would reflect unfavorably on the government.[27]

Wiener's summary ended the intradepartmental hesitation. Less than three weeks later, Quinn received a letter from the United States District Attorney in the Canal Zone describing how he would proceed in presenting the d'Aquino case to the grand jury. That man was none other than Tom DeWolfe. Although he had disagreed with Wiener's views in discussions with John Hogan and Raymond Whearty, DeWolfe ultimately succumbed to superior directives—and, of course, served them. DeWolfe found himself in the classic bureaucratic crunch. As late as January 1949—after he had secured an indictment—he informed the Department that he had reviewed all treason investigations in the San Francisco area. These included Ince, d'Aquino, Mark Streeter, and John Provoo —all suspected of collaboration with the Japanese. He evaluated the importance of their actions and the comparative evidence in the following order: (1) Provoo, (2) Streeter, (3) Toguri (d'Aquino), (4) Ince. Of the four, however, only d'Aquino ever was successfully prosecuted and convicted.[28] But DeWolfe continued to follow higher orders.

With the decision made to seek an indictment, the way was at last open for d'Aquino's return—not, of course, in a manner of her choosing. In contrast to the casual treatment of her departure and attempts to return in 1941, the United States government now displayed extraordinary concern about her voyage home in 1948.

D'Aquino returned to the United States for indictment on the transport ship *General H. F. Hodges*, accompanied by army guards. She departed Yokohama on September 15, 1948, and arrived in San Francisco on the twenty-fifth, where a familiar figure, FBI Special Agent Tillman, took custody of the prisoner. The route home was curious, almost leisurely, like a lengthy holiday cruise. From Japan, the ship sailed to Naha, Okinawa, and then to Inchon, Korea, to discharge troops. From there, the *Hodges* sailed directly to California, avoiding an obvious resting or refueling stop in Hawaii. This was a carefully calculated maneuver to avoid berthing in any American port prior to landing in California. For if the ship had stopped in Hawaii, or any other American territory in the Pacific, jurisdiction would lie in the local federal court. Attorney General Clark had made his preference clear to Justice Department subordinates: the case was to be presented in the Northern District of California. Apparently, the Attorney General found no comfort or security in risking the probability of a polyglot jury in Hawaii, or anywhere off the mainland. Given then current Nisei enthusiasm to demonstrate their loyalty, Clark's fears may have been misplaced.[29]

The Justice Department's dealings with Secretary of the Army Kenneth Royall to arrange passage home offer a model for bureaucratic dissembling. Assistant Attorney General Alexander Campbell, Quinn's successor in the Criminal Division, told Royall that Justice would be very anxious to know if there was any planned diversion in the ship's route back to the United States. He frankly admitted the intention to seek indictment in San Francisco, and noted that a prior stop in any territory might vest jurisdiction in a territorial court. But he explained that the Department's desire to avoid the territories was based on "budgetary and financial restrictions, and for other reasons." Campbell requested confirmation from Royall that the ship would not make a call in the territories of Alaska or Hawaii. In the meantime, Royall was to hold this seemingly innocuous request in strictest confidence.

Disingenuousness was supplemented with a final touch of surliness. Campbell noted that d'Aquino had a husband and that she was "believed to be the mother of a minor child." Persecutors, it would seem, should know simple biographical facts; d'Aquino's child had been stillborn in January 1948. In any event, Campbell said that Justice would not defray the costs of transporting the husband and child. But Campbell was not without heart. He told John Hogan to interview d'Aquino on arrival, "but don't delay so that they can say we used a hose."[30]

The decision to try the case in San Francisco did not meet with universal approval. The presidents of both the California Federation for Civic Unity and its San Francisco Council asked Tom Clark to consider the possible adverse affects upon racial feelings in the area. They emphasized that they "unquestionably assume[d]" there were ample grounds for prosecution, but expressed concern that the trial would hamper efforts to "weld together" the different, loyal racial elements in the community. Campbell merely replied that the action was "foreclosed by statutory provisions" for venue.[31]

Whatever public pressures the Department experienced for prosecuting d'Aquino, the fact is that Tom DeWolfe had no easy time persuading the grand jury in San Francisco to return a true bill. He nonetheless succeeded in doing so in October 1948. "It was necessary for me to practically make a fourth of July speech in order to obtain an indictment," he reported to Washington on November 12. Still, two jurors voted against the government. The same day, in a more formal message to Campbell, DeWolfe reported he personally presented the case "in a rather forceful manner." Apparently the grand jury was disturbed that the government was asking for an indictment against d'Aquino without similar action against Ince. As a result, DeWolfe told the jurors Ince's case would be presented "in the immediate future" after further investigation in the Orient. (It never was.) DeWolfe pressed both Whearty and Campbell to apprise Clark and Ford of the situation so that they, in turn, could secure J. Edgar Hoover's cooperation for post-indictment investigation.

The FBI Director initially balked at further participation. Agent Tillman had done his work in 1946 and early 1948, and apparently Hoover believed that sufficient. Or perhaps Hoover, always eager to chalk up victories, was reluctant to involve his agency in a potentially losing cause. Ultimately, however, he consented and Tillman returned to Japan on December 28 to secure more witnesses.[32]

It is impossible to know exactly what had troubled the grand jury besides the Ince matter. Perhaps the jurors detected a lack of credibility surrounding one of the key Japanese witnesses, Hiromi Yagi. Yagi, it will be recalled, was discovered and interviewed by Hogan and Brundidge during their trip to Tokyo in March 1948. In his grand jury testimony, Yagi claimed that, while in the company of a friend, he witnessed Iva doing one broadcast. The "friend" was the same one Brundidge had hidden in his Tokyo hotel room because the man allegedly feared the military authorities. Yagi's evasiveness before the grand jury, however, definitely disturbed the FBI, who questioned him "many times" while he was in San Francisco, trying to learn the identity of his "friend." By then Yagi must have been terrified, for he consulted with Brundidge, who then was living in Monterey, and identified his friend to the FBI as one Toshikatsu Kodaira.

The FBI agents informed DeWolfe and Hogan, who were then in San Francisco. The Justice attorneys asked the Army Counter-Intelligence Corps (CIC) agent who had escorted the Japanese witnesses to conduct further investigations in Japan and to locate and interrogate Kodaira. The subsequent CIC report was devastating and sent shock waves throughout the bureaucracy that had developed the case. Kodaira "emphatically" denied having attended any broadcasts with Yagi. Yagi stuck to his original story until November 5, when the CIC man threatened to bring Yagi and Kodaira together to resolve the conflict. Thereupon, the investigator reported:

Yagi begged [him] . . . not to do so, stating, "I will tell you the truth this time."
Yagi then advised, "My friend, Harry T. Brundidge, came to Japan in March or April
1948. He asked me to go to the United States of America as a witness against Toguri.
I told him I never seen Toguri broadcasting. He stated, "If you tell the story to Mr.
Hogan then you will make a trip to the United States and we will have a nice time
together." At this point of the interview, Yagi seemed to gain his composure. In
response to a question . . . whether he would make a sworn statement to the above,
he replied, "Yes, I want to tell the truth now even though it gets me in lots of
trouble." Yagi continued, "The statement I signed [that is, the statement given to
Hogan in Tokyo in March or April 1948] was not the truth."

Assistant Attorney General Campbell duly reported all this to Clark on December 2. The Attorney General's assistant, Ford, took the all-important first step
in a cover-up that ultimately tarnished the whole affair. The report had a handwritten notation stating, "I would run this darn carefully. Confront Brundidge
with it, etc."[33]

Less than a fortnight later, Campbell sent a rather formal letter to Brundidge
at his New York residence, asking him to come to Washington to talk about
"certain matters" relating to the indictment. The letter was written "For the
Attorney General." Brundidge was on vacation at the time and did not receive
the letter until December 23. He thereupon called his old traveling companion
Hogan, demanding to know what was happening. Hogan informed his superiors
he replied to Brundidge that he "was unable to tell him." Brundidge refused to
come to Washington at his own expense and told Hogan to inform Campbell
that the Department should send a representative to see him in New York—
preferably John Hogan. Brundidge, however, finally appeared in Washington on
January 5, 1949, and conferred with Campbell, Hugh Fisher, a special assistant
to Clark, and Dean Schedler, Director of Public Information for the Department
and an old acquaintance. He categorically denied he had prompted Yagi's testimony. He could offer no explanation for the witness's recantation except to say
that he probably had "been stricken with fear" since his return to Japan. Clearly,
there now were serious doubts about Yagi and Brundidge among some people in
the bureaucracy. But Hogan at least still knew the proper course for the Department. On Campbell's report to Clark of his interview with Brundidge, Ford
noted to the Attorney General that "we can still make the case according to my
information from Hogan."[34]

The chummy relationship between Hogan and Brundidge continued through
the spring of 1949. Hogan told the reporter of a postponement in the trial and
that the government still intended to subpoena him and keep him on the witness
list. In May, Brundidge called Hogan from New York to offer confidential
information he believed the government should know. Apparently Brundidge's
former colleague, Clark Lee, was outraged at the persecution of d'Aquino and

had prepared a series of six articles for his employer, International News Service. (In his 1947 book, Lee already had referred to Mrs. d'Aquino as a "fall guy.") According to Brundidge's information, the articles "included a most bitter and vitriolic denunciation of the Government for having even considered a prosecution . . . in this case." The chief editor of INS refused to publish the articles because they were so hostile. Brundidge drew the obvious conclusion: Lee would be "extremely sympathetic" to the defendant if called as a witness by the government. Curiously, Hogan prepared all this information only for "The Files" and apparently did not relay it to his superiors.[35]

Whatever doubts existed in the Department about the existence and nature of the Yagi-Brundidge link were resolved with a report from Criminal Division attorney Noel E. Story, who was in Japan with FBI agent Tillman in the spring of 1949. On May 27, Story informed Campbell and DeWolfe that Theodore Tamba, one of d'Aquino's lawyers, had found Yagi and confronted him with the charge of perjury before the grand jury. Tamba was in Japan at the time gathering depositions and interviewing prospective witnesses. Yagi admitted the perjury to Tamba and then went to Tillman to offer a complete confession. Tamba also located Kodaira, from whom Story and Tillman then secured a deposition confirming Yagi's duplicity. Tamba desperately tried to get a deposition to this effect from Yagi himself, but Story advised the Japanese he did not have to do so and that it could be used against him in subsequent proceedings. Story was fully aware of Tamba's questioning of Yagi, as army censors regularly monitored Tamba's calls to Wayne Collins, d'Aquino's chief lawyer in San Francisco. According to Story, Yagi then left Tokyo and could not be found. Story also reported that Brundidge represented himself to Kodaira as an official representative of the Justice Department. Because of the "serious nature" of the allegations against Brundidge, Story recommended that the Department launch a "vigorous investigation" of his actions "with a view of possible prosecution action."[36]

But Brundidge had powerful friends. Moreover, Justice Department officials realized that any prosecution of Brundidge would "completely destroy any chance of a conviction" of d'Aquino, as Campbell admitted to Clark on June 8. Not only was there a final wrap put on the cover-up, but it was done with a disingenuous twist. Campbell told Clark it would be unwise to prosecute Brundidge, for there was only a slight chance of convicting a white man in California on the testimony of two Japanese.[37] Brundidge's case was not only dropped for the present; there would be no future action—for if d'Aquino was convicted, prosecution of Brundidge would reveal his machinations in securing d'Aquino's prosecution and conviction, casting doubt on the evidence and likely constituting grounds for reversal on appeal; if she was acquitted, the same revelations from a trial of Brundidge could render the Department vulnerable for having undertaken d'Aquino's prosecution and subject it to charges of covering up an obstruction of justice.

Better yet for Brundidge, he would not have to testify in d'Aquino's public trial. The government would not call him to the stand, and the defense could not: the common law rule then in effect required one to vouch for the veracity and truthfulness of one's own witness. Harry Brundidge sat in the proverbial catbird seat.

iv

The Cold War summer and autumn of 1949 marked a particularly grim moment for the United States. The "fall of China" and the Soviet Union's explosion of an atomic device occurred in rapid succession in August and September. Both events ultimately were viewed from within the United States as calamities facilitated by the connivance and disloyalty of Americans who aided and abetted those ominous, sinister developments. That perception had profound internal consequences in the United States. The external events confirmed rising fears of international Communism, fears that already had led to increased persecution of alleged subversives and spies, as well as an increased demand for patriotic conformity. The ever-fragile supporting props for diversity and civil liberty virtually collapsed as national governmental institutions and the media successfully peddled the idea of a domestic "Red Menace."

Resorting to legal institutions and processes legitimates dubious public policy. Thus the period is noteworthy for more than "Red baiting," whether by the President, other executive branch officers, or congressional committees. From 1949 through the next half decade, the federal government initiated a wave of criminal trials involving alleged subversives and spies. The charges, of course, were criminal; yet political purposes heavily freighted the prosecutions. The lengthy trial of the Communist Party leadership for violating the Smith Act heads the list. The summer of 1949 also brought Alger Hiss's first trial for perjury. More sweeping, and more indicative of the times, were the new, not so subtle demands for loyalty from ordinary citizens. The mania for loyalty, officially sanctioned since 1947 by Executive Order 9835 (which established the Federal Employee Loyalty Program), spread throughout the country, insistently demanding that varied individuals, however notorious or ordinary, publicly attest to their past, present, and future loyalty. The Board of Regents of the University of California, for example, implemented a loyalty oath program for professors in 1949, provoking bitter institutional divisions that persisted for a generation.

The world was choosing up sides, so to speak, and individuals, like nations, could not avoid involvement. The times dictated a premium on conformity and loyalty, however adverse and trying to one's personal situation. And this was the cold reality that Iva Ikuko Toguri d'Aquino confronted in her treason trial from July to September 1949. Her alleged crimes had been committed during World War II. But the immediate popular and official concerns for loyalty, coupled with a merciless, publicity-seeking pursuit by a few self-appointed persecutors—with both aided and nurtured by bureaucratic inertia, timidity, and, at times, chicanery —explain Mrs. d'Aquino's indictment, trial, and conviction far more than do the distant events of 1941–45.

The war with Japan was four years past; it might as well have been four light-years. Japan's place as the linchpin of the United States' East Asian defense perimeter was established, and economic reconstruction, with American aid, was in full bloom. Just before the d'Aquino trial began, the San Francisco *Chronicle* carried a long feature on changes in Japan and American plans for the area. The article particularly emphasized that reconstruction would accelerate in order to make Japan "the workshop of Asia." Equally symbolic, perhaps, was the Naval Academy's appointment at this time of its first Nisei, a young man who had spent the war years in the Minidoka Relocation Center in Idaho.[38]

The d'Aquino trial opened on July 5, 1949, with Federal District Judge Michael J. Roche presiding. While it began amid fanfare and sensationalism appropriate to the public's perception of the notorious "Tokyo Rose," the trial pales in contrast to the drama of the case's covert aspects. The adversaries were experienced and skillful. Tom DeWolfe was a veteran prosecutor, and he was on familiar terrain as a result of his experiences with the Nazi broadcasters. Defense lawyer Wayne Collins similarly had extensive trial experience, and he was familiar with the force of governmental power, having taken an active role in most of the major cases involving the rights of Japanese-Americans since 1942. Until his death in 1974, he devoted much of his time and practice to serving these clients in myriad cases and issues. The d'Aquino trial lasted nearly three months, but mostly it was uneventful and tedious, save for Collins' desperate, unavailing attempts to offer depositions discrediting government witnesses and to prove the taint of perjury. Judge Roche excluded as hearsay Kodaira's deposition denying that he and Yagi had attended any broadcast together, but Collins managed to get a statement from Tillman on the record that Yagi had confessed to him he had been bribed to come to San Francisco and give false testimony to the grand jury.[39] Yagi, of course, having thoroughly recanted his original statements as given to the grand jury, was never called during the trial.

The government prosecuted the case in San Francisco to ensure an all-white jury, and it secured one with little difficulty. The prosecution used only seven of twenty peremptory challenges, disqualifying six blacks and one Chinese, an army veteran who had fought in the China-Burma-India theater. Following prevailing fashion, the government segregated witnesses during the trial, whites in one room, Orientals and blacks in another. The jurors consisted of middle-class professionals and housewives, equally divided between men and women.[40] They were not sequestered during the fifty-two days of testimony. The long parade of witnesses they heard offered conflicting views on the nature of d'Aquino's role as broadcaster, with prosecution witnesses portraying her as an active participant in Radio Tokyo's propaganda purposes and those for the defense emphasizing her working under duress and as a ready accomplice in attempts to undermine the Japanese Army's propaganda goals.

The indictment voted by the grand jury the previous October alleged eight overt acts of treason that involved the defendant's broadcasting for the enemy. Overt Act No. 6 quickly emerged as the focus of the government's case, with its charge that the defendant had broadcast information "concerning the loss of ships" during October 1944. As distinguished from Japanese or Allied soldier witnesses who claimed to have *heard* these remarks, two key witnesses testified they *saw* d'Aquino deliver the broadcast. George Nakamato Mitsushio was chief of the Overseas Section of Radio Tokyo and Kenkichi Oki was production supervisor at the station. (Oki's wife had been a radio announcer.) Both men were California Nisei who had gone to Japan in 1940 and subsequently renounced their American citizenship. Both claimed to have witnessed the broadcast cited in Act No. 6, and Mitsushio testified he directed her to make the remarks. Mitsushio quoted d'Aquino as saying:

> Now you have lost all your ships. You really are orphans of the Pacific. How do you think you will ever get home?

And Oki:

> Now you fellows have lost all your ships. You really are orphans of the Pacific. Now how do you think you will ever get home?

These statements concerned the heavy American naval losses caused by a ty-phoon following a decisive victory over the Japanese in the Second Battle of the Philippine Sea. D'Aquino emphatically denied the testimony, but the government had its required two witnesses. The jury had to decide who was telling the truth.[41]

The jurors began their deliberations on the afternoon of September 26. From statements issued after the verdict, and from the foreman's memoir, we know the jury wrangled bitterly for nearly four days. While there was "a general opinion" that the overt acts had been committed, the problem was whether there was sufficient proof of the defendant's intent to betray the United States. Specifically, they divided 9–3 on overt Act No. 6. On several occasions, the jurors returned to the courtroom, telling Judge Roche they were "hopelessly deadlocked," but the judge refused to dismiss them. In the late afternoon of September 29, the jurors asked for clarification of the judge's instructions. Roche had instructed the jury that when overt acts were judged "in the light of related events, [they] may turn out to be acts which were not of aid and comfort to the enemy." The holdouts wanted clarification on this point in order to use the evidence of d'Aquino's assistance to prisoners of war as demonstrating a lack of intent to commit treason. But Roche refused to elaborate on his point, insisting the jury must give "uniform consideration" to all of his instructions. According to Foreman John Mann, Roche's position and pressure for a verdict led to the capitulation of the holdouts. In the early evening of the twenty-ninth the jury delivered its verdict, finding d'Aquino guilty of one count of treason. The decision shocked not only the defense but the reporters covering the trial, who had voted among themselves by a 9–1 count that the jury would acquit.[42]

Judge Roche imposed a sentence of ten years' imprisonment and a $10,000 fine on October 6, 1949. Speaking for his client, Wayne Collins said that "her own conscience is clear. She is sorry because she wishes she could say the Government's witnesses' consciences were also clear."[43] Neither Collins nor d'Aquino had the information to question the consciences of the bureaucrats who had determined her fate.

Appeals to the Ninth Circuit Court of Appeals and to the Supreme Court failed, and the defendant was sent to her new prison, the Federal Women's Reformatory at Alderson, West Virginia. She was released in January 1956—the first convicted traitor to return to freedom—and then went to Chicago, where her father had established a successful business following the war. There were talks of deportation—but to where? The treason conviction ironically confirmed d'Aquino's persistent, almost pathetic claim of American citizenship. Nor was this the end of d'Aquino's encounters with bureaucracy. Her attorneys made several attempts to secure a pardon after her release from prison, but to no avail. In fact, the Department counterattacked by pursuing d'Aquino for full payment of the $10,000 fine, the final demand coming in 1971 from Attorney General John Mitchell. The papers requesting a presidential pardon worked through the bureaucratic labyrinths in the White House and the Justice Department through successive administrations. Finally, on his last day in office, President Gerald R. Ford, notoriously open-handed with pardons, pardoned Iva Ikuko Toguri d'Aquino.[44]

v

Mrs. d'Aquino was an isolated, relatively insignificant individual who classically confronted political justice. She symbolically served the government's goals and purposes. Her acknowledged acts of broadcasting for the enemy took on a legendary mystique that heightened her importance far beyond the innocuous substance of her activities. Similarly, she served the professional and political needs of a few relentless lay persecutors who successfully mounted enough pressure to enlist the cooperation of both ambitious and timid bureaucrats. D'Aquino was a symbolic sacrifice for their energies and fears; furthermore, they used her to symbolize the stringent, politically expedient meaning of loyalty. She was a pawn, and nothing more, from 1941 to 1949. In her desperate plea to Walter Winchell in 1948, d'Aquino perceptively captured the essence of her situation. "Under normal circumstances I should be called a 'bad girl' but there were so many complicated cobwebs . . . I . . . had to find a way to survive," she told Winchell. "I . . . had little chance in choosing a way to survive."[45] She was speaking of her Japanese experiences, of course; she had no idea of how well that explained her Kafkaesque experiences after 1945.

2

"SHE WHO HESITATES . . ."
The Agony of Beatrice B.

Someone must have traduced Joseph K., for without having done anything wrong, he was arrested one fine morning.

—FRANZ KAFKA, *The Trial*

Plaintiff dealt with an institution, the U.S. Government, one where, in any administration, no one gets to sign the letters he writes, or to write the letters he signs.

—JUDGE PHILIP NICHOLS, JR.

i

BEATRICE Braude assumed her new duties in the United States Information Agency in December 1953. She had worked for the Office of Strategic Services and the State Department since her arrival in Washington ten years earlier. After an unpleasant tour of duty in Germany, she looked forward to her new position. Her employment evaluations consistently had been high and she carried out her new duties in her usual efficient manner. She read documents on French political developments and prepared a weekly report for the Agency's intelligence digest. On December 30, 1953, her supervisor praised her work and told her she was being recommended for a salary increase. But the next day, USIA Director Theodore C. Streibert informed Braude that for budgetary reasons she was terminated as of that day. But he did offer her a temporary, month-long appointment in order to find a new job.[1] Time would show how meaningless the gesture was.

Braude's well-ordered world, and her steadily advancing career, suddenly and unexpectedly disintegrated. The days of commendation and reward were over. Instead, Braude found herself jobless. That, of course, she knew at once. She did not know, however, that she really lost her job for security reasons; she also did not realize that in effect she was blacklisted from federal employment.

33

The USIA was a particular target for loyalty probers under the new Republican administration in 1953. But Braude already had been extensively examined and cleared by the State Department's loyalty board. When she was dismissed, Braude believed that budgetary considerations dictated her firing. For years afterward, she accepted that explanation. The year 1953 was still an "age of belief" in the credibility of government. Twenty years later, however, after the sobering experiences of Vietnam and Watergate, it was easier to suspend such belief. And a little help from the Freedom of Information and Privacy Acts would provide documentary support.

The Freedom of Information and Privacy Acts certainly have enriched our historical knowledge. They also have confounded it at times. Unique as they are, these laws, despite their flaws and the frustrations they occasionally generate, have given us another window to see how we are governed. For individuals, the laws offer a more sophisticated means for making Everyman his own historian.

The revelations of secret files can be frightening as well as informative. One can find, for example, that one's life amounted to a dual existence, where on one level "reality" was consciously experienced, sometimes understood completely, partly, or not at all; while on the other level, the actual reality of life was manipulated behind the scenes by unseen forces rendering the first level as nothing more than a charade or a delusion.

So it was for Beatrice Braude. For years, she faithfully accepted the government's explanation of her dismissal. Slowly, however, almost in spite of herself, she came to suspect that her life was not all it seemed. To discover the reality, she had to penetrate lies, obfuscations, and cover-ups. Curiously, those who manipulated the reality of her life also operated on two levels. They provided more paper, more explanations, to perpetuate their lies and cover-ups. Remarkably, they simultaneously provided more paper, more explanations, to reveal the fact that they had lied and covered up. They thus provided the ultimate corroboration for the wrongs done to Beatrice Braude in 1953 and thereafter. And all of it comes down to a classic case of bureaucratic self-conviction.

ii

The loyalty probes of the postwar period were a heady elixir for a nation beset by dissension and fears. Conflicts with the Soviet Union inevitably sharpened fears of disloyalty, infiltration, and subversion within the government and other American institutions. The disclosures of the *Amerasia* case in 1945 and the Soviet spy ring in Canada in 1946, and the blunderbuss charges of the House Committee on Un-American Activities, all seemed to substantiate such fears. Whatever the reality, political partisans could hardly resist the temptations to capitalize on the issue.

The chronic state of hot and cold war in the twentieth century forced the government to confront real problems of security. Since 1884, civil service rules forbade any inquiry into the political affiliations of government workers. But by the 1940s, "political affiliation" involved something more complex than association with the major political parties or one of their factions. External, hostile ideologies found receptive audiences and raised new concerns for loyalty. Political opportunists could not resist exploiting a public mania for loyalty, a mania heavily infused with fear and paranoia. From World War I into the 1930s, the World War II period, and the Cold War, Washington and the states developed various political criteria of loyalty for government employment. Loyalty oaths, tests, and inquiries affected government employees from the highest levels of policy making to teachers, clerks, and custodians. By the late 1940s, the process of loyalty checks had become one of the most ambitious, amorphous, and ambiguous of government functions.[2]

Civil service legislation since 1884 had sought to protect government employment by prohibiting partisan affiliation as a criterion. The Hatch Act of 1939 primarily prohibited political and electioneering activity by federal employees. But Section 9A of the act was directed toward preventing "pernicious political activity," specifically barring federal employees from belonging to any political party or organization advocating the overthrow of the existing constitutional form of government. The legislation amounted to a significant historical departure from the 1884 norm that "no question . . . be so framed as to elicit information concerning the political or religious opinions or affiliations of any applicant."

The wartime conditions in the early 1940s prompted new measures to grapple with disloyalty. In 1940 Congress authorized the Secretaries of the War and Navy Departments summarily to suspend employees in the interest of national security without regard to any existing laws or regulations governing dismissal of federal employees. (The so-called McCarran Rider granted the same authority to the Secretary of State in 1947.) Shortly after the Pearl Harbor attack, the President and the Civil Service Commission issued War Service Regulations providing for dismissal if there was a reasonable doubt as to one's loyalty to the United States. Even before our entrance into the war, the Attorney General, in October 1941, authorized the Federal Bureau of Investigation to scrutinize complaints against allegedly disloyal employees. The FBI's findings were given to the various employing agencies, action being left wholly to the discretion of the agency concerned. In February 1943, President Roosevelt established an Interdepartmental Committee on Employee Investigations to process loyalty cases. Upon investigation, it could declare a permanent federal employee removable on loyalty grounds if he belonged to an organization advocating the overthrow of the government or the use of violence to change existing political institutions. The committee, however, was only advisory and had no authority to discharge employees.

The Cold War conflicts heightened fears of domestic subversion. In July 1946, a subcommittee of the House Civil Service Committee pointedly declared existing loyalty checks inadequate. It criticized the lack of uniform effort and called for the centralization of loyalty procedures. Finally, the subcommittee urged the establishment of a commission to present "a complete and unified program."[3]

Truman's advisers considered the possibility of creating such a commission by executive order, but for the moment the President chose not to act. While Congress did nothing, individual members continued to exploit the issue, particularly criticizing the executive branch. The issue was largely partisan and Republicans effectively used it in the November 1946 congressional elections. Two weeks after the election, Truman finally decided to take the initiative and he appointed a Temporary Commission on Employee Loyalty. The political cause and effect of the action was obvious, and the commission's report of March 2, 1947, reflected the demands for a coherent, centralized policy of loyalty checks. The report found existing security procedures inadequate since the government now had to protect itself against those who were "expert in the techniques of deception," who resisted "candid revelation" of facts, and who had no regard "for the sacredness of an oath." The commission also articulated some significant uncertainties. Acknowledging that the employment of disloyal persons constituted "more than a speculative threat," the commission still could not "state with any degree of certainty how far-reaching that threat is."[4]

President Truman adopted the report with few changes, and on March 21, 1947, he announced Executive Order 9835, prescribing procedures for an employee loyalty program. The program initiated the most sweeping inquiry into employee loyalty in the nation's history, immediately affecting over two million civil service workers. The presidential order established loyalty review boards for executive departments to evaluate any negative information turned in by FBI or Civil Service Commission investigations. A central Loyalty Review Board was created to coordinate procedures. The standard for dismissal required "reasonable grounds for belief in disloyalty." Such grounds included obvious and statutory crimes such as treason, sedition, espionage, and sabotage; the Hatch Act prohibition against advocacy of force and violence to overthrow the government; and a wholly new category: namely, any affiliation with an organization which the Attorney General deemed "totalitarian, Fascist, Communist, or subversive." Three years later, his program having failed to mollify critics, Truman significantly altered the standard for dismissal. Executive Order 10241 (April 28, 1951) provided for dismissal if there was a "reasonable doubt" of one's loyalty. In short, the burden of proof shifted to the accused or suspected.[5]

Executive Order 9835 provoked broad criticism, much of it obvious and predictable. Those on the extreme left raised the cry of witch hunt, while partisan critics of the President and those long connected with anti-Communist crusades complained that the program did not go far enough. The most prescient remarks, however, came from legal analysts who contended that the program violated traditional standards of due process and fair hearing. The combination of political imperatives and growing fears of subversion, however, made the program acceptable, indeed irresistible. Congress gave its blessing on July 30, 1947, when it granted the President $11 million to operate the program for the first year. The authorization not only implemented Truman's order, but it augmented the scope of FBI power and activities. Truman clearly had intended that the Civil Service Commission bear the largest burden of the investigations, requesting funds at a 2–1 ratio for the commission over the FBI. But somewhere in the legislative process, the figures were reversed. However ambiguous the intentions of Truman's loyalty program may have been, it proved an unqualified boon to J. Edgar Hoover's imperial drives.[6]

Despite widespread dismissals and the pervasiveness of the program, the political pressures for still stronger loyalty checks continued. In 1950, Congress enacted the Internal Security Act over Truman's veto, but more pertinent to the loyalty mania, it also passed Public Law 733, which permitted eleven "sensitive" agencies (such as State, Commerce, and Justice) to suspend immediately alleged security risks, pending formal notice and hearing of charges. Even that was not enough. By then, the Republican congressional leadership had unleashed Joseph McCarthy, and during the next several years, through the presidential election of 1952, political rhetoric revolved around the charge that Washington had been infected with "twenty years of treason." The triumph of Dwight Eisenhower carried to power new concepts of loyalty and Republican officials determined to do something about the "traitors."

However harsh the historical judgment of Truman for originating the sweeping loyalty program, his contemporary critics insisted he never went far enough. Eisenhower later complained that Truman's policy ignored the security liabilities of loyal employees. He suggested that homosexuals, alcoholics, or those who had some ties that would make them prey to blackmailers had to be investigated and, if necessary, dismissed. For Eisenhower, the Truman program reflected "a complacency or skepticism toward security risks in government." Eisenhower's Executive Order 10450 (April 1953) made security, not loyalty, the prime concern. The catchall standard for determining security risks boiled down to a "bad tendency" doctrine. Section 8 (I) (i) provided for immediate suspension if there were "any behavior, activities or associations which tend to show that the individual is not reliable or trustworthy." In effect, the basic idea of Public Law 733 was extended throughout all federal agencies. Heads of departments selected hearings boards from outside their own agencies, but the panels had only the power to study and recommend. Department heads had the final authority to recommend dismissal.

Eisenhower naturally applauded the effectiveness of his program as the dismissals and resignations mounted. Yet, in November 1954, the chairman of the Civil Service Commission admitted that no Communist or fellow traveler had been uncovered and fired by the Eisenhower administration.[7]

The loyalty probes produced mountains of paper and staffs equal to small armies. Questionnaires, investigations, and hearings abounded. During the Truman years, approximately 1,200 federal employees were dismissed and 6,000 resigned because of the inquiries. Between 1953 and 1956, 1,500 persons were dismissed and another 6,000 resigned. Precise figures are difficult to project. The key weapon in the security programs was immediate suspension without pay, and many employees undoubtedly resigned to save themselves the stigma and expense of fighting charges, however flimsy.[8]

The direct and indirect pressures, as well as the casualties, of the loyalty and security programs probably never can be tabulated with certainty. These programs quickly assumed a life of their own, generating a vast enterprise for specified agencies such as the FBI and the Civil Service Commission and a wholly new investigative function for every executive agency. Newly created security offices checked people, not locked doors. They also spawned a climate of fear, suspicion, and timidity that unquestionably undermined morale, initiative, and courage. Furthermore, loyalty and security considerations provided an added weapon in the ever-present jungle of bureaucratic politics, stifling independence and encouraging a bland orthodoxy.

Any challenge to the program required extraordinary financial and emotional expense, not to say extraordinary courage and persistence. Dr. John Peters lost his position because of the testimony of secret informers. Yet how many, like Peters, challenged that action? Kendrick Cole successfully appealed his dismissal, which had been based on some brief, remote flirtation with an allegedly subversive group. But how many others similarly situated did so? John Stewart Service, one of several State Department diplomats who were pilloried for the "loss" of China, was dismissed by John Foster Dulles. But how many, like Service, had influential friends in the government and media who exposed the political chicanery of his superiors?[9]

The times and program dictated conformity, and conformity included a substantial dose of acquiescence in whatever fate the loyalty/security game decreed. Legal expenses, emotional trauma, embarrassment, and long-term ostracism seemed the most likely results of any challenge; understandably, few ventured to fight. Finally, complicating matters even further was the shroud of secrecy under which the program operated. Those accused could not easily challenge what they could not know for sure.

The loyalty probes proceeded largely in private and in an administrative fashion, only occasionally punctuated by a dramatic, public incident. But the arrest of Judith Coplon, a Justice Department employee in March 1949, made credible years of charges that Communist spies had infiltrated and subverted the American government. When she was apprehended with a Soviet United Nations employee, her purse contained numerous Justice Department documents labeled "top secret." She was the first American civilian arrested and tried for Soviet espionage.[10]

At the time, the government was preparing to try Alger Hiss—but on a charge of perjury, not espionage as so many passionately believed or wished. The trial of the top American Communist Party leaders was entering its third month. Despite their alleged clandestine activities, the defendants were well-known, avowed Communists. Coplon, however, was another matter. The Cassandras seemed vindicated, for she was living proof that the Kremlin had done its work well, what with an ordinary, nondescript American bureaucrat passing sensitive secret documents to an agent posing as an innocent United Nations employee. It was easy for Americans to find convincing the accusations in 1949 of an obscure senator from Wisconsin that there were 205—or was it 57?—Communists influencing State Department policy. Who else of the millions of government employees was suspect?

Coplon was found guilty in two trials, the first in Washington in the summer of 1949 and the second in New York early in 1950. She was convicted on separate charges of having stolen government documents for a foreign power and for having transmitted those documents to a foreign agent. Her trials revealed that she was indeed the epitome of the eager, dedicated Washington careerist. She alleged, without much credibility, that the stolen documents were helpful background material for a novel she claimed to be writing.

Coplon's convictions eventually were reversed. In two appellate court proceedings the judges held that the evidence did not justify an arrest without a warrant, that the government's wiretap information had to be divulged to the defense, that the government had to demonstrate that its "confidential informant" testimony did not come from a wiretap, and that the FBI had improperly monitored conversations between Coplon and her lawyer. Although new trials were ordered, Coplon never again was prosecuted, as the government apparently decided it could not comply with the judicial requirements. Yet prevailing opinion undoubtedly shared Judge Learned Hand's assumption that Coplon's "guilt is plain."[11] And that assumption both sharpened and heightened the demands for tighter loyalty and security checks among government employees.

iii

Like Judith Coplon, Beatrice Braude left New York to work in wartime Washington. After a chance meeting, they developed a friendship, which soon fell apart over personal differences, and following Coplon's arrest in 1949, investigators found Braude's name in Coplon's address book. Braude's ephemeral encounter with Coplon cost her heavily, as she lost her federal position and never again worked for the government. She also suffered thirty years of confusion, hardship, and grief.

Braude was born in New York City in 1913. Her father had emigrated from Eastern Europe and he worked in the clothing business after settling in America. Beatrice graduated from Hunter College and attended Columbia, where she received an M.A. degree in French. After briefly working in New York for the Home Relief Bureau, she went to Washington in August 1943 to work for the Office of Strategic Services (OSS). She first served in the Secret Operations Division, but soon transferred to the Research and Analysis Division. Braude harbored ambitions of becoming a *Time* magazine correspondent and she hoped her OSS experience ultimately would give her credentials to work for *Time* as a researcher on French politics. Failing that, and more realistically, she looked forward to a career in public service where she could use her language skills.

Braude's OSS years were happy ones. She worked as a research assistant for Franz Neumann, a distinguished scholar who was the Principal Research Analyst of the Central European Division of the OSS. For a young woman of self-confessed intellectual pretentions, her associates in the OSS offered impressive company. John Clive, Felix Gilbert, John Herz, H. Stuart Hughes, Leonard Krieger, Herbert Marcuse, and Carl Schorske all worked in her section. One of her favorites was Otto Kirchheimer, already known for his pathbreaking studies on the subject of political justice. Some of Braude's OSS work was sensitive. She remembered compiling a list of exiled German Socialists (including Willy Brandt) for Neumann. At other times, she did ordinary research analysis on such topics as German youth, culture, and the press.

In October 1947, Braude transferred to the State Department, which found her talents useful in its European Research Division. Three months later, the Department reclassified her to its Foreign Service Staff. She was assigned to the Paris embassy as a research assistant and eventually worked her way up to an assistant cultural affairs officer. Again, she found her work satisfying and enjoyable. In May 1953, she was reassigned to Bonn, but she never was comfortable in Germany. "I hated Germany; I couldn't bear it," she later recalled. While serving in Bonn, Braude received word of her father's death on December 1. She returned home immediately. At the same time, the State Department reassigned her as a permanent Foreign Service Staff Officer in the Washington headquarters of the newly organized United States Information Agency. After only a few weeks on the job, Braude suddenly was dismissed.

USIA Director Streibert justified Braude's dismissal on economic grounds. Specifically, he cited the "personnel rider" of Public Law 207, part of the

Congressional Appropriation Act (Fiscal 1954), which authorized him to terminate employees above the GS-7 grade. (Braude's Foreign Service rating was FSS-9, which was above the GS-7 standard.) In his letter, Streibert explained that Congress had funded the Agency at a level 27 percent below what the President had requested. Many activities consequently were eliminated or reduced, with a corresponding "reduction in force." The Agency's "changing needs and reduced activities," Streibert said, made it impossible to "make full use" of Braude's services and therefore it was necessary to terminate her. Streibert closed with the usual expressions of regret, but he went much further. There was no intent, he maintained, "that this action could possibly jeopardize your future employment." He closed wishing her success in finding another position.[12] No such intent? No jeopardy? Given the information he acted upon—information unknown to Braude—Streibert was naïve at best; at worst, cynical.

Streibert's public position on Braude's dismissal remained fixed on fiscal considerations. While his letter of December 31 did not provide for any appeal, on January 22, 1954, Braude requested that Streibert review his decision. A week later he replied that he had done so and again insisted that the original decision was made only on "consideration [of] the various factors" mentioned in his original letter. He added a personal, handwritten note to his formal reply, assuring Braude that he personally had reviewed the decision and was satisfied that "the action taken was fully justified." In the meantime, Braude had asked New York senator Irving Ives to inquire whether the decision could be reversed. In response to Ives, Streibert again gave no indication that the reasons were any other than budgetary.[13]

By the time of Braude's dismissal, the Eisenhower administration had been in office for a year. Long-promised Republican programs for governmental austerity were beginning to take effect. The USIA's budget reductions were part of a larger pattern. It was also, however, a time which witnessed a significant upsurge in the dismissal of "security risks." What was Braude to believe? "While I was puzzled and felt that I might not have been told the entire story behind Mr. Streibert's action," she later testified, "I had no alternative but to believe, as I had been told, that my termination was related solely to budget cutbacks." Several years later, she reported to the Civil Service Commission that she had been "reduced in force" from the USIA.[14]

In Braude's case, the calendar was a key determinant of her fate. The austerity demands placed upon Director Streibert required him to reduce his staff by January 1, 1954. The personnel rider was in effect from August through December. If the State Department had reassigned her one month later than it did— that is, in January rather than December—Streibert would have had no authority to dismiss her as he did. Chances are that Braude never would have been reviewed and would have lived happily ever after in her government career.

To implement the rider, Streibert ordered the USIA's Office of Security to review the security files of all employees subject to the rider and for whom "possible questions existed." Streibert listed criteria for termination, such as an inability to get along with superiors, poor performance, mental or moral infirmities, and "past activities or associations which might suggest possible questions as to loyalty." Personnel files were reviewed, and in cases where "derogatory information" existed, security files also were checked. Apparently all employees over grade GS-7 were reviewed. The largest group was terminated in September, but further cuts followed in October and November. A final check was made the third week in December—after Braude had joined the Agency. Streibert's policy served the concerns for both austerity and security articulated by the new administration. Braude was tailor-made: she was above grade and she had a security record.

The recommendations for termination were reviewed by an informal, in-house committee which then transmitted final recommendations to Streibert. According to the Director's report, supervisors were instructed "not to get into 'specifics' as to the reasons why each employee was selected for termination." Those dismissed were only to be told that budgetary constraints dictated the Agency's action.[15] As so often is the case, the cover-up began almost simultaneously with the illegal act of commission.

The USIA Office of Security reviewed Braude's file and completed its report on December 28—just before the January 1 deadline. The report specified a series of allegations against Braude that had accumulated over a five-year period. But most startling is the lack of attention to Braude's responses to those allegations —responses that were in her record and which over two years earlier had been judged completely to exonerate her.

The Security Office's report opened with the kind of charge that was so devastating in those days: "A reliable FBI informant advised that in November 1946 Mary Jane Keeney (Communist) was in contact with the subject on 'several' occasions." The report then moved to a subject familiar to any Washington hand at that time: Judith Coplon. When the FBI arrested Coplon in March 1949 they found that her address book contained Braude's name and address. On this point, at least, the Security Office report included Braude's explanation of her acquaintance with Coplon. Third, the report noted that Braude briefly was a member of the Washington Book Shop, an organization cited by the Attorney General as subversive. Finally, Braude had been a member of a Communist-dominated federal workers' union, although she claimed to belong to the anti-Communist faction. The report concluded that existing personnel regulations on security matters justified Braude's termination. In particular, any "behavior, activities, or associations which tend to show that the individual is not reliable or trustworthy"; any "sympathetic association" with a secret agent of a foreign power; or any fact which suggested that the individual might "act contrary to the best interests of the national security" applied to Braude. This report, of course, was unknown to Braude at the time.

The Office of Security flatly recommended termination of Braude.[16] In short, she was fired for security reasons. Or was she? The Office of Security's action was based on the personnel rider of P.L. 207. As such, the USIA was able to skirt the requirement of certain procedural rights for Braude. If dismissed as a security risk, she clearly was entitled to a statement of the charges and an opportunity for a hearing. But Streibert wanted quick, simple dismissals. He had, it may be remembered, instructed supervisors "not to get into 'specifics' as to the reasons" for termination. A hearing would disrupt his budgetary arrangements. More than that, it could well have led to exoneration for Braude and embarrassment for the Agency.

Braude's security difficulties in late 1953—and the enormity of the wrongs done to her—can only be understood against the backdrop of her "security history." Following President Truman's Executive Order 9835, Braude became a subject for intensive field investigation by the FBI beginning in February 1948. When the FBI inquiries began Braude was a research analyst for the State Department in the American Embassy at Paris. The inquiry apparently was launched when Braude's name was discovered on a 1944 list of delinquent dues of members of the Washington Book Shop. Membership in the Book Shop was considered sufficient grounds by the Attorney General to justify further investigation of a person's loyalty. The Book Shop was a well-known rendezvous for politically left-wing people, a place for lectures, discussions, and recreation.

Five detailed reports from February 1948 turned up repetitious information: Braude was an efficient, industrious worker, with strong anti-Nazi and mild liberal political views. Above all, she was unquestionably loyal—"100 percent American," as a number of respondents put it. FBI field offices participated widely in the investigation. Reports were filed from New York City, Albany, Omaha, Boston, as well as a very extensive one from Washington headquarters. J. Edgar Hoover duly transmitted the reports, without a recommendation, to the Investigations Division of the Civil Service Commission. The Loyalty Review Board informed Hoover in September 1948 that Braude had been retained.[17] The reports must have satisfied whatever curiosity existed about Braude, for there was no further interest in her for three years.

Braude's personnel file was reviewed again in May 1951 in the State Department. The apparent cause was the FBI's discovery of Braude's name and Paris address in Judith Coplon's pocket address book. Either the FBI delayed transmitting the information or the State Department's security apparatus worked slowly. Coplon had been arrested on March 4, 1949, in New York. FBI agents immediately searched her purse and found the address book. Yet nothing happened for over two years. Then in the spring and summer of 1951, FBI agents made numerous inquiries about the nature of the Braude-Coplon relationship. Once again, they found unanimous praise for Braude's loyalty. As for her friendship with Coplon, the agents learned it was brief, not very close, and ended as a result of a spat.[18]

In September 1951, the State Department's Loyalty Security Board nevertheless notified Braude that "certain information" in its possession necessitated further investigation and consideration. Accordingly, the board submitted eleven interrogatories for Braude to answer in triplicate and to have notarized.[19] Four questions involved Braude's association with Mary Jane Keeney, another centered on Braude's membership in the Washington Book Shop, three focused on Judith Coplon, and three asked about any possible links to Communist activity.

Keeney allegedly was a Communist Party activist, employed at the United Nations. In her reply, Braude acknowledged having spoken twice with Keeney and having met her once in 1946. According to Braude, Keeney was anxious to send clothing to someone in occupied Germany. (Braude later learned that the clothing went to a woman who became a prominent official in the East German government.) The women were introduced by a third party actively aiding Nazi victims after the war. Braude denied any knowledge of Keeney's political beliefs or her alleged Communist sympathies. As Braude characterized it, the Keeney meeting was only a "transitory experience."

Braude's answers about her connections with the Washington Book Shop revealed more of her personal character than her political beliefs. She admitted that after her arrival in Washington in September 1943, she had a desperate need to meet "congenial new people." A friend, knowing her love of music, suggested she join the Book Shop, where musical evenings were held. As a result, she addressed envelopes on a few occasions—which explained the charge that she was a "worker" at the Book Shop. In any event, she let her membership lapse when it expired.

Braude acknowledged she was sensitive to "the undercurrent of sympathy with the Russian cause" at the Book Shop. But she reminded her inquisitors that this was a time of close U.S.-Soviet collaboration and even if she had been aware of Communist domination of the group, she would not have thought it very significant. She could not tolerate, however, the intense internal politics of the group and insisted that, as a result, she lost interest. She added that essentially she was an "anti-organization" person who found such internal politics distasteful.

Braude readily admitted knowing Coplon. They had attended a class taught by Herbert Marcuse at American University in the summer of 1945, but apparently did not meet until the following spring. Braude thought Coplon to be very good-looking and well-dressed—an ideal date for her brother, then visiting Washington. She and Coplon also joined in giving a pre-nuptial party for a mutual friend.

After that, they saw each other "infrequently," their friendship essentially reduced to a "clothes and men" level, as Braude described it. (According to Braude, Coplon, when arrested, was wearing a coat and beret Braude had sold her.)

Braude left for Paris in January 1948. Six weeks later, Coplon wrote saying she was coming to Paris in May and asked Braude to find her a hotel room. Braude located one in her own Left Bank hotel and Coplon stayed for approximately six weeks. They saw a good deal of each other during Coplon's first weekend in Paris, but met only infrequently afterward. Braude claimed to have found Coplon "very trying," as did her roommates, and said that Coplon found her very disagreeable. Braude strongly disapproved of Coplon's sexual behavior—a subject much discussed in Coplon's trials. After Coplon left Paris in July, Braude heard nothing from or about her until she read of the arrest. But while on home leave in December 1950, Braude encountered Coplon in a department store. They had, according to Braude's responses, "a short and naturally thoroughly unsatisfactory talk." Coplon, by then married and free as a result of her appeal, told Braude how happy she was. Afterward, Braude remarked to a mutual friend that "the wages of sin were not very heavy in this case." She never saw Coplon again.

Braude insisted that her acquaintanceship with Coplon was purely social and that she had no knowledge of Coplon's political and economic views. Braude had allied herself with a woman who led the anti-Communist faction of the State Department unit of the Federal Workers Union. She reported that when the two discussed the matter in front of Coplon, the latter never interrupted or argued with them, leaving Braude and her friend with the assumption that Coplon agreed with them. Significantly, Braude realized that Coplon was "very well informed" about the Soviet Union, but she attributed this to Coplon's graduate thesis on the subject. Finally, she denied any knowledge whatsoever of Coplon's espionage activities. "My astonishment and sorrow over this revelation were intense," she concluded.

In the final set of queries, Braude flatly denied any affiliation or activity with the Communist Party or Communist-front groups. Finally, although accepting the necessity of loyalty investigations in the context of the Cold War, she nevertheless disputed condemnations based on "ephemeral past associations." For one living in New York in the 1930s with "intellectual pretensions," it was difficult, she said, not to have some contact with Communists or sympathizers. Although she maintained she was not a "political person," Braude pointed out that she had voted for La Guardia and Roosevelt and had fought Communist attempts to dominate her State Department union. She wrote that her European experience gave her firsthand knowledge of victims of Communist terror and consequently she had become "even more anti-Communist." She "sincerely" believed herself to be a loyal citizen and had worked diligently abroad to gain friends for the United States.[20]

Braude submitted her responses to the Loyalty Security Board on October 9, 1951. The board promptly considered her case and on October 30 unanimously decided that the evidence did not warrant any charges of disloyalty or security risk. It recommended that the case be closed. There was another review in early February 1952 before the board sent Braude a formal notice of clearance that same month. The results clearly were known to the USIA's Office of Security. A Civil Service Commission Official Personnel File Memorandum, dated January 5, 1952, noted that Braude's report was favorable and that no further action was contemplated in her case.[21] Nevertheless, the USIA Office of Security, privy to the FBI reports, Braude's responses to the interrogatories, and the Loyalty Security Board's report—in fact, *on the basis of those materials*—flatly recommended Braude's termination.

After leaving the USIA, Braude returned to New York, moved in with her mother, and worked first for the French Cultural Services and then for the Institute of International Education. Her salary was about half what she had been earning at the State Department and the USIA. Ignorant of the real reason for her USIA dismissal, she repeatedly tried to find employment with the federal government. Coincidentally, early in 1956, she discovered that her old position as French analyst in the Research Branch of the USIA was vacant. She called her former supervisor about the opening, but he reported that he was under pressure from the Personnel Office to fill the job from among current employees. Finally, the supervisor suggested that Braude visit Washington and speak to the Security Chief of the USIA and discuss her "possibilities frankly with him." She did not, primarily because of the expense involved. Despite the lack of encouragement, Braude applied for the position, but was rejected in October. The recruitment officer bluntly told her that "we have no current or anticipated vacancies where your particular background and skills can be affectively [*sic*] utilized."[22]

Still Braude persisted. She took the Civil Service typing examination, scoring 100 percent. Her federal government application and score were referred to the USIA, but again there was no job offer. In the next eighteen months, she applied for positions with the U.S. delegation to UNESCO, the Civil Aeronautics Board, Department of Commerce, Department of the Interior, and State Department. Again, there were no offers. In 1964, she reapplied to the USIA but was told there were no "suitable" openings. Braude then spent about three years applying for various positions in the Office of Education of the Department of Health, Education, and Welfare. The Department's Civil Service Examiners rated her as eligible for a GS-11 position, but she never was hired despite repeated efforts on her part.[23]

Braude had an inkling that the problem went beyond a lack of "suitable" openings. In the spring of 1954 she was interviewed for a position with a private French banker in Paris. She considered the interview with the banker's American assistant to be "extremely successful" and was told that she soon would hear from the banker personally. She never did. Two years later, she learned that the banker had written a friend for a recommendation. But the banker also revealed that he had called the State Department Personnel Office and learned that Braude was "on the blacklist."[24]

Thus in 1956 Braude had the first firm indication that her firing had not been routine or all that it purported to be. She immediately hired an attorney, former California congressman Byron Scott. He urged her to take the Civil Service examination and renew her quest for federal employment. Six months after her typing examination, and two months following her rejection for a clerical post at the USIA, Scott wrote a lengthy letter to the Civil Service Commission. He contended that the USIA's lack of "suitable" openings was "not the real reason for her rejection, and is not a rejection that makes sense"—not when Braude had a 100 percent score and when a typing vacancy existed in the USIA.[25] Scott charged that Braude's adventures with her application clearly indicated that her file contained derogatory information. He demanded that the Civil Service Commission investigate the situation and allow Braude an opportunity to respond to any charges and clear her record. Four months later, Scott renewed his request and finally received an answer in May 1957.

The commission's general counsel told Scott that employment powers were vested in individual agencies; the commission could only refer people for a position. Furthermore, the commission had no power to review an agency decision (except when a non-veteran was hired over a veteran) "even if it is granted" that Braude was rejected because of derogatory information in her file. The counsel then pleaded that the commission's clerks had misinterpreted Braude's reply to the referral, thinking that she had been offered, and had accepted, the USIA appointment. Hence there had been no more referrals. Finally, he noted Braude's eligibility and offered to certify her to other agencies. Braude's fruitless search continued. Nearly a year later, she requested help from Senator Jacob Javits, who wrote to the commission in her behalf. A staff assistant informed the senator that the commission could only certify, not hire, her. He also claimed the commission's files offered no indication that Braude was fired on security grounds.[26]

Unable to find a government job, Braude looked for new career prospects. She studied educational television at New York University between 1959 and 1960. For several years, she worked in Boston for the educational television station. In the summer of 1962, she learned of a job possibility with the new television division of the USIA, but again nothing materialized.

In November 1963, Braude wrote a desperate, pleading letter to John Macy, Chairman of the Civil Service Commission. Fifty years old at the time, and without substantial career prospects, she remained anxious to resume her governmental career. She recounted to Macy the alleged facts of her 1953 USIA termination, her information about the blacklist, and her lawyer's previous encounters with the commission. Despite the commission's determination of her eligibility, she still had not been hired. She closed by asking for an appointment "to talk frankly with you and go over the whole situation, to learn what you think the possibilities are for me."

Two weeks later, Kimbell Johnson, Director of the commission's Bureau of Personnel Investigation, replied for Macy. He claimed to have reviewed Braude's file and insisted that it contained nothing to preclude her consideration for appointment. To be charitable, perhaps the operative word here was "consideration"; in any event, there was no acknowledgment of the reasons behind her 1953 dismissal from the USIA. Johnson told Braude that a personal conference with Macy would serve no useful purpose, but offered to have her meet with himself or a staff member.[27]

Beatrice Braude was a persistent woman. Despite a decade of rejections from USIA, she tried again in 1964. She did not secure a position, but she may have gained something more valuable: namely, information that came very close to revealing the truth.

Braude sent her 1964 inquiry to Reed Harris, Director of the Information Center Service of the USIA. Harris was no stranger to suspicion and calumny himself, having been one of Senator McCarthy's victims a decade earlier. Harris had been a student at Columbia in the early 1930s and was expelled for writing radical editorials in the student newspaper. The Communist-dominated chapter of the National Student League led a strike supporting his reinstatement. A number of his other radical associations and flirtations were dredged up two decades later. Perhaps Harris' greatest notoriety came as a result of his essays on "King Football," a devastating critique of football at Columbia. By the early 1950s, however, all that was past and Harris had risen to high position in the International Information Agency, the forerunner of the USIA. The IIA and the Voice of America were McCarthy targets at the time, and despite Harris' frank acknowledgment of his youthful activities and his insistence that he had long ago disavowed his earlier radical beliefs, Harris was pressured to resign in April 1953. In 1961, the new chief of the USIA, Edward R. Murrow, brought Harris back to the Agency.[28]

Braude read about Harris' return to government service in _Newsweek_'s "Where They Are Now" column and she thought that a direct approach to him would be worthwhile. She candidly told him her impression was that she had been dismissed in 1953 because of her fleeting association with Coplon. She also recounted her decade-long quest for other federal positions and her growing suspicion that something in her personnel file poisoned her chances for federal employment. Harris thereupon took the perfectly plausible course of asking the

USIA's Office of Security whether it would object to employing Braude in the Agency.

Two days later, the Office of Security briefed—"instructed" might be a better word—Harris on Braude's case. He was told that she had been let go on Security's recommendation. The briefing officer said that a new check could be run, and if her record was clear since 1953, then she might be given clearance. But he suggested that the Agency might wish to formulate a general policy about rehiring such people before a background check was initiated. Harris obliged by in effect devising policy on the spot. He told the briefing officer that people such as Braude who had been terminated should be re-employed only "if they had a particularly outstanding contribution to make to the Agency mission." He added that he did not think this was true of Braude and had no intention of pursuing the matter any further. The memorandum summarizing this exchange abounded in euphemisms. Harris was told that Braude had been terminated under the provisions of Public Law 207.[29] His reply to the Security Office clearly indicated that such a dismissal was recognized within the Agency as a stigma—and he knew that only an extraordinary individual could surmount that obstacle.

Six weeks later Harris replied to Braude. He told her he had explored numerous personnel opportunities in the Agency but there only were "discouraging conclusions." Without any specific details, he acknowledged that there were "past problems" in her employment record but insisted that they would not matter if an appropriate position opened up. But Harris' letter was a model of "if this, but on the other hand" jargon, for he quickly negated the concession. If an opening developed, and there were several equal candidates, including Braude, "obviously," Harris asserted, "there could be a tendency to lean toward others."[30]

Thus Harris had it both ways: Braude's past record would not debar her from a position, but her past record weighted the scales against her. What was one to conclude? Either Harris could not write a clear letter, or he deliberately chose to be ambiguous or obscure, or he deliberately sought to give Braude a hint as to the true nature of her situation.

Whatever Harris' intentions, Braude renewed her efforts and now turned to the American Civil Liberties Union, whose Washington office brought the case directly to John Macy, Chairman of the Civil Service Commission. At the time, the Washington office had been discussing with Macy whether it was advisable that interrogatories remain in personnel files after a person supposedly had been cleared. Braude's case presented a perfect example of the perniciousness of such policy. The ACLU quoted Harris' letter (without identifying him) about a tendency to lean toward others as illustrative of the point. For Braude's immediate relief, the ACLU requested that the interrogatories in her file be destroyed or at least not be forwarded to reviewing agencies.[31]

Harris' statement to Braude, inadvertent or not, plus Braude's complaints to the ACLU and Senator Javits at last had some effect. If nothing else, the events unnerved some of the affected bureaucrats. But typically they continued to conceal the real cause of Braude's termination. First, Kimbell Johnson of the Civil Service Commission checked with USIA Security. He reported the ACLU complaint and quoted the passage from Harris' letter, without knowing the author's identity. The Security people at the USIA, however, quickly determined Harris' role and queried him about his letter to Braude. Harris insisted that the quotation was taken "out of context." Clearly, at this point there was concern that Harris' statement could possibly reveal the real reason for Braude's employment difficulties. Johnson thought that the letter "might make a difference." Did he, in other words, fear that the cover-up might unravel?

A few days later, after a visit from a USIA Security officer, Johnson seemed satisfied that he "could handle the response to the American Civil Liberties Union adequately." The two men determined that the State Department interrogatories and the FBI reports on Braude had been transferred from the USIA to the Civil Service Commission in June 1954 and therefore could not have been circulated. All this involved some playing with words. True enough, the materials pertinent to Braude's Loyalty Security Board investigation had been transferred to the commission. But the reports recommending her discharge—including the key Office of Security memorandum of December 28, 1953—remained at the USIA. They certainly were there when Reed Harris discussed the prospect of Braude's possible re-employment in June 1965. "I briefed Mr. Harris," the Security officer wrote in a memo that month, "with regard to the information contained in *the security file* of Miss Beatrice Braude."[32]

The Security man also told Johnson that Braude's dismissal had been carried out under authority of Public Law 207 and definitely "was not a security termination." Again the men toyed with words and technicalities. Apparently, the Security officer did not tell Johnson that the Office of Security had recommended Braude's firing. The verbiage was important, for it masked some devious circular logic. Since Braude never had been given the proper procedural rights in conjunction with a security discharge, this "proved" her dismissal was not a security termination. *Post hoc, ergo propter hoc.*

Macy's reply to the ACLU was based on an extensive staff report, probably prepared under Johnson's direction. The report pinned Braude's difficulties on her own actions, and even hinted at some paranoia on her part. First, the staff contended she sought a very few positions for which there were many candidates. Second, the report blamed her for "scaring off" prospective employers by an over-eager volunteering of her past loyalty problems. Furthermore, she erroneously believed her record "was following her around." Macy's letter grasped for the offensive in what was a defensive situation. Beatrice Braude, Macy argued, not unseen bureaucrats, perpetuated the "big lie."

The staff report first offered a brief chronology of Braude's government career. Its most startling omission was its failure to mention her USIA termination. The only mention of her USIA connection involved her temporary thirty-day appointment in January 1954—an appointment given *after* her formal termination at the end of 1953, which the report completely ignored. "No significance can be attached to [the] fact that appointment was of limited duration," the report noted.[33] That line certainly would impress any superior unfamiliar with the facts of the case. It innocently suggested that Braude's appointment was temporary and was not to exceed thirty days. Indeed, on that basis, it was easy to presume that Braude was causing the proverbial tempest in a teapot. To give Chief Macy the benefit of the doubt, he was at the mercy of his Indians.

The rest of the report contained some shaving of the truth and outright fabrications. For example, it mentioned that the USIA Security Office had stated there would be no reason to deny Braude security clearance. But discussions within the USIA's Security Office had already decided that Braude would have to be reinvestigated if considered for hiring and that no one be hired who had been terminated as she had. That decision, made largely in response to Braude's case in 1965—which Johnson of the Civil Service Commission knew quite well and which is completely ignored in this report—gave the lie to the staff's conclusion that Braude never had been denied appointment because of an unfavorable security determination by a federal agency.

Macy's letter outraged Braude. She denied his accusation that she had stigmatized herself, claiming she had told prospective employers only that she had been part of an RIF—bureaucratic jargon for a reduction in force—in 1953. There were two exceptions. The first was the interview with Reed Harris in 1965 for obvious reasons and the second, just one month earlier, in January 1967, with the Regional Director of HEW, a woman personally known by Braude.[34]

But there was some hope. Friends of Braude's in Binghamton, New York, had contacted John Burns, chairman of the New York Democratic Party, who in turn wrote to Marvin Watson, a Lyndon Johnson assistant in the White House. Probably this direct political pressure had more influence on Macy than the ACLU's intervention. In any event, both Macy and Watson now urged the New York Regional Office of HEW to assist Braude in securing a position. Braude must have been terribly tempted to reply to the lies and half-truths of the Civil Service report, yet she feared jeopardizing what seemed like a newfound job opportunity. Three months later, however, the New York office of HEW had found nothing for her. A year later, in May 1968, the Regional Director told her "there has been no change with respect to the development of a position for which you could qualify."[35] So much for political clout.

Throughout the 1960s Braude pursued alternative careers. She did some educational television work in Boston. WGBH selected her to help produce Eleanor

Roosevelt's *Prospects of Mankind,* and after that she participated in the creation of Julia Child's cooking programs. But television, she decided, was "a young people's game—you had to have pull," and she soon drifted away from it. In 1968, after her rejection by HEW, she decided to seek a Ph.D. in French at the City University of New York. The years in school proved refreshing, exciting, and, fortunately, led her to a new career. In 1972, her fortunes changed. The University of Massachusetts needed a French instructor with radio-TV experience—a position made to order for Braude. She was hired—with no loyalty oath required, although she gladly would have taken one. She published scholarly articles and reviews, worked on textbooks, and ultimately received what had so long eluded her and what had become a rare commodity by the late 1970s—tenure.

iv

Braude's hurt and confusion caused by her employment experiences lingered on, however. In 1971, she had an interview with one of her former bosses in the Paris embassy who was interested in hiring her for the State Department's exchange programs. He later reported that he could not make the appointment, saying that reduced hiring policies were in effect.

This incident prompted her again to seek legal counsel. She approached a former co-worker, whom she once had recommended for law school and who was now an associate at the New York firm of Cadwalader & Taft. The woman's husband formerly had worked in Javits' office and, according to Braude, advised his wife against taking the case. Braude then approached Stuart Land (whose mother-in-law she knew), a senior partner in Arnold & Porter in Washington. The firm took the case under its *pro bono publico* program. Using the Privacy Act of 1974, Land secured Braude's USIA file and in 1976 uncovered the true circumstances of her dismissal. Maxwell J. Mehlman, an associate at Arnold & Porter, took over active direction of the case.[36]

Armed with the government's own documents, Braude's lawyers brought suit in the U.S. District Court in the District of Columbia in December 1976. The suit was filed against James Keogh, Director of the USIA, and Robert E. Hampton, Chairman of the Civil Service Commission. The complaint alleged that Braude had been illegally terminated in 1953 and had been subject to a de facto blacklist ever since. The civil action was for a declaratory judgment, reinstatement, and back pay.

Braude's complaint charged that she was dismissed for security reasons and that for twenty-three years the government had camouflaged the fact. In addition, the Civil Service Commission's 1965 "investigation" discovered and perpetuated the cover-up, thus effectively precluding Braude from further pursuing the matter at that time. Not until she secured the relevant documents in her files could Braude fully grasp the true nature of her dismissal. All this, her lawyers contended, violated Braude's right to free speech, free association, and due process. They charged that the termination was arbitrary, an abuse of discretion, and unsupported by any substantial evidence. The failure to give Braude proper notice, a hearing, and an opportunity for review violated the USIA's own regulations and the due process clause of the federal constitution.

The government's response was simple, denying every allegation put forward by Braude's lawyers despite the weight of documentary evidence. Indeed the government still persisted in its cover-up. Braude "was not dismissed for security reasons," the government answered, and "her lack of success in obtaining reemployment with the Federal Government was due to the numbers of qualified applicants and for other similar reasons." Finally, the government moved to dismiss the plaintiff's motion on the grounds that the District Court lacked jurisdiction. While not explicitly accepting the government's position that Braude's claim was without support, in August 1977 Judge June L. Green granted the defendants' motion because the case involved a monetary claim exceeding $10,000, thereby giving jurisdiction to the Court of Claims.[37]

Three months later, Braude's lawyers carried the case to the Court of Claims. Given what appeared to be the incontrovertible evidence, Braude's attorneys moved for a partial summary judgment on the liability issue. This move would have avoided a trial and any complicated determination of relief for Braude until after a decision on the merits of the cause. Braude's brief reiterated the facts of her firing, the cover-up, and the subsequent blacklisting. Again, her lawyers projected the constitutional issues, but relied on the proposition that her termination had been unlawful under applicable USIA regulations and was unauthorized by statute.

The plaintiff's argument relied heavily on the Supreme Court's 1957 decision in *Service* v. *Dulles*. The Court then held that the State Department could not arbitrarily fire an employee on security grounds. Service had been dismissed after seven investigations had cleared him, quite simply because of political pressures from supporters of Nationalist China in Congress. Dulles ostensibly acted on the authority of a McCarran Rider, a congressional authorization of dismissal authority similar to that of Public Law 207, the basis of Braude's dismissal. Dulles argued that security regulations and procedural guarantees did not apply to terminations under the McCarran Rider; furthermore, Service had not been discharged for security reasons. The Supreme Court, however, rejected these positions and held that Dulles was bound by the security regulations promulgated by his own department even though he contended he had acted under the McCarran authority. Braude's lawyers argued that Public Law 207, like the

McCarran Rider, was not intended to negate the procedural safeguards for security discharges.

The McCarran Rider basically was aimed at the "security risk." Public Law 207, however, was designed to enable the USIA Director to terminate unqualified employees who had too much tenure and seniority to be discharged through the usual reduction-in-force techniques. Its legislative history revealed that the law's clear purpose was to give the USIA Director "the latitude and responsibility that go with his position, in an effort to get technically-trained people to fill the highly technical positions in the agency." One isolated congressman suggested the authority might be used to rid the agency of "Communist sympathizers," but he was exceptional. A number of prominent senators from both sides of the aisle (Democrats Fulbright and Magnuson and Republicans Ferguson and Hickenlooper, for example) emphasized that the USIA had an "unusual" need to separate incompetents—not security risks—who had drifted into the Agency from numerous other executive offices. The fact that Congress had repealed the McCarran Rider just prior to passage of Public Law 207 buttressed the plaintiff's case. The prevailing sentiment was that the rider had been unfairly used to effect discharges without procedural safeguards. It was hardly likely that Congress would immediately re-enact legislation to perpetuate the same abuses.

In sum, Public Law 207 was designed to eliminate incompetent workers. Braude's employment ratings, however, always had been favorable, she was qualified for her job, and she had been commended by her supervisor the day prior to her discharge. Finally, the USIA documents themselves conclusively demonstrated that her superiors had used Public Law 207 to dismiss her on security grounds, and without proper notice and hearing procedures.[38]

When the original suit had been filed, the government disputed the material facts. But in the Court of Claims, lawyers for the Justice Department's Civil Division significantly shifted strategy and offered a cross-motion for summary judgment, contending that Braude's suit was time-barred, first by the statute of limitations and second by the doctrine of laches (an undue delay in asserting a right). The government developed a two-pronged, no-lose proposition: either Braude had not been dismissed for security reasons as she alleged; or, if she had been, the six-year statute of limitations and/or the doctrine of laches nullified any claim to damages.[39] The government's syllogistic defense reached new heights of imagination:

• Braude consistently complained that the USIA had wrongfully determined she was a security risk;

• the government, with equal consistency, had told her she was not terminated for that reason;

• despite her belief she had been wronged, Braude did not file any action until 1977.

Ergo: Braude's failure to sue demonstrated a lack of diligence that was inexcusable. Or to put it another way, Braude never should have believed what the government told her.

Braude's lawyers recognized the potential threat of the government's position. They accordingly responded that the government's cover-up from the time of her discharge, and for the next twenty-four years, prevented her from determining the true cause of her dismissal. Braude consequently could not have been expected to have been aware of any cause for action until she obtained the necessary documentation from her files in 1975 and 1976. "In the face of the clear and unconscionable deception of plaintiff by defendant," they concluded, "the government's argument that plaintiff's suit is time-barred must be soundly rejected."[40]

Such arguments were in vain, for the limitations issue and not the facts or merits of the case proved decisive. Two of the three Court of Claims judges ruled in October 1978 that for more than six years prior to her filing, Braude had been "on inquiry" that she had a potential claim. Senior Judge Byron G. Skelton, writing for himself and Judge Robert L. Kunzig, said that the plaintiff had the burden of proof to establish either that the government had concealed its actions so that she was unaware of their existence or that her injury was "inherently unknowable" at the accrual date. Skelton said that the injury resulting from the loss of her position was "obviously knowable." The government's concealment, he added, was no excuse to halt the running of the statute of limitations. The rules of discovery and other pretrial procedures to flesh out claims could have been used by Braude once she was "on inquiry" that she had a claim.[41]

Following Braude's recital of the facts and the incidents of her ordeal, Skelton contended she had a potential claim prior to September 1971—six years before she filed suit in the Court of Claims. For example, he cited her hiring of Byron Scott as a lawyer in 1956 "to find out the truth" of her dismissal; her telling Reed Harris in 1964 that she had the "impression" she was discharged for security reasons, and Harris' response about a "tendency to lean toward" other equal job candidates; her approach to the ACLU, among others—all of which ought to have indicated to her that her dismissal was more than it appeared to be. This, Skelton concluded, was enough to show she was "on inquiry" for projecting a potential claim.[42] With that, the majority granted the government's motion for summary judgment and dismissed Braude's petition.

Judge Philip Nichols, Jr., dissented in part from his colleagues and favored remanding the case to the trial division to try both the limitations issue and the merits of the case together, as they were closely related. He agreed that Braude's actions prior to 1971 demonstrated her awareness that she had a grievance. But Nichols also recognized that the issue was more complex than that. Should the statute of limitations be tolled when the government deliberately and successfully prevented Braude from obtaining the evidence necessary to support a claim, despite her repeated efforts to gain information? Nichols approached the problem with a willingness to construe the facts in favor of the defendant because of the government's motion for summary judgment. Nevertheless, he was impressed that the government made virtually no attempt to deny the cover-up allegations —allegations, he noted, amply supported by the USIA files.[43]

For Nichols, the heart of the matter was that nothing in her record (or in the majority opinion) showed that Braude knew—or even suspected—that she had been illegally fired. She may have suspected she was blacklisted, but that was not a matter for the Court of Claims. Furthermore, the record satisfied him that the government had made "a calculated effort" to prevent Braude from learning the real cause of her termination. Braude herself, her attorneys, and friends had, through the years, used "all due diligence" to discover the truth in her record. That record, as represented to Braude before she secured her file, contained nothing to show she had been illegally discharged. With obvious disdain, Nichols said that the government could not come to court and contend Braude was time-barred because she should have disbelieved the government's own representations. Statutes of limitation had their origins in equitable considerations. The passage of time often erodes evidence, making the proof of charges or claims difficult, regardless of merit. But, Nichols maintained, the rationale of the statute of limitations simply was not applicable when the plaintiff was "confronted with the problem of litigating against a governmental organization which has as one of its primary purposes the preservation of secrecy and the power to obstruct" investigations of potential claims.[44]

In a concluding paragraph, Nichols wrote an eloquent epitaph both to the case and to the times that spawned it. The falsification charges in the case involved persons once well known. They were, he said, entitled to the presumption of good faith, and may have acted on a well-intentioned (but misguided) view of security requirements. He charitably conceded that these officials had perpetuated no personal fraud. But Braude had to deal with the United States government—an institution, Nichols said, in which "no one gets to sign the letters he writes, or to write the letters he signs." Superiors are dependent on subordinates for the facts in the letters; and thus the "Indians," not the "Chiefs," often wield the greater power. The Civil Service Commission's staff report to Chairman Macy vividly underscored the point. Nichols perceptively noted that "many nameless executive branch" workers made Senator McCarthy's rise possible, "and many were burrowed deep in the bureaucracy after he was gone." And there, as in Braude's case, they continued to behave the same way. With the governmental apparatus so constructed, with victims and Chiefs alike manipulated at will, the institution could not cure its security-related wrongs. "Some of the brightest and the best," Nichols concluded, "may have unwittingly lent their names in the way none other than Dean Acheson" figured in John Service's ordeal. The Court of Claims only had to pass "on what the institution did respecting Ms. Braude."[45]

V

Following the decision, Braude's lawyers filed motions for a rehearing and for a rehearing *en banc* in the Court of Claims. Both were denied a month later by votes of 2–1 and 5–2, respectively. Her lawyers believed that the Supreme Court would not reverse a Court of Claims ruling interpreting the statute of limitations as applicable to its own proceedings. The judicial remedies were exhausted. Beatrice Braude understood very well. "They are saying 'you should have sued,' but it wasn't possible to sue. It's Catch-22," she concluded.[46] Braude had had her day in court. But it was a day frighteningly similar to the day of her firing, when she received the forms, and not the substance, of justice.

Braude's lawyers advised her that the most promising alternative was a private congressional act waiving the time limitation and allowing her a hearing on the merits of the claim. New York senators Jacob Javits and Daniel Moynihan introduced such a bill in 1979 and eventually secured unanimous Senate consent on January 29, 1980. But the measure lingered in a House Judiciary subcommittee for nearly a year because the minority Republicans and the Justice Department objected. In a public hearing on August 22, 1980, Representative Robert McClory (Rep.-Ill.) contended that Braude had been dismissed as part of a typical reduction in force. He expressed concern that the bill would lead to a flood of similar claims. McClory ignored the fact that Braude's firing was not an original economy move, and that if it had been, Braude then was denied her civil service rights entitling her to another position. Finally, in the waning hours of the 96th Congress in January 1981, some Republicans let it be known that they would not allow the necessary unanimous consent for passage of the bill. The effort collapsed and for all intents and purposes Braude's long fight was over.[47] The Republicans' insensitivity was an ominous sign of the times, reminiscent of the grim days of the 1950s. The drifting political mood in 1981 was accompanied by renewed demands for governmental secrecy and a revival of loyalty programs.

Braude had wanted justice, and for her justice meant damages and, above all, an apology for the wrongs done to her. Those wrongs were predicated on trivial findings: that Braude briefly had belonged to a leftist political salon, that she had talked to a known Communist, and that her name had appeared in Judith Coplon's address book. Those facts might have implicated her as being anything from an espionage associate to a Mah-Jongg partner of Coplon's. She was neither. Extensive investigations found that she was not a security risk, but the files produced by those investigations "followed her around" and ultimately left her in the cold. We know, and to some extent understand, how such trivialities operated in the dark days of loyalty purges. Less comprehensible, and even less defensible, is that a self-serving, malevolent bureaucracy compounded and perpetuated the wrongs long after the political context had changed.

For more than a quarter century, Braude confronted a bureaucratic bodyguard determined to protect its own actions—but a body which ultimately convicted itself. The lies and deceit damaged not only Braude but the standards of fair play and due process the government devised for itself in the loyalty program. And that may be the most heinous of crimes in a government of laws, for as Justice Brandeis once wrote: "Our government is the potent, the omnipotent teacher. For good or for ill, it teaches the whole people by its example. Crime is contagious. If the government becomes a lawbreaker, it breeds contempt for law; it invites every man to become a law unto himself; it invites anarchy."[48]

Beatrice Braude's case vividly and personally reveals how the loyalty program could work and how difficult it was to challenge its decrees. Her adventure offers some insight into bureaucratic caprice and the techniques of official abuse. Her story also highlights the difficulty of unraveling one's own story against nameless, faceless accusers, aided and abetted by an ongoing cover-up. Not least, it is a story of rare courage and perseverance.

3

"THIS NOTORIOUS PATIENT"
The Asylum of Ezra Pound

> . . . you must decide whether I am to be cured or
> punished.
> —EZRA POUND, PSYCHIATRIC INTERVIEW, 1945

> Overholser's word is final in the matter.
> —JUSTICE DEPARTMENT MEMO, 1947

> At any rate, my thanks.
> —EZRA POUND TO DR. WINFRED OVERHOLSER, 1959

i

Ezra Pound is one of the towering figures of twentieth-century literature: poet, critic, and patron of such contemporaries as T. S. Eliot, Robert Frost, and James Joyce. But Pound also was a notorious Fascist and an anti-Semite, and he was indicted for treason in 1945 for broadcasting for the enemy during World War II.

Pound was never tried. Judged insane and incapable of trial in 1946, he was incarcerated in St. Elizabeth's mental asylum in Washington. He remained there for over twelve years—"a closet which contain[ed] a national skeleton," it was charged. Opinion has been divided on Pound's guilt. To some, the insanity judgment has served to mitigate the seriousness of Pound's wartime behavior. Others, however, have charged that the government institutionalized Pound because it neither understood him nor dared to confront him in open court. In their view the American government used the asylum as a convenient means for dealing with its most famous political prisoner.[1]

But as long-suppressed government files clearly demonstrate, Ezra Pound was not insane. He was not "railroaded" as a consequence of a malicious, vindictive conspiracy. Pound elected to plead insanity and incompetency to avoid the kind of trial that had resulted in the conviction and disgrace of others similarly accused. Once institutionalized, he chose to remain until he could walk out totally

59

free on his own terms. Pound was hardly the victim of a capricious use of psychiatry; if anything, psychiatric testimony blocked and then aborted the legal process in his favor. Furthermore, his "custodian," Dr. Winfred Overholser, Superintendent of St. Elizabeth's, protected him by arguing that Pound was insane, a position he maintained despite overwhelming evidence and professional opinion to the contrary. Overholser's cooperation, authority, and prestige, significantly aided and abetted by the ineptness and timidity of the government's prosecutors, gave Pound the safe martyrdom and asylum he desperately needed.

ii

Ezra Pound was born in 1885, in Hailey, Idaho, where his father worked as a federal registrar of mine claims. Eighteen months later, the family returned to his father's original Wisconsin home. Pound occasionally referred to his "frontier experiences," but in fact his formative years were spent in the East. When he was four, his father became an assayer at the Philadelphia mint—a fact that has led to endless speculation for its connections to Pound's later preoccupation with gold, money, and interest. The family lived a comfortable Main Line existence, and Pound attended a Quaker private school. He entered the University of Pennsylvania by examination when he was fifteen. After two years, he left and finished his degree at Hamilton College. He returned for an M.A. degree at Penn in 1906. While there, he formed a turbulent, lifelong friendship with William Carlos Williams.

Pound received a fellowship in 1906 for doctoral research in England and Spain. By that time, he already had made two trips to Europe. For some reason, the fellowship was revoked and Pound never completed his degree. He then accepted a position as head of the Romance Language Department at Wabash College. But after an episode involving a stranded burlesque dancer whom he had taken into his rooms, he was forced to leave the college in 1908 and abruptly took off for Europe and his destiny. Except for a brief visit in 1939, he did not return to the United States until he was brought back as a prisoner in 1945.

Pound settled in London, and in the next twelve years established himself as an innovative poet and literary critic during one of the most dramatic periods in twentieth-century literary and cultural history. In London he was in constant contact with Yeats, Joyce, and Ford, as well as fellow American expatriates, among them Frost, Eliot, and Amy Lowell. Aside from his own work, notably his *Cantos,* Pound editorially reconstructed Eliot's epic poem *The Waste Land.* After the war, he went to Paris, where he became involved with the Imagists and Dadaists.

In 1924 Pound moved to Rapallo, Italy, and there continued writing his monumental *Cantos,* a work that stretched out over the next four decades. But political, rather than artistic, pursuits dominated Pound's life. The 1920s and 1930s were a time when powerful political ideologies deeply moved countless artists. For many, the traditional bourgeois culture of the West seemed on the wane. Some saw Bolshevism as the wave of the future; others chose the equally disciplined appeal of Fascism. Pound's guru was Benito Mussolini, who in a flight of fantasy he compared favorably to Thomas Jefferson.

Mussolini's Fascism offered Pound a ready prescription for the world's ills. Obsessively, he concentrated on financial and monetary issues, believing that usury and the manipulations of international bankers lay at the root of economic distress. He coupled that view with an anti-Semitism that was pervasive and obscene. He established links with the Social Credit movements in England and the United States, which, like Pound, contended that financial manipulations largely accounted for political and monetary problems. But Pound's anti-Semitism and Fascist solutions generally proved more embarrassing than helpful to other critics of the existing order.

As the depression deepened and the world moved closer to war in the 1930s, Pound grandiosely believed that he could solve both problems. Returning to the United States in 1939 to receive an honorary degree from Hamilton College, he frantically sought out a number of politicians to offer his advice. The President refused to see him. Frustrated and angry, he returned to Italy, where he escalated his criticism of American policy, blaming its failures largely on Franklin D. Roosevelt, Jews, and bankers.[2]

Late in 1940 Pound began to write scripts in English for broadcast from Rome. The combination of his commitment, pique, and the easy money motivated him. In January 1941 he recorded his own scripts, which were broadcast by the Mussolini regime approximately twice a week. After the United States entered the war, he continued the broadcasts until the Italian surrender in 1943. An Italian announcer regularly introduced him with a statement Pound wrote himself: "Rome Radio, acting in accordance with the fascist policy of intellectual freedom and free expression of opinion by those who are qualified to hold it, has offered Dr. Ezra Pound the use of the microphone twice a week. It is understood that he will not be asked to say anything whatsoever that goes against his conscience, or anything incompatible with his duties as a citizen of the United States of America."

Pound's broadcasts, though in substance little more than what he had been saying for years, were now harsher and more vitriolic. He consistently attacked the American entry into the war and he contended that the Axis regimes had been misrepresented by Roosevelt. The United States and its allies, Pound insisted, were the true aggressors. He particularly focused on Roosevelt, bitterly criticizing the President for having joined forces with Churchill and Jewish bankers to rescue the British Empire. In one typical assault, Pound asserted that it was an outrage that the "sub-Jew in the White House should send American lads to die for their Jewsoons and Sassoons and the private interest of the skum of the English earth, and the still lower dregs of the Parsee and Levantine importations. . . . To send boys from Omaha to Singapore to die for British monopoly and brutality is not the act of an American patriot."[3]

One might wish to dismiss such remarks as having little more value than country club prattle or simply to equate them to the rantings of anti-Roosevelt, anti-Semitic speakers and pamphleteers who enjoyed occasional attention. But Pound was not in Union or Pershing Square. He was in an enemy nation during wartime, and therefore, to use constitutional language, did appear to be adhering to the nation's enemy and giving it aid and comfort.

Typically, controversy surrounds Pound's alleged efforts to leave Italy just before and after the outbreak of the war. The most recent analysis, largely based on State Department documents, concludes that Pound made no serious effort to return to the United States. Why did Pound stay? His own letters reveal his concern for his aging, ailing parents, who lived with him and could not travel, as well as his need to remain with his books—his "tools," as he called them. But he also believed that his "work must continue. Twenty or, more visibly, ten years of work for a New Europe," he wrote.[4] Pound, in short, was committed to what he saw as the emerging New Order and to translating his ideas into action. Yet always he insisted that his actions were not treasonable. Two grand juries thought otherwise.

After the successful military coup against Mussolini in July 1943, Pound left Rome and returned to Rapallo. He worked fitfully on the Italian translations of his broadcasts, articles, and books from the 1930s, and wrote articles praising Italian Fascism and the Duce and attacking the Allied governments. He actively supported Mussolini's rump government in Salò in northern Italy. The Fascist regime continued to pay him a monthly salary through the Ministry of Popular Culture, whose chief described him as "the collaborator Ezra Pound, American writer, old and proven friend of Italy, in the service of which he has placed his intellectual bearing."[5]

Pound first was indicted in July 1943, along with six other persons charged with broadcasting from Germany. The indictments accused the seven of intentionally and treasonably aiding and abetting the enemy during war. After Pound's return to the United States in October 1945, he was reindicted and charged with accepting employment from an enemy nation to dissuade the American people from supporting their government's war effort. Specifically, the indictment alleged nineteen overt acts in the "prosecution, performance and execution" of treason.

Word of his first treason indictment reached Pound in Rapallo in August 1943. He promptly wrote to Attorney General Francis Biddle to deny the charges and justify his actions. He maintained that his broadcasts constituted an exercise of his right to free speech and that they set out facts that he knew to be true. The expression of his conscience, he asserted, was his duty as an American citizen. "[A] man's duties increase with his knowledge," he told Biddle.[6] Pound's surprisingly temperate letter—perhaps he realized the seriousness of his situation—showed no recognition of the meaning of treason. Either from falsehood or from ignorance, he denied that his broadcasts were beamed to American troops. He also failed to acknowledge that all of his scripts were approved by the Ministry of Popular Culture before he broadcast.

Whether Pound appreciated his peril or not, American army commanders were alerted to find and arrest him. But armed Communist partisans reached him first in April 1945. Pound wisely demanded that they turn him over to American authorities. American MPs then drove him to the Counter-Intelligence Center in Genoa, where he was questioned for several weeks. He signed a lengthy statement that forthrightly admitted and defended his actions, as well as expressed his willingness to stand trial. Finally, on May 27, he was taken to the Detention Training Center (DTC) near Pisa. Army orders provided for the "utmost security measures" and specified that he was to be given no preferential treatment.[7]

The DTC harbored some of the Army's most unsavory criminals, among them deserters, rapists, and murderers. But the camp was also a rehabilitation center for soldiers convicted of lesser crimes, who were later returned to combat. While certainly no country club, neither was it Alcatraz.

A number of army officers have described Pound's seven months in the DTC. The commanding officer extended significant privileges to Pound, including the use of a typewriter and writing paper. He and "Uncle Ezra," as Pound was called, talked about economics, a subject the officer had taught before the war. Quite naturally, the commanding officer later resented the charges of sadism leveled by Pound's supporters. Another officer, even more sympathetic, noted Pound's apprehension when it was time to leave. Pound was no doubt thinking "of the solicitude, friendliness, and productiveness" of his latter days in the DTC, this officer recalled.[8]

Pound undoubtedly suffered in the DTC, as the *Pisan Cantos* remind us. When he arrived, he was placed in what he called an open-air "gorilla cage." Yet he received extraordinary working privileges, and here Pound produced the poetry that won the Bollingen Prize in 1949. In addition, Pound's wife, as well as his mistress and their daughter, were allowed to visit him.

The Pisa experience is crucial to any understanding of Pound's case and condition. He periodically referred to it as the time of his "breakdown." His advisers and supporters later claimed that it explained Pound's incompetency to stand trial. But contemporary medical accounts offer a very different picture.

After Pound complained of "confusion" and "claustrophobia," two army psychiatrists examined him extensively in the DTC and both found "no evidence of psychosis, neurosis or psychopathy." While noting Pound's complaints of confinement and certain minor fears, the doctors found "no paranoia, delusions nor hallucinations." Routine neurological tests proved negative. The doctors in Pisa found Pound voluble, of superior intelligence, and without notable personality defects. One doctor added that Pound's age, coupled with a "loss of personality resilience," could precipitate a mental breakdown—"of which premonitory symptoms are discernible"—unless he was transferred to the United States or to a more adequate institution in Italy. Three days later, Pound was moved to a tent with officer prisoners and provided with reading and writing materials. His "warden" noted a satisfactory mental adjustment and further psychiatric reports of Pound's mental competency.[9]

Several weeks later, the Justice Department relayed to army headquarters in Washington an FBI report that a military psychiatrist had found strong indications of a mental breakdown. The report was wrong, but the Army responded to Justice's request for a further psychiatric interview. Another examination, reported on July 17, delved more deeply into Pound's family history and his personal affairs. He was evasive only with regard to his marital and extramarital situation, as he would be for the next thirteen years. But again, the doctor found no evidence of psychosis, neurosis, or depression. The "transitory anxiety state" resulting from Pound's capture, close confinement, and "apprehension over his future" had eased once Pound was made more physically comfortable.

This doctor discussed Pound's economic theories and radio broadcasts with the patient. He found a "prodigious flow of thought," somewhat repetitious, but "on the whole relevant and coherent." Pound maintained that his ideas and radio broadcasts were designed to prevent war and to uphold the Constitution. Not for the last time, Pound offered his expert knowledge of foreign affairs to the government. And again, he defended his broadcasts as exercises in free speech and denied that his actions were treasonable. Significantly, the doctor noted no evidence of hallucinations or delusions.[10]

Shortly before leaving the DTC, Pound had written a lengthy letter to his English lawyers discussing his political situation as well as literary and business affairs. The letter was neatly typed, lucid, and detailed, albeit haphazardly organized. In it, Pound discussed the "essential facts" of his case and clearly indicated his understanding of his acts and their implications. He denied having broadcast "axis propaganda"; instead, he insisted that the views were his own and he had said nothing contrary to his conscience or duties as an American citizen. He refused to recant any of his opinions; indeed, he felt some vindication given the priority the British Labor government assigned to nationalizing the Bank of England. "After 25 years of study," he wrote, "I can no longer be treated as a whimsical child in these matters." Finally, he believed that his actions could be defended on free speech grounds.[11] Pound's views reflected his familiar grandiosity and egocentrism. Yet he clearly realized the seriousness and complexity of the charges against him. In his own extravagant way, he believed that he could defend against them.

In mid-November, Pound was flown to Washington to face charges of treason. On the trip, Pound subjected his fellow travelers to lengthy discourses on his economic theories, the Jewish conspiracy, the moral dishonesty of Franklin D. Roosevelt, and his special contacts in Japan and China that could aid the United States. Again professing innocence, Pound worried about finding an American attorney with sufficient knowledge of his work to conduct a proper defense. Since his "mental capacity and studies placed him in a sphere above that of ordinary mortals," it would, he said, "require a 'superman' to conduct his own defense."[12] The grandiosity that became so familiar to those involved in the case was evident here, but grandiosity is not incompetence, let alone psychosis.

Following Pound's transfer to civilian authority, Julien Cornell, a lawyer retained by Pound's American publisher, James Laughlin, visited him. To Cornell, Pound gave a lurid description of his Pisa confinement, claiming he suffered a complete loss of memory until September—a statement wholly at variance with his behavior and interviews with the army doctors in Italy throughout the summer of 1945. Cornell naïvely believed that the government would not strenuously oppose an application for bail, thinking that the government regarded the case as "a mild one of its kind." Cornell did not yet know, of course, that the Justice Department lawyers were fully committed to the presentation of a lengthy list of treason charges.

Cornell also decided to pursue an insanity defense, an idea first suggested to him by Laughlin. More importantly, Pound informed Cornell that he already had settled on the same strategy. Cornell anticipated the normal contradictory psychiatric testimony, but he was prepared to rely on a sympathetic jury. In the meantime, his client sent word that he wished to publish some cantos written at the DTC in Pisa.[13]

The 1945 grand jury indictment against Pound was based on evidence amassed since August 1943, when the Justice Department first dispatched FBI investigators to Italy. The FBI file contained excerpts from Pound's broadcasts, his communications with the Italian government, records of payments to him, and statements from witnesses to his broadcasts. The evidence was impressive enough so that the grand jury charged Pound with nineteen overt acts of treason.[14]

Following the grand jury's action, Cornell promptly filed a motion for bail so that Pound could be sent to a hospital. On November 27, Pound was brought from the District of Columbia jail for arraignment before Federal Judge Bolitha Laws. Pound said nothing, but Cornell entered a not guilty plea. Responding to

Cornell's motion, Laws held over a decision on bail but remanded Pound to Gallinger Hospital for examination and treatment. Cornell had to arrange for a psychiatrist to represent the defendant. His first choice was Dr. Winfred Overholser, Superintendent of St. Elizabeth's Hospital in Washington, and perhaps the nation's most reputable forensic psychiatrist. Overholser declined because of his government position. Cornell then secured Dr. Wendell Muncie of Johns Hopkins University. Overholser, meanwhile, joined with Dr. Marion King, Chief Medical Officer of the U.S. Bureau of Prisons and the Public Health Service, and Joseph Gilbert, Chief Psychiatrist at Gallinger Hospital, to examine Pound on behalf of the government. Overholser's prestige made him the unofficial leader of the doctors.

Overholser had begun his psychiatric specialization during World War I when he treated soldiers suffering from war neuroses. Following that, he worked in Massachusetts mental hospitals, becoming Commissioner of the Massachusetts Department of Mental Diseases in 1934. He went to St. Elizabeth's as superintendent in 1937, remaining there until his retirement in 1962. In Washington, Overholser pioneered in outpatient treatment and programs enabling patients to work outside the hospital. He founded the American Psychiatric Association's section on forensic psychiatry, and later served as president of the Association in 1947–48. He wrote an early, basic text on psychiatry and the law, in which he forcefully argued that defendants suffering from any mental disease or defect were not responsible for their crimes.[15]

While the doctors began their examinations, Cornell reported to Pound's English lawyer that he doubted whether Pound ever would be able to withstand the rigors of a long trial. He thought the government would have to assume responsibility for restoring Pound's physical and mental health. Once again, Cornell, acting on instructions from Pound, began arrangements for publication of additional cantos and translations from Confucius. Pound specifically asked that T. S. Eliot's publisher, Faber and Faber, undertake the publication.[16]

The four doctors—Muncie plus the three government psychiatrists—saw Pound on several occasions, both separately and together. Within two weeks, they were ready with a unanimous report to the court—much to the pleasant surprise of Cornell and to the dismay of the prosecutors. Dr. Muncie told Cornell that Dr. Overholser did not want the usual farce of psychiatric disagreement, which forced a jury decision on a matter that really was the responsibility of medical people. Muncie's initial impression was that Pound was a "plain psychopath," but apparently after talking to the other doctors, he too concluded that Pound was insane.[17]

Overholser subsequently told the court that the doctors had met on December 13 and readily agreed on a report. But on the eleventh, Dr. King submitted an examination report riddled with ambiguity. King's report apparently is the only extant recorded opinion of the four doctors in this period. He found Pound astute, intelligent, cooperative, apparently sincere, rather tense, with no regrets for his acts, and steadfast in support of his convictions. Pound exhibited his familiar grandiosity, claiming he had information of "atomic bomb" capacity and expressing a desire to learn Russian with a Georgian dialect so he could deal directly with Stalin. Despite Pound's complaints about the Pisa confinement, King accepted the findings of the doctors in Italy and concluded that Pound had suffered an understandable hysterical reaction to his situation.

King noted the "querulous, egocentric, arrogant, critical and eccentric traits" that had characterized Pound's career both before and during his Italian experience. Admittedly, he was "far different" from the "average" person. Nevertheless, King insisted "he cannot be considered mentally ill and thus absolved from responsibility simply because he is different and encountered trouble due to his own folly. This would be an unreasonable extreme and tantamount to absolving other outstanding artists and even statesmen from their errors on psychiatric grounds."

But King qualified his judgment by finding that "rather ill-defined yet definite symptoms of mental illness exist." To King, Pound's grandiose proposals, his exaggerated sense of self-importance, and his naïve reaction to the charges against him indicated "mental instability." Those symptoms, King concluded, characterized "a paranoid state of psychotic proportions," and he recommended hospital care.[18]

King's report originally was written on December 11. He revised it after a joint examination and conference with the other doctors two days later to include the conclusion that Pound's condition took on "psychotic proportions." Nothing in the bulk of the report justified such a deviation. What is more, King's revisions were made after the four doctors had filed their opinion on December 14 to the court, which Judge Laws made public on December 21. Their joint statement contended that Pound suffered from "a paranoid state" which rendered him "mentally unfit" to participate reasonably in his own defense. He was, they concluded, "insane and mentally unfit for trial, and is in need of care in a mental hospital."[19]

Judge Laws quickly complied and ordered Pound delivered to St. Elizabeth's Hospital on December 21 to begin what became a thirteen-year stay. Sensitive to public opinion and pressures from their superiors, federal prosecutors pressed for a jury trial on Pound's sanity. Meanwhile, Overholser and the staff doctors at St. Elizabeth's had further opportunity to interview Pound. For several weeks, Pound was subjected to the most intensive examinations of his long incarceration. Strangely, no official diagnosis was ever made. The doctors refused to render a judgment of psychosis, and their observations tended to portray Pound as competent to stand trial. None of this, however, impressed Superintendent Overholser.

On the night of Pound's arrival at St. Elizabeth's he had a thorough physical examination and an extensive psychiatric interview. In every respect his physical condition was normal. When the doctor asked Pound to give a brief account of himself, the patient launched into a lengthy explanation of his Pisa confinement and his broadcasts from Italy. He claimed that he broadcast because he could not find any other outlet for his views. He insisted that his actions were not treasonable and that his speeches consisted of materials he had used long before the war. Pound defended the broadcasts as reflecting his "sense of patriotic duty" and "sense of duty to humanity." Throughout, he attacked Roosevelt and Congress for having violated the Constitution.

The doctor noted Pound's egotism, haughtiness, dogmatism, and belief in his infallibility and omniscience. Pound specifically denied any past bizarre behavior on his part, and the doctor found no evidence of it in the interview. Concluding, the doctor said that Pound displayed "no marked deviations from the normal in degree or kind" and "no outright deficiency in orientation." Equally significant, he concluded that Pound was "quite complacent if not actually pleased with his present status."[20]

After Pound settled in St. Elizabeth's, Dr. Jerome Kavka, a young resident, conducted extensive interviews with him for several weeks, covering his family and personal history. Kavka's interviews produced the basic background material for the hospital records. With the formal sanity trial only several weeks away, it was a crucial time.

Pound occasionally was sullen and uncooperative, and most of the interviews were brief, since he complained of fatigue. Yet Kavka found Pound evasive only with regard to his marital and sexual affairs. Pound was his familiar animated self, soliloquizing, gesticulating, and using "the most" profane language. Pound performed judgment problems accurately, but Kavka believed that Pound failed to appreciate the seriousness of his situation since he continued to maintain that he could defend himself. Pound claimed to have questioned his sanity in the past, but he told Kavka: "No, I don't think I am insane, but I am so shot to pieces that it would take me years to write a sensible piece of prose. I think I am of unsound mind, and I don't think I have been shown good treatment here. I am absolutely unfit to transact any business."

On February 6, one week before the trial, Kavka summarized his interviews. He concluded that Pound was intellectually alert, well oriented, and "gave no evidence of clear cut abnormal mental content," although his self-evaluation as a significant world figure bordered on the "delusional."[21]

A week earlier, Kavka and five other doctors met to review the case. Their report mentioned no evidence of mental depression or psychomotor retardation. The doctors found him "an odd character," who probably had been egocentric and eccentric for many years. One doctor suggested that Pound might have had a psychopathic personality because of "certain asocial and antisocial behavior with some disturbance of interpersonal relationships." Beyond that vague judgment, there was no conclusion of insanity or psychosis, and no suggestion whatsoever that Pound was incompetent to stand trial. But when the findings were delivered to Overholser, he suggested further observation before reaching a final decision.

During the examination period, a staff psychologist administered a Rorschach test. He found a long-standing, marked personality disorder, essentially narcissistic and egocentric. He also reported that while Pound displayed some paranoid attitudes, there was "no evidence of psychosis."[22]

As the trial neared for his most famous patient, Superintendent Overholser had precious little in his file from his own staff to support any conclusion of either insanity or incompetency to stand trial. In mid-January he obtained the complete file on Pound's Italian activities from the Justice Department to aid his psychiatric evaluation.[23] But he kept his own counsel. Except for a brief report of a visit by the court-appointed doctors on February 7, 1946, the hospital files contain no record or notes of Overholser's interviews with Pound; this would be true throughout Pound's long stay at St. Elizabeth's.

Cornell, meanwhile, was in touch with the court-appointed doctors. He knew they believed Pound incompetent for trial. Cornell also claimed that the doctors told him they did not expect any changes in Pound's condition and therefore it would not be necessary to keep him in the hospital for long. He expected that the government would soon drop the case and that Pound would be freed. He assured Dorothy Pound that her husband's condition was "just about normal," although the doctors recognized a paranoid state which affected his judgment and his ability to defend himself.[24]

On February 12, a day before the hearing, Cornell visited with Overholser. To his surprise, the superintendent related the staff's division on Pound's true condition. Overholser reportedly said that their judgment was "distorted by patriotism," but he remained firm in his belief that Pound was unfit for trial. He also told Cornell that he would take the doctors' reports to the trial and refute them, if necessary. Cornell apparently was unworried, confident that the prestige and authority of Overholser and the other doctors would outweigh any dissenting voices. Some years later, after Pound's release, Cornell asked Overholser if he could quote the superintendent's statement that the staff "almost unanimously" opposed him. Overholser replied that although the remark was not "strictly accurate," he preferred that Cornell remain silent.[25] By that time, Overholser was terribly anxious to conceal any doubts or criticism of his position.

Pound appeared at his sanity hearing on February 13—his only formal trial. It was a brief and one-sided affair. Cornell initiated the questioning, followed by the government's cross-examination, largely conducted by Isaiah Matlack. Muncie, as the defense psychiatrist, appeared as the first witness. Twice he flirted with the truth: once he testified that the staff doctors' findings were similar to those of the four court-appointed psychiatrists, and again when he said that there had been no disagreement among the four doctors. He also admitted that he had little experience examining accused criminals.

Muncie was convinced that Pound could not participate in his own defense. His general mental condition was marked by grandiosity, vagueness, and distractibility. But he emphasized that Pound's system of reasoning made it impossible for him to think outside that pattern and respond to the reality of his situation. Muncie described Pound as a "peculiar personality," with marked neurotic and paranoid states. On cross-examination, however, he admitted that queer and peculiar ideas did not necessarily constitute insanity. He also acknowledged that Pound understood the charges and knew he could be tried for treason, while steadfastly insisting he had not committed treason. Matlack raised the consideration that Pound's delusional and grandiose qualities were no different from the attitudes of leaders who thought they could conquer the world. Muncie simply replied that he had not examined such people.

Dr. King's testimony was the most forthright and clinically vivid. He admitted he had changed his mind about Pound, claiming that further interviews persuaded him that much of Pound's talk was "abnormal." Yet when queried about the St. Elizabeth staff reports, he referred only to the physical examinations. King flatly asserted that Pound was a paranoid of psychotic proportions and unfit for trial. He admitted that a psychotic person with paranoid tendencies could stand trial, but he insisted that Pound's confusion and distractibility were such that he never could participate in his own defense. Furthermore, his emotional state, his easy exhaustion, and his inability to reason might lead to a physical or a mental collapse if he was tried.

In the light of his central involvement with the case, Overholser's testimony is the most interesting. The superintendent essentially emphasized Pound's inability to stand trial. Pound's rambling, illogical, vague method of talking would make it difficult for his attorney to keep him in a straight line of conversation, the doctor said. He believed that Pound's present state was the end product of a lifelong pattern of antagonism, eccentricity, egocentricity, and querulousness. Overholser indicated that he did not anticipate any fundamental change in Pound's condition and added that such a paranoid state tended, if anything, to worsen.

Responding to Cornell, Overholser admitted he had seen the reports of his staff doctors, but saw no reason to change his opinion. Matlack picked up that point on cross-examination and asked the superintendent if he had the hospital records with him. Overholser replied that they were in his briefcase, but Matlack inexplicably dropped the point. "I smiled to myself at Dr. Overholser's confidence and daring," Cornell later noted.[26] Perhaps even more startling was Overholser's casual admission that the extensive staff examination of Pound had not yet produced a formal diagnosis. Matlack apparently expressed some surprise and asked Overholser to repeat the point. But he dropped that line of questioning and the subject was not raised again.

Matlack displayed a similar diffidence when he questioned Overholser about the army psychiatrists' reports. Overholser admitted that those doctors concluded that Pound was not psychotic, but he casually dismissed their findings, saying that they were only "interested in prison facts" and that he did not know how long they had seen Pound. Matlack—who had copies of the reports—made no effort to enter on the record the extent of the examinations or compare their depth to those presented by Muncie, King, Gilbert, and Overholser.

Matlack made one extended effort to determine Pound's understanding of the charges. Overholser acknowledged that Pound knew the nature of the indictment and the meaning of treason, but that he did not comprehend how those charges could apply to him. Responsibility for his actions, and responsibility for understanding their meaning, were somewhat beside the point, the doctor insisted; Pound's mental state precluded any ability on his part coherently to explain or defend his actions.

The four doctors carefully and consistently presented their expert observations. They described a patient given to extreme volubility, while complaining of exhaustion, and whose statements exhibited excessive grandiosity, while given to vagueness and easy distractibility. They reported his belief that the British Secret Service and Communists had instigated his troubles, a belief that Overholser described as "pathological" and consistent with paranoid tendencies. Although King described the paranoia as of "psychotic proportions," the doctors only vaguely suggested that Pound was of unsound mind. The doctors all agreed that Pound simply was unfit for trial since no lawyer could communicate effectively with him.[27]

In his charge to the jury, Judge Laws focused on the doctors' chief contentions. He emphasized that an accused person must be able to cooperate with his counsel, and he reminded the jury that the law was humane to the extent that a trial could not be held if there was a possibility of the defendant's breakdown. He also stressed the qualifications of the four doctors. While the jurors were not bound by the doctors' testimony, Laws told them that inasmuch as they had "united in a clear and unequivocal view with regard to the situation, I presume you will have no difficulty in making up your mind." The jury then retired, only to return in three minutes with a unanimous verdict that Ezra Pound was of "unsound mind."

With that judgment, Pound returned to St. Elizabeth's, where he remained for over twelve years. He received visitors regularly, wrote, and conducted his business affairs. There were some isolated protests over the outcome, but in 1946 Pound's friends and supporters had no reason to complain. He had found sanctuary from the processes of criminal justice. Ironically, the government—by the actions of Dr. Overholser—itself provided the sanctuary. Pound was in good hands.

There were some criticisms of the handling of the case and recurrent rumors of disagreement within the government, but the attempts to secure documented evidence proved fruitless. A reporter for New York's *PM* newspaper was aware of the army reports, but neither the Justice Department nor the Army would release them.[28]

Several weeks after the sanity hearing, J. M. McInerney, one of Matlack's superiors in the Criminal Division, received a visit from a *Newsweek* reporter who claimed that three St. Elizabeth's staff doctors would testify that Pound was sane. The reporter may have discovered the staff's disagreement, but one of the doctors he named has since denied any inclination on their part to "go public" with the story. In any event, McInerney was unimpressed, for he blandly told Matlack that the story did not offer a "sufficient basis" for reopening the case. Matlack readily agreed. He recalled that Overholser had indicated that "one or two of his staff" disagreed with him. Matlack also reported that Overholser privately told him that "the majority of the staff was in agreement with him"—a remark somewhat different from what he told Cornell. Matlack saw no "useful purpose" in reopening the sanity hearing, for the dissidents would be opposed by the court-appointed psychiatrist "plus five or six" other staff members.[29]

The hospital records do not corroborate the claims that Overholser alleged to have made to Matlack. But the government's prosecutor simply was reluctant to pursue the matter and confront Overholser. One did not lightly contest expertise within the bureaucracy. Overholser was a formidable figure, in and out of the government. He was an oracle of sorts, comparable (albeit on a smaller scale) to J. Edgar Hoover; as with Hoover, Overholser's judgments largely went unchallenged within his domain. Perhaps also, Matlack was content to let matters rest where they were because the case was growing cold. It had "looked good" in late 1945 and early 1946, but Pound, Matlack realized, was not as "rabid" as those who had broadcast for the Nazis. In late 1947 Matlack suspected that Pound's eccentricity might persuade a jury that he was not to be taken seriously.[30]

iii

Dr. Overholser was a man of learning, with a keen respect for cultural and literary endeavors. He never revealed his personal opinion of Pound's political views. Given his character and his professional associations, as well as the memories of those who knew him, he probably was repulsed by Pound's outrageous social and racial views. Yet Overholser liked and admired Pound. After Pound's release, Overholser recalled their personal relations as "always most pleasant." He acknowledged Pound's "eminent standing" as a poet. Professional dealings aside, Overholser's own literary interests frequently led him to visit Pound to discuss "persons and things" of mutual interest. Pound's non-literary opinions probably best explain Overholser's comments that his patient was bombastic, opinionated, and supercilious. He proudly noted, however, that Pound's attitude toward him "was always friendly," despite the fact that Overholser was "technically" his "custodian."[31]

The superintendent was more than that; he was his protector from adverse publicity, from his lawyer, and from the ever-present threat of prosecution. Overholser resolutely screened visitors who sought interviews for publication. "EP does not grant interviews," the patient told his doctor, and Overholser followed Pound's wishes. Pound set his own schedule, and he often used the superintendent to ward off undesirable visitors. Overholser generally required visitors to secure his permission, but he admitted that "invariably" he discussed such matters first with Pound. Thus Pound could see H. L. Mencken but at the same time complain that he was too "fatigued" to see someone else. He also refused to allow his son to visit. Overholser facilitated the recording of Pound's poetry readings. He consistently extended visiting hours for Pound, even allowing "his closest disciples and helpers" to visit at any hour. Overholser naturally bristled at outside reports that Pound was mistreated; he correctly told his superior at one point that Pound had more privileges than did other patients.[32] Many of Pound's well-intentioned supporters failed to see, or to admit, how comfortable his situation was.

The superintendent also advised Pound's lawyer on legal matters that might undermine his judgment and position. Shortly after the hearing, Cornell sent Pound a document requiring his signature to give Cornell the power of attorney for transacting publishing business. The letter was prepared at Pound's request. Overholser returned the document unsigned, contending that Pound's legal status of incompetency would be inconsistent with conferring the power of attorney. He then suggested the appointment of a guardian to protect Pound's interests. Cornell quickly agreed, but said that it would have to await the arrival of Pound's wife. In the meantime, he continued to press for Pound's signature. He thought that in publishing and business matters, Pound had an "extraordinary clarity of mind, even shrewdness, . . . which is in striking contrast to his lack of comprehension of social and political issues and his own relation thereto." He thought Pound legally competent to conduct business although he was unfit for trial. As a layman, he thought it possible for a person to be sane on some subjects and insane on others. He suggested that Pound qualify his power of attorney by adding a statement that he was "of unsound mind to an extent I am unable to stand trial on charges of treason."[33] The matter soon became moot as Dorothy Pound arrived to assume guardianship.

Overholser resisted numerous suggestions that he consent to Pound's release to a private sanitarium. As long as the indictment stood and as long as Pound's mental condition remained the same, the court order obligated Overholser to keep him at St. Elizabeth's. He admitted that if Pound were an ordinary patient, without any pending criminal charges, he would not hesitate to permit his removal. Dr. William Carlos Williams, acting upon Dorothy Pound's urging, asked Overholser if Pound could be removed to his custody and care. Again, Overholser said he could do so only if the pending charges were dropped.[34]

Throughout the years of confinement, Overholser regularly had to respond to Justice Department inquiries regarding Pound's condition. The continued political sensitivity of the case dictated periodic review. Overholser's replies revealed a persistent vagueness regarding Pound's mental condition and some interesting contradictions.

William Foley, Chief of the Internal Security Section in the Justice Department, received a report in October 1948 from a doctor whose son had visited Pound. The doctor told Foley that Pound had considerable freedom at the hospital and that he was in constant communication with all kinds of persons. The doctor thought Pound "obviously sane" and believed he should be released immediately or brought to trial.

The doctor's report prompted a Justice Department inquiry to Overholser on Pound's current condition. Overholser readily acknowledged that Pound had a steady stream of visitors, but he claimed that none had ever told him that Pound was sane. Besides, there had been "no essential change" in Pound since his admission to St. Elizabeth's. He remained "extremely bombastic and opinionated, highly disorganized in his train of thought, and possessed of a considerable number of extremely grandiose ideas about himself as well as ideas of persecution against others." Overholser repeated his court opinion that Pound was mentally incompetent to stand trial and added that he considered it unlikely that there would be any substantial improvement in Pound's condition, "which is a singularly deep-seated one."[35]

But some of Pound's oldest and closest friends had told Overholser that they thought he was in relatively good condition. William Carlos Williams, Pound's friend since college days, a fellow poet, and a medical doctor, found Pound "about as he has always been." "The quality of his ideas has so far as I can tell undergone no change," Williams noted, and "he is interesting, amusing and even profound in many of his observations." He thought Pound a "fool" but hardly dangerous.[36] The disagreement of the two doctors is striking. Overholser's impressions of Pound's grandiosity struck Williams as just what he had observed in the man for forty years. Furthermore, in Williams' view Pound was "interesting and profound," not "bombastic and opinionated," as Overholser saw him. To some extent, Overholser also thought Pound was a fool—"supercilious," was his favorite description—yet he realized the danger for Pound if he left St. Elizabeth's.

But the most significant refutation of Overholser's public and official pronouncements on Pound's condition came from within the hospital itself. As a patient, Pound periodically was examined and interviewed by staff psychiatrists and neurologists. For the years between 1946 and 1953 the hospital file contains several reports a year. The doctors' notes are remarkably uniform in their clinical observations of Pound's mental state. No staff doctor supported or substantiated the conclusion that Pound was insane and incompetent to stand trial. Just before the 1946 trial, Overholser noted the court-appointed doctors' unanimous conclusion that Pound suffered from a "paranoid condition with a considerable psychoneurotic coloring."[37] But the staff doctors then, and throughout Pound's confinement, never corroborated even that non-psychotic conclusion. Not until 1955 did a single doctor dictate a "diagnosis" of psychosis. That doctor was Overholser himself.

Some of the doctors' reports are detailed; others are brief. Basically, they contain similar information. The doctors commented on Pound's personal appearance, the condition of his room, his refusal to do hospital work, his reading and writing, his aloofness from other patients, his alleged fatigue, his disdain for psychiatrists, his streams of obscenities, his political, social, and economic diatribes, and his justification of his wartime activities. But their observations and conclusions reveal their consistent professional judgment that Pound was not psychotic.[38]

March 31, 1946: A prominent staff neurologist referred to Pound's "obviously feigned infirmities," an observation confirmed two weeks later by a psychiatrist who found Pound's "sudden outburst of energy and enthusiasm" inconsistent with a "marked preoccupation with his weakness and exhaustion." The neurologist claimed that Pound "effected [*sic*] an elaborate caricature of fatigue" when asked if he wished to stand trial. Yet he also found that Pound apparently appreciated his predicament. This doctor experienced little difficulty in understanding Pound's economic and social views. While these ideas were admittedly unorthodox, he found them "logical and coherent."

May 9, 1946: Another doctor was skeptical about Pound's fatigue. "He forgets for a period of time his pose of fatigue," only to be reminded of it when the questions became difficult. This doctor similarly found that Pound fully appreciated his predicament.

July 3, 1946: Pound vigorously defended his broadcasts, insisting he had not uttered treason. The doctor noted that Pound spent "most of his time writing."

August 12, 1946: Pound was found to be eating and sleeping well, but spent most of his "complaining time" lying on his bed. In general, Pound continued "in his invariable, immutable, undeviating[,] steadfast[,] constant way without perceptible vicissitudes."

October 8, 1946: Pound described himself as a war "casualty." The doctor found "no evidence of other mental states" than fatigue. He did, however, refer to "some mild paranoid trends" that Pound exhibited when he talked about international bankers and his attempts to prevent World War II.

(In January 1947 Cornell attempted to secure bail for Pound. The court refused, but with the consent of the Justice Department and Overholser, Pound was transferred to a private room with more pleasant surroundings and fewer restraints.)

March 28, 1947: Following his transfer to a room in the Chestnut Ward, with a view of the Potomac, Pound was found to have made a good adjustment in his new surroundings. But his ideas on the war and his role in it had not changed at all. The examining doctor found "no abnormal content" in his ideas, except that some of them bordered on the delusional.

June 27, 1947: Pound was found to be characteristically contemptuous of others, but nevertheless he was "well oriented in all spheres," demonstrating "excellent comprehension, attention and perception." Pound's days were largely spent writing and conducting his enormous correspondence. Finally, this doctor noted that "apparently [the] patient does not exhibit any delusional or other psychotic material."

October 17, 1947: In one of Pound's lengthier interviews, another doctor reported that Pound complained of fatigue, but then would be highly animated and would attempt to take over the interview. The doctor was convinced that Pound had a particular genius and that he was "eccentric, is a poseur, and has a general flair for histrionics." Perhaps most significantly, this doctor was struck by what he called the "obscureness" of Pound's mental illness. Now, nearly two years after the trial, this observer discovered there had been no diagnosis, and it appeared that Pound did not fit any of the current classification categories of mental illness. He acknowledged that some of Pound's ideas could be considered paranoid and delusional, but he suggested that this would be true only in terms of our own cultural framework, and not necessarily so in others. He compared Pound's "ideational activity and his particular distortion" to such other socially destructive philosophies as those of Wagner, Hitler, and Mussolini. Finally, he suggested that Pound might best be understood in terms of a "social illness" or of a "mild illness."

March 12, 1948: The doctor found "no perceptible change" in "this notorious patient" from a year earlier. In this interview Pound launched into obscenities to describe the government and foreign policy. Pointing to the Capitol, he complained about the "drivel that comes out of that ——— house."

June 1, 1948: Pound still was doing "a lot of writing." He suggested to the doctor that he be allowed "ground parole," complaining that all kinds of "blithering idiots" were free. He attacked the Attorney General and the President for persecuting him in particular.

September 30, 1948: Pound complained that no psychiatrist could possibly understand him, and neither could the American people, who were twenty to thirty years behind the times. The psychiatrist did understand, however, that Pound's memory was intact, that he was "precisely oriented," and that his insight and judgment were unimpaired.

March 19, 1949: Pound complained vigorously about having to submit to another interview. He was particularly insulting to the doctor, who had a common Jewish name. The doctor noted that Pound stayed in his room almost all day and typed continuously. He also was impressed with Pound's ability to turn off his alleged fatigue at will.

July 29, 1949: The examining doctor found that Pound spent most of his time reading and typing and he reported "no abnormal mental trends." After this occasion no psychiatric interviews were recorded for nearly two years. Pound's periodic complaints apparently gave him a respite.

April 12, 1951: Using a metaphor that he occasionally employed, Pound complained that his "main spring is broken and his conning tower doesn't seem to be functioning as it was." He continued to display exceptional hostility toward psychiatrists. Psychoanalysis, he said, "is a bunch of sh—, that the psychoanalysts don't know the difference between clean seamen [*sic*] and sh—." Although Pound discussed Roosevelt and politics "with almost too much emotion," the doctor found "no definite delusional trends." In summary, the doctor noted "no gross psychotic behavior."

September 29, 1951. The doctor found Pound well oriented. The patient complained that he had served longer than "that damned" Alger Hiss.

January 21, 1952: The doctor observed that Pound did a great deal of writing and that he had a "friendly, rather supercilious and condescending attitude." He also was "unable to elicit any psychotic content at this time."

October 16, 1952: Pound attacked that "fart" Roosevelt and the "s.o.b.'s in London." He complained that people should have listened to him twelve years ago. Once again, however, the doctor found him "precisely oriented and no abnormal mental content was elicited."

March 20, 1953: One of the doctors who examined him in January 1946, just before the trial, and one of the few with more than one recorded opinion, reported: "No psychotic ideation was manifested."

In July 1953, Dr. Stanley Krumbiegel, Medical Director of the Bureau of Prisons, asked Overholser for a report on Pound's condition and a statement of diagnosis and prognosis. After more than seven years in St. Elizabeth's, and seven years after Overholser acknowledged in open court that no diagnosis had been made, Pound still had not been formally diagnosed. Overholser ordered further examinations and interviews in order to answer Krumbiegel.

Dr. Bernard Cruvant, the examining psychiatrist, considered Pound's political, social, economic, and artistic opinions at great length. He believed that Pound represented an "unfortunate parachronism," fixed on antiquated social and scientific theories. He acknowledged Pound's complexity and the difficulty of confining him to any accepted category of diagnosis. But from his own interviews, as well as the testimony of old friends such as William Carlos Williams, the doctor concluded that Pound's most outstanding personality feature was his "profound, incredible, overweening narcissism."

Cruvant observed that there was much of the "poseur" in Pound and that his professed neurasthenia was easily forgotten since he could become very animated in conversations. There were features of hysterical, obsessive-compulsive, and schizoid personality, and Pound occasionally demonstrated "marked emotional instability." Nevertheless, Cruvant found that Wilhelm Reich's characterization of the phallic-narcissistic personality dominated all understanding. Cruvant believed that Pound needed the "narcissistic supplies" from his admirers more than they needed his critical genius. For reinforcement he was dependent upon many people, including his wife, his disciples, and "above all, his enemies and detractors." Pound's destructive philosophy, with its sadistic overtones, fit his narcissistic personality. Finally, Cruvant offered his diagnosis: "Personality trait disturbance, other. Narcissistic personality."[39] That diagnosis, of course, was of a non-psychotic condition; indeed, Cruvant offered no suggestion whatsoever of psychosis.

Several weeks later Overholser interviewed Pound and then replied personally to Krumbiegel. Pound's condition, he said, had not essentially changed through the years. He described Pound as uninterested in his personal appearance and, despite knowing otherwise, he reported that Pound did "no writing and very little reading." He remained extremely egocentric, supercilious, and critical—"to the extreme of a decidedly paranoid attitude, with particular emphasis on the outstanding nature of his abilities." Overholser maintained that Pound had no grasp whatsoever of the charges against him and that he was still mentally incompetent to stand trial. While he admitted that Pound's illness was hard to classify, he duly reported Cruvant's diagnosis. He acknowledged that the category was non-psychotic, but he nevertheless argued that the personality disturbance was so great as to constitute incompetence. "In our opinion," he concluded, "one may be incompetent without being technically psychotic."[40]

Thus Pound was not insane—at least, he was not classified as such in 1953— but he remained unfit to stand trial. Overholser, however, was contradictory on the extent and manner of Pound's incompetence. A year later he told the Justice Department that there was no evidence that Pound had done productive work in the hospital. The Department had noted the recent publication of Pound's translation of Confucius and questioned whether anyone mentally fit to write poetry was unfit to stand trial. Overholser carefully denied that Pound had written that work while in St. Elizabeth's. He also insisted, quite properly, that one could be insane and mentally incompetent and still produce poetry.

In fact, Pound was writing and reading a good deal, as Overholser knew full well. After Pound left the hospital, he acknowledged his debts to his keeper and protector: "I don't know whether you will ever get credit for making possible the Confucian Anthology and for two volumes of Cantos." Overholser replied that he was glad to have contributed to Pound's literary efforts while at St. Elizabeth's.[41]

Pound's literary activities and correspondence were sensitive matters. Pound complemented Overholser's concern for maintaining discretion. Louis Dudek, one of Pound's more active supporters, issued a public call in 1953 for Pound's release. Dudek termed Pound's insanity "questionable," noting that Pound had translated "difficult" prose and poetry into "imperishable" English, edited and proofread his own work, guided biographers and bibliographers, and carried on a far flung "voluminous, practical, benevolent correspondence." Dudek himself had corresponded extensively with Pound.

Dudek had touched a sensitive nerve and Pound reacted vehemently. "God bloody DAMN it and save one from ones friends," he told Dudek. "SHUT UP. You are NOT supposed to receive ANY letters from E.P. . . . Who the HELL told YOU that E.P. has carried on correspondence?" Dudek was exiled to a purgatory for one year as Pound refused to write to him. Dudek naïvely interpreted Pound's letter as "an index of his frustration in that terrible mental hospital." Yet Pound obviously did not want his "insanity" questioned, realizing that public discussion of his activities jeopardized his delicate legal position.[42]

In October 1954 another psychiatrist found Pound's speech clear, with a great deal of circumlocution, yet without any remarkable effect. Pound complained that publication of his work had been blocked by numerous people and he insisted that he had produced no new work during his hospitalization. The doctor found some paranoid elements in Pound's belief that he had been hospitalized because of the machinations of Harry Dexter White, among others. The country, he complained, had been run by traitors since 1913, the year Woodrow Wilson became President and the Federal Reserve System was created—two of his favorite targets. He lamented that so much was expected of him by others: "Oh why must all of this weight fall upon my shoulders—I can't bear it."[43]

Two years after the Cruvant diagnosis, it was abruptly altered to "Psychotic Disorder, Undifferentiated." The change was made in a one-sentence statement inserted in Pound's file. The doctor who signed that statement noted that it had been suggested and authorized by Overholser. The superintendent then used the new diagnosis in a 1957 letter to the Bureau of Prisons and added that the prognosis was "not particularly good."[44]

After the 1955 diagnosis no more psychiatric interviews were recorded, although a note mentioned that Overholser interviewed Pound before his discharge. An outside psychiatrist (also a poet) visited Pound in July 1955. He told Overholser that Pound was "suffering from paranoid schizophrenia with strong affective components, such as hypomanic and megalomanic tendencies." He said that Pound had a "genuine respect" for the staff except for the Jewish members. Pound also told this doctor that he was "working hard on the Cantos."[45]

iv

Throughout the long years of Pound's incarceration, there was only one formal legal attempt to free him. In February 1948 Cornell filed a petition for a writ of habeas corpus in Washington. Cornell apparently contrived the idea after consulting with Dorothy Pound. Whatever chance it had for success ended when Pound himself aborted the proceedings.

Cornell's petition challenged the legality of Pound's detention. The petition argued that Overholser had concluded that Pound would never recover his sanity and thus would never be mentally fit for trial. Cornell also claimed that Overholser had told him that Pound did not require hospitalization and that he would benefit from greater freedom—a claim that Overholser flatly denied to the Justice Department. (Dr. Muncie later told the FBI in 1956 that he informed Cornell in 1946 that Pound need not be institutionalized.) Legally, Cornell knew that the relevant statutes made no provision for releasing a person declared permanently insane and consequently unable to be tried. Yet he argued that given the unlikelihood of Pound's recovery, the effect of his confinement was to deprive him of his liberty without due process. Judge Laws summarily denied the petition.

Cornell prepared to appeal but Dorothy Pound abruptly ordered him to withdraw. She claimed that her husband could not be upset—"the least thing shakes up his nerves terribly," she wrote. She then added that she wanted nothing further attempted until after the forthcoming presidential election. But as in other similar instances, Dorothy Pound was only the medium: the decision was Ezra Pound's.[46]

Why did Pound choose to stay in St. Elizabeth's? Given the fact that Pound clearly understood the charges against him, and steadfastly maintained his innocence, he wanted complete vindication. He told his publisher that he would not "come out except with colors flying and a personal apology from the president." He also did not want to be at the mercy of a "corrupt" Supreme Court. Once again using Dorothy Pound as his voice, he told Cornell that he was not interested in the question of his sanity, but rather in proving he did not commit treason. "The treason was in the White House, not in Rapallo."

Pound was not willing to leave the hospital and live under the threat of an outstanding indictment. Overholser correctly told the FBI in 1956 that while Pound desired to return to Italy, he had "never made any attempt to be released from St. Elizabeth's." He also added that Pound seemingly enjoyed his situation —his wife visited every day; he held court, expressing himself on a variety of subjects; and he regularly had distinguished visitors. It was indeed a good situation for a man who enjoyed and needed such exceptional treatment.[47]

It is difficult to say with precision whether an appeal in the habeas corpus proceeding would have succeeded. Years later, Thurman Arnold, who finally negotiated Pound's release, thought an appeals court might have granted the writ. But without the writ, Arnold noted that the "philosophical legal logic" of the situation dictated that Pound could not be released unless the indictment was quashed.[48] Ezra Pound understood that very well.

Public demands and private efforts for Pound's release gathered momentum by the mid-1950s. In 1954 Ernest Hemingway told Italian reporters that it was "a good year to release poets." Winner of that year's Nobel Prize, he thought that Pound might have won the award. The Vatican Radio broadcast a vigorous defense of Pound. At the same time, Pound's daughter and friends regularly urged the Italian government to press for Pound's freedom. Their representations reached the American Embassy and were duly reported to the State Department by Ambassador Clare Boothe Luce. The envoy supported the pleas, but the State Department did little but make routine inquiries to the Justice Department and the hospital. Luce's concern undoubtedly inspired her husband's *Life* magazine editorial in January 1956 calling for Pound's release. Noting the recent release of "Tokyo Rose" and numerous war criminals, *Life* contended that World War II crimes had "aged to the point of requital, parole or forgiveness." The editorial urged public consideration for quashing the indictment against Pound.[49]

The calls for action widened and gained respectability. But the movement received a severe setback in the fall of 1956 when one of Pound's disciples, John Kasper, was arrested for conspiring to interfere with court-ordered desegregation in Tennessee. Kasper regularly visited Pound and he coordinated an "Ez for Prez" campaign in 1956. He organized the Seaboard White Citizens Council and denounced desegregation in Tennessee with vicious assaults upon blacks and Jews. He encouraged resistance and, after the bombing of a desegregated school, he was arrested and subsequently convicted. Critics quickly connected Kasper's bigoted actions to Pound. Overholser was compelled to make a rare public statement, disclaiming any responsibility for the hospital.[50]

Dwight Eisenhower's re-election in November 1956 stimulated new efforts by

Pound's supporters to win his release. With the election over, the belief was widespread, and largely justified, that the Administration would have a freer hand and particularly would not have to fear any potential Jewish backlash. But Pound's release involved a delicate mix of political, medical, and legal tactics. While the original stimulus came from outside the government, Overholser served as tactician and counselor for the effort. And, in all probability, he coordinated his advice with the wishes of his ward.

Archibald MacLeish assumed responsibility for organizing a plea from such writers as Eliot, Frost, and Hemingway to have the government drop the case. MacLeish proposed appealing to the Attorney General on the grounds that Pound had been incarcerated for nearly eleven years, that St. Elizabeth's psychiatrists now believed he was sane, and that a trial probably would cause a complete mental breakdown and make him a permanent charge of the government. But first MacLeish asked Overholser to confirm these points.

MacLeish was a lawyer, but Overholser had a firmer grasp of the legal implications. He told MacLeish that "we should not bring up the question of his 'insanity,'" but concentrate instead on Pound's unfitness for trial. More important, he distinguished the matter of Pound's incompetence and his suitability for release. Indeed, he suggested avoiding the question of Pound's release, for it "would merely confuse the situation."

Overholser's key point was that Pound never would be fit for trial, a conclusion that Overholser already had given to the Justice Department, and consequently he thought it "unnecessary" to keep the charges alive. He later explained to MacLeish that he believed it "high time" that the charges were dropped, but that Pound's release prior to such a move "would muddy the waters to an undesirable extent." Pound, of course, was uninterested in being released unless the charges were quashed; and Overholser was his skillful and influential advocate on this point.[51]

MacLeish understood and accepted the advice. He subsequently told his old friend Milton Eisenhower, the President's brother, that Pound's doctors thought he would never recover. Given that, MacLeish thought it "irrelevant" for the government to perpetuate the charges of treason. MacLeish's real purpose in writing to Eisenhower, however, was to tell him that he had "the very best reason to believe" that Pound would receive a Nobel Prize. He feared that would invite ridicule of the United States if it held a Nobel laureate in an insane asylum. He frankly urged Milton Eisenhower to use his position "to bring about the desired action"—the quashing of the charges.[52]

Overholser's advice also was evident in a formal letter sent by MacLeish, Eliot, Frost, and Hemingway to Attorney General Herbert Brownell in January 1957. The writers told Brownell that they considered the perpetuation of the charges as unfortunate and "indefensible" in view of the certainty that Pound never would be fit for trial. They urged the Justice Department to drop the charges and remit the case to medical authorities for disposition.[53]

The effort to release Pound encountered a formidable new adversary in April 1957 when J. Edgar Hoover strongly recommended to the Attorney General that the charges against Pound not be dismissed. Hoover was primarily concerned with the possibility of creating a "dangerous precedent" because the federal government then held more than forty other prisoners who had been declared mentally incompetent to stand trial. Hoover also believed that in the light of the recent Kasper incident, the government could show that Pound's release might be dangerous to the nation's interest.[54] Hoover expressed no interest in the merits of the case. Good bureaucrat that he was, his concern focused on the precedential value of the matter. He also was aware of the "difficulty" in diagnosing Pound, and the reports on the hospital situation left him uneasy. But whatever Hoover's doubts, he had little chance to counter the authority and prestige of Winfred Overholser.

Pound's supporters nevertheless gained significant political support within the government in the next months. Dr. Gabriel Hauge, a presidential assistant with connections to Pound's publisher, actively supported the release efforts. Representative Usher Burdick of North Dakota secured a congressional resolution in August authorizing the Library of Congress to prepare a complete report on the subject.

But obstacles remained. In November 1957 Robert Frost visited the new Attorney General, William Rogers, and learned that the government would quash the charges only if Pound agreed to be transferred to a private institution. Rogers added that such a plan depended upon Overholser's consent. The superintendent, however, told MacLeish that "nothing would be gained" by moving Pound to a private sanitarium. While he did not indicate whether he had consulted with Pound on the matter, he told MacLeish that Pound much preferred to return to Italy. Overholser was "sure" that he would be happier there and would be no menace to the government. He urged MacLeish to explore State Department channels to secure backing for the idea of Pound's return to Italy. In any event, he stressed to MacLeish that Rogers' proposal did "not represent much progress" if he insisted on Pound's commitment to a private institution.

MacLeish well knew Pound's position on the matter. In July 1956, Eliot had told him that the Pounds did not want him released from St. Elizabeth's "unless he can have a passport and return to Italy." They told Eliot that it would be too expensive to stay in the United States. But Pound certainly had other reasons, including some sort of vindication and total freedom from the threat of prosecution. And Eliot knew his friend well: "I believe he would prefer to stay where he is" rather than go to a private sanitarium, Eliot told MacLeish. "It would depend on HOW I got out," Pound wrote to a friend.

In December 1957, however, Rogers still insisted on his plan. MacLeish realized it would require Overholser's consent, which was unlikely, and Pound's, which was even more unlikely. Besides, Rogers said nothing of dropping the indictment. MacLeish met privately with Overholser just after Christmas, and apparently Overholser confirmed his earlier positions.[55]

Pound's supporters did not realize that Rogers was playing a weak hand. By 1956 the Justice Department had neither the inclination nor the resources to press the indictment against Pound. In July the lawyers most familiar with the case favored dismissal of the charges.

Dorothy F. Green, a lawyer in the Subversive Activities Section, had followed the case closely for over six years. At the request of her superiors, she prepared a detailed summary and analysis of it in May 1956. Green had written a similar report in April 1950, and nothing had changed in the intervening years except her final recommendation. After carefully examining the nineteen alleged acts of treason by Pound, Green concluded in both reports that the evidence for only one was sufficient to meet the constitutional requirement that treasonable action be proved by two witnesses or that Pound's actions could properly be construed as giving aid and comfort to the enemy. Green had personal doubts about the validity of the one charge, but she concluded that it satisfied constitutional requirements.

Green, however, now believed that "practical," not legal considerations, should dictate the government's course. Recalling that both "Tokyo Rose" and "Axis Sally" had been convicted on only one count of treason (though charged with others), Green believed that it was terribly risky to present a case resting on only one clear overt act. In addition, she noted that the Department had no knowledge of the existence or whereabouts of the necessary Italian witnesses, having had no contact with them since 1946. Finally, she suggested that the trial might strain relations with the present Italian government.

Green coupled her practical arguments with "humanitarian" ones. Taking note of Pound's age (then seventy), his ten years in St. Elizabeth's, and the official judgment that he would never be mentally competent to stand trial, she realized that some might contend that the interests of justice had been served and there was no useful purpose in further detaining Pound. Although she believed that Pound's actions were as reprehensible as those of others who had been convicted for similar charges, she concluded, "with great reluctance," that the Department should seek dismissal of the charges because of the insufficiency of evidence and the unlikelihood that Pound ever would be able to stand trial.[56]

Green's chief in the Subversive Activities Section, however, did not endorse her report and recommended that the Department do nothing. He feared "an avalanche of criticism" if the charges were dropped, and favored waiting until Pound was declared mentally fit before moving for a dismissal. But William

Foley, former chief of the section and then executive assistant to the Assistant Attorney General for the Internal Security Division, completely supported Green's proposal. He had worked closely with her on the case through the years, and had decisively backed her 1950 recommendation against dismissing the charges. Now, in 1956, Foley believed that the government should seek a dismissal "on the sound legal ground" that it no longer had the evidence to gain a conviction. He minimized the threat of adverse political criticism.[57]

Pound's insistence on a return to Italy also inevitably involved the State Department, although it had no formal jurisdiction in the case. In December 1957, Overholser asked MacLeish to determine State's attitude. MacLeish promptly saw Undersecretary Christian Herter, who had known Overholser in Massachusetts. Herter invited the superintendent to see him and discuss Pound —"this difficult individual," as Herter described him. But even after Overholser's visit, Herter told MacLeish that it was "impractical" to allow Pound to leave the country. Herter had spoken to the Attorney General and both remained concerned about the political consequences. As late as March 30, 1958, the State Department apparently did not yet realize what terms were acceptable to Pound. Herter suggested to MacLeish that Pound live "in some inconspicuous place" in the United States and be an outpatient of a private sanitarium. Pound quickly let MacLeish know that he objected to any such plan.[58]

The Administration's dilatoriness can only be attributed to political sensitivity. Congressman Emanuel Celler, chairman of the House Judiciary Committee, urged that Pound be kept in St. Elizabeth's. "I can't understand how they'd let him out scot free. . . . Many of our men lost their lives as a result of his exhortations." But Celler was virtually alone and eventually Rogers and others realized there was little to fear. In early April 1958, Rogers told a press conference that Pound might escape trial and be allowed to return to Italy.[59] The reaction was favorable.

Almost simultaneously, on April 14, Washington lawyer Thurman Arnold filed a motion to dismiss the case. (Arnold had attended Wabash College when Pound taught there and had been Cornell's teacher at Yale.) He appended an affidavit by Overholser, stating that Pound was incurably insane and forever unfit for trial. Overholser added a new twist—one cherished by Pound's supporters—when he stated that Pound probably was insane when he committed the alleged crimes. Arnold also mobilized support from various writers and a special appeal by Frost. Frost acknowledged Pound's disgrace and registered his strong disapproval of Pound's political statements. Yet he tied his plea for Pound's freedom to Overholser's pronouncement that Pound was too insane to be tried but not too dangerous to be released in his wife's care—"a very nice distinction," Frost concluded.

Four days later Arnold and United States Attorney Oliver Gasch appeared before Judge Laws, who had presided over the sanity trial in 1946. Gasch perfunctorily told the court that the government did not oppose the motion. "I am satisfied as to the present competency of the defendant to stand trial," he said. "Therefore, I do not oppose; in fact I consent to Mr. Arnold's motion." Laws immediately granted the motion. Pound, who was in court, rose and immediately shook hands with Overholser. The hearing had lasted nine minutes. After some dental care at the hospital, Pound was formally discharged on May 7. He arrived in Naples in early July, offered the Fascist salute, and announced that "all America is an insane asylum."[60]

Three years after Pound's release Overholser must have been amused when he learned that some people believed that the hospital had "pushed or cast Pound out." On the contrary, he told another psychiatrist, "we were instrumental in securing [the] dropping of his charges, and, indeed, were very happy, as was Pound, that he could return to Italy."[61]

Overholser nevertheless had to protect his position and his diagnosis. In February 1959, Pound wrote to the superintendent stating that he wished to end his wife's legal guardianship because he had never been mentally ill. Overholser wisely forwarded the letter to the Arnold law firm. Arnold quickly realized that such a claim could invite a reindictment and he wrote to Pound suggesting a "passive course of action," warning that a formal petition to the court was "inconsistent with Dr. Overholser's representations" in support of dismissing the indictment. If a court determined that Pound's sanity had been restored, Arnold feared a possible reindictment since there was no statute of limitations on treason.[62] Pound's "victory" was thus incomplete, for he could never run the risk of a formal, legal declaration of his sanity. At the same time, his legal status preserved the appearances of Overholser's consistency, integrity, and professional judgment. It was a small price for Pound to pay.

V

Ezra Pound was not insane in any accepted clinical or legal sense. He deliberately selected his insanity defense, which succeeded after a perfunctory court trial, and then was maintained for more than twelve years with the crucial assistance of Dr. Overholser, who adhered to his "diagnosis" that Pound was insane, despite the consistent, contrary judgments of his staff. Pound's marked eccentricity and egocentricity lent some credibility to his plea, but such traits do not constitute psychosis.

Pound's purposes are not difficult to fathom. He pleaded insanity to avoid a treason trial, a trial which may well have resulted in his conviction and disgrace. However much he believed himself innocent, he recognized the risks of a treason trial in the charged postwar atmosphere. The convictions of others similarly accused of broadcasting for the enemy (including his publisher's cousin) undoubtedly confirmed his worst fears. The insanity plea and Dr. Overholser's efforts sheltered him and eventually made possible the vindication and freedom he had sought from the outset. The sanctuary of the asylum preserved—perhaps even enhanced—his literary reputation. But Pound's decision and his retreat into St. Elizabeth's betrayed the Confucian ideals of commitment he dearly advocated and which he had expressed when he chose to remain in Italy in 1941 and when he was first interrogated in Genoa in 1945.

Overholser's motives are a bit more complicated. Pound's literary reputation aroused Overholser's sympathies and through the years of Pound's stay in the hospital the two developed a close, warm relationship. Overholser genuinely seemed to enjoy his famous ward, however much he professed to find Pound's political and social views outrageous.[63] Professionally, Overholser may well have been compassionate toward a man he believed to be so eccentric he could not have been tried according to the traditional processes. Whatever his motives, Overholser's actions single-handedly made possible the protection and then the freedom that Pound desired.

Overholser's cover-up of Pound's true condition was the real conspiracy in the case. The failure to try Pound for treason, coupled with the eventual dismissal of the charges, has reinforced the contention that Pound's incarceration offered the government a convenient means for punishing a political opponent. There is no evidence for *that* conspiracy. But on another level, some critics have harshly judged the uses of psychiatry which, they argue, skewed the legal process and prevented a resolution of the issues.

The noted psychiatrists Frederic Wertham and Thomas Szasz both charged that the government contrived the declaration of insanity. From the meager public record, Wertham thought Pound sane in 1949. He considered that the insanity judgment rationalized "profound defects in society by placing them outside society, in the sphere of individual pathology." Both doctors found Overholser's conclusions imprecise and unsubstantiated either in the record or in Pound's previous career. They favored trying Pound on the facts and then, if he was found guilty, possibly granting him clemency. Szasz particularly criticized the role of psychiatrists in the case as substituting the "Rule of Men for the Rule of Law" and saw the affair as an exception to the principle that everyone must be responsible for his behavior. Szasz later likened Pound's incarceration to the Soviet Union's use of mental hospitals for political dissidents, with both being a "pseudo-medical system of social controls." Finally, Szasz believed that "Pound played the game against the United States, played it well and honorably—but lost."[64]

Wertham and Szasz were correct in large part, but for the wrong reasons. Certainly psychiatry abused the legal process in this case. But the government's prosecutors had only a peripheral and perhaps unconscious part in determining Pound's fate. Pound himself elected to go to St. Elizabeth's and certainly Overholser's efforts were not the somewhat sinister ones that Wertham and Szasz portrayed. In a sense, Pound had played a "game" against the United States. By 1946 he had "lost"; but that was only the beginning. By the end, however, he won the game, for he never was tried, as he argued he should not have been. He did not quite receive the apology he demanded, but he walked away a free man.

Pound's alleged treason can never be decisively determined. But certainly his defenders cannot absolve him from responsibility for his actions and words during the war. And they cannot contend that the government "railroaded" him into the asylum. For that journey, Pound bought the ticket, willingly boarded the train, had his ticket validated by Overholser, and then took over as engineer. The trip was his refuge and asylum.

4

GOVERNMENT BY DISCRETION
The Queendom of Passports

The [Passport] Division acts rather as a law unto itself.
—HOOVER COMMISSION REPORT, 1949

Don't you think that after twenty-eight years, I should know what's needed?
—RUTH B. SHIPLEY, CHIEF, PASSPORT OFFICE, 1927–55

This [is] government by a woman rather than by law.
—SENATOR WAYNE MORSE, 1952

i

LINUS Pauling certainly has been one of the towering figures of science in the twentieth century. His early major work, published as *The Nature of the Chemical Bond* in 1939, led to a Nobel Prize in chemistry in 1954. His textbook *General Chemistry,* published just after World War II, influenced several generations of students. But unlike many of his scientific colleagues, Pauling's inquiring mind led him into other, quite diverse interests.

Pauling is one of three persons to receive two Nobel awards, his second being the 1962 Peace Prize for his role in bringing about the treaty banning atmospheric nuclear tests. The universal approbation he received for his scientific work did not, however, carry over to his politically related endeavors, especially not in his own country. In the late 1940s and 1950s, Pauling stood in the vanguard of a relatively small group of prominent scientists who had the temerity to criticize American foreign and defense policies. Secretary of State Dean G. Acheson ridiculed the activities of such dilettantes and neophytes. Pauling, Acheson wrote, may have known a great deal about biochemistry (which was *not* his field) but had little understanding of world affairs. Pauling replied with characteristic puckishness: "If Dean Acheson had studied biochemistry as much as I have

89

studied world affairs, then I would say we *ought to listen* to what he had to say about biochemistry." Undaunted, Pauling campaigned for the banning of nuclear tests and weapons. He also opposed the development of the hydrogen bomb. As a nonconformist on such issues, Pauling was often seen as a man who did not "represent the best interests of the United States."

On January 24, 1952, Pauling routinely submitted a passport application to the State Department. He planned to travel abroad to lecture, to receive an honorary degree at the University of Toulouse, and to discuss the chemical structure of proteins at a meeting on May 1 arranged by the Royal Society of London. Three weeks later, the Passport Office rejected his application, telling him that his "proposed travel would not be in the best interests of the United States." Bewildered, Pauling wrote directly to President Truman on February 29, protesting the decision. A month later Truman's secretary notified him that his letter had been referred to the State Department for an appropriate reply. That meant, of course, the letter ultimately would be routed to the Passport Office. Apparently anticipating this, Pauling wrote to the Passport Office, asking for a reconsideration. Not knowing that a negative reply was already en route, on April 21 Pauling and his wife called on Ruth B. Shipley, Chief of the Passport Office. She briefly discussed the situation with him, but then suggested he see her superior, S. D. Boykin, Chief of the Office of Security and Consular Affairs.

Boykin asked Pauling why he had not refuted the "charges" against him. But there had been no charges; furthermore, the rejection letter offered no modes of redress or appeal. Boykin then told Pauling he was a suspected Communist and that he had made numerous statements critical of the United States and its policies. Boykin refused, however, to document the charges. For his part, Pauling ridiculed the accusations and retorted that the Soviets had been critical of his advocacy of the theory of resonance. The security chief invited Pauling to submit additional materials to the State Department for a further review. The next day, Pauling brought what he thought were relevant documents, as well as an affidavit that he was not nor ever had been a Communist.

Pauling scheduled his departure for London from New York on April 28 at 6 P.M. Throughout that day, he waited at the National Academy of Sciences in Washington for some word. Finally, at four o'clock, Shipley called him to say that the Department had upheld her decision. A month later when Pauling reapplied for a passport in order to participate in an August meeting of the Faraday Society in London, the Passport Office simply ignored his request.

The denial of a passport to Pauling involved questionable political and legal practices by the State Department. Such policy was not, of course, confined to Pauling. Hundreds of prominent and not so prominent individuals experienced similar difficulties. Pauling's case, however, may have been unique. It has been suggested that by blocking Pauling's trip to England, the Passport Office may have cost him an unprecedented third Nobel Prize. Pauling was one of the first Americans working on the chemical structure of biological molecules. Others, meanwhile, were studying the function of genes as an approach to the nature of life. Ultimately, these two rather antithetical approaches coalesced in the discovery of the structure of DNA. Had Pauling made his London trip in 1952, he might well have seen the X-ray pictures of DNA from Rosalind Franklin and Maurice Wilkins' laboratory. That information possibly could have given him the stimulus and information necessary to retrace his own steps and solve the DNA structure.[1] We will never know, of course. But we can know and understand the political process that prevented such an intriguing possibility.

ii

Linus Pauling probably was a minor irritant to the politically harassed Dean Acheson. At the time Pauling was denied a passport, public and congressional criticism of Acheson was particularly harsh. The Korean War, Truman's dismissal of General MacArthur, the "loss" of China to the Communists, and the charges of Communist infiltration into the State Department left Acheson vulnerable and subject to repeated assaults of Cold Warriors more militant than he. Even Acheson's control over his own department was open to question.

In his memoirs, Acheson candidly discussed his tenuous authority. He virtually acknowledged that published tables of line and staff arrangements reflected public administration textbooks, not authority. Acheson likened divisional heads to a feudal system of barons, wracked by mutual jealousies and suspicions, and constantly at war with each other. Yet the barons always consolidated their bases, to the point that a Secretary of State had to recognize their power within their own domain. Real authority, Acheson admitted, belonged to those "who could take and hold it." Among other fiefdoms, Acheson referred to "the Queendom of Passports ruled over by Mrs. Ruth Shipley."[2] Acheson's passing, apparently witty reference to the Passport Office underplayed the seriousness of the problem.

Ruth B. Shipley and her successor, Frances G. Knight, headed the Passport Division for a half century, from 1927 to 1977. Together they served ten Presidents. Like J. Edgar Hoover, these women were independent, knew how to use power, and lived a long time. They, too, ruled their fief almost wholly oblivious to the wishes of their putative masters. Also like Hoover, they had formed political alliances outside their realm that served to neutralize potential enemies within. And like Hoover, Frances Knight succeeded in gaining two extensions for her appointment beyond the mandatory retirement age of seventy.

Shipley began her government service in the Patent Office in 1908. She married the next year and quickly resigned her job, following the custom of the time. In 1914 she returned to work, this time in the State Department, where she remained for the next four decades. She became Chief of the Passport Division in 1927. Through most of the years, she and her staff labored in deserved obscurity. But by the early 1950s, her attempts to deny passports to many prominent persons won Shipley her share of publicity. Much of the popular press depicted Shipley as the epitome of a quiet, self-effacing, efficient government official, carrying out her appointed tasks with dispatch and orderliness. Supposedly known as "Ma" in State Department circles, she was affectionately acknowledged to be a tough but lovable bureaucratic infighter.

Criticism of Shipley's methods occasionally surfaced, but the source almost always was "unidentified." At the time of the Pauling incident, however, Oregon's maverick senator Wayne Morse launched a sharp attack on the high-handedness of the Passport Office and on Shipley in particular. In June 1952 he publicly criticized the "growing tyranny" and the "star-chamber proceedings" of Ruth Shipley's domain. Shipley's actions, he charged, had abused the rights of American citizens. Morse spared no targets. He excoriated Acheson for tolerating and lauding Shipley's actions while self-righteously defending his department against charges that it maintained undesirable employees. Morse added that Congress itself had to share much of the blame for so long condoning such "arbitrary and capricious discretion."

Morse's speech was a preface to a series of amendments that he offered to existing passport legislation. Morse proposed the creation of an independent board of review to permit appeals of Passport Office decisions. He emphasized that such a board should not be made up of State Department officials. A departmental board, Morse believed, would be susceptible to alibis of secrecy or the excuse that the nation's security might be threatened if relevant facts were disclosed. For too long, Morse insisted, the Department had claimed secrecy and security needs to justify the exercise of unchecked power. The secrecy surrounding passport decisions clearly aroused Morse's wrath. In May he had written to Acheson asking for an explanation for the denial of a passport to "Professor X" —who turned out to be Pauling. As usual, Shipley replied for the secretary. She told Morse that the "confidential nature of the passport files" prevented the Department from disclosing detailed information. It was Catch-22. But Morse perceptively gauged the extent of Shipley's power and demanded that her "attitude of infallibility" be brought under surveillance.[3]

Secretary Acheson, gallant and politically attuned, came to Shipley's defense. "I do not know any person in the service of the government," he said, "who brings to her work greater devotion, greater sense of public obligation and public duty, greater knowledge of the field, and greater skill than does Mrs. Shipley." Others rushed to the counterattack. Senator Pat McCarran (Dem.-Nev.), one of Acheson's most persistent critics and a sponsor of some of the most notorious immigration restriction and anti-subversive legislation (which included authorizations for passport controls), credited Shipley with helping to formulate parts of those acts. Shipley returned the compliment, noting that "the McCarran and un-American committees have done a grand job."[4]

Shipley generally maintained a low public profile, confining herself to statements citing the growth of travel and business for her office. But on one score, her opinion was clear and absolutely open. "One of the things I believe in is refusing passports to Communists. They've been working against us for a long time," she said. Her interest in Communists extended beyond simply denying them passports. Passports, visas, and immigration matters were, to her, all related to the security of the United States. As such, her office regularly collected information on individuals from embassies and consulates, newspapers, and investigative agencies. She even used her brothers, who formerly had served in the FBI and the OSS and who later worked as private investigators. Ultimately, she proudly claimed data on more than twelve million persons, filling over 1,250 filing cabinets.

When Shipley prepared to retire in 1955—and travel abroad—she openly bragged: "Yes, my successor has been chosen—by me. We have a good ship. Don't you think that after twenty-eight years, I should know what's needed?"[5] That appointment, however, was a bit more complex.

The designated heiress was Frances G. Knight. Like Shipley, Knight worked her way through a variety of clerical government jobs before rising to a position of authority and power. But unlike Shipley's climb, which is rather obscured in the record, Knight's path and vital network of political patrons are fairly clear.

Born in 1905, Knight started her government service as a typist in the National Recovery Administration in 1934. After that agency collapsed, she moved to the Works Progress Administration as Deputy Information Director. When her superior suddenly died, she took over his desk temporarily, but soon lost the position, apparently for political reasons. She now shifted her allegiance and joined the staff of the Republican Congressional Campaign Committee. The trail of upward mobility then took her to the office of Representative John Taber, a conservative New York Republican and a power in the House. In 1949, Taber helped Knight move into the State Department, where she remained for nearly thirty years and became a power in her own right. She began as a radio information specialist, soon moving to the Voice of America, where she concentrated on Czechoslovakian affairs. Early on, she tested herself in the sport of bureaucratic politics by trying to have a separate desk established for Slovakian interests. (At the time, she had close contacts with a Slovak separatist movement founded by a priest once active in the wartime Nazi puppet government.) She lost that battle —but her superior lost his post when Knight leapfrogged ahead of him in the Department.[6]

Knight's key move came with the partisan changeover in 1953. John Foster

Dulles, anxious to appease congressional critics who believed the State Department "soft" on Communism, named Scott McLeod to head the Department's Bureau of Security and Consular Affairs. The newly appointed Secretary of State preferred to run American foreign policy by whispered conversations in the Oval Office, working on airplanes, or through personal meetings with foreign leaders. He willingly left day-to-day operations of the Department to subordinates such as McLeod. But real power, as Acheson acknowledged, is deceptive, and the net effect of Dulles' decision was to relinquish substantial power to others.

McLeod's chief qualifications for his post were his service as an FBI agent in Manchester, New Hampshire, and his staff work for conservative Senator Styles Bridges (Rep.-N.H.). He cultivated close contacts with Senator Joseph McCarthy's staff and later with McCarthy himself. Most credited McCarthy with McLeod's appointment to the State Department.[7] Just as McCarthy begat McLeod, so McLeod begat Frances Knight when he named her his chief assistant in 1953.

Knight was reputed to be part of what McCarthy called his "loyal American underground" in the State Department. Indeed, McLeod acknowledged that she had passed information to McCarthy exposing "subversives" in the Voice of America. In her work for McLeod, Knight served as a liaison with congressmen. To some this meant she checked the security files of jobholders to determine whether they could be replaced by favorites of friendly congressmen.[8] Given Ruth Shipley's public statements on alleged subversives or Communists, she, too, must have been cozy with McLeod, and undoubtedly, as she said, she could appoint her own successor. If she could have observed Frances Knight for the next twenty-two years, she would have been as pleased as if she herself had continued in the post. Indeed, Knight scrupulously kept the half dozen old-fashioned hot irons for affixing photographs to passports.

Joseph L. Rauh, Jr., national chairman of the Americans for Democratic Action, protested that Dulles must have been aware of Knight's connections to McCarthy, and he called her appointment "shocking to all who wish to preserve American freedom." Dulles later denied ever hearing the comment that Knight was part of the "loyal American underground." In any event, he claimed that would not have influenced his choice of her to head the Passport Office.[9]

Knight clearly shared Shipley's antipathies to Communists and alleged subversives. She inherited the policy of prohibiting passports to such people, and even raised the level of her office's vigilance and scrutiny. But times were changing, and Knight had to confront mounting public and legal challenges that ultimately diminished the scope of her authority and arbitrary rulings. Yet she proved as unrelenting and adroit as her predecessor in imposing her preferences on the State Department—a classic example of the tail wagging the dog. Knight nevertheless projected the image of the dutiful and disinterested public servant.

Twenty years after her appointment, and then seventy years of age, Knight received two successive one-year extensions, including one framed by Secretary of State Henry Kissinger's office and hand-delivered to her. At the time, she said she had to "outlive the opposition." That opposition—the "nervous nellies," as she labeled them—consisted of congressmen and State Department officials who had the temerity to criticize her arbitrary methods and politicization of passport procedures. To the end, she insisted her office never denied passports to suspected or known Communists. "Obviously, that's absolutely untrue. You can ask anybody in the shop. We never made that type of decision." Her office, she argued, was "pretty far down the line and simply had no such power."[10]

Knight thus would have had people believe that Acheson and Dulles themselves initiated cases against Linus Pauling, Otto Nathan, Paul Robeson, Max Schachtman, Leonard Boudin, Walter Briehl, and Rockwell Kent, among others, and that 596 alleged Communists were denied passports as of 1958 because the Secretary of State so decided. Like all good bureaucrats, Knight and Shipley left ample records demonstrating their policy-making authority. Their modest public poses and disclaimers belied their determination to impose their personal predilections.

iii

The Magna Carta in 1215 provided a libertarian benchmark in Anglo-American law for a "right to travel." Article 42 provided that every free man had the right to leave the realm in time of peace. In practice, however, English law developed some restraints on the ideal. The *ne exeat regno* writ reflected royal prerogative and was used to prevent foreign travel by those the Crown feared might act in a manner prejudicial to its interests. The writ was given a statutory basis in 1381 and various kings and parliaments used it for political reasons. For example, travel abroad was denied to archers and artificers, "lest they instruct foreigners," and after the break with Rome, Parliament forbade the sending of children to Catholic seminaries abroad. But in 1606 Parliament repealed the 1381 statute and the writ largely fell into disuse, certainly in its political, prerogative sense. British law thereafter followed the spirit of Magna Carta and allowed subjects to leave the realm at their pleasure, except in time of war. By the eighteenth century, William Blackstone included "locomotion" and freedom of movement as part of one's personal liberty.[11]

The formal, regularized issuance and control of passports in the United States is largely a post-World War I phenomenon. Until 1914, except for brief wartime interludes, passports generally were not necessary for foreign travel. Prior to that, the State Department's Passport Clerk ran a very modest operation. Through the mid-nineteenth century, the State Department competed with governors, mayors, and at times notaries public in issuing passports. In 1835 the Supreme Court found no federal laws regulating the issuance of passports or declaring their legal effect. While it was a matter of practice for the Secretary of State to require proof of citizenship before granting passports, the Court found that was entirely discretionary with him.

The fraudulent use of American passports by non-citizens prompted congressional action in 1856. A statute passed that year became the foundation for all subsequent regulation. It stipulated that only the Secretary of State could grant passports, and then only to American citizens. Later revisions in 1902 and 1926 provided for criminal sanctions and authorized consular officials abroad to issue passports.[12]

After passport control was nationalized in 1856, citizens received passports as a matter of right. Aside from mechanical stipulations such as the payment of fees and the submission of an application demonstrating citizenship, the State Department largely regarded the issuance of passports as a duty to certify the citizenship of Americans traveling abroad.[13] This practice, of course, prevailed in a day of relatively scant foreign travel and when the lines between war and peace were clear.

The 1856 act provided that State Department regulations must conform to presidential directives. Executive orders regularly established rules governing the issuance of passports, and in the twentieth century, virtually every President provided for new procedural standards. These included information required on the application, where applications could be made, the dimensions of the photograph required, and so forth. None established policy regarding citizen access to a passport. Neither the Secretary of State nor his Passport Division were authorized to make substantive policy on their own.

The rare occasions when the government restricted travel largely confirmed the general understanding of a right to travel. During the Civil War, Secretary of State William Seward prohibited travel without a passport; in 1918, Congress acted similarly as a result of war; and in 1941, Congress again applied the prohibition to "national emergencies."

As late as 1952, a three-judge federal court panel rejected any contention that the secretary had absolute discretion to revoke or deny a passport. The judges ruled that passport regulation must be administered "not arbitrarily or capriciously, but fairly, applying the law equally to all citizens without discrimination, and with due process adapted to the exigencies of the situation." Yet the court made an important concession, holding that the secretary could "establish reasonable classifications" of persons who might be denied passports.[14]

Following the Bolshevik Revolution, the Department occasionally denied passports to Soviet sympathizers. The undersecretary issued a memorandum in November 1920 designed to establish a consistent policy. He "recommended" that passports be denied to (1) any person who advocated the overthrow of organized governments anywhere by force (such as members of the Communist Party, the Communist Labor Party, or the Industrial Workers of the World); (2) any person who actively supported the cause of the Soviet government; (3) any person directly or indirectly working for the Soviet government. The memorandum contended that granting passports to such persons would interfere with prevailing policy which was directed toward the "hope" that the Russian people would overcome their existing anarchical situation and "again take a leading place in the world." A month later, the Chief of Passport Control extended the ban to American anarchists. Several other political categories were added in May 1921. Ruth Shipley offered her own touch with a list of instructions in July 1937. She maintained that passports might be denied to persons guilty of disloyal acts, persons suspected of an intention to commit a crime or otherwise "to bring grave discredit on this country," evaders of justice, and "political adventurers." The chief kept a firm grasp on discretionary authority, as she provided that all cases coming within such categories had to be referred to her for a final decision.[15]

The Cold War created new political considerations for government action. The Internal Security Act of 1950 prohibited members of Communist or Communist-front organizations from applying for or using passports. The law created a Subversive Activities Control Board to determine whether particular groups (e.g., the Communist Party) must register as a subversive organization. Although the SACB had not made any such recommendation, the State Department relied on the Internal Security Act to justify its increasing refusal after 1950 to allow Communists, real or alleged, to travel abroad. Specifically, the Department announced in August 1952 that members of the Communist Party, those who supported its goals, or those whose activities abroad would advance the Communist movement could be denied passports. Here was the first formal declaration of substantive policy, giving the Department discretionary control over individual applications. The policy implemented the Department's announcement in June that the secretary had discretionary authority "as a power inherent in the exercise of the Presidential authority to conduct foreign relations and as a matter of statutory law."[16] But clearly such a reading of statutes conflicted with their original and clear intent and the administrative practices of nearly a century.

The Pauling incident in 1952 proved to be just one of the more prominent instances in which the State Department denied a person permission to travel. In truth the Department's formal declaration of policy in 1952 rationalized and justified practices already in effect. After that, the more vigilant Scott McLeod and Ruth Shipley regularly saw to it that passports were denied to well-known or suspected left-wingers, such as Otto Nathan (the executor of Albert Einstein's estate), Rockwell Kent, Paul Robeson, Max Schachtman, Corliss Lamont, Clark Foreman, Howard Fast, Leonard Boudin, and scientists such as Martin Kamen,

Ralph Spitzers, Edward Corson, and Bernard Peters. Some pressed the State Department for an explanation. Dr. Nathan was told he had been charged with membership in the National Council of Art, Sciences, and Professions and the Teachers Union; Foreman's presidency of the Southern Conference for Human Welfare and affiliation with the National Committee to Abolish the Poll Tax offered grounds for denial; Dr. Kamen, who had discussed radioactive treatment of leukemia with a Soviet vice-consul, had been cleared of any willful or deliberate disclosure of secrets, but still was denied a passport; and a minor political functionary for the American Labor Party was denied his passport because in 1941 he had been a poll watcher for his party.[17]

The 1952 regulations set up a Board of Passport Appeals, ostensibly to provide an administrative procedure for those denied passports. The board's creation clearly was a response to Wayne Morse's attack on the Passport Office and effectively short-circuited legislative reforms. But the cards were stacked against any appellant. The board was not independent and it existed basically as a coordinate entity with the Passport Office—exactly as Senator Morse had feared. An appellant was required to deny under oath the charges offered by the Passport Office, even though he had no opportunity to review or impeach the agency's reports or evidence. The board could take other testimony in its hearing, but was not required to disclose it to the appellant. The board's recommendation went to the Secretary of State, with no opportunity for the appellant to see or refute it. Finally, the board would entertain no appeal unless the appellant signed a non-Communist affidavit.

Ten months after the announcement of the creation of the board, Shipley admitted that the board actually did not exist and that panel members would be designated only when they were needed. The implication—and the fact—was that the board would consist of State Department employees. Despite passport denials, pressure by aggrieved individuals, and pending litigation, the Department had no Board of Appeals until a successful suit by Martin Kamen in 1955 forced its creation. By that time, eight years had elapsed since Kamen first had been denied a passport.[18]

Leonard Boudin, the general counsel for the Emergency Civil Liberties Committee, represented a significant number of persons denied passports—including himself. Few were in a better position to observe and experience the arbitrariness and capriciousness of the Passport Office's actions. Boudin had been refused a passport in 1954 because he sought to travel abroad in behalf of clients who were suing the Department and because he wished to represent UNESCO employees before the International Labor Organization in Geneva. Such travel, he was told, was contrary to American policy and interests. Boudin charged that the Department's regulations combined "an unconstitutional vagueness with a tone more reminiscent of political controversy than of the conventional language of statutes" and that they impinged on First Amendment rights.[19]

Vagueness, Boudin contended, was the most serious problem in the field of "political crime." In particular, Shipley's rampaging presumptions offered scant respect for orderly procedures. And the vaguest, most utilized criterion used by the State Department in denying passports was that applicants sympathized with Communists. Membership or participation in organizations listed as subversive by the Attorney General, friendship with Communists or Soviet officials, participation in "peace" conferences, or even opposition to Attorney General Tom Clark's nomination to the Supreme Court, were all deemed sufficient to prevent one's travel as not being "in the interests of the United States." The Attorney General's list of subversive organizations was published in 1947, yet none was given a hearing as required by law until 1956. The list served meanwhile as official policy and contributed to the prevailing notions of guilt by association.[20]

Prior to the 1950s the Supreme Court considered only one case involving the right to a passport. That decision, in 1939, involved the petitioner's citizenship status and in no way touched on the kind of administrative actions or regulations that emerged during the Cold War.[21] But the incidents of the 1950s raised new, and legally more difficult, questions. The persons denied passports in that period were all citizens, all politically active critics of American policies, and many were prominent. The last point cannot be overly emphasized. Passports consistently were denied to rank-and-file Communist Party members or to those who belonged to other political fringe groups. But few such people had the means to carry out lengthy formal, legal challenges.

Anne Bauer, a naturalized citizen and a journalist who had worked for the Office of War Information, had her passport revoked in Paris in 1951, six months prior to its expiration. American consular officials in Paris refused to give her any reason except to state the Department's contention that her activities ran counter "to the best interests of the United States." Bauer challenged that action as a denial of due process. A three-judge district court panel held that she had been unfairly deprived of proper notice and hearing and directed that the Department grant her a passport.[22] The Department promptly issued its August 1952 regulations defining the scope of its authority, the categories of persons to be denied passports, and the machinery for a hearing and appeal.

A year later, Dr. Otto Nathan applied for a passport to travel to Europe to fulfill his responsibilities as executor of Albert Einstein's will. After nearly two years of waiting for a final answer from the Passport Office, Boudin, on behalf of Nathan, filed a complaint asking for a declaratory judgment directing that a passport be issued. A district court in March 1955 ordered that Nathan promptly be granted an appropriate hearing. Three months later, a hearing still had not been held, and the judge ordered the Department to grant Nathan a passport. An appellate order the next day, however, allowed the Department a few more weeks to hold the hearing but set a specific schedule. The Board of Passport Appeals promptly reviewed the application and recommended its approval, thus making the case moot.[23] The Department apparently chose to avoid a full-scale review of the constitutional issues.

A parallel case, however, clarified some of the constitutional questions regarding passport restraints. Max Schachtman, chairman of the Independent Socialist League, a group cited on the Attorney General's subversive list, challenged the Department's denial of his passport application. In 1955, the Court of Appeals held that the Secretary of State's discretion was subject to judicial scrutiny. The passport was no longer a simple document certifying citizenship, the judges held. It was a necessary prerequisite for travel abroad; accordingly, it could be withheld only if standards of due process were applied. The court was particularly concerned with the State Department's arbitrary policies. Finally, the court noted that the League had made at least fifteen attempts in six years to secure a hearing from the Attorney General to challenge his inclusion of the group as subversive. This especially heightened the judges' due process concerns: "For us to hold that the restraint thus imposed upon appellant is not arbitrary would amount to judicial approval of a deprivation of liberty without a reasonable relation to the conduct of foreign affairs." The failure to provide Schachtman and the League with a hearing in regard to the subversive list made it impossible for him to remove the cause of his passport denial, and thus he had no opportunity to secure any relief or reconsideration from that action.[24] Apparently desirous of avoiding any definitive ruling on either its passport policies or the Attorney General's list, the government chose not to appeal. Schachtman received his passport soon afterward.

The legal assaults chipped away at individual actions by the State Department, but the courts and the Department seemed equally reluctant to confront the basic issues of control and discretionary authority. Shortly after the Schachtman decision, a district court held in *Boudin* v. *Dulles* that the Secretary of State had no power to deny a passport on the basis of evidence not in the record. Boudin had followed the procedural requirements of the 1952 regulations and had carried his plea to the Board of Passport Appeals. The board had denied his appeal and based its decision on evidence unknown to Boudin and which he had no opportunity to refute. The court ordered a new hearing. In this case, both parties appealed. The Court of Appeals held that the Department must offer open factual findings to bring the applicant within one of the categories of persons to be denied passports. It found none had been made and ruled Boudin was entitled to his passport. The court specifically declined to consider whether the Department could use confidential information (information which Boudin denied), but said that it would have to state whether its findings were based on such evidence.[25]

Paul Robeson's passport denial probably was the most prominent case of the period. Robeson flatly refused to sign the non-Communist affidavit. He went to court and asked for a declaratory judgment that the passport rules were unconstitutional and for a decree ordering the Secretary of State to issue him a passport immediately. The Court of Appeals, however, invoked the standard rule that a plaintiff had to exhaust administrative remedies before coming to court, holding: "We cannot assume the invalidity of a hearing which has not been held or the illegality of questions which have not been asked."[26]

Whatever the reluctance of the courts and the Department to bring the whole question of passport policy under judicial scrutiny, the decisions of the mid-1950s inevitably pointed the way to just such a resolution. The courts already had heard many challenges to the administrative, bureaucratic, and legislative caprice of the previous decade. The loyalty program was under increasing attack, bold new appeals against the continued harassment of the Communist Party were pending, and the courts were hospitable to demands that restraints be imposed on the more abusive techniques of congressional investigations. The time was ripe. What was needed was a case that would raise the proper questions for judicial scrutiny of the State Department's passport policy.

iv

Rockwell Kent typified the activist, leftist intellectual of the interwar and early Cold War periods. Born in 1882 in Tarrytown Heights, New York, of native-born parents, Kent was educated at Horace Mann High School in New York City and at New York University and Columbia. He characterized himself as writer, lecturer, dairy farmer, carpenter, and architectural draftsman. Kent was, of course, most famous as an artist, widely known for his paintings, wood engravings, and, perhaps most prominently, as an illustrator of popular editions of Shakespeare, *The Decameron*, and *Moby Dick*. His stark paintings of seascapes and barren landmasses fit the artistic realism of the 1930s and 1940s.

The Federal Bureau of Investigation was a connoisseur of Kent's politics, not his art. The Bureau reported in 1951 that Kent had been affiliated with at least eighty-five Communist-front organizations, basing its investigation on publications, witnesses, and Kent's own admissions. The FBI traced Kent's interest in Communism at least back to 1936, when he had published an article in the *New Masses*. He argued then that a "true American" must have the will to right social wrongs. "For me," Kent said, "the way is Communism." During the 1930s, Kent vigorously spoke out against the capitalistic forces that had caused the Great Depression, and he warmly supported the Loyalist cause during the Spanish Civil War. Through the years, he published political statements in both the Communist and the non-Communist press and made repeated public appearances for such organizations as the American Youth for Democracy, the International Workers Order, the National Council of American-Soviet Friendship, the American Council for the Protection of the Foreign-Born, and the Trenton Emergency Civil Rights Conference. He readily sponsored groups like the Abraham Lincoln Brigade, the American People's Meeting, the National Federation for Constitutional Liberties, the Committee for Free Political Advocacy, the World Peace Congress, and the National Council of the Arts, Sciences, and Professions. All these groups, the FBI noted, were on the Attorney General's list of subversive organizations.

Kent also had been an outspoken defender of Earl Browder and Harry Bridges when they were prosecuted by the government. He had entertained Soviet students and diplomatic officials. He had been a longtime subscriber to the *Daily Worker* and the Soviet Embassy's *U.S.S.R. Information Bulletin.* In 1953 the FBI reported that Kent had advocated the repeal of the McCarran-Walter Act, had urged clemency for the Rosenbergs, and had spoken at a memorial meeting for Joseph Stalin. The FBI's informants, particularly ex-Communist Party members, identified Kent as a Communist.[27]

The FBI undoubtedly had its own reasons for keeping tabs on Kent. But the Passport Office was particularly interested in amassing such information, for Kent's criticism of American policy and unabashed apologies for the Soviet Union had aroused Ruth Shipley's animosities. By the early 1950s, Kent already had attended several international "Peace Congresses." His participation and comments abroad raised concerns that Kent was not representative of the "best interests of the United States."

Kent secured a passport to attend the World Congress of Partisans for Peace in Paris in April 1949. The French Communist Party organized the Congress as a protest against NATO. Shortly before the conference, the House Committee on Un-American Activities denounced the sponsors, topping the list with Kent, who was affiliated, the committee said (obviously privy to the FBI reports), with at least eighty-five Communist-front organizations. The State Department quickly condemned the Paris Congress, labeling the participants as "performers."[28]

In February 1950, Kent requested that his passport be amended to permit travel to Norway, Denmark, and Sweden, as well as France and England. Apparently Kent anticipated some difficulty, for he engaged a Washington lawyer to support his application. The attorney informed Shipley that Kent's purposes were "journalistic" and that he was to appear before a committee of the French Parliament. The passport was promptly extended to include the additional countries, but it was restricted to the places specified and only for a duration of three months. Kent made no objections. But while traveling the next month, he visited Czechoslovakia, Finland, and the Soviet Union. In the Soviet Union, Kent prominently figured as one of the few Americans participating in the gathering of the Permanent Committee of the World Congress Partisans of Peace. The

American Embassy cabled Washington that Kent followed a "straight Communist line." The embassy's reporting officer thought Kent's most notable contribution was a remark on the cleanliness of Moscow's streets, with the implication that that was not true for American cities. Kent also laid a wreath on the grave of John Reed. The embassy reported that while in Helsinki Kent had visited the Soviet legation.[29]

The American delegation then proceeded to Stockholm to attend the Stockholm Peace Congress. O. John Rogge, a former Assistant Attorney General (who had prosecuted the Washington sedition trial in 1944 and later represented David and Ruth Greenglass in the Rosenbergs' spy trial), Johannes Steel and Albert Kahn, both prominent left-wingers at the time, and Kent were the American participants. Rogge publicly asserted that none of the delegates was a Communist. The American Embassy observer in Stockholm reported that the group was somewhat divided over the Congress, describing Rogge and Kent as "lukewarm" in their support. Yet when Kent returned to the United States he actively served on the committee publicizing the "Stockholm Peace Appeal" and urged people to sign it. The statement included only the Soviet proposal to outlaw atomic weapons.[30]

After returning home, Kent received an invitation to be the American juror on an international panel for awards in the arts to those who had advanced the cause of peace. The sponsor was the World Congress of Defenders of Peace, and the jury was to assemble in Prague in August 1950. Kent wrote to Shipley on July 21 asking that his passport be extended for travel to Czechoslovakia. He included his passport and the five-dollar renewal fee. Earlier, when Kent's lawyer had called Shipley about the extension, she brusquely told him there was no need for an intermediary and that Kent should deal directly with her.[31]

On August 1, Shipley informed Kent that the State Department could not consider extending his passport until he prepared an affidavit explaining why he traveled to countries not specified on his passport. She also asked for the details of his previous trip. Kent planned to depart on August 9. Before receiving Shipley's response of August 1, he had written on July 29 stressing the urgency of the approaching date. Similarly, on August 3, he called Shipley but was told she was occupied. A secretary promised to look into the matter and call him back promptly. She did not, and Kent wrote again on August 4—still not having received Shipley's response. He again pleaded for prompt action and courteously maintained he had followed the correct application procedures, despite his belief that a passport was "no more than an official authentication of citizenship and [was] not to be construed as a permission to travel." He insisted he was not "begging" for an extension, for he thought that the passport itself was evidence of his unquestionable right to an extension. Finally, he added that "in this crisis in world affairs, the importance of my mission is deserving of priority."[32]

Shipley telephoned Kent on August 7. Kent's description of the conversation indicates that her call must have alarmed him and that he had little inclination to challenge her ruling. She told him that his previous unauthorized travel placed him in violation of federal law and made him liable for prosecution. He well realized that the passport decision was designed to prevent him from attending the Prague peace meeting, but he also understood that he was vulnerable to retaliation for his illegal action. "If I have broken a law—and I appear to have —they are perfectly justified in punishing me by not granting me a passport," he told a friend. "I won't stick my neck out unless my feet are planted on firm ground—and in this case they are not," he concluded. A few days later, Shipley's assistant formally denied the passport extension and warned Kent of his liability for prosecution.[33]

Publicly, however, Kent remained irascible. He contended he had violated regulations unwittingly. The only country specifically excluded on the passport was Yugoslavia, and he had decided to visit the Soviet Union only after he arrived in Europe. He admitted a "transgression," but insisted that he was working for peace, and that he would do so with anyone, Communist or non-Communist. The Prague conference, he acknowledged, was "of course, led by Communists." Nevertheless, "anything that the Communists say about peace sounds good to me." The Passport Office returned Mrs. Kent's passport on August 30, but retained Kent's.[34]

Six months later, Kent learned that his passport difficulties affected not only his political activities but his work as well. In February 1951 he wrote Shipley asking whether he could have a passport to paint pictures either in Ireland or in Peru. He insisted he intended to paint and do nothing else. If the matter needed discussion, he offered to travel to Washington to see Shipley. Two weeks later, he renewed his request. After another eight days, Shipley replied with a curt refusal: "the Department is not willing at this time to grant you passport facilities for travel to any countries for any purpose."[35]

Not for four years did Kent approach the State Department with another passport request. But out of sight was not necessarily out of mind. In August 1953 —two and one half years after his last application—Shipley reported Kent's 1950 travel violations to the Justice Department and recommended that he be prosecuted. The lengthy delay doubtless resulted from departmental bureaucratic politics and policies. John Foster Dulles' stewardship of the Department, beginning in early 1953, resulted in a tightening up of loyalty investigations and security matters in general. Scott McLeod, the newly appointed head of the Bureau of Security and Consular Affairs, and Shipley worked closely on passport matters, and no doubt they found each other most congenial.

Shipley reported to the Justice Department that Kent's travel to the Soviet Union, Finland, and Czechoslovakia in 1950 violated Section 1544 of Title 18 of the U.S. Code. The law, clearly stamped on all passports, specified that any person who used it in violation of the conditions or restrictions contained therein was liable to prosecution. The Justice Department initially displayed enthusiasm for making a case. In October 1953, Assistant Attorney General Warren Olney III, head of the Criminal Division, turned the matter over to the U.S. Attorney in New York City, J. Edward Lumbard. Since Kent had admitted the violations, and they could be corroborated, Olney wanted Lumbard to present the case to the grand jury and secure a three-count indictment, regarding the travel in the three countries not authorized by Kent's passport. Olney then asked Dulles to secure corroborating evidence from the Finnish government. Both departments assumed it would have been impossible to gain such cooperation from either the Soviet or the Czech government. All the while, Olney and his staff kept in mind the implications of the case, owing to Kent's political and artistic prominence and the fact that this would be the first case ever prosecuted charging the wrongful use of a passport.[36]

U.S. Attorney Lumbard clearly was not enthusiastic. The unique character of the charge, Kent's advanced age, and his "innocuous background" made Lumbard wary of prosecution. He asked Olney to request the FBI's security file on Kent, for he believed it would "benefit the prosecution to have Kent's views on Communism before the jury." He also wanted to know if the State Department was submitting similar cases for prosecution. Finally, and most important, he said it would be crucial to demonstrate that Kent's activities abroad were detrimental to American interests.

The Justice Department promptly put Lumbard in touch with the FBI, but he was warned not to use any Bureau reports or informants in court without permission. Lumbard's replies to Washington continued to reveal his concern about the weakness of the case. As matters stood, he doubted that Kent "willfully and knowingly" misused his passport; Kent's admissions, in fact, denied criminal intent. But Lumbard suggested that the FBI might be able to develop direct or circumstantial evidence demonstrating such intent, either in his writings or in statements prior to his unauthorized travel. Again, he expressed concern about the need to compile details and evidence that Kent's presence abroad harmed the national interest. Lumbard urged the Justice Department to contact Shipley, who had indicated she possessed the relevant facts.[37]

Shipley promptly prepared a summary of her office's evidence against Kent. To demonstrate Kent's criminal intent, she cited his passport application of 1950. At the time, he asked that Sweden, Norway, and Denmark be added to his previous passport approval for France and the British Isles. Kent's actions demonstrated that he knew he could travel only where authorized, Shipley argued. Accordingly, when he traveled to the Soviet Union, she said it was reasonable to assume he realized he was making an unauthorized journey. For evidence of

Kent's damages to American interests while in Moscow, Shipley submitted two comments from a CIA summary of Soviet press dispatches. First, there was the remark contrasting Moscow's cleanliness with New York's filth. Second, Kent had allegedly said that anti-Soviet remarks in the United States were designed to create hostility among the American people toward Russians.[38] Lumbard could hardly have been overwhelmed by such "evidence."

Shipley subsequently submitted copies of Kent's various passport applications dating back to 1934. Apparently she found in this further evidence that Kent acknowledged the Department's right to authorize specific travels. Secretary of State Dulles himself sent a long cable to the Paris embassy requesting information on Kent's activities in France just prior to his departure for Moscow in 1950 and whether he used the embassy for passport services. But Paris had no information on Kent's whereabouts while he was in France.[39]

Shipley's case against Kent failed to impress the Justice Department. The Passport Office files contain no further communication on the case for the rest of Shipley's tenure into early 1955. Frances Knight, her successor, approached the new head of the Internal Security Division, William F. Tompkins, about the case in July 1955. Tompkins, however, was reluctant to proceed. Contrary to information Shipley had provided, the Justice Department learned that Kent's traveling companions in 1950, Rogge and Steel, also had visited the Soviet Union without proper authorization. Tompkins advised Knight that State should check on this matter and learn if there was any criminal intent on the part of Rogge and Steel. Knight quickly responded that the others had valid passports "which did not preclude travel to the Soviet Union." She did not say they had specific authorization.[40] In any event, the brief exchange between Tompkins and Knight reflected the Justice Department's last serious consideration for the Passport Office's desire for prosecuting Kent. As for the State Department, it soon found itself a defendant in a suit brought by Kent.

Kent's political concerns, rather than his vocational pursuits, appropriately dictated his next clash with the Passport Office. In May 1955 he received an invitation from the Secretariat of the World Council of Peace to participate in an international peace assembly, scheduled for Helsinki in late June.[41] Organized by intellectuals, artists, and authors, the Helsinki meeting was different from the Communist-dominated gatherings in Paris and Stockholm that Kent had attended. It reflected a growing international concern with domination by the superpowers and fear of nuclear war. The conference was devised to discuss controls on atomic weapons, disarmament, and the promotion of economic, cultural, and social cooperation among all nations. Such topics, of course, instinctively aroused suspicion among the security-oriented minds in the Passport Office.

Kent submitted a new application on May 28 for a passport to Finland and England, where he wished to visit friends. The Helsinki meeting had been scheduled for June 22. Receiving no response from the Passport Office, Kent wrote to President Eisenhower on June 24 stressing the importance of the meeting and how it squared with the President's public calls for increased cultural contacts, and calling his attention to the "great negligence or extreme discourtesy" of the Passport Office.[42] The wheels of Frances Knight's office were grinding, slowly, of course. On June 28, an office memorandum noted the decision to refuse Kent a passport on the grounds that he was a Communist. The next day Knight sent Kent a lengthy letter detailing the decision.

Knight told Kent that he fell afoul of Section 51.135 of the Regulations; he allegedly was a Communist; the evidence indicated his consistent adherence to the Communist Party line; and his visit abroad seemed designed to further the Communist movement. To support the charges, Knight offered three closely typed pages detailing Kent's activities dating back to 1936. She cited his affiliation in over twenty "front" groups, his subscriptions to the *Daily Worker,* his support for clemency for the Rosenbergs, his speech at a dinner honoring Paul Robeson, his opposition to the McCarran Internal Security Act, his criticism of the Attorney General for using paid informers, his participation in a memorial meeting for Stalin, his support of a ban on atomic weapons, and his sponsorship of Communist Party candidates. All this, of course, was based on the numerous FBI reports available to Knight and her staff.

Knight informed Kent that the Regulations allowed him "informally" to present his case before a hearing officer, and with benefit of counsel. But she warned Kent that if he asked for a hearing, he would be required to offer a sworn statement as to whether he was or ever had been a Communist. She also offered him the option of simply submitting a written appeal, provided he included the non-Communist disclaimer. No longer was the case one of simply denying Kent his passport; instead, Knight and her staff chose a new battleground in the ongoing imbroglio.

The relevant section of the Regulations provided that a person refused a passport who then had a hearing "will, upon request, confirm his oral statements in an affidavit for the record" (Section 51.137). Knight thus clearly put Kent on notice about what would be asked of him in a hearing. If he balked at the affidavit, then she could congratulate herself on saving the Passport Office the time and expense of a hearing.[43] Kent did refuse, and the refusal was the cutting edge for his struggle of the next three years.

Kent replied on the Fourth of July, protesting that he had been judged guilty without a hearing and then was offered an opportunity to prove his innocence. A hearing before a group which devised the rules, and interpreted them, would be, he said, "nothing less than a grotesque disregard for basic principles of American justice." He also charged that the information against him had been obtained through wiretapping and mail openings. Finally, he contended that recent court rulings held that a passport was the right of every American citizen and was no more than an official certification of fact. Travel could not be forbidden without due process of law, and the ruling against him circumvented his constitutional rights. In his reply, Kent did not specifically refuse the offer to sign an affidavit. But a few days later, he publicly declared: "I am not a Communist and I have never been a Communist, but I'm damned if I will sign one of those things." The remarks were published in the New York *Times* and an upstate newspaper. An unidentified correspondent sent Knight a clipping from the latter with a typed note claiming that the enrollment records of Essex County showed that Kent had voted the Communist ticket in the late 1920s.[44]

The most immediate aid and comfort to Kent came from Clark Foreman, director of the Emergency Civil Liberties Committee. The committee's general counsel, Leonard B. Boudin, had just successfully argued the Nathan case. In reply to Foreman's support for his stand, Kent said that he would be willing to go to court and that he, like Foreman, desired a definitive judicial ruling. He said he would gladly reapply for a passport in order to raise a test case. Foreman was delighted. The judgment in the Nathan case was a limited one, and the Passport Office still required an affidavit. He was anxious for a test case in which one swore he was an American citizen, but offered nothing more. If Kent were willing to use Boudin as his counsel, there would be no charge for the legal service, Foreman wrote. Kent himself would be liable for expenses and court costs. Kent eagerly accepted. Once he agreed, Boudin wasted little time in setting the stage for a new confrontation. He suggested that Kent apply for a new passport to visit Europe for work and pleasure. To give the Passport Office a reasonable period for action, Boudin proposed a departure date of November 1.[45]

Kent applied for a new passport on August 2. Almost three weeks later, he received an acknowledgment from Knight—much to his surprise, for he expected a perfunctory denial based on the previous ruling. Kent obviously had little understanding how such an expeditious handling would have violated customary procedure. But on September 2, Boudin wrote to the Passport Office requesting an immediate decision. Furthermore, he suggested an "informal hearing" if it was a necessary condition for rendering a verdict. Hearing nothing, he renewed his call for action ten days later.

Knight finally responded on September 14 with a terse statement that Kent's records were being re-examined and that an evaluation report could be expected "in the near future." Boudin's reply was equally blunt. There was no need for a further evaluation, for the Department had two alternatives: (1) either to grant a passport immediately based on the Schachtman and Nathan decisions or to support its refusal with a quasi-judicial hearing; or (2) adhere to its letter to Kent of June 29, 1955, and offer a hearing under Section 51.137 despite its conflict with court decisions. Again, he urged promptness. Knight refused to be hurried, reserving a decision pending the evaluation report. She did, however, offer the informal hearing under Section 51.137 if Kent wished to explain or deny the allegations contained in her previous letter.[46]

Knight was not sitting idly waiting for whatever report she expected. For example, she replied to a New Yorker who regularly corresponded to the Passport Office to complain about Kent. She thanked this good citizen for the information—already in the FBI files—that Kent had signed a brief urging the Supreme Court to invalidate the Internal Security Act. Also, on October 3, two months after its receipt, she forwarded Kent's application to the Security Office "for evaluation." She suggested that Security "continue its evaluation," for it appeared Kent would pursue further action. Kent had planned his travel for November 1. As the date approached, Boudin's Washington associate, David Rein, called the Passport Office to inquire about the matter. He spoke to a clerk, who told him the Office would be in touch with him, but possibly not by November 1.[47]

Boudin telegraphed Scott McLeod on October 26 asking that the "person in charge" of Kent's case telephone him immediately. Orson Trueworthy, McLeod's special assistant, promptly called. The conversation largely clarified the procedure preparatory to a formal suit. Trueworthy opened by offering an informal hearing for Kent on November 4 before Ashley Nicholas, Chief of the Legal Division of the Passport Office. The catch, of course, was that in order to receive a passport or a final decision in the hearing, Kent had to submit an affidavit. And there was one more bind: the Board of Passport Appeals had decided it would not entertain any appeals without an affidavit or a decision by the hearing officer. It was a dead end. The Department insisted that the affidavit requirement was a lawful condition; Boudin adamantly took the contrary view.[48] Accordingly, Boudin saw no need of going through with the proposed hearing.

Kent, meanwhile, anticipating a suit, arranged an exhibit of his paintings at a New York hotel. Calling his show "The Right to Travel," Kent displayed some of his noteworthy paintings and drawings done around the world. The two-week exhibit raised $2,000 from admissions, enough, Kent and Foreman said, to cover Kent's legal expenses. At the end of the exhibit on October 30, Kent announced he would file suit in Washington on November 9.[49]

After Boudin's October 27 conversation with Trueworthy, the State Department reconsidered its views and developed a more defensible position. Instead of flatly contending that without an affidavit there would be no passport, it now said that Kent would be *requested* to present an affidavit. The Department's subsequent action then would "be based on all of the pertinent information and evidence before it." Presumably, this would include Kent's refusal, but the Department avoided the pitfall of saying that would be the only reason. The hearing thus was a necessity for Kent.[50]

Kent appeared at the State Department on November 8. He was repeatedly pressed to swear he was not a Communist and questioned about statements in his recently published autobiography. He refused to respond, contending that the inquiries were beside the point. He insisted once again that a passport merely certified citizenship and that as an American citizen he was entitled to one as of right. Kent demanded that he receive a passport or be confronted with the evidence and sources the Department had used to deny him the document.

After the hearing Kent flatly declared to waiting reporters, "I am not now and never have been a member of the Communist Party." Before the hearing ended, hearing officer Nicholas promised "an early decision." It took three weeks for the obvious decision to emerge: no affidavit, no passport. The Department decided to adhere to Section 51.142 of the Regulations, providing that an applicant may be required to submit an affidavit. The permissive form became an imperative presumably because of the lengthy file detailing Kent's pro-Communist activities. Finally, Knight told Kent that he would receive further consideration when he complied with the rules.[51]

Despite the new refusal, the Passport Office and related sections still seemed reluctant to let the matter proceed to court. Before serving a complaint, Boudin had one more hurdle to clear. The Regulations provided for an appeal to the Board of Passport Appeals. In its previous rulings in the Nathan and Foreman cases, and most recently in that of Dr. Walter Briehl, which Boudin was currently handling, the board had held that it would not entertain an appeal without an affidavit. Boudin made several inquiries whether the policy would hold for Kent. John W. Sipes, the board's counsel, finally replied with an ambiguous answer on December 12. Before that, one of his subordinates advised him that the board's previous policy denied applicants the constitutional right of a hearing to which courts ruled they were entitled. Two days after receiving Sipes's letter, Kent's attorneys served Knight with a complaint and summons. Boudin bluntly charged that by its delays the Department was avoiding a resolution of the issue. If the Board of Passport Appeals instituted an immediate hearing, he offered to have Kent appear, without prejudice to his rights in subsequent litigation. But he warned that he would permit no further delays.[52]

The dilatory tactics of Knight, Sipes, the Security Office, and various other functionaries who had been involved in Kent's case abruptly ceased once the case moved to the State Department's legal office. The correspondence between Herman Phleger, the Legal Adviser, and Warren E. Burger, then Assistant Attorney General for the Civil Division, indicated a genuine desire to secure definitive judicial rulings on the Secretary of State's power over passports. In reality, this meant decisions involving the power of the virtually autonomous fiefdom, the Passport Office.

Phleger well understood that the passport regulations were jeopardized by a district court ruling six weeks earlier in Boudin's own passport case. Judge Luther Youngdahl (who earlier had ruffled official feathers in Owen Lattimore's case) held that the secretary had no power to deny a passport on the basis of evidence not introduced in the record and which the applicant could not impeach. The denial of due process was clearly apparent, for Boudin had appealed to the Board of Passport Appeals. At issue was the seemingly limitless authority of the board. But Youngdahl pointedly refused to grant the government the right to deny passports "in an uncontrolled manner." It was not enough, he maintained, for the board to take into consideration the applicant's inability to counter unseen evidence or attack the credibility of confidential informants, for "whether the Board does or does not do this no one can ever know."[53]

As the State Department considered an appeal of Boudin's case and the new challenge of Kent's, Phleger urged Burger to raise the fundamental question of control over passports. These included the secretary's right to refuse a passport for any reason believed to be in the public interest; the secretary's right to refuse a passport based on confidential information not disclosed to the applicant; the right to refuse based upon testimony not heard in the applicant's presence; and the right to refuse because of the applicant's failure to answer under oath questions deemed pertinent by the secretary. Phleger reported to Burger that the Department had neither the apparatus, subpoena power, nor funds to carry out hearings according to Youngdahl's prescription. If that decision stood, then Phleger predicted a complete breakdown of the Passport Office mechanism. It would, he fretted, become necessary to issue passports "indiscriminately" to all applicants—exactly what Boudin and Kent and other litigants had asked. But Phleger, reflecting typical lawman thinking on the efficacy of courts, preferred that such changes come "as a result of final decisions by the Court."[54] A judicial ruling also would relieve the Department from making a decision that might stimulate political criticism. Given the entrenched power of the Passport Office bureaucrats, perhaps Phleger's response offered the only solution. Reform and self-abnegation simply were not in Frances Knight's lexicon.

Phleger thought that from the due process perspective, the government was not as vulnerable in Kent's case as in previous ones. He told Burger that Kent's application was processed "relatively quickly" (without defining what was quick), that Kent had notice of the derogatory information ("to the extent possible short of disclosing the precise sources"), and that he had a transcript of his informal hearing. Substantively, too, Phleger thought the case to be a better one. He conceded that Kent might merely be "a politically naive dupe" rather than a disciplined Communist. Nevertheless, he thought it arguable "that such persons can be just as dangerous as inveterate Communists and that both types are within the letter and spirit of the Regulations."[55]

Rockwell Kent's initial venture into the federal courts in March 1956 was not very comforting to him. Federal Judge Joseph C. McGarraghy in the District of Columbia District Court granted summary judgment to the government and denied Kent's request for a preliminary injunction. Kent's attorneys argued that his alleged ideological views had no bearing on his need to travel for his work and that the regulation was an unconstitutional infringement of his right to travel. The government insisted that the affidavit requirement was authorized by statute and that Kent had not fulfilled it. A year later, the Circuit Court upheld Judge McGarraghy by a 5–3 vote.[56]

Despite the decision favorable to the Passport Division, Secretary of State Dulles admitted shortly afterward that "the whole legal area as regards passports is somewhat in doubt." Pointing to other pending cases, Dulles thought that the Supreme Court eventually might offer an authoritative decision on his functions and responsibilities. Until then, he said he would continue to hold that the issuance of passports involved foreign policy considerations, and that he would act in accord with what he believed the best interests of the nation. Asked whether he would welcome a court test of that policy, Dulles said yes.[57]

The Supreme Court granted certiorari in November 1957 and heard arguments the following April. (Kent's case was joined to Dr. Walter Briehl's.) Kent's persistence combined with the State Department's willingness to pursue the issues virtually ensured a major test of the government's passport policy. A closely divided Supreme Court finally ruled in favor of Kent in 1958 and the effect was sharply to curtail the wide-ranging discretionary authority the Department had exercised with such impunity for nearly a decade.

Justice William O. Douglas, speaking for the five majority justices, acknowledged the long-standing construction, by Presidents, Secretaries of State, courts, and Attorneys General, that the issuance of passports was wholly discretionary. But the problem, he contended, was the manner of exercising that discretion and not the power itself. Furthermore, Douglas in a sweeping statement asserted that "the right to travel is part of the 'liberty' of which the citizen cannot be deprived without due process of law." He found such a right dating back to Magna Carta and running through most of our history. Freedom of movement was "necessary for a livelihood"; it had "large social values"; and it was "as close to the heart of the individual as the choice of what he eats, or wears, or reads."[58]

The Court, Douglas stated, need not determine the degree to which freedom of travel could be curtailed; rather, the question was the extent to which Congress had limited that liberty. Statutory authority for the refusal of passports consisted specifically of the Secretary of State's right to determine one's citizenship, or whether one was engaged in illegal conduct or trying to escape the enforcement of the laws. He acknowledged that the State Department had used a broader range of activities to justify some of its passport refusals, but with respect to Communists or Communist sympathizers, they were not consistent. Administrative practice had "jelled" only around the two statutory categories. While Congress made a passport necessary for foreign travel in 1952, and left its issuance to the Department's discretion, there was no basis for contending that the Secretary of State could withhold a passport for any substantive reason he might choose.[59]

Douglas cited the Japanese-American removal cases as an exceptional example of the Court's willingness to sustain any restriction of freedom of movement. But that involved a showing, he claimed, by the government of " 'the gravest imminent danger to the public safety.' " Congress and the executive then had moved in step, and the nation was at war. But no similar condition, and no similar coordination, had prompted the present passport policies of the State Department. And given the constitutional protection that Douglas found for the right to travel, he flatly contended that the Court would "not readily infer that Congress gave the secretary of state unbridled discretion to grant or withhold it."[60]

Passports traditionally functioned as a notice of citizenship, as a request to allow one to travel safely and freely, and in the event of need, to request all lawful aid and protection for the traveler. But under present law and practice, Douglas noted, the passport's crucial function was to control exit and thus impinge on one's freedom of movement. Such infringement required either congressional authorization or, if such power were delegated, then "the standards must be adequate to pass scrutiny by the accepted tests." In brief, the Court would "construe narrowly" all delegated powers that curtailed or diluted anyone's liberty. Congress had not specifically authorized the denial of passports for political beliefs or associations. Therefore it was unnecessary to deal with the constitutionality of any legislation; and without such legislation, the State Department could not "employ that standard to restrict the citizens' right of free movement." Such policy was directed against citizens who had been neither accused nor convicted of crimes. Citizens could not be denied their freedom of movement because they refused to allow an inquiry into their political thought.[61]

The majority opinion was a typical Douglas performance, combining sweeping, bold statements of constitutional liberty with a relatively narrow holding that an administrative agency had exceeded the scope of its authority. Strictly reading the relevant statutes, Douglas avoided any clash with congressional authority. Yet Kent's arguments were upheld: a citizen had a right to travel, a passport merely affirmed one's citizenship, and administrative agencies could not deny the passport on the basis of one's real or alleged political beliefs. The repressive political policies of the Passport Division stood repudiated.

The Justice Department quickly informed State that it regarded the Kent case as definitive. The Internal Security Division determined that the existing regulations could not be defended as a basis for future passport denials. State's Legal

Adviser agreed and said that passports would be issued in the other outstanding appeals, such as those of Paul Robeson, Anna Louise Strong, and Corliss Lamont. J. Edgar Hoover responded in his own special petulant way. He asked his staff to search for any statements by Justice Douglas that Communism was not dangerous.[62]

Eleven days after the Court's decision, on June 27, Boudin submitted a new application for Kent's request to travel abroad on July 15. Kent noted his intention to visit England, Denmark, France, Sweden, Poland, Czechoslovakia, and the Soviet Union. The Passport Division complied within four days and Kent seemingly was treated as an ordinary citizen. But State Department records reveal that the Passport Division maintained a lively interest in Kent's political activities. A memo of March 12, 1959, contained a story from the Communist Party newspaper, *The Worker,* describing Kent's visit to the Soviet Union. His letter to the New York *Times* of May 25, 1960, criticizing President Eisenhower's "open skies" plan and supporting Soviet military secrecy, was duly filed. And then there was a dispatch from the American Embassy in Moscow reporting Kent's Soviet television appearance in November 1960, when he remarked that the Bolshevik Revolution was "the birthday of the future of mankind." In June 1959, Kent wrote the Department regarding a peace appeal sponsored by Norman Thomas, taking the occasion to dispute the Department's position that the Soviet Union aimed to subject the entire world to Communism. That letter promptly was dispatched to the Passport Division.[63]

Kent's next passport application in January 1962 demonstrated anew the Passport Division's determination to control his activities and to preserve its long-standing prerogatives. Knight requested that the Security Office and the FBI consider whether Kent was subject to the provisions of Section 6 of the Subversive Activities Control Act (SACA). After several weeks of delay, Kent wrote to Knight requesting action by February 15 so that he could pay the required deposit for his passage. But the Department's Legal Division did not prepare its report until the twentieth. The reviewer reported to Knight that the security files offered "no indication of CP membership" and therefore that Kent was not subject to Section 6 of the SACA or any part of Title I of the Internal Security Act of 1950. The passport finally was mailed on the twentieth. Ironically, Kent himself may have precipitated the new flurry of activity. For some unexplained reason, Kent signed the non-Communist affidavit in his 1962 application. Four years after his victory, he handed one to Knight.[64]

v

The Supreme Court's decision did not immediately or decisively affect the long-nurtured behavior and beliefs of the State Department bureaucracy, and particularly the Passport Division. While passports were granted rapidly in a number of outstanding cases such as those of Kent, Robeson, Strong, Lamont, and Briehl, Frances Knight's office periodically engaged in guerrilla and diversionary tactics in an attempt to re-establish its prerogatives. Right-wing partisans reacted predictably to the Douglas opinion, and probably encouraged resistance from passport officials.

Columnist David Lawrence suggested that the Supreme Court had come close to legalizing treason and he berated the majority for their naïveté toward the "menace of Communist imperialism" and its acts of subversion in the United States. Communists were different, he concluded, and the government had every right to restrict their activities in ways different from those of other citizens.[65]

Secretary Dulles meanwhile announced his department's willingness to comply with the decision, while noting the ruling was based on a determination that existing legislation could not support the discretionary policy. He therefore directed his staff to work with the Justice Department to draft new legislation to justify the previous regulations. Exactly three weeks after *Kent* v. *Dulles*, the President submitted a special message to Congress on the need for passport control legislation. He insisted that it was "essential" for the Secretary of State to deny passports when their possession "would seriously impair the conduct of the foreign relations . . . or would be inimical to the security of the United States." He requested statutory authority for the State Department to continue its "historical" policy of limiting the issuance of passports. The President offered the traditional concern for balancing security objectives with the "inherent rights" of American citizens. "Any limitations on the right to travel," he concluded, "can only be tolerated in terms of overriding requirements of our national security, and must be subject to substantive and procedural guarantees."[66]

Dulles transmitted a draft bill to Congress the same day and supported it with his best Cold War rhetoric. The proposed legislation essentially restored the secretary's previously accepted discretionary authority. He reminded Congress that the nation was engaged "in a bitter struggle against the International Communist Movement." Issuing passports to supporters of that movement, he contended, afforded them another means "to encircle the United States and subordinate us to its will." Undersecretary Robert Murphy appeared on July 16 before the Senate Foreign Relations Committee to support the bill and to stress the urgency of the situation. He complained that since the Court's decision more than sixty applicants who supported Communist activities had been issued passports and were in a position to aid international Communism. Another seventy such applications were pending. The "heightened tension of the present state of the cold war," Murphy argued, made congressional action imperative. The Administration remained convinced that freedom of movement for Communist supporters threatened national security. He concluded by challenging the senators to deny "that a hardened Communist who alleges he is going abroad for innocent purposes is not in fact travelling for some more sinister purpose."[67]

Murphy's appeal apparently made little impression, as the Senate took no action. In the House, however, the Committee on Un-American Activities ironically criticized Frances Knight for her prompt compliance with the Supreme Court's decision. Chairman Francis Walter (Dem.-Pa.) charged Knight with "going out of her way" promptly to issue passports to "outstanding Communist agents or espionage suspects." In a letter to Dulles on July 10, Walter urged that passports be withheld from such people pending congressional passage of corrective legislation.[68] Walter clearly was grasping at straws and engaging in political posturing. Since the government chose not to ask for a rehearing in the case, the Court's mandate became official on July 11. Walter, then, was asking for the impossible: committee hearings and floor action for corrective legislation in both houses in one day's time. To their credit, State Department officials chose to follow the Court's lead rather than to anticipate such rapid congressional action.

While the Department offered prompt compliance, it continued to sponsor calls for new legislation and to criticize the effect of the Court's ruling. Concerted pressure from some parts of the Department stressed the dangers of the new policy—or, as they would characterize it, the lack of policy. In a speech to the Veterans of Foreign Wars, Roderic L. O'Connor, McLeod's successor in the Bureau of Security and Consular Affairs, complained that within four months of the decision, the Department had received 596 applications for passports from Communist sympathizers. The unrestricted travel of such persons, he warned, constituted "a real danger" to American security and he urged the VFW to support new legislation. Uninhibited travel allowed international Communism to carry on its worldwide operation, "the very essence of which," O'Connor added, "is espionage, subversion and sabotage."

The House of Representatives supported the Administration's efforts and approved new discretionary authority. But the Senate failed to act. The next year, O'Connor's successor, John W. Hanes, Jr., renewed the drive for legislation to circumvent the Kent decision. The arguments largely were the same, stressing the imminent danger of international Communism and the probable subversive acts of domestic sympathizers who sought to travel abroad. Congress again failed to respond and the State Department continued to issue passports to those it characterized as an "unprecedented threat both to our liberty and to our very existence."[69]

Frances Knight remained at her post, despite the shifting fashions. Her duties were largely routine and outwardly she seemed concerned only with her ceremonial functions. Presidents and Secretaries of State changed, but Knight stayed. Under Dean Rusk, the Department issued new regulations on January 12, 1962, giving applicants denied passports the right to review derogatory security information in their files. They also could confront witnesses and informants in open hearings. Rather than risk exposure of its informants, the FBI preferred to avoid confrontations. But in May 1962, Knight appeared on her own before a closed hearing of the Senate Internal Security Subcommittee and bitterly complained that the new regulations "in effect forbids us to protect ourselves."

The new controversy over passports, heavily laden as it was with shades of the 1950s, arose directly out of the Supreme Court's June 1961 decision in *Communist Party* v. *Subversive Activities Control Board.* In a 5–4 decision, the Court upheld a 1950 law requiring registration of the Communist Party and its members. That act also made it a crime for registered groups or their members to apply for a passport. The State Department thus had to deny passports to Communists, but in the spirit of the Kent decision it had to allow applicants to confront the evidence and witnesses used against them. The January 1962 regulations tried to solve the dilemma. But those regulations also aroused Frances Knight's ideological animus and her territorial imperatives.

Following the Court's registration decision, Knight revoked the passports of five top Party officials. National Chairman Elizabeth Gurley Flynn, however, challenged the order and asked for a hearing. According to Knight, her superiors ordered her to reissue the passport and avoid a hearing. Abba P. Schwartz, head of Security and Consular Affairs, and Knight's immediate superior, was, according to Knight, the chief culprit in the affair. It was widely known in Washington that Schwartz was anxious to break Knight's power either through transfer or dismissal. Her appearance before the Internal Security Subcommittee clearly signaled her determination to resist. With her civil service tenure, however, she remained serenely confident. "It is hard to see how they can get me out," she told reporters. "They have tried it before."[70] "They," of course failed; indeed, before long, Schwartz was eased out of the State Department.

A decade later, Knight still was at the same stand, occasionally reviving older concerns. In 1975 she advocated a national identification card for every citizen to deter fraud, to guarantee identity, and to serve as "a valuable tool" in crime detection. In the post-Watergate climate, Knight's proposal was virtually ignored. But it may have been a shrewd gimmick on her part to attract attention as she approached the compulsory retirement age of seventy. If so, it worked, and she received two successive one-year extensions. Two years later, however, the State Department's Retirement Division notified her that she would have to retire on July 31, 1977.[71]

Knight chose to leave quietly. And thus the half-century-old Queendom of Passports faded into history, unlamented, and best remembered as a reign of excessive, misguided zeal, but sadly all too reflective of its time and place in the past.

5

"IF AT FIRST . . ."
The Trials of Harry Bridges

The evidence . . . establishes neither that Harry R. Bridges is a member of nor affiliated with the Communist Party of the United States of America.
—HEARING EXAMINER JAMES M. LANDIS, 1939

Everybody knows Harry Bridges is a communist.
—AFL PRESIDENT WILLIAM GREEN, 1939

The record in this case will stand forever as a monument to man's intolerance of man.
—JUSTICE FRANK MURPHY, 1945

Tarry, Jew:
The law hath yet another hold on you.
—SHAKESPEARE, *The Merchant of Venice*

i

HARRY Bridges was one of the most prominent, powerful, and controversial labor leaders in the United States for nearly three decades. And for much of this time, the massed resources of governments, national and local, often in league with segments of the business community and organized labor, were raised against him. These forces combined to seek Bridges' deportation on the grounds that he was a dangerous alien radical. Why they did so appeared obvious throughout the lengthy proceedings; the intricacies of how they did it speaks volumes on the nature of legal, political, and bureaucratic processes.

Harry Bridges' labor record is familiar and well documented. His accusers and enemies, however, have been only vaguely depicted and they lie behind a veil of cold, lifeless public documents. Their tactics, methods, and purposes deserve similar revelation and understanding.

Bridges endured numerous court trials on a variety of charges, several congressional hearings, repeated investigations, and two deportation proceedings. They began in the tumultuous depression years of the 1930s and continued through the affluent 1950s. At first, non-governmental groups such as the Industrial Association in San Francisco and the American Legion sought to discredit Bridges as a labor leader and to have him deported. To a significant extent, federal authorities, at least in Washington, tended to disparage and deflect assaults on Bridges. But the situation changed after 1940 when new political imperatives and bureaucratic considerations stimulated a vigorous drive by the federal government to deport Bridges.

But Harry Bridges survived and prevailed. He became an American citizen and led his once militant union to a new era of accommodation with old antagonists. Finally, to the amusement or dismay of some, he received an accolade that certainly would have made a younger Harry Bridges cringe: "responsible labor statesman."

ii

As a boy in Australia, Harry Bridges read the early novels of Jack London. Those seafaring adventures, laced with a strong hostility toward capitalism (reinforced by an uncle who was a Labor Party official), apparently left an enduring impression on the youngster. His real-life adventure with the sea began in 1915, when as a fifteen-year-old he shipped out on a sailing vessel to Tasmania. He also furthered his political education when he encountered seamen members of the Industrial Workers of the World (IWW) on these runs. He then worked on Australian ships throughout the world until he arrived in San Francisco in April 1920 when he was nineteen. He paid the ten-dollar head tax required of landed immigrants and became a resident alien. In line with his new allegiance, he transferred his union membership from an Australian union to the American Sailors' Union of the Pacific. A year later, he was caught up in a seamen's strike in New Orleans and he briefly joined the IWW. He came away from that strike with two lessons: the Wobblies' syndicalism and lack of a political program impressed him as purposeless, and the accommodationist tactics of the American Federation of Labor (AFL) left him equally disillusioned with traditional trade unionism.

Bridges drifted back to San Francisco, where he decided to settle and work as a longshoreman. The San Francisco waterfront, unlike East Coast ports, had successfully resisted unionization by the mid-1920s although a classic company union, known as the Blue Book, operated. Nevertheless, the men were subject to the uncertainties of hiring (the shape-up), undermanned gangs, speedups, and the unregulated physical hazards of the job. Economic necessity and the shippers' power left workers with little choice. Bridges characteristically resisted joining the company union; instead he tried to revive the International Longshoremen's Association (ILA), an AFL affiliate well entrenched on the East Coast but long moribund along the Pacific. For his trouble, Bridges was blacklisted until he eventually joined the Blue Book in 1926.

While Bridges tried to order his working life, he was rather casual about his citizenship. He obtained his first papers in 1921. As the seven-year limit approached in June 1928, Bridges contacted the San Francisco immigration office and was told to appear in federal court the following September. He was misinformed, however, as the papers had expired in July. Although Bridges quickly refiled, his laxity was to cost him dearly.[1]

Unionism was Harry Bridges' all-consuming passion. The depression and a new administration in Washington revived labor militancy throughout the nation. Section 7 (a) of the National Industrial Recovery Act (NIRA) in 1933 provided nascent governmental support for union organization, and the West Coast dock workers enthusiastically responded to the opportunity for their union. Several factions emerged, but the struggle lay chiefly between a traditional trade-union group chartered by the ILA, dominated by conservative Irish Catholics, and a smaller one sparked by radicals and led by Bridges. Typical of the period, Communist cadres provided organizing skills and efforts. Whether Bridges himself belonged to the Party became a legal question debated for the next two decades; but he never denied his cooperation with Communists. He later publicly testified that they were "militant and sincere" and good union men. While he admitted they supported him, he denied he had ever courted them as Communists.

Bridges' faction encouraged militancy among the dock workers. Job actions, boycotts, and slowdowns disrupted the shippers' tight control and steadily gained new recruits for the ILA. By November 1933, Bridges and his allies controlled a majority of the business agents and the executive board. At the same time, the ILA clearly commanded the loyalty of most workers. The shippers, of course, continued to support the Blue Book, and the NRA Board in San Francisco supported the validity of their contract with the company union.

Up and down the Pacific coast, from Seattle to Los Angeles, the ILA continued to grow and demand recognition. Despite opposition by the nominal leadership in San Francisco and the International office in New York, Bridges secured an overwhelming vote for a strike in March 1934. He personally took command in San Francisco and the longshoremen struck on May 9.

Joseph P. Ryan, longtime conservative leader of the ILA, supported the traditional faction in San Francisco, and he rushed to the West Coast to take control of the strike. Unaccustomed to the rank-and-file politics that Bridges and his associates so expertly practiced, Ryan foolishly negotiated a settlement with the shippers that completely ignored the men's basic demands. The workers, prodded by Bridges and other militants, overwhelmingly rejected Ryan's efforts and booed him off the platform. Bridges maintained his leadership, but he also succeeded in making an enemy of Ryan, an influential labor baron in the AFL hierarchy.

The longshoremen's action brought prompt support from the seamen. As their ships docked in San Francisco, the sailors, many of whom belonged to the AFL Seamen's International Union (SIU), joined the picket lines. The SIU leadership hesitated to support the strike, but the Marine Workers' Industrial Union (MWIU), an affiliate of the Communist Party's Trade Union Unity League, ordered its 2,000 men off the job on May 19. Bridges later claimed that the MWIU action forced the more conservative unions to follow suit. Within a week, more than 15,000 men had effectively struck the Pacific Coast ports.

San Francisco police consistently supported the shippers' efforts to open the port. Police and pickets battled regularly for nearly two months. The business community meanwhile tried other, more subtle methods of breaking the strike. The San Francisco Chamber of Commerce sent a widely publicized telegram to President Roosevelt denouncing the strike as a Communist plot. "There can be no hope for industrial peace until communistic agitators are removed as the official spokesmen of labor and American leaders are chosen to settle their differences along American lines," the Chamber told the President.

On July 5—"Bloody Thursday"—waterfront clashes caused the deaths of two strikers and a bystander. The Teamsters, who had been supporting the dock workers, struck throughout the city. By July 16, the hitherto cautious Central Labor Council sanctioned a citywide general strike. The strike involved nearly 150,000 workers, but it collapsed after four days, largely because of the apathy of the older, more traditional unions. Several clear results emerged: the ILA won recognition and a six-hour day (to spread the work), and a jointly run employer-employee hiring hall replaced the barbarities of the shape-up. Those victories also left Harry Bridges a marked man. For the next two decades, his enemies in the shipping industry, aided by "patriotic" groups and Red-baiters, and then by various governmental agencies, relentlessly and vindictively tried to break Bridges' power and influence. The Industrial Association left no doubt as to the grounds of the struggle: "We must retrieve control of the waterfront from the Communistic leadership of the Longshoremen's Union and restore to the people of this community the serenity to which they are entitled in their transaction of their business and daily affairs."

For its part, the Communist Party willingly acknowledged its role in the strike. Testifying in August 1934 before the House Special Committee on Un-American Activities, California Party secretary Laurence Ross claimed that CP members "guided" the longshoremen's "dissatisfaction into organizational action."[2]

Washington officials responded tentatively, yet nervously, to the events in San Francisco. The San Francisco *Commercial News* charged that the Immigration and Naturalization Service (INS) was afraid of the unions and Harry Bridges.

Squarely blaming Bridges, "a professional labor agitator from Australia," for the strike, the *Commercial News* excoriated the agency for failing to perform its duties. Turner Battle, executive assistant to Labor Secretary Frances Perkins, reported that the White House had complaints about Bridges. He promptly ordered the INS (then part of the Labor Department) to secure a field report on Bridges from the San Francisco office.[3]

The San Francisco district office, already familiar with Bridges, launched an intensive investigation. Inspector T. V. Donoghue closely observed Bridges for the next eight months, regularly reporting on his activities. During the June 1934 strike, he reported that Bridges' speeches were confined to labor issues. He noted that Bridges had severely criticized police behavior, and had suggested that if the strike were not promptly settled, then steps should be taken for a general strike. Although several Communist-controlled unions and their spokesmen had participated with Bridges in a rally, Donoghue was satisfied that they had not "in any way" controlled or influenced events. The following February, the inspector reported that his investigation had failed to demonstrate that Bridges was "in any manner connected with the Communist Party, or with any radical organization." He added that the Crime Prevention Detail of the San Francisco police, which intensely surveyed radical and alien activities, likewise had not turned up any incriminating evidence. District Commissioner Edward Haff duly forwarded Donoghue's findings to Washington. Nothing, he believed, had been developed to indicate that Bridges was subject to deportation; specifically, no evidence existed establishing his membership in the Communist Party. Haff acknowledged the widespread belief that Bridges had "leanings toward communism," but again his office had not "as yet" secured any concrete evidence.[4]

Haff's conclusion gave him a loophole and the basis for an ongoing investigation. Officials in the INS Washington bureaucracy meanwhile consistently cited the San Francisco police reports and those of its own inspectors in response to demands that the Service do something about Bridges.

INS inspectors in the San Francisco office characteristically worked at cross-purposes. One agent, following the case of an alleged Communist from Japan, used his report to make totally different assumptions about Bridges. He found that the American League Against War and Fascism, of which Bridges was a member, had invited the Japanese. The League, he contended, was a Communist organization—"provable" by the fact that Roger Baldwin of the American Civil Liberties Union was also a member. The agent found it useful to discredit the Japanese Communist by identifying him with Bridges, "whose affiliations," he claimed, "are communistic." Much of the report was based on the charges of Paul Scharrenberg, head of the rival AFL Seamen's Union and secretary of the California Federation of Labor, that Bridges and the Communist Party sought total control of the Pacific ports.[5]

Despite the INS's low-key estimate of events, the general strike frightened some top officials of the Roosevelt administration. Secretary of State Cordell Hull and Attorney General Homer Cummings particularly reacted with alarm. According to Labor Secretary Frances Perkins, they proposed that FDR send troops to San Francisco. The President, who was then cruising toward Hawaii on a warship, declined to order intervention. Several months later, Roosevelt acknowledged that some of his people had panicked. "Everybody demanded that I sail into San Francisco Bay, all flags flying and guns double shotted, and end the strike. They went completely off the handle," he told reporters. The strike, said the President, was the work of "hot-headed young leaders," inexperienced in organized labor, along with the "old, conservative crowd," including the editors of the Hearst newspapers and the Los Angeles *Times*, who wanted a general strike, knowing it would fail and discredit the labor leaders. Admitting that he lacked legal proof, the President spoke off the record, but he remained convinced that the "old, conservative crowd" "baited the other fellows" into the general strike.[6]

The official government position, however, was that Bridges had legal status in the United States as an alien and that he had done nothing under the immigration laws to justify action against him. INS Commissioner Daniel W. McCormack maintained that Bridges' radical views did not make him deportable; rather, there had to be a clear showing that he advocated the overthrow of the government by force. Privately, however, FDR asked Perkins to discuss with the Attorney General whether a case could be made against Bridges for uttering "propaganda directed at the destruction of the government."[7]

But the pressures on Washington officials did not ease. In December 1935, Harper L. Knowles, chairman of the Subversive Activities Commission of the American Legion in California, demanded that the INS take action against Bridges. Knowles offered statements from rival labor leaders that Bridges was a Communist, and noted that Bridges persistently refused to deny the allegation. Like others on the West Coast, Knowles accused the INS of giving Bridges preferential treatment and ignoring Bridges' dilatoriness in acquiring citizenship. Bridges' behavior, Knowles concluded, demonstrated that he had no serious intention of becoming a citizen, and Knowles urged that he be deported immediately. In subsequent letters, Knowles cited Bridges' repeated favorable comments on the Soviet Union.

The legal staffs for both the Labor Department and the INS resolutely urged their superiors to resist Knowles's pressure. Acting Solicitor for the Department, Gerard D. Reilly, found that Bridges' statements during the 1934 strike did not advise, advocate, or teach unlawful damage to property—all valid grounds for deportation. He firmly warned against pursuing the matter in court. Federal courts traditionally had accepted the government's findings in such cases, but

Reilly feared that a court would reject this case as capricious and totally without foundation. Most important, Reilly recognized that Knowles sought to use the "deportation facilities as a means of controlling labor disputes by getting rid of leaders like Bridges." Reflecting the larger concerns of Labor Department policy, Reilly realized that the Department's credibility for mediation and conciliation efforts would be destroyed. Some months later, the INS's own legal advisers reviewed Knowles's lengthy correspondence with the agency, much of which had gone unanswered. They concluded that Knowles clearly was prejudiced, that he was merely engaged in "heckling," and that his language was "intemperate and overbearing." They brusquely recommended that Commissioner McCormack not "prolong a useless correspondence."[8]

Bridges' rising prominence continued to alarm his antagonists. Restless with the conservative AFL leadership, Bridges worked closely with the new unions that eventually formed the Congress of Industrial Organizations (CIO). The AFL expelled him in 1937 and Bridges took his newly named International Longshoremen's and Warehousemen's Union (ILWU) into the CIO. CIO president John L. Lewis promptly appointed Bridges as Pacific Coast Director of the national organization. Bridges' new affiliation undoubtedly frightened his enemies. The CIO, with its concept of an industrial union, its militancy, Communist connections, and political activism, must have struck them as Harry Bridges writ large.

Acting Commissioner Edward J. Shaughnessy reviewed and defended the INS's investigation of Bridges early in 1937. In a memorandum to Perkins, he reported that "every question" relating to the longshoremen's leader had been "promptly and carefully investigated" by the Service. Shaughnessy noted that Bridges still was casual about his citizenship. After allowing two declarations of intention to expire, Bridges submitted a new application in San Francisco in May 1936, but seven months later he had not yet formally filed the declaration in the district court.

Washington officials felt sufficiently fortified to cope with criticism from without, such as Knowles's complaints and frequent editorial comments. But a new assault on Bridges from within the ranks of the INS apparently shocked the official hierarchy. In the summer of 1937, Raphael P. Bonham, District Director of the Seattle office, surprised his Washington superiors with affidavits charging that Bridges was a member of the Communist Party. The information was relayed to Secretary Perkins, who considered it vague and largely hearsay. Nevertheless, she promptly went to Hyde Park to consult with Roosevelt. According to her account, the President reacted as "an ordinary American liberal." Had Bridges done anything to overthrow the government? he asked. When Perkins said he had not, the President replied: "Then why in the world should a man be punished for what he thinks, for what he believes. That's against the Constitution." Roosevelt finally advised Perkins to "carry out the law," but "not to let our imagination run away."[9]

Meanwhile, pressure mounted from formidable congressional sources. Senator Royal S. Copeland, a conservative New York Democrat, chaired the Senate Commerce Committee, which had jurisdiction in maritime matters. The senator had long-standing ties to old-line AFL leaders in New York, notably Joseph Ryan, president of the ILA. In October 1937, the two had joined to oppose Mayor Fiorello La Guardia's re-election bid and denounced La Guardia for accepting support from the CIO. Ryan was particularly sensitive where the CIO was concerned, for it, "through non-citizen Harry Bridges," as he labeled his rival, now controlled the Pacific Coast longshoremen. Several weeks later, Copeland let it be known that he would introduce legislation requiring that the heads of all labor unions be American citizens. He frankly admitted he was aiming at Bridges.

But Copeland also chose less direct action. In early February 1938, he convened hearings on proposed amendments to the Maritime Act that would impose federal mediation on maritime disputes and thus restrict strikes. Maritime Commission Chairman Joseph P. Kennedy endorsed Copeland's suggestion. Copeland's conduct of the hearings, however, focused on Bridges, his alien status, and his radical activities. He demanded that Secretary Perkins turn over the INS file on Bridges to the committee. Against her "better judgment," Perkins complied. Several days later, the senator complained that several items were missing, particularly Bonham's Seattle reports. Nevertheless, the available material satisfied him that Bridges was a menace and should be deported. He was convinced that Bridges and his lieutenants were Communists, an opinion promptly endorsed by Ryan.[10]

In his formal testimony before the committee, Ryan stated that Bridges as well as Ryan's East Coast rival, Joseph Curran, head of the CIO National Maritime Union, were on the Communist Party payroll. Ryan insisted that his East Coast union had kept Bridges and the CP from an absolute control of American shipping. He complained, however, that Secretary Perkins' support of the leftist unions handicapped his efforts. The committee also heard from Paul Scharrenberg, Bridges' old AFL foe from California, and now the Federation's national legislative representative. Scharrenberg similarly attacked Bridges and made several references to "red" domination of the waterfront.

The committee rejected Bridges' and Curran's demands that they be allowed to appear and respond. With characteristic blunt language, Bridges told Copeland that the committee was a "mouthpiece of shipowners and reactionary interests." Curran charged that Ryan, Copeland, and the shippers were in league against the interests of seamen and longshoremen.[11]

Political realities, and not her "imagination," finally forced Perkins and her legal advisers to bring deportation proceedings against Bridges early in 1938. Coping with outside "hecklers" such as Knowles proved relatively simple compared to confronting strategically placed middle-level bureaucrats and formidable political forces, each of which had strong ties to outside private interests. Bridges' enemies were powerful. Perkins' assistant told her in September 1937 that the Teamsters, the AFL, shippers, and business organizations were in league "to crush Bridges." A warrant was issued in Baltimore and served on Bridges and his attorney, Lee Pressman, on March 2, 1938. Bridges was charged with having violated the alien laws when he joined a group advocating the overthrow of the government by force. A deportation hearing in San Francisco was set for April 25.[12]

In the "Red Scare" climate of 1918, Congress provided for the deportation of those aliens who were anarchists, who believed in the overthrow of the government by force or violence, who advocated the unlawful destruction of property, or who were members of or affiliated with any organization that believed, taught, or advocated the violent overthrow of the government. Any alien who, at any time after entry, was found to belong to any of those classes could be deported. The act was amended in 1920 to cover aliens who belonged to the IWW.[13]

Washington officials obviously were unsure of their case. Newly appointed INS Commissioner James Houghteling pressed Bonham for harder evidence, and he clearly had serious doubts about the quality of some of the affidavits. Bonham, meanwhile, was annoyed that the proceeding would be out of his bailiwick, and he expressed concern for the safety of his witnesses. Knowles demanded closed hearings in order to protect witnesses and the right of the American Legion to have its own attorney present. Bridges' lawyer similarly demanded closed hearings in order to prevent distortion by the hostile media.[14] But another deportation case, seemingly unrelated to Bridges', raised havoc with the government's efforts.

For over five years, immigration officials in New Orleans and Washington had sought to deport Joseph George Strecker. A citizen of the Austro-Hungarian Empire, Strecker entered the United States in 1912. Undisputed evidence demonstrated that he joined the Communist Party in November 1932 and that he was a member until February 1933, when he ceased paying dues. Several months later, he applied for citizenship in Arkansas. On the basis of his own admissions of Communist Party membership, he was arrested in November 1933 and held for a deportation hearing. The government's chief evidence consisted of Strecker's Party membership book, which summarized the Party's purposes and which contained his dues stamps for a four-month period ending in February 1933. The book cited a rule that failure to pay dues for three months automatically canceled membership. Following the hearing, the Department of Labor issued a deportation order, finding that Strecker believed in, and that he was then affiliated with, a group advocating the overthrow of the government by force.

Strecker applied for a writ of habeas corpus in the federal district court in New

Orleans, alleging that the proceedings had been unfair and that the findings were unsupported by the evidence. The court dismissed the writ, but Strecker successfully appealed to the Fifth Circuit Court of Appeals. That tribunal found no evidence linking Strecker to the Communist Party at the time of his arrest and no record that he had ever taught or believed in the violent overthrow of the government. Judge Joseph C. Hutcheson, speaking for the majority, said that Strecker merely was "a small 'bourgeoisie' merchant, with a little capital, some canniness, a fair amount of human kindness, some bad habits, and apparently no quarrel with the Government of the United States, but only with what he regards as the evils of Capitalism . . . , and with grafters holding Government offices." The government's findings of Strecker's anti-capitalist animus, Hutcheson stated, dramatically illustrated "the tyranny of labels over certain types of minds." Finally, Hutcheson charged the government with "Pecksniffian righteousness," "hypocrisy," and "party bigotry" when it assumed that because Strecker once joined the Communist Party, he therefore advocated the violent overthrow of the government.[15]

The Strecker decision left the Labor Department in a quandary. Bridges' CP membership no longer was the only issue at stake; according to the Strecker ruling, the government had to prove that he advocated the overthrow of the government by violence and force. The Labor Department therefore logically chose to delay its proceedings against Bridges pending a definitive ruling on the Strecker case from the Supreme Court. Departmental officials had little stomach for running the risk of having their efforts negated (and their witnesses exposed) if the high court affirmed the Strecker ruling.

Commissioner Houghteling, presumably acting on the advice of his legal staff, suggested to Perkins on April 15, 1938, that the Bridges case be continued pending a Supreme Court review of the Strecker case. On the same day, he informed Bonham that he was "considerably worried" about the Strecker decision. Four days later, the Justice Department decided to appeal, and Perkins promptly ordered a continuance in the Bridges proceedings.[16]

Bonham was furious. In a telegram to Houghteling he criticized the INS's efforts in the Strecker case, charging that it had failed to introduce adequate proof that the Communist Party advocated the violent overthrow of the government. He assured Houghteling that his evidence against Bridges was ample and pleaded that he be allowed to continue.

Houghteling's reply reflected the caution and concern in the Labor and Justice Departments. He emphasized the widespread consensus that it "would be a mistake of the first class" to hold the Bridges hearing at that time, as the Supreme Court might develop an alternative ruling for deportation requirements under the 1918 law. The thinking was that if the government proceeded against Bridges, it could fail to cover the points that the Court might require in its review of the

Strecker case. A subsequent rehearing for Bridges would then involve "old stuff," with the government's witnesses exposed and more liable to refutation. Houghteling also used the occasion to reprimand Bonham severely. Calling the latter's telegram "ill-judged," Houghteling countered that Bonham had only "an imperfect knowledge" of the Strecker case. He accused the Seattle commissioner of an "arrogance of judgment and apparent zeal to put your superiors in the wrong," and he deplored his lack of cooperation. Houghteling also reminded Bonham that he did not have a monopoly of concern; "no one," he said, was "more anxious than myself to enforce the law in the Bridges case."[17]

The Supreme Court's decision, announced a year later in April 1939, disappointed those who had hoped for clear guidelines in the Bridges case. Citing the language and legislative history of the 1918 statute, the justices found that it did not provide for the deportation of an alien who had ceased to be a member of the CP. Typically limiting the scope of judicial inquiry, Justice Owen J. Roberts held that the Court's construction of the statute made it unnecessary for it to pass on the adequacy of the evidence regarding the aims and purposes of the CP.[18]

The Strecker case offered no new definitive directions for Labor and Immigration officials. But Judge Hutcheson's Circuit Court opinion offered an alternative to traditional, long-standing rulings that the CP automatically fell within the statutory ban of advocating or teaching the violent overthrow of the government. His charge that such thinking reeked of "hypocrisy" and "party bigotry" proved not to be an isolated one.

The decision to postpone the Bridges hearing meanwhile had revived both the bureaucracy's determination and outside political pressures to pursue the case. Seattle District Director Bonham remained disgruntled. He offered a halfhearted apology to Houghteling, yet he insisted that the existing evidence was sufficient to secure deportation. He pointed to his extensive experience in Communist Party cases and claimed that he had never lost a case in which he submitted Party literature to demonstrate advocacy of the violent overthrow of government. Bonham petulantly told Houghteling that perhaps he had "presumed too much that my experience and opinions might possibly have something of value in them to you." Several weeks later, he offered to submit briefs detailing Communist plans and methods from Party literature. He was certain that this would buttress the testimony against Bridges by ex-Party members.[19]

Harper Knowles (now heading the "Radical Research Bureau" of the California American Legion) also vehemently protested the delay. He called it "unwarranted" and a "dereliction of duty," and he demanded a more detailed explanation for the action. Knowles contended that the Strecker case was not parallel. The government, he said, had ample witnesses and evidence for the Bridges case to demonstrate that the Communist Party advocated violent overthrow. Ominously, he told Houghteling that the Labor Department's action "proves that there is someone in a position of authority in the Department who does not wish all of the facts in the case to become known."

Houghteling's reply clearly indicated a new decision to treat Knowles gingerly and with courtesy—a far cry from the firm, brusque dismissal of his complaints two years earlier. The commissioner assured Knowles of the Service's good intentions. He nevertheless defended the postponement as desirable to avoid any appeals by Bridges on the basis of the Strecker case. Finally, Houghteling refused to confront the more sinister implications of Knowles's charges, merely stating that they were based on "unofficial and inaccurate information."[20]

Knowles sensed and appreciated Houghteling's courtesy and gentleness. He believed that Houghteling was a prisoner of his superiors, and Knowles pressed the commissioner to urge reconsideration. Houghteling assured Knowles, however, that he was not guided entirely by his legal staff and Solicitor Reilly, but had relied on his own evaluation of the Strecker case. He refuted Knowles's citation of a specific affidavit alleging that Bridges advocated violent overthrow. The sworn statements, he said, merely demonstrated that Bridges indicated a preference for the Soviet system but "certainly" did not advise revolution by force. Houghteling nevertheless politely urged Knowles to continue his search for evidence. For his part, Knowles (and similar "patriotic" spokesmen) persisted in distinguishing between the Strecker case and the Bridges case and pressed for an immediate deportation hearing.[21]

Martin Dies's House Special Committee on Un-American Activities inevitably developed an interest in Bridges during the summer of 1938. John Frey, head of the Metal Trades Department of the AFL, testified for several days on Communist domination of the CIO and charged that Bridges and other leading figures in the CIO were Party members. He offered a photostat of a Communist Party membership book under the name of Harry Dorgan, which he alleged was Bridges' Party name. At the same time, a committee investigator charged that "an outstanding official" in the Labor Department advised, instructed, and protected Bridges. He also contended that "unbridled and unchecked Communist activity" on the West Coast had cost employers and employees millions of dollars. Industrial peace and prosperity, he concluded, required Bridges' deportation. Dies demanded prompt action from Perkins. In a lengthy public reply, the secretary accused Dies of usurping executive and judicial functions, and she staunchly defended the continuance of the case pending an appeal of the Strecker decision.

Despite Perkins's sharp retort, the Roosevelt administration sought to appease Dies. In late October, Solicitor General Robert H. Jackson invited Dies to participate in preparing the government's brief in the Strecker appeal. Dies was not mollified. He told Jackson that Perkins was using the Justice Department to "pull her chestnuts out of the fire" while she persisted in protecting Bridges.

Dies's response repeated the now familiar political charges; it also revealed that Seattle District Director Bonham had relayed to the Un-American Activities Committee his charges and affidavits against Bridges, as well as his dissatisfaction with his superiors' handling of the case. The intramural conflict in the INS inevitably resulted in the recruitment of outside supporters. For his allies, Bonham shrewdly chose Dies and his committee. And Dies, appreciative of Bonham's complaints that Bridges was receiving special protection, duly defended Bonham.

In December 1938, Captain John J. Keegan of the Portland Police Department offered the committee several affidavits attesting that Bridges was a member of the Communist Party and that he had advocated the violent overthrow of the government. Keegan, as later developments demonstrated, had close ties to both Bonham and Harper Knowles. And Knowles's superior, the national commander of the American Legion, demanded an end to the delays in the Bridges case. Several weeks later the Dies Committee's report followed this line and said there was no justification for the Labor Department's behavior.[22]

The frustration of Bridges' enemies with the Labor Department eventually resulted in a House of Representatives resolution in January 1939 calling for an investigation into the conduct of Secretary Perkins, Solicitor Reilly, and Commissioner Houghteling. J. Parnell Thomas, the ranking Republican member of the Special Committee on Un-American Activities, charged that the three were guilty of high crimes and misdemeanors resulting from their conspiracy "to defer and to defeat" Bridges' deportation. Thomas' resolution also accused the three of conspiring to defraud the United States by appealing the Circuit Court decision in the Strecker case rather than retrying it with more evidence.

The House Committee on the Judiciary met on January 25 and appointed subcommittees to examine the records and briefs of the Strecker case, the Labor Department's Bridges file, and the Dies Committee's reports. Thomas twice testified before the Judiciary Committee, and each of the accused was questioned at length. At Thomas' urging, the committee invited R. P. Bonham and R. J. Norene, from the INS's Seattle and Portland offices. Chairman Dies of the Un-American Activities Committee was asked to testify, but he was ill at the time. The Judiciary Committee's interrogation of Bonham and Norene followed questions submitted by Thomas and his staff.

In its report to the House on March 24, 1939, the committee flatly rejected the impeachment request and forcefully repudiated the individual charges. Bonham and Norene, publicly loyal to their superiors, testified (correctly) that they had been encouraged to build the strongest case possible against Bridges, thus undermining Thomas' contention that Labor Department officials had frustrated efforts to deport Bridges. The Strecker appeal, the committee concluded, was taken in good faith and was not deliberately designed to further delay action against Bridges. Although the committee's report was unanimous, the minority

Republicans appended additional views, clearly indicating that the Bridges case remained a contentious political issue. They charged that the three officials had been "lenient and indulgent" toward Bridges "to an unprecedented extent," and the three deserved condemnation and censure. Bridges' radical and Communist sympathies, if not his active participation as a Party member, were well known, they insisted, and sufficient to have disposed of his case speedily. While the conduct of the accused officials did not justify impeachment, the Republicans insisted that it called for the committee's "official and public disapproval." Although the labor officials were exonerated on legal grounds, their Republican critics may have won the political war. The Labor Department retained jurisdiction over Harry Bridges for only another eighteen months, and during that time Perkins and her staff remained politically suspect and under constant assault.[23]

Despite the limitations imposed by the Supreme Court in the Strecker decision, the Labor Department decided to proceed with a deportation hearing against Bridges. Two months after the Court's ruling, the warrant against Bridges was amended and served in San Francisco. The political demands for action against Bridges were too compelling, whatever doubts existed. Political conditions also dictated that a hearing examiner be selected from outside the Department. In 1938, Perkins had planned on using Donald Hiss, who had been in the Solicitor's office earlier and who apparently had some familiarity with the case. But in 1939, Hiss was in the State Department and his superiors refused to assign him to Labor. Finally, after considering others, Perkins settled on James M. Landis, former chairman of the Securities and Exchange Commission and now dean of the Harvard Law School. Perhaps the most prominent of Felix Frankfurter's numerous protégés who descended on Washington in the 1930s, Landis had made an enormous impression during those years. He cultivated close ties with Joseph P. Kennedy and eventually was a power in his own right. Above all, he was a highly respected authority on administrative law.[24]

Dean Landis opened the hearing on July 10, 1939, on Angel Island, the INS's San Francisco headquarters. The proceeding, covering forty-five days of testimony, lasted until September 14. Thomas Shoemaker, from the INS's Washington legal staff, conducted the government's case, with the active assistance of Seattle District Director Bonham. Carol King from New York, along with Richard Gladstein, Aubrey Grossman, and Ben Margolis from San Francisco, represented Bridges. The alien's lawyers all had extensive experience representing radical persons and causes, and all periodically were identified as alleged CP members. The government called thirty-two witnesses, while the defense summoned another twenty-seven, and the hearing record totaled nearly 8,000 pages.

Landis transmitted a 150-page report to Secretary Perkins on December 28. The basic issues, Landis believed, were whether the Communist Party advocated or taught the violent overthrow of the government and whether Bridges was deportable because he was a member of, or affiliated with, that party. Based on his analysis of the testimony, Landis flatly declared that the evidence failed to establish either of the required links to the Communist Party. His conclusion made it unnecessary for him to consider the nature of the Party. But Landis clearly indicated his sympathy for the Fifth Circuit ruling in the Strecker case. He suggested it was possible not only that the characteristics and objectives of the CP had changed through the years, but that "in the light of changing economic and political conditions," the Party's radical advocacy might possibly be viewed "as now so indefinitely related to force or violence as to cast doubt upon its appropriate inclusion within the ban of the statute."[25]

Landis simply did not believe the government's witnesses. He consistently assailed their general credibility and their specific testimony. Moreover, he strongly hinted that key witnesses had been coerced and even bribed by public officials and interested outsiders. In a lengthy analysis of the testimony of the government's witnesses, Landis carefully disentangled what he saw as a web of perjury, pressure, and official wrongdoing.

Bridges' lawyers effectively refuted the testimony of dissident Communists and union members. The inconsistencies of testimony obviously impressed the hearing examiner, but the activities of Harper Knowles and local law enforcement officials apparently convinced Landis of the soundness of the defense's contention that a public and private conspiracy existed to secure Bridges' deportation at any cost.

Landis had harsh words for Knowles's conduct. He scoffed at Knowles's simple contention that aliens could be deported merely because they were "undesirables." More important, he found that Knowles's links with employer groups (such as the Industrial Association and the Associated Farmers) revealed that his primary purpose was to combat militant unionism. As such, Landis suggested, Knowles did not always properly distinguish labor agitators from those truly engaged in subversive activities. Knowles was "neither a candid nor a forthright witness," Landis concluded, and he dismissed Knowles as a man who liked "to fish in troubled waters."[26]

"If the government becomes a lawbreaker, it breeds contempt for law," Justice Brandeis wrote in a 1928 wiretapping case. Landis, who had been Brandeis' clerk in 1926, knew the lesson well, and it clearly informed his report, particularly as he discussed the activities of Captain John J. Keegan, Chief of Detectives of the Portland Police Department. Landis found Keegan's interest in Bridges disturbing and extraordinary since Bridges' alleged Communism was more properly the concern of immigration officials than of local police. Keegan's large expenditures, and the extent of his activity from Los Angeles to Seattle, hardly constituted a "normal" investigation, Landis contended. Landis pointed to persuasive evidence showing payments to Keegan by the International Brotherhood of Teamsters.

The Teamsters then were widely engaged in jurisdictional disputes with the ILWU and naturally had some interest in action against Bridges. Keegan had recruited a significant number of witnesses, and he had worked closely with Bonham in preparing the affidavits which originally persuaded the INS and Labor Department hierarchy to proceed against Bridges. Keegan's efforts, as well as his testimony, drew harsh criticism from Landis. Landis charged that Keegan had lied in one important matter, that his testimony was frequently contradictory, and that he repeatedly had misled the trial examiner. Finally, Landis found solid basis "for indulging in suspicious inferences" regarding Keegan's possible bribing of witnesses.

Landis completely rejected most of the key witnesses who testified that they knew Bridges to be a CP member or who had seen him at Party gatherings. Others had testified that Bridges consistently had opposed "red-baiting," but for Landis this did not prove Party membership. By contrast, the "candor" of Bridges' testimony enormously impressed the examiner. "It was," he said, "a fighting apologia that refused to temper itself to the winds of caution." He acknowledged that Bridges' views were "energetically radical," but he found no proof that Bridges advocated them in any way other than that permitted by "the framework of democratic and constitutional government."[27]

Landis' decision left the government's case in shambles. With its witnesses and the tactics of Knowles and Keegan discredited, Landis cast serious doubt as to the government's control of its own case. Equally important, Landis on several occasions came down hard on Raphael Bonham's activities, clearly linking him to some of the more dubious tactics of Knowles and Keegan. Such a conclusion could not have surprised INS officials who had on file complaints and affidavits regarding the coercive tactics of Bonham and his close ties to Knowles. Bonham's vested interest in Bridges' deportation appeared, at times, to extend beyond mere bureaucratic fervor. Secretary Perkins quickly approved Landis' report and dismissed the proceedings on January 8, 1940.[28]

iii

The reaction to the Landis report was predictable. The dean was inundated with mail, almost all of it uncomplimentary. The Bridges Defense Committee labeled Landis' actions a "vindication" of Bridges' leadership and of CIO unionism. AFL president William Green was unimpressed. Landis' decision, he said, was "not in accordance with the facts. Everybody knows Harry Bridges is a communist." In Congress, Utah's senators, both Democrats, lined up on opposite sides. Senator Elbert D. Thomas thought that Landis had "cleared up" the matter very well. "I don't think we should deport anybody because of their political beliefs. I think most people would agree with that, although I'm afraid there are some who don't." And that included his fellow Utahan, Senator William H. King, who still demanded action against Bridges. "Undoubtedly," he said, "Mr. Bridges is not an American and is not in sympathy with our system and should be deported as an undesirable alien." Martin Dies claimed he was not surprised, and hinted at renewed efforts. "It will take an outraged public sentiment to put a stop to the coddling of undesirable aliens." Finally, Captain Keegan, one of Dies's most important informants, lashed back at Landis. The hearing, he claimed, was a "setup" and Landis had been sent to San Francisco for a "whitewash." The San Francisco *Chronicle*'s labor writer, offering a rare defense of Bridges, complimented Landis for seeing through the patently anti-labor purpose of the proceeding. But he also recognized that the hearing would not change much. Bridges' friends would remain constant while his foes remained bent on destroying the longshoremen's leader.[29]

An ominous and far-reaching result of the Landis hearing was to shift the INS to the Justice Department. On the surface, the move appeared to reflect the Administration's belief that it would be best to integrate all national security activities under one agency. Actually, FDR made the proposal to Congress in May 1940, some months after he had submitted an elaborate Executive Reorganization Plan. Later official documents described the change as a national security measure, designed to provide more effective control over aliens. Clearly, however, the Administration was sensitive and responsive to growing congressional hostility toward Perkins and her management of alien problems. Congress promptly voted for the transfer. During the debate, numerous congressmen made it clear that they supported the plan only to free the INS from the "influence and mismanagement" of Secretary Perkins. Some representatives viciously assaulted Perkins' administration of labor laws in general, but unquestionably the Bridges affair motivated most of the approving vote. Perkins was well aware of the political dynamics and privately resented the Administration's action. Senators George Norris and Burton Wheeler opposed the move because it would make aliens subject to the control of the FBI, which, they charged, consistently had violated the civil liberties of citizens.[30]

The most heated response to Landis' report came from the House of Representatives. On June 13, 1940, the House passed an extraordinary bill directing the Secretary of Labor to arrest and deport Harry Bridges. A lengthy rhetorical blend of Fourth of July oratory laced with language befitting the Spanish Inquisition enabled many congressmen to vent their wrath against Bridges, subversion, militant labor, and government officials who had failed to perceive the danger from these sources. Prominent conservatives with long records of anti-labor bias, such as Hamilton Fish, Everett Dirksen, and J. Parnell Thomas, insisted that Bridges was a menace and that Congress could deal with aliens in any manner it wished. Only left-leaning Vito Marcantonio of New York defended Bridges as a worthy labor leader and as a victim of a sinister conspiracy. A handful of congressmen raised the issue of due process. Adolph Sabath, chairman of the Judiciary Committee, argued that the measure was nothing less than a bill of attainder—but in vain. The bill passed overwhelmingly, 330–42.[31]

Somewhat cooler—but no less determined—heads prevailed in the Senate. Senators Richard Russell (Dem.-Ga.) and Warren Austin (Rep.-Vt.) of the Immigration Committee called on Attorney General Robert Jackson. They told him that they did not like the House bill but that there was strong sentiment for action against Bridges. Anxious to spare the President a possible veto, Jackson and the senators struck a bargain. Section 23 was hastily added to the then pending Alien Registration Bill—eventually known by its more popular title as the Smith Act—making it unlawful for a resident alien at any time to belong to a group advocating the violent overthrow of the government. The paragraph in effect nullified the Strecker holding that required affiliation at the time of deportation proceedings. The bill's proponents unabashedly admitted that it was directed at Bridges. Jackson wrote the senators on June 18 assuring them he would institute a new hearing on Bridges. Appalled at the special House bill, Jackson believed that the Senate "compromise" was "the best that could be had."[32]

The transfer of the INS to the Justice Department introduced a new dimension to the case—and a new actor: J. Edgar Hoover. In August 1940, Jackson ordered Hoover to make a "thorough investigation" of the Bridges case. Hoover wasted little time expanding his already burgeoning empire of files as he requested all of the INS's voluminous exhibits, summaries, and documents. Never again did the INS play the featured role in proceedings against Bridges.[33]

Hoover's concern with Bridges coincided with his renewed interest in the Communist Party, resulting from the recently passed Smith Act. In a series of reports from November 26 to December 9, totaling more than 2,500 pages, Hoover offered all the "pertinent evidence" he believed necessary for the Attorney General to rule on Bridges. As an added bonus, Hoover presented what probably was his first recommendation for prosecuting CP leadership. Attorney General Jackson waited nearly two months before responding, despite numerous reminders from Hoover. Finally, on February 12, 1941, Jackson approved of new deportation proceedings against Bridges. He solemnly maintained that the FBI's report was purely factual and quite properly contained no conclusions or recommendations—a statement which skirted the edges of truth, for Hoover consistently offered a "recommendation" for "consideration" of a hearing or prosecution.[34]

Hoover's memos to Jackson reveal that the FBI chief was characteristically prodding his reluctant superiors to action. Yet this time his investigation was mere window dressing for a decision Jackson had made at the time of his dealings with the Senate in June 1940. In fact, Jackson later recalled that he had promised

Senators Russell and Austin that he would appoint a person "of real judicial stature and experience" to conduct a hearing on Bridges. The description obviously was a swipe at Landis. The Attorney General accordingly selected a long-time "friend and sponsor," retired New York Court of Appeals judge Charles B. Sears. Jackson regarded Sears as a "liberal," but noted that he had been nominated for the New York judgeship by both the Democrats and Republicans.[35]

The political climate had changed drastically and abruptly. Until 1939 organized labor and its leaders were important allies of the New Deal and could do little wrong in the eyes of the Administration. Communist infiltration of labor unions—alleged or real—was not a matter of great concern. The Popular Front mentality was still in vogue. Enemies on the left were minimized, and the Communist Party's political activism generally served the Administration's purposes. After Landis delivered his report, FDR told him that it was a "Scotch verdict" but an apparently sound one. If by that FDR reflected his concern for maintaining good relations with the left, he soon changed his mind.

In 1940, FDR perceived the full impact of the cynical Nazi-Soviet Pact which had been announced less than one month before Bridges' hearing. Both the pact and the loyal lockstep of American Stalinists disillusioned and angered him. According to Robert Jackson, the ready acquiescence of the American Communist Party convinced FDR of its subservience and primary loyalty to Moscow. Consequently, "Roosevelt became very anti-Communist—militantly so," Jackson observed. The President specifically demanded Bridges' deportation. "He was fed up with Bridges and with all those people," Jackson later said. Jackson himself saw Bridges as the typical "tough, left-wing labor leader, who was ruthless in his methods and had no regard for the interests of the country as a whole."[36] Jackson did not note Bridges' endorsement of Wendell Willkie in the 1940 presidential election; the President undoubtedly remembered it.

Roosevelt's changed attitude helps to explain the renewed, determined effort to deport Bridges. Although congressional pressures were real, they had been resisted before and might have been deflected again. Certainly J. Edgar Hoover was a formidable force, with his own drives and purposes in pursuing Bridges. But in this case, at least, Hoover's efforts had the blessing of a higher power.

Bridges' hearing before Presiding Inspector Sears was almost a rerun of the hearing two years earlier. Again it was held in San Francisco. Bridges' defense team remained intact but the government prosecutors were new. Sears heard forty-four days of testimony between March 31 and June 12, compiling a transcript of more than 7,500 pages. The INS examiners went through familiar terrain to demonstrate Communist infiltration into the labor movement and the CP's program for forcible overthrow of the government. Now, however, the INS offered new witnesses, many of them ex-Communists or former union allies of

Bridges'. No Harper Knowles or John Keegan clouded the government's case. And this time, the government got a different verdict.

Sears found that Bridges was affiliated with the Communist Party and that the Party was committed to the violent overthrow of the government. Specifically, he determined that Bridges' cooperation with the Party and with the MWIU during the 1934 strike demonstrated his affiliation. The testimony of two witnesses, Harry Lundeberg and James O'Neil, proved decisive on the matter of membership.

Lundeberg was involved with the Sailors' Union of the Pacific, the Seafarers' International Union, and the Maritime Federation of the Pacific. Although he and Bridges had cooperated during the 1934 strike, the men began to drift apart the next year, with Lundeberg remaining active in the AFL. He testified that he had dinner at Bridges' house in the summer of 1935, along with Sam Darcy, a prominent California CP leader. Darcy allegedly asked Lundeberg to join the Party and Bridges supported him, saying that there was no need to be afraid "because I am one too." Bridges denied the conversation ever took place. Lundeberg admitted that he consistently had told government agents until the hearing that he had no knowledge of Bridges as a Communist. Sears acknowledged Lundeberg's rivalry and antagonism toward Bridges, yet he believed him. What swayed him was that Bridges failed to call as witnesses his wife, stepson, and former secretary, all of whom had been at the dinner.[37]

O'Neil's testimony was more complicated. O'Neil had served as an administrative assistant to Bridges for about three years. Unquestionably, he was close to Bridges in that time. O'Neil was interviewed twice by the FBI in October 1940, with a stenographer present. The government claimed that O'Neil admitted his own CP membership and that he had seen Bridges affixing dues stamps in his own membership book. During the hearing, however, O'Neil denied having made the statements, claiming that the whole FBI report was garbled and was an incorrect summary of several interviews. Major Lemuel Schofield, head of the INS, testified that the night before O'Neil's appearance, O'Neil said he did not want to appear for fear of being called a "rat." Sears chose to believe Schofield and the earlier stenographic statement and found that Bridges had been a member of the Communist Party in 1937.[38]

Finally, Sears ruled that Bridges' continual cooperation with Communist-front groups and his sympathetic attitude toward Communist-sponsored programs and policies formed a consistent pattern of affiliation with the Communist Party, "rather than as a matter of chance coincidence." His attitude of non-discrimination against Communists and his attacks on "Red Baiters," Sears concluded, "strongly" corroborated the findings of membership and affiliation.[39]

Justice Department procedure provided for a review of Sears's ruling by the

Board of Immigration Appeals. Attorney General Francis Biddle later claimed that his predecessor, Robert Jackson, warned him to bypass the board because it was "pro-Bridges." Biddle, however, chose to follow normal procedures, and Jackson proved right as to the outcome. The board, composed of "fair and conscientious men"—as Biddle characterized them—unanimously recommended in January 1942 that the warrant for Bridges' deportation be canceled.

The board's 100-page report largely followed Landis' earlier judgments on affiliation and his analysis of Bridges' cooperation with Communists. But almost half of the board's report was devoted to an extensive repudiation of the Lundeberg and O'Neil testimony. The board members concluded that Lundeberg's testimony was at times evasive and contradictory; they also found it incredible that Darcy and Bridges would attempt to recruit Lundeberg, who already was a prominent anti-Communist. They dismissed O'Neil's statements for their evasiveness and contradictions. More important, the board held that O'Neil's statements were inadmissible, for they had not been made under oath or signed, as INS regulations required.[40]

A few years earlier, the top echelon of the INS had been pilloried for "protecting" Harry Bridges. Following the board's decision the INS counterattacked with a fury that would have delighted Copeland, Dies, and Bonham. Commissioner Lemuel B. Schofield submitted a lengthy memorandum to Biddle on February 14, 1942, bitterly assailing the board, calling its decision "erroneous" and urging the Attorney General to set it aside. Schofield, to be sure, was no disinterested party. During the Sears hearing, he had testified that Harry Bridges was one of the leading Communists in the United States and he had supported O'Neil's "statement."

Schofield complained that the board had not really reviewed Sears's decision; rather it had proceeded on the assumption that Landis' report was "sacrosanct" and had looked at Sears's decision only to see if it contained additional evidence to warrant any departure from Landis'. That procedure, Schofield insisted, was unjustified both by departmental regulations and by any rules of legal or administrative procedure. Finally, he maintained that Sears's findings and conclusions were amply supported by the evidence and should be sustained. Throughout his memorandum, Schofield used language to exalt Sears and diminish Landis. Sears was the "experienced trial judge," the "distinguished judge," the "open-minded jurist," and a man of "great learning," while Landis merely was the "hearing examiner."

Schofield analyzed the conflicts between the board's ruling and Sears's decision with copious references to the record. He noted that the board had greatly relied on the sections of Sears's decision that had been adverse to the government. Indeed, Schofield suggested that at times Sears may have been "overprotective" of Bridges. In his own way, Schofield "overruled" Sears, for he insisted that evidence the judge had found inadequate had a high probative value. Were it not for Sears's "extreme fairness," such evidence would have compelled a verdict against Bridges, he said. The rest of Schofield's analysis, however, stridently defended Sears's findings on Bridges' CP membership and affiliation. He was outraged that the board habitually found Bridges' testimony "more likely" to be true than that of the corroborated witnesses which Sears accepted.[41]

Biddle finally acted in May 1942. He largely followed Schofield's critique and issued the deportation order. Lundeberg's and O'Neil's statements were most decisive, though Bridges' support of a recent Communist-led strike in the southern California aircraft industry also influenced Biddle, reflecting the Administration's disgust with Communist tactics in the 1940–41 period.[42]

FDR had different Attorneys General, and typically he told them different things, depending on the political moment. Given his character and his finely tuned political antennae, he responded to Biddle's decision in a decidedly different fashion than he had a year earlier to Jackson's. According to Biddle, the President said, "I'm sorry to hear that," when he learned that Biddle would issue the deportation order. Biddle claimed that the President thought the order was a mistake. But if the President truly was convinced of that, he could have stopped the order. (Two weeks earlier, despite Biddle's objections, FDR pardoned Communist Party leader Earl Browder, who had been jailed for an old passport violation.) Privately, the President sharply rebuked his wife, who argued in behalf of Bridges, perhaps revealing his real thoughts on the matter. The President, however, allowed the Bridges order to proceed, while keeping some distance from Biddle's activities. Probably, that was the wise political course. But FDR certainly was prophetic when he told Biddle: "I'll bet the Supreme Court will never let him be deported." Then, smiling, he added: "And the decision is a long way off."[43]

As the government pressed its case against Bridges, the labor leader found strange bedfellows to support his cause. The Nazi attack on the Soviet Union transformed Bridges' position on international affairs, and he promoted labor harmony so as not to hinder shipments of war materials. As early as the Sears hearing, *Business Week* magazine calculated that deportation might have high costs since "businessmen have learned to work with Australian Harry and they are concerned about the instability of labor relations which might follow in the wake of his martyrdom." Cynically noting the change in Bridges' attitude, Robert Jackson petulantly remarked that Bridges "became something of a darling" to the "big shipping interests," and consequently they were less interested in doing anything about him.

After Biddle's order, and through the war years, letters and petitions inundated the White House and the Justice Department as Bridges appealed. The range was impressive. Traditional AFL craft unions, the Brotherhood of Railroad Trainmen, the California and Washington state legislatures, California senators and congressmen, the California Department of the Veterans of Foreign Wars, and San Francisco District Attorney Edmund G. Brown, among others, urged the President and the Attorney General to cancel the deportation order. Without exception, they praised Bridges' crucial efforts to prevent strikes and work stoppages during the war and protested the "grave injustice" of the persecution. Chinese-owned shipping companies reminded Biddle that Bridges had opposed the transportation of scrap metal to Japan as far back as 1937. A survey of West Coast businessmen praised Bridges as "a seasoned and responsible labor leader." He was regarded as an "investment," and many expressed fear that they would find a racketeer or a "hothead" in his place.[44] Patriotism and stability offered convenient refuges for Bridges' born-again admirers.

Shortly after Biddle's order came down, a special meeting of the CIO Executive Board convened to discuss Bridges' case and offer its support. Bridges complained that Biddle was "playing around with political guinea pigs . . . , making test cases out of something that can split the CIO . . . , and sabotage the entire war effort." President Philip Murray expressed amazement at Biddle's action, and reported that both Jackson and Biddle had told him they did not believe Bridges should be deported. But was all this merely a surface show of support? Jackson claimed that Murray told him that Bridges was a Communist or at least followed the CP line.[45]

Bridges immediately appealed the deportation order to the courts. In early 1942, however, the federal district court in San Francisco denied Bridges' petition for a writ of habeas corpus. Judge Martin Welsh held that no double jeopardy was involved; that the amendment to the Alien Registration Act applied to Bridges and was not *ex post facto;* that Landis' findings were not binding as *res judicata;* that the court could not question Congress's motivation as to whether Bridges was the sole object of the 1940 legislation; and that the court would not inquire into issues of free speech, suggesting at one point that congressional power over aliens need not be exercised within constitutional bounds. Beyond that, Welsh denied Bridges' remaining claims against the unfairness of the Sears hearing and the inadequacy of evidence to support a deportation order.[46]

The Circuit Court similarly denied Bridges' appeal late in June 1944, but the 3–2 decision indicated that the issues remained divisive and debatable. Judge William Healy in dissent found it "patent" "to any candid person who takes the trouble to examine the record" that the accusations against Bridges were not proven. For Healy, the most significant aspect of the case was "the paucity of the evidentiary product as contrasted with the magnitude of the effort expended in producing it." He particularly criticized Biddle's acceptance of the O'Neil testimony as probative evidence. Biddle, it will be recalled, had used O'Neil's unsworn, and later disavowed, oral statement for proving Bridges' Party membership. That action violated the INS's own regulations requiring sworn, written statements. Biddle had excused Sears's acceptance of the O'Neil statement because the administrative regulations had not been called to his attention. But Healy questioned why Biddle, who certainly was aware of the rules, chose to disregard them. In any event, the Attorney General's action satisfied Healy that Bridges had been denied due process.[47]

When the Bridges case finally reached the Supreme Court a year later, the "liberal-conservative" conflict of the Roosevelt Court was at its peak. The combatants divided ideologically to some extent, but more precisely they differed over the nature of the judicial function and its relation to issues of civil rights and liberties. The hard-core libertarian activists—Black, Douglas, Murphy, and Rutledge—favored judicial intervention in behalf of a preferred status for fundamental liberties. Felix Frankfurter, long schooled in the virtues of judicial restraint, insisted (ideology aside) that democratically chosen legislators and officials should be given the same benefit of the doubt in these cases as the Court was willing to grant in economic matters. By 1945, Frankfurter usually found himself in a minority, as the activists periodically picked up votes from either Jackson, Stone, or Reed. For the Bridges case, Justice Jackson properly took no part. Justice Reed joined his four activist colleagues to provide a majority for a stunning reversal of the government's case.

Douglas' majority opinion held that the evidence offered of Bridges' Communist Party membership was given without a fair hearing and that the finding of affiliation was based on a misconstruction of the term. Douglas followed Healy's lower court dissent in relying on the issue of procedural safeguards, and like Healy, he found the use of O'Neil's statements procedurally defective. Those statements were hearsay and admissible only for the purpose of impeachment, not as substantive evidence, he said. Although the courts often had relaxed ordinary rules of evidence in administrative hearings, Douglas insisted on the importance of procedural fairness when liberty was at stake. "Though deportation is not technically a criminal proceeding, it visits a great hardship on the individual and deprives him of the right to stay and live and work in this land of freedom. That deportation is a penalty—at times a most serious one—cannot be doubted. Meticulous care must be exercised lest the procedure by which he is deprived of that liberty not meet the essential standards of fairness."[48] It was prejudicial for Biddle to lump O'Neil's statements with the Lundeberg testimony to, as Biddle had acknowledged, "tip the scales" against Bridges; as such, the government's determination of Party membership could not be sustained.

The majority also repudiated Sears and Biddle's position on the meaning of affiliation. Douglas borrowed heavily from Landis on this point. One who contributed financially to an organization could generally be said to approve its aims.

"But he who cooperates with such an organization only in its *wholly lawful activities* cannot by that fact be said as a matter of law to be 'affiliated' with it," Douglas said. The facts of the Bridges case merely revealed that Bridges had cooperated with Communists "for the attainment of wholly lawful objectives."[49]

The decision aligned the Court with Landis' original findings, reaffirmed by the Board of Immigration Appeals, as opposed to those of Sears, Schofield, and Biddle. Perhaps mindful of the need to hold Justice Reed's vote, Douglas confined himself to a rather dry analysis of the issues and carefully avoided imputing any improper motives to government officials as Healy had done in the lower court.

Justice Murphy felt no such constraints, and he used a concurring opinion to expose a record that he said would "stand forever as a monument to man's intolerance of man." Murphy had preceded Jackson and Biddle as Attorney General, and while the Bridges case was not in his jurisdiction, he had to be aware of its contents. In his opinion, he deplored the "concentrated and relentless crusade" by "powerful economic and social forces . . . combined with public and private agencies" to secure Bridges' deportation. He noted Biddle's admission that much of the evidence was "untrustworthy, contradictory, or unreliable"; but for Murphy, the remainder could not be described in any more generous terms. Finally, Murphy went beyond the other majority justices by insisting on applying the full panoply of constitutional rights to resident aliens. Attorney General Biddle heard the opinions, and Murphy's infuriated him. "What a windbag he was," Biddle later recalled.[50]

Chief Justice Stone's dissent (with Frankfurter and Roberts) emphasized the Court's limited role in a deportation proceeding. If the findings of administrative officers and agencies were supported by evidence of any probative value, courts could not set aside such holdings, Stone maintained. While not conceding that O'Neil's statements had been improperly admitted, Stone held that the Lundeberg testimony sufficiently demonstrated Bridges' CP membership—yet ignored the fact that Biddle *had* tied it to O'Neil's statements. Most important, Stone rejected the majority arguments that O'Neil's statements were used in violation of INS regulations and merely were hearsay. Contrary to Murphy, Stone said this case was not "novel." For him, it simply involved sustaining the right of an administrative officer to determine the credibility and weight of evidence not unbelievable on its face.[51]

iv

The Supreme Court decision cleared the way for Bridges to secure citizenship. He wasted little time, filing a petition for a hearing on August 8, 1945, which the court scheduled for the following September 17. (Bridges' last declaration of intention had been filed on March 28, 1939, and was still valid.) INS Commissioner Ugo Carusi, with the approval of Attorney General Tom Clark, dispatched a memorandum to the San Francisco office summarizing the history of the case. Significantly, the memorandum noted that "no adverse evidence" against Bridges had been obtained since the Court's decision. The government apparently had no inclination to pursue the matter further.[52]

But Bridges had a new enemy. Three days before the scheduled hearing, his former wife offered an affidavit and a sworn statement to INS officials in which she stated that Bridges had presided over Communist Party meetings in their kitchen in 1934 and that she hid his Party membership book for him. San Francisco District Director Wixon dispatched a coded telegram requesting instructions, but he was told to proceed with the hearing. Agnes Bridges was an angry woman. Some months earlier, she had filed a cross-complaint in a divorce action alleging that Bridges had fathered a child by a New York dancer. The court, however, found her allegations unsupported by proof.

Thomas Foley, presiding during Bridges' naturalization hearing, chose not to give much credence to Agnes' new claims. The judge advised the government's naturalization examiner that the affidavit was inadmissible since she could be called to testify directly. In the formal hearing, however, the government submitted it to Foley, who used it only as a basis for further questioning. Bridges denied every one of his ex-wife's allegations. (Foley duly noted that Agnes' testimony in the divorce trial impeached the affidavit.) Finally, Bridges formally denied he belonged to the Communist Party or that he advocated the violent overthrow of the government. After a quarter century of residence in the United States, Bridges at last was granted citizenship. Two of his loyal union lieutenants, J. R. Robertson and Henry Schmidt, supported his application by swearing they had no knowledge of his ever belonging to the Communist Party. The government would remember them well.

Richard Gladstein, now Bridges' primary lawyer, was uneasy despite his client's success. Following the naturalization hearing, he wrote to District Director Wixon asking for a copy of Agnes' affidavit, claiming that the government's examiner had promised to provide one. Since it had been used, Gladstein argued, there could be no claim for confidentiality. Gladstein sensed that Bridges' troubles were far from over. He told Wixon that Agnes had been exploited by Bridges' traditional enemies and the affidavit underlined the fact that those "enemies" still sought, "no matter how foul the means, to achieve their sordid ambitions." He wanted a copy of the affidavit in order to meet future attacks "which we have every right to expect from these same forces who have been laboring all these years to accomplish their vicious aims." Washington officials decided not to accommodate Gladstein, believing his fears were only "speculative." On a more sanguine note, INS's legal counsel said that the case was "closed both from immigration and naturalization standpoint[s], and we are not going to keep this thing going on forever."[53]

Gladstein's pessimistic assessment proved to be correct, and the case seemed to go on "forever." Harry Bridges was no less controversial as a naturalized citizen. His views and activities after the war was over once again provoked a broad, formidable array of enemies who redoubled their efforts to get him. His public opposition to the Truman Doctrine, the Marshall Plan, and later the Korean War left him easily suspect as a Communist sympathizer, a fellow traveler, or the real thing. With the revival of Red-baiting during the Cold War, Bridges was an obvious target.

The postwar years also witnessed a resurgence of anti-labor militancy in the business community and to some extent among the public at large. The West Coast shipping industry, combining its long-standing animosity toward Bridges with a frustrated yearning for management dominance, jumped at the opportunity to do something about Bridges and the union. Encouraged by the new Taft-Hartley labor legislation, with its requirement of non-Communist affidavits on the part of labor officials and its ban on the closed shop, the shippers adopted a hard-line stance in their negotiations with the union. But after an 80-day injunction for a "cooling off" period, the longshoremen unanimously refused to vote to accept the shippers' final offer, and a 95-day strike began in September 1948. A shippers' spokesman later admitted that the maritime industry had based its public position on the proposition "that it would no longer, or could no longer, do business with Communists, [and] with Mr. Bridges."[54] But the ILWU rank and file held firm and the strike confirmed the union's power and appeal. More pragmatic elements among the employers finally recognized certain realities, not the least of which was that Harry Bridges was thoroughly capable of "business unionism," whatever his anti-capitalist rhetoric and alleged affiliations.

In the 1930s, Bridges' primary enemies largely were localized on the West Coast. National governmental and labor officials either protected him or responded benignly to his enemies. But by the late 1940s and early 1950s, the situation was exactly reversed. Bridges' traditional enemies now were ready to sit down and "do business" with him so they could carry on their own. Officials in the national government and the CIO hierarchy, however, diligently pursued various means for punishing Bridges. The CIO's traditional tolerance of political diversity within its ranks while pursuing "bread and butter" goals fell victim to the increasing demands for political conformity. CIO president Philip Murray long had been uncomfortable working with leftist elements. Pushed by anti-Communist militants such as Walter Reuther and James Carey, Murray and other leaders expelled the Communist-dominated unions within the CIO in 1949. The CIO policy reflected the public's attitude which supported loyalty oaths, investigations, and the branding of subversive groups. Although subjected to intense criticism, Bridges maintained a tenuous tie with the CIO until August 1950, when, after a lengthy "trial" within the organization, he was expelled.

The Justice Department's attitude in this period differed markedly from that of the Labor Department in the 1930s. Whether responding to congressional pressures or acting on its own, the Department, particularly under Attorney General Tom Clark, and with the prodding of J. Edgar Hoover, generated a number of investigations, condemnations, indictments, and trials of Communists or Communist groups. In this environment, a number of INS officials renewed their pursuit of Bridges. And perhaps it was more than coincidental that the government's moves followed Murray's removal of Bridges as CIO Regional Director for California.

Concurrent with the outbreak of renewed strife on the San Francisco waterfront in early 1948, the INS launched an investigation to determine whether there was any possibility of revoking Bridges' citizenship. Deputy Commissioner John P. Boyd visited Seattle District Director Bonham in early 1948. Bonham, of course, long had been intimately involved in the case, and Boyd apparently believed that Bonham could be most helpful. He also enlisted assistance from J. Edgar Hoover. Leading CIO officials, such as Director of Organization Allan Haywood and UAW president R. J. Thomas, were interviewed and offered to assist the INS, although they had no personal knowledge of Bridges' Communism. But Boyd worked most closely with Bruce Barber, a lawyer in the INS's Los Angeles office. By autumn, Barber had interviewed Mervyn Rathborne and John Schomaker, both of whom would become key government witnesses against Bridges. Significantly, the CIO officials had suggested meeting Rathborne.

Rathborne and Schomaker had been intimates of Bridges in union affairs in the 1930s. Both also had belonged to the Communist Party. Schomaker once had stated under oath that Bridges was not a Communist, while Rathborne had refused to testify against him. Now, however, they dramatically supported the government's case against Bridges. Rathborne told Barber that he had been at several meetings of the Communist Party National Committee with Bridges in the 1930s. Rathborne also claimed that he was at a meeting in 1941 when Bridges' lawyers "worked on" James O'Neil to repudiate his statement on Bridges' Party membership in the hearing before Judge Sears. O'Neil subsequently corroborated that story in an October interview with Barber. O'Neil claimed that his original account of Bridges affixing Party stamps was true and that he changed his story because he feared Bridges' attorneys and publicly exposing himself as a Communist.[55]

As Barber and Boyd prepared their case for the government, a snag developed as to whether the three-year statute of limitations applied. Someone in the bureaucratic labyrinth discovered that the limitations might operate in this case, but Barber countered with the Wartime Suspension of Limitations Act, which made limitations inapplicable to any offense involving fraud against the United States during war. Satisfied that the government could proceed because Bridges' naturalization occurred before the formal cessation of hostilities (December 31, 1946), both Barber and Boyd recommended to the Attorney General that the case be brought to a grand jury in San Francisco. In the meantime, Tom Clark had commissioned his former assistant, Buffalo lawyer Robert M. Hitchcock, to evaluate the evidence. Hitchcock reported that Rathborne's testimony would "insure a successful result." He urged Clark to meet Rathborne and appeal to his newborn anti-Communism in order to secure his testimony. Finally, Hitchcock recommended that no action be taken until the longshoremen's strike was settled.[56] The pending elections in November also may have influenced some delay. Contrary to all expectations, Bridges never endorsed Progressive Party presidential candidate Henry Wallace.

In May 1949 the grand jury heard the government's arguments that Bridges had lied at his naturalization hearing in September 1945 and that his union friends, Robertson and Schmidt, had knowingly lied when they vouched for his loyalty. The jurors voted a three-count indictment, charging the three with a conspiracy to defraud the government by impairing the proper administration of the naturalization laws. Bridges himself was charged with perjury. The defendants immediately sought a dismissal on several grounds, including a contention that the indictment was barred by the statute of limitations. After a lengthy trial between November 1949 and April 1950, a jury found the defendants guilty on all counts. Bridges received concurrent sentences of two and five years.

The government's case, while remaining substantially the same, had a whole new cast of witnesses. In the 1939 Landis hearing, the INS assembled thirty-two witnesses, yet none of them was used during the Sears hearing two years later. In that proceeding, thirty-three new witnesses appeared; only two mattered for the decision, however, and they were repudiated on appeal. Of the whole new group in the 1949 trial, one admitted perjury during the trial and two did so later.[57]

The Justice Department frankly acknowledged in June 1949 that its case against Bridges was political. As part of the frenzied counter-assault against charges that the Truman administration was lackadaisical in its effort to combat subversion, the Department listed numerous prosecutions, such as those of the leading officials of the CP, as well as the Hollywood Ten, Alger Hiss, and Judith Coplon. The press release then noted the indictment of Bridges, which, if proven, would both jail and denaturalize him. Several days later, Attorney General Clark, speaking in Milwaukee, linked the prosecution of Bridges to the goal of breaking Communist labor influence in Hawaii. Naturally, the Department did not acknowledge any coordination between its policy and that of the CIO. But again, it may have been more than coincidence that the grand jury indictment followed by one week the CIO Executive Board's demand that the ILWU rid itself of Communist influence.[58]

Following Bridges' conviction in April, the government moved for a hearing to revoke his citizenship. Judge George Harris, who presided at the jury trial, voided Bridges' naturalization papers on June 20. As the case headed for appeal, government lawyers again appeared before Harris to request revocation of Bridges' $25,000 bail on the grounds that he was pursuing a course of conduct "dangerous" to the nation's security and welfare. On August 5, Harris granted the motion and ordered Bridges jailed immediately.

Harris relied on the Federal Rules of Criminal Procedure, Rule 46 (a) (2), allowing judges to revoke bail at any time. The constitutional right to bail did not apply after a conviction and during a pending appeal. Satisfied "to a moral certainty" that Bridges was a Communist agent "dedicated to execute the Communist program," Harris added that Bridges was a constant danger to American security. The labor leader's outspoken, frank opposition to the Korean War outraged the judge, and he feared that Bridges' influence could disrupt the military effort. "The Army, Navy and Marine Corps will hold the beachheads in Korea," he said, while "our duty here at home is plain, to protect the 'beachheads' involving internal and national security." A hastily assembled Ninth Circuit panel, however, voted 2–1 to overturn Harris' order. The judges found Harris' conclusions on the implication of Bridges' political activities "startling" and "novel." Satisfied that Bridges' appeal from his conviction was both substantial and serious, and given no suggestion that he might flee American jurisdiction, the court concluded that bail then was "a matter of right, not of grace." But a different panel of circuit judges heard Bridges' trial appeal and unanimously upheld the conviction in September 1952.[59]

The Supreme Court had changed substantially since the 1945 decision. The two most outspoken libertarians, Murphy and Rutledge, were dead. Nevertheless, a narrow and unusual majority reversed the conviction. Black and Douglas, the prominent remaining libertarians, joined their more conservative brethren, Frankfurter and Burton, to overturn the verdict. Reed, Minton, and Chief Justice Vinson dissented. Both Frankfurter and Reed had switched from their 1945 positions. (The two former Attorneys General, Jackson and Clark, did not participate.) The decision lacked the emotional arguments and division of the earlier case as the justices focused on the construction of the Wartime Suspension of Limitations Act. Burton, speaking for the majority, found it had been designed to deal with pecuniary frauds and was not intended to cover offenses included in Bridges' indictment. Those offenses allegedly occurred in 1945 and the indictment was not brought until 1949, and Burton held that the district court should have dismissed it, as Bridges' attorneys had requested at the time. Burton privately told his majority colleagues that his solution was "disarmingly simple and reasonable, [and] it also disposes of the *Bridges* case in a readily understandable manner."[60] The four majority justices were the only judges who at any time in the case accepted the defense's statutory arguments.

Supreme Court decisions determine only specific questions presented to the Court—or those framed by the justices themselves. In 1953 the Court decided that the statute of limitations prevented the government from instituting criminal proceedings against Bridges for his alleged fraud in acquiring citizenship. But the effect of that narrow holding was to invite a new governmental initiative, utilizing yet another procedural weapon against Bridges.

On the same day in May 1949 that the grand jury returned a criminal indictment against Bridges, the government filed a civil suit to cancel his naturalization on the grounds that it had been fraudulently secured. Judge Harris, however, stayed all proceedings in the civil action pending the result of the criminal trial. Following that trial, the government promptly asked Harris to revoke Bridges' citizenship because of the conviction. Although Bridges obviously intended to appeal, the INS equated its plea of revocation to a recent successful petition for disbarment of Alger Hiss following his perjury conviction. Harris granted the government's request. When the Supreme Court reversed the conviction in 1953, it also handed down a separate ruling reversing the order on denaturalization. One month later, however, the general counsel for the INS was ready with a report recommending that the civil case be reactivated and brought to trial.[61]

The government's civil action largely followed the pattern of the 1949 criminal trial. Curiously, however, Mervyn Rathborne, the government's most effective witness in 1949, was not called and the government was forced to rely chiefly on John Schomaker's testimony. Bridges' strategists made two major changes: they decided to forgo a jury trial, and they brought in Telford Taylor, the distinguished Nuremberg prosecutor, as chief counsel. In his opening statement, Taylor argued that naturalized citizenship is not second-class citizenship, "held under the sword of Damocles." The history of the earlier proceedings against Bridges, he maintained, increased the burden of proof on the government. Finally, Taylor countered the notion of Bridges as a dedicated, fanatical, secret revolutionary by appealing to his record as a labor leader. That record, Taylor concluded, had stimulated "mutual trust" and a recognition of "mutual interest" between labor and management.

The trial in San Francisco before Judge Louis Goodman lasted from June 20 to July 22, 1955. Goodman made clear his opinion that an alien who "knowingly consorted" with advocates of violent revolution should never be naturalized. But he admitted that was not the issue, as the government sought to prove nothing less than Bridges' membership in the Communist Party. On that point, Goodman found the government vulnerable because of its witnesses. In particular, he found Schomaker's testimony improbable and unacceptable. Goodman complained that Schomaker's charges, along with those of other ex-Communists, were "tinged and colored with discrepancies, animosities, vituperations, hates and above all, with lengthy speeches, . . . which, it is not unfair to say, is a disease with which Communists are afflicted." To find the truth in their welter of words was "a task for the omniscient." While mindful of the "extra-judicial clamor" for denaturalizing Bridges, Goodman simply did not find the witnesses credible and he concluded that the government had failed to prove its case.[62]

Goodman's decision apparently exhausted the government's legal arsenal. Both criminal and civil proceedings against Bridges had failed, and the government simply had to accept the fact of Bridges' citizenship. But the government made one more petulant move. In 1958, nearly three years after Goodman's decision, the Internal Revenue Service notified Bridges, Robertson, and Schmidt that they were liable for $82,000 in back taxes on money raised in their behalf between 1949 and 1953. The IRS contended that the defense funds provided income that was taxable, no matter how it was spent. After several years of negotiations, the union decided in 1961 to accept a settlement offer of $11,000—a mere pittance considering the costs of defending Harry Bridges for nearly a quarter century and what the union's challenge to the tax bill would have cost. Bridges himself recognized the harassment: "It's pretty chicken—, a cheap thing for the U.S. Government to do." But the government had a "victory" at last.[63]

V

Harry Bridges was a colorful labor leader whose accomplishments on behalf of his followers were enormous. Under his leadership, the West Coast longshoremen rose from near peonage to a respectable level of working conditions and wages. As his legal and political troubles ceased in the late 1950s, Bridges confronted the technological problems of the waterfront. The longshoremen's contracts he negotiated in the 1960s may have satisfied the shippers more than his rank and file, as he accepted automation, containerization, and fewer jobs. Accommodation, it seems, is the true path for a "seasoned and responsible labor leader." Yet Bridges undoubtedly will fade into relative obscurity and eventually his work probably will merit little more than a footnote in the history of labor relations.

The tactics of his persecutors, however, have a timeless quality. They illuminate the awesome resources of public power, exploiting the intricacies of the legal system to pursue avowedly political goals. The effort was considerable: extensive investigations by different government agencies, two deportation hearings, three trials, and two appellate proceedings. The costs are beyond any reasonable accounting—for both sides. Innumerable government agencies, officials, and bureaucrats consumed public expenses; the defense burden for lawyers, investigations, and publicity similarly was enormous.[64] But for both sides, time, energy, and costs were irrelevant.

The government effort, once committed, took on a momentum of its own. Originally undertaken as a reluctant response to the ambitions and vindictiveness of Bridges' enemies, the government drives became intertwined with those of private interests, and simply would not cease. Each government move responded to a political calculus. Political concerns, fears, and imperatives dictated every decision to proceed against Bridges.

Motivation aside, was there any substance to the government's charges? Was Harry Bridges a Communist? Paul Jacobs, who prepared the CIO's expulsion case against Bridges yet was somewhat sympathetic to him, said that Bridges' arrangement with the CP was a *"quid pro quo* working alliance." Bridges used Party people to build and control the ILWU, while the Party used Bridges' ILWU and CIO positions as respectable fronts for articulating and promoting its programs. Bert Cochran, in his perceptive study of labor and Communism, conceded that Bridges may not legally have been a member of the Communist Party, but "sociologically" he was an ally and followed Party policies and tolerated the Communist faction inside his union. "He was also," Cochran added, "an egotistic, opinionated and willful individual who must have given many hours of agony to the commissars assigned to handle him." Finally, Joseph Starobin, former foreign affairs editor for the *Daily Worker,* claimed that Communists enabled Bridges "to become a foremost radical unionist." Yet Starobin found Bridges somewhat of an ingrate, for he was "close to anarcho-syndicalism and never was a Communist."[65]

Bridges always candidly acknowledged his close ties and cooperation with Communists. He consistently admitted that Communist policies and goals often coincided with union purposes; as such, he had no hesitation in allying himself with them. Government investigators and prosecutors nevertheless relentlessly compiled a wealth of data, evidence, and witnesses to confirm what was obvious, only to be undone by its own procedural irregularities and questionable cast of witnesses.

Why in the face of Bridges' egregiousness, provocativeness, and varied cast of enemies did he prevail? How did the integrity of due process survive amid the massed resources and diligent tactics of official power? Why did Bridges "triumph" where others failed?

Bridges represented a viable, successful union that was bound to social and economic reality. He held high office, he negotiated agreements, and he signed contracts, all tasks which he carried out within the mainstream of American economic life. Yet his links to Communists imperiled his standing and security. Justice Hugo Black during the 1945 Supreme Court conferences on his case contended that the charges against Bridges resulted from his prominence and success, which had offended powerful interest groups. And Justice Douglas noted in his opinion that Bridges had cooperated with Communists only to attain "wholly lawful objectives." The massive support for Bridges from diverse sources, as evidenced by the letters and petitions to the President, confirmed that reality.

Bridges, in short, was cloaked with a legitimacy and respectability that the courts acknowledged. Admittedly, Communist influence in some unions was both destructive and self-serving; yet the evidence indicates that Bridges well served the market-oriented collective bargaining desires of his membership. Whatever Bridges' links to the Communist Party, he subordinated them to the primary end of striking satisfactory market bargains, and the law ultimately regarded those links as extraneous and irrelevant. Bridges was part of a movement that was inextricably bound to the society. The CP, on the other hand, essentially represented only a foreign power and itself. And within a few years, the Supreme Court was to decide that the Party's flagrant subservience to Soviet direction left it outside the pale of legitimacy.

Bridges' travails provided a paradox: the law was used against him as a vexatious, almost fatal weapon; yet the context dictated a certain integrity, even autonomy, for the law that rebuked other power authorities and provided the eventual victory for Harry Bridges.

6

"KILL THE LAWYERS"
Guilt by Representation

> The lawyer owes entire "devotion to the interest of the client, warm zeal in the maintenance and defense of his rights and the exertion of his utmost learning and ability," to the end that nothing be taken or be withheld from him, save by the rules of law, legally applied. No fear of judicial disfavor or public unpopularity should restrain him from the full discharge of his duty.
> —*Canons of Professional Ethics*, CANON 15

> In every particular [a judge's] conduct should be above reproach. He should be conscientious, studious, thorough, courteous, patient, punctual, just, impartial, fearless of public clamor, regardless of public praise, and indifferent to private political or partisan influences.
> —*Canons of Judicial Ethics*, CANON 15

i

THE Smith Act prosecution of the Communist Party leadership in 1949 marked the most blatant political trial in American history, a trial of the Party's purposes, ideology, and organization, as well as of its leaders. The indictments in July 1948 reflected a growing national demand to counter the expanding international menace of Communism and signaled a national commitment to destroy domestic Communism.

The passage of the Smith Act of 1940, making it a crime to teach and advocate the overthrow of the government by force, or to belong to a group advocating such overthrow, threatened long-standing traditions of civil liberties and political dissent. The law reflected a fear of growing Fascist and Communist powers in the world and their use of domestic subversive groups. Before 1948, the government invoked the Smith Act twice; first, to prosecute a group of Minneapolis

Trotskyites who headed a local Teamsters union, and again to try a group of alleged Fascist sympathizers. The initial test resulted in a number of convictions (with the hearty approval of such disparate groups as the International Teamsters Union and the Communist Party) and the second ended in a mistrial when the judge died of a heart attack.[1]

The FBI and Justice Department lawyers formally began to build a possible Smith Act case against the Communist Party as early as June 1945. By 1947 the FBI had prepared a brief running over 1,800 pages, including some 800 exhibits. When Republican members of the House Committee on Un-American Activities learned of the brief in early 1948, they pressed Attorney General Tom Clark to push the prosecution. Clark responded by calling on John F. X. McGohey, United States Attorney in New York City, to determine the feasibility of prosecution. Political currents in the nation and in the Administration in the spring of 1948 sharply fluctuated on the issue of proscribing the Communist Party. Clark apparently resisted prosecution as late as June 1948, but McGohey presented his superiors with a *fait accompli* when he informed them that he intended to secure indictments. On July 20 the grand jury returned true bills against twelve national leaders of the Party. With that, the government pursued a course that consumed enormous human and financial resources over the next three years. The ultimate cost for the Communist Party was far more substantial.

The New York trial—the "Battle of Foley Square," as it was popularly known —began in January 1949 and lasted nine months, with the first two taken up by the defense's elaborate challenge to jury selection procedure. The trial tediously explored the nuances of Marxist-Leninist-Stalinist texts on Communism and revolution. But bitter acrimony between Judge Harold Medina and the defense lawyers over procedure and the admissibility of evidence regularly punctuated the proceedings. Those episodes assumed a life of their own separate from the trial issues and quickly propelled the judge into national prominence.

For their part, the defense lawyers were cited for contempt and served varying jail sentences. Afterward, they found themselves subjected to continuing disciplinary actions by their peers, including disbarment. The legal and political responses to the lawyers' conduct raised important questions regarding representation and the bar's role as an extension of official power to conduct political harassment.

Attorney General Tom Clark had set the tone in a widely publicized talk before the Chicago Bar Association in June 1946. The speech focused primarily on the nature of federalism and the national government's responsibility for protecting civil rights. Although Clark emphasized the growing need for national action to preserve the rights and liberties of all, and particularly blacks, he highlighted Communist and Fascist exploitation of the civil rights issue. Warning that such extremists followed a classic "divide and rule" tactic, he charged that they subverted the honest aims of those protesting injustice.

Lawyers, Clark insisted, had a special responsibility for protecting the people against the false preachments of extremists. While admitting there were two sides to many legal questions, the Attorney General urged lawyers to "view the present with open eyes so that [they] may not be blind in the future." In other words, he said, lawyers should be careful in their choices of clients and causes. Yet what of those who chose to represent extremists? For them, Clark urged his fellow lawyers vigilantly to police their own ranks. "I do not think there is anyone more subject to censure in our profession than the revolutionary who enters our ranks, takes the solemn oath of our calling," he asserted, "and then uses every device in the legal category to further the interests of those who would destroy our government by force, if necessary." Denying any interest in purges, he nevertheless called on the bar associations to take "those too brilliant brothers of ours to the legal woodshed for a definite and well-deserved admonition."[2]

Clark's Chicago address was not an isolated episode. In the midst of the Foley Square trial—and just after he had been appointed to the Supreme Court—Clark reiterated his concerns about lawyers who served Communist causes. In a *Look* magazine article, he questioned the right of Communists to practice and urged bar associations to closely scrutinize the conduct of such lawyers. Clark cast a wide net: even those lawyers who were not members of the Party, "but who act like Communists and carry out Communist missions in offensives against the dignity and order of our courts," should be questioned, he said. Finally, in an obvious reference to Judge Medina's difficulty in the then current Smith Act trial, Clark praised judges who upheld "the majesty of the law against destructive tactics [while] still maintaining fair trial standards." Clark's remarks found a receptive and most important audience—the American Bar Association. By 1951 the ABA's House of Delegates recommended that bar groups throughout the nation expel Communist Party members and advocates of Marxist-Leninist doctrines.[3]

"Over the years the bar shared the prevailing religious, racial and national prejudices of middle-class Americans," Willard Hurst has written. The Attorney General of the United States added a gloss to that characterization when he decreed that those who stood outside such shared values did not deserve the benefits of legal representation. Clark more ominously suggested a judgment of "guilt by representation" for lawyers who insisted upon serving such clients. In effect, he provided a hunting license for bar associations to punish those who strayed from the prescribed line of orthodoxy.

"The first thing we do, let's kill all the lawyers," one of Jack Cade's revolutionaries said in fifteenth-century England. Although hardly a revolutionary, Clark offered a corollary suggestion: a legal process that would benefit some and exclude others from protection. Unlike Cade's exhortation, it was implemented for a time, so that a "black silence of fear," as Justice William O. Douglas characterized it, engulfed the legal profession.[4]

ii

Harold Medina was a relative newcomer to the federal bench, having been appointed in 1947. The son of wealthy Mexican immigrants, Medina had been educated at private military academies, Princeton, and the Columbia Law School, where he graduated in 1912 with high honors. He established a very successful private practice in New York City, first as an appellate attorney and then as a trial lawyer. In fourteen years of trial work, Medina claimed that he had never lost a case. He periodically taught at Columbia and for twenty-five years conducted a very popular bar review course. Many of Medina's associates regarded him as excessively aggressive and an "insufferable egotist"—qualities that later emerged in the Foley Square trial.

In preparation for that trial, Medina reviewed the 1944 Washington, D.C., Smith Act trial of thirty-one neo-Fascists, one of the most bizarre episodes in American courtroom history. Defense lawyers and defendants alike constantly interrupted, objected to nearly every prosecution witness and exhibit, and generally insulted and harassed Judge Edward Eicher. After nearly eight months, the prosecution still had not concluded its case. Ill and tired from the lengthy proceedings, Eicher suddenly died and the case ended in a mistrial. Medina absorbed the lesson and determined to conserve his strength. Throughout the New York trial, he refrained from any social or other outside activities. After the trial began, Medina became convinced that the defense lawyers and defendants were determined to wear him down and break his health. In his various exchanges with the lawyers, Medina often referred to his physical condition and to what he regarded as the attorneys' plot to destroy his health. The more the trial dragged on, the more it reinforced Medina's conviction that he was the victim of a defense conspiracy to obstruct and possibly prevent the continuation of the trial.[5] Whether his fear was real or imagined, the defense lawyers would pay a heavy price because of it.

The defense team of five lawyers possessed varying degrees of skill and experience. All were members of the National Lawyers Guild, and some had a long identification with leftist causes. Harry Sacher of New York had represented left-leaning labor unions including the Transport Workers and the Furriers. Abraham J. Isserman of New Jersey was similarly active in labor affairs as well as civil liberties causes. He had been a member of the National Board of the American Civil Liberties Union until his resignation (or ouster) as a result of the ACLU's decision to expel Communist members in 1940. Richard Gladstein from

San Francisco was the most experienced trial lawyer of the group and was best known for his successful defenses of Harry Bridges in the 1930s and 1940s. Gladstein, like Sacher and Isserman, was Jewish. George Crockett of Detroit had served with the Labor Department, the Fair Employment Practices Committee, and the United Automobile Workers. Crockett knew full well that he was in the case primarily because he was black. Louis McCabe, an able criminal lawyer from Philadelphia, rounded out the defense. After the trial opened, the leading defendant, Communist Party secretary-general Eugene Dennis, acted as his own lawyer.

However competent and qualified, the defense lawyers labored under enormous handicaps. Obviously, it was a difficult case, compounded by the prevailing hostile climate of opinion toward their clients and their cause. Although the lawyers were aware of FBI surveillance, they did not realize the extent to which the Bureau had penetrated defense conferences and strategy-planning sessions. Judge Medina would appear in due course to be more of an adversary than an arbiter, but the lawyers' own internal differences undermined their efforts and significantly contributed to their later problems.

The defense lawyers suffered from bruising personality clashes, with their egos and pride very much on the line. Sacher and Gladstein were the most prominent of the five lawyers, and both fancied themselves as chief counsel in the case. Sacher was on his home ground and was most familiar with the defendants, but Gladstein was far more experienced as a trial lawyer and was brought into the case primarily for his skills at cross-examination. There was constant tension between the two, and their differences eventually required the intervention of the defendants themselves. Crockett later described working with Sacher and Gladstein as "a two-ring circus," with "one trying to outdo the other."

The lawyers and their clients divided over the nature of the defense. Isserman advocated a strategy modeled on Georgi Dimitrov's audacious defense during the Reichstag Fire trial in 1934. (Crockett later admitted he did not know who Dimitrov was.) Sacher believed that there was no way to win an acquittal and that the trial should be conducted so as to establish a record which would make possible a favorable verdict on appeal. Gladstein contended that they might win through bold, aggressive tactics, including an imaginative challenge to the jury selection procedure. The differences were never really resolved. The varying approaches all were tried, and all failed.

Three decades later Gladstein observed that the defendants "should never have had lawyers at all; they should have defended themselves." The lawyers simply were not in control of either their clients or their case. And that, of course, reduced their effectiveness. Gladstein recalled that the defendants insisted on offering stock Marxist-Leninist recitations in their testimony instead of allowing him to elicit impromptu answers in language the jury could understand. Further, the defendants insisted on reading and correcting Gladstein's summation word for word in advance, thus preventing him from delivering a spontaneous and more convincing argument. It was clear, Gladstein recalled, that "we were not our own masters."[6]

Finally, the lawyers' very participation in the case cast a stigma upon them, a stigma that made them indistinguishable from their clients. At best, they were seen as fellow travelers; at worst, as Communist Party hacks chosen to make a mockery and spectacle of American justice. Were they Party members? Probably some were, but no matter. They were identified as Communists in the mass media and public consciousness, by large parts of the legal profession, and, to some extent, by Medina. Despite professional tradition and the popular maxim that every man was entitled to fair representation, there was a widespread belief that only sympathetic, compatible lawyers could defend such reprehensible defendants. It was a belief fostered on the highest level of government, and reinforced from within the profession.

iii

It was shortly before noon, October 14, 1949. To no one's great surprise, the jury delivered a guilty verdict against all the Communist Party defendants after less than seven hours of deliberation. Judge Medina promptly polled the jurors and dismissed them with the usual thanks and admonitions. It is noteworthy that the judge stressed the importance of the case after he had insisted throughout the trial that it was an ordinary proceeding.

Although it was time for the usual defense motions relative to the verdict, the mercurial judge had higher drama in mind. "Now I turn to some unfinished business," Medina announced, and he thereupon read a portion of a lengthy certificate of contempt, containing forty specifications against the six lawyers. The heart of Medina's judgment was Specification I, charging counsel with having joined in a deliberate, premeditated conspiracy to obstruct the trial. In "a cold and calculating manner," he asserted, they had delayed and confused the proceedings, provoked incidents, and impaired his health in order to create a mistrial. To divert attention from the issues of the trial, Medina contended, the defense had attacked him, the jury system, the Department of Justice, the President, the police, and the press.

The judge then listed thirteen broad categories of contemptuous, unjustified behavior to carry out this plan, including delaying tactics, long and repetitious arguments, insinuations of collusion between the court and the prosecution, and disregard for rulings on the admissibility of evidence. As if to purge himself of any possible wrongdoing, Medina added that the lawyers had provoked intemperate and undignified responses from him to demonstrate his unfitness or bias.

The conspiracy charge, however, was crucial. In his preliminary remarks, Medina admitted that normally he would have been tempted to overlook or merely reprimand the lawyers for conduct which occurred in the heat of controversy or because of an overzealousness in their defense of clients. But early in the trial, Medina concluded that the lawyers' actions and statements had resulted from "an agreement" among themselves. Through the years, the heart of Medina's case has often been overlooked. But by his own admission, the judgment rested on his perception of the lawyers' "agreement."

One by one, Medina tolled the specifications and sentences against the lawyers. He found Sacher guilty of twenty-three counts of contempt, and sentenced him to six months' imprisonment on each charge, the sentences to run concurrently; for Gladstein, eighteen counts and six months; for Crockett, nine counts and four months; for McCabe, six counts and thirty days; and for Isserman, seven counts and four months. (Eugene Dennis, who had acted as his own counsel, had only five counts of contempt, but forsaking mathematical symmetry, Medina sentenced him to six months.) All, of course, were found guilty of the conspiracy specification. And with the pronouncement of guilt and sentences, Medina blithely asked if there were any motions. He meant motions regarding the trial verdict, not for what had just occurred.

The lawyers stood stunned, dazed, barely believing what they had heard. Isserman was the first to recover. Sharply objecting to the contempt finding, he contended that it further reflected Medina's bias and prejudice. He also remarked that Tom Clark's threatened punishment of lawyers who defended Communists had now become a frightening reality. With that, Isserman moved to vacate the certificate. Medina denied the motion, saying he would hear only motions regarding the trial verdict. Sacher thereupon pleaded for more time, but quickly returned to the judge's summary judgment of contempt. While not questioning Medina's power, Sacher complained that the judge's discretion and judgment did not give the lawyers a "running chance"—a reference to Medina's unwillingness to allow them to say anything in their defense or to purge themselves. Medina heatedly responded that Sacher was continuing "in the same brazen manner" he had used throughout the trial. He charged that Sacher had no desire to "amend" his ways, and was persisting in "the same old mealy-mouth" manner.

Gladstein, the veteran of the Bridges cases and other political controversies, was eloquent and forceful. He insisted that he had rightfully defended his clients with zeal, earnestness, and fervor. Crockett called his contempt citation a "badge of honor" and had no regrets for having waged a vigorous fight. McCabe categorically denied the charges and, like Gladstein, contended that he had faithfully carried out the mandates of the American Bar Association's Canon 15 regarding a lawyer's obligation to his client. McCabe alone indicated some regret for any possible misbehavior before the court.[7]

Daily wire service accounts of the trial had emphasized Judge Medina's encounters with obstreperous, overzealous defense lawyers. His contempt judgment accordingly received immediate acclaim. Medina received thousands of letters, warmly endorsing his conduct of the trial. One was simply addressed to "The *American* Judge, New York, New York." A Pasadena woman complimented him on his "sentencing Defense Council [*sic*]" and hoped that time would not be wasted on appeals to the Supreme Court. A Madison, Wisconsin, attorney praised Medina for having the "patience of Job" and for punishing attorneys who "tried to burlesque the trial and make mockery out of our courts of justice." Attorney General J. Howard McGrath warmly praised Medina's "patience and steadfastness." Medina insisted that he was surprised to find himself in the limelight and "more or less" a national hero. As for his avalanche of mail, he told one correspondent, "Everyone seems to have gone crazy."[8]

Some individuals and groups—notably the National Lawyers Guild—expressed criticism of Medina's behavior and concern for the possible chilling effect of his action on lawyers willing to represent unpopular clients. But in the prevailing atmosphere it appeared unlikely that appellate judges would overturn the substance of Medina's charge. The appeals therefore focused on the proper scope of Medina's authority to deliver the judgment. Rule 42 (a) of the Federal Rules of Criminal Procedure allowed the presiding judge to determine and punish contempt himself; Rule 42 (b) provided for an alternative determination by another judge after notice, hearing, and an opportunity for the accused to defend. In their appeal, the lawyers contended that Medina had no power to punish them summarily because the alleged conduct contained in Specification I—the conspiracy count—was not committed in the presence of the court as required in Rule 42 (a); furthermore, they argued, Medina erred in not imposing punishment immediately following the contemptuous acts.

After confrontation with the neophyte Medina, the convicted lawyers might have taken some comfort from the panel of distinguished judges they faced on the appellate level. Augustus Hand, Jerome Frank, and Charles Clark were widely respected and experienced, and the latter two had deserved liberal reputations. Small comfort, as it turned out. The judges sustained the citations and sentences in April 1950, although they handed down separate opinions somewhat diluting Medina's ruling.

Hand followed the contempt certificate in nearly every particular and upheld Medina without equivocation. The timing and execution of judgment Hand found to be of no consequence, and flatly rejected the petitioners' argument that the conspiracy, if it existed, required Medina to follow Rule 42 (b). Medina's conclusion that counsels' acts were the result of an agreement "meant no more than that they were deliberate, and it was quite unimportant whether he believed that a prior conspiracy had been entered into." Hand went on to isolate certain trial incidents he believed amply justified the conspiracy specification. Finally, Judge Hand delicately maneuvered through contradictory precedents on the question of immediate punishment, but was quite willing to leave the matter in the domain of the trial judge and dependent on the facts and circumstances of the particular case. Hand found that immediate punishment need not be imposed if it "would endanger the defense in a criminal case, or interfere with its conduct."[9]

Judge Frank agreed with Hand on all matters but one. Given his reputation as a legal theorist and as one of the most prominent New Deal liberals of the 1930s, his remarks on the lawyers' behavior were devastating. He brusquely denied that affirming the contempt orders would intimidate future defenses on behalf of labor unions, minority groups, or unpopular persons. The Foley Square lawyers' conduct was "outrageous," not "courageous," Frank declared. Their "crude antics," their attempt "to throw a wrench in the machinery of justice," were acts which "no sensible man" could approve. Yet Frank held that Medina had erred on the conspiracy specification and that the charge required a hearing under the terms of Rule 42 (b).[10]

Frank nevertheless chose to regard Specification I as entirely superfluous to the other specifications. The latter all occurred within the courtroom and thus, he held, were properly punishable by Medina. Yet Medina's own words undermined any such interpretation. In his remarks preliminary to the enumeration of the specific contempt charges, Medina stated that the individual acts "were the result of an agreement between these defendants, deliberately entered into in a cold and calculating manner."[11] The conspiracy arrangement was the very basis of his contempt adjudication and punishment; there can be no other interpretation of his words. And without the conspiracy finding, Medina admitted he would have tended to overlook the other acts.

Judge Clark dissented on all counts, largely because he considered the conspiracy charge central and crucial. For Clark, intent was basic to any conspiracy, and its determination required a hearing as a proper "prerequisite to punishment." Clark insisted that Medina's admission that he was punishing for conspiracy underlined the importance of the charge. Clark himself found little substance to the conspiracy idea. The trial, he said, "was not being and was not broken up," and actually proceeded to an orderly conclusion.[12]

Frank's ambiguous opinion revealed a sharp division among the judges, but the split was actually much deeper than indicated in the published reports. Some months later, Clark confided to Supreme Court Justice Hugo Black that the contempt case involved an "emotional strain." Older colleagues on the circuit bench, Clark reported, subjected him to enormous pressure. His doubts, furthermore, increased when "a younger colleague"—obviously Frank—who originally had sided with Clark, changed his vote to create the tenuous majority. Clark confessed that his final decision to stand alone caused him great concern.[13]

The conflict within the intermediate court was a harbinger of similar tensions in the highest court. The Supreme Court first denied an appeal for certiorari on May 18, 1951.[14] Yet the terse order actually masked a narrow 4–3 division within the Court. Chief Justice Fred M. Vinson, Justices Stanley Reed, Robert H. Jackson, and Harold H. Burton formed the majority, with Hugo Black, Felix Frankfurter, and William O. Douglas in dissent. Sherman Minton was absent and Tom Clark naturally recused himself. The Court's traditional practice required four votes for granting a writ of certiorari, and thus the matter appeared closed. But deeply felt passions and vigorous politicking boiled beneath the seemingly placid surface.

In the fall of 1951 the justices confronted a routine request for reconsideration. Frankfurter, Black, and Douglas, for varying reasons, pressed for granting the plea. Black and Douglas openly sympathized with the defendants. Frankfurter, however, was extremely agitated by the growing hostility to Communist lawyers. In February he told his colleagues that he favored an order against the American Bar Association to show cause why it should not be cited for contempt for its recent resolution calling for the disbarment of Communist lawyers.

But as of October 8 the Court's voting lineup remained intact from that of May. Frankfurter, however, lobbied hard with Jackson, perhaps his most kindred colleague. He told Jackson that the case presented an opportunity to speak out on what was important—"the responsibilities of both the bar and bench as parts of the trial process, as well as the obligations of an independent bar in a democratic society." The signs of the time dismayed Frankfurter. He was profoundly disturbed by the reluctance of approximately half a dozen "reputable" lawyers who had refused to appear with Henry Wallace before a congressional committee. Frankfurter reminded Jackson of Brandeis' dictum that the Court's most important function was that of a "rational educator." In that vein, he urged Jackson to take the lead, for he could offer an opinion that "would be a powerful lifter of fear, a dissipator of a good deal of nonsense, and an instiller of traditional manliness in our profession."[15]

Frankfurter's prodding (and typical flattery) brought quick and positive results. On October 9 Jackson circulated a memorandum emphasizing the importance of the case and suggested a limited review. Jackson's views neatly belie the notion of a cloistered judge, wholly devoid of political and social sensitivities. While disavowing any sympathy for the defense lawyers, Jackson said that a "concern for the reputation and the reality of fairness, of neutrality and freedom from partisanship in our judicial system," prompted his change of heart. Noting the government's acceleration of Communist prosecutions, he warned his colleagues that their earlier denial of review had increased the difficulties which confronted new defendants in obtaining adequate counsel. In such cases he said, lawyers might find it necessary to press "unwelcome arguments upon the bench"; Jackson therefore believed it imperative for the Court to consider the nature and limits of punishment for contempt in order that counsel could proceed confidently.

Jackson reiterated his belief that the Foley Square attorneys had engaged in obstructive behavior. But Medina, he argued, had "unnecessarily" included the conspiracy and personal injury charges. This raised, then, the one question that Jackson suggested be considered: namely, whether Medina properly followed the requirements of Rule 42 in adjudging and punishing the offending lawyers himself.[16]

Jackson's change of heart meant four votes for reconsideration. The Court's practice, however, required a majority in such cases. Frankfurter invoked what he called a "rule of deference," and he urged Burton to change his decision. But Burton already had told the Chief Justice that he would vote for reconsideration.[17] The case was argued in January 1952, and two months later, Jackson delivered the Court's opinion upholding the contempt convictions.

Jackson now muted his earlier clarion call. He confined himself to a narrow holding, offered no real criticism of Medina, and soft-pedaled any of his prior concern for the chilling effects on the profession. Following the Circuit Court's determination of the facts, Jackson held that the lawyers had violated professional decorum in the jury's presence and in the face of repeated warnings from the bench. The incidents were not isolated, and they had "prejudiced the expeditious, orderly and dispassionate conduct of the trial." Jackson's conclusion actually sharpened the petitioners' chief contention that Medina should have acted during the trial, and not afterward when obstruction was moot. Jackson, however, held that Rule 42 allowed judicial discretion in timing if a trial judge deemed immediate action inexpedient.[18]

The lawyers, obviously encouraged by the split in the Circuit Court, had stressed the vulnerability of Medina's conspiracy specification. If a conspiracy existed, they contended, it was not made in his presence and thus required proper notice, preparation time for a defense, and a hearing before another judge as provided in Rule 42 (b). But here Jackson relied on Judge Frank's "swing" position in the lower court decision and noted that the substantive offenses were separable, independent, and amply sustained without the conspiracy charge. There was then no inextricable link despite Medina's own words to that effect; the charge, as Frank had said, was mere "surplusage."

Jackson vaguely addressed the possible ramifications of the contempt holdings. He agreed that the contempt power could be abused and exercised in arbitrary fashion. But he noted that every judge who had examined the record had condemned the lawyers' conduct. Although he acknowledged his fear that defendants identified with unpopular causes might find it difficult to secure counsel of their choice, Jackson now insisted that such reasons were remote and it was more important to uphold the power to punish contempt. Finally, Jackson sought to resolve some of the contradictions seemingly raised in the lawyers' canons of ethics. The Court, he asserted, would "unhesitatingly" protect lawyers in the "fearless, vigorous and effective performance of every duty pertaining to the office of the advocate on behalf of any person whatsoever." But he would not equate contempt with courage or insults with independence. Above all, he concluded, the Court would protect the process of orderly trial—"the supreme object of the lawyers' calling."[19]

Justice Black (joined by Douglas) offered a pithy dissent, stressing Medina's prejudice and constitutional arguments justifying a jury trial in such contempt cases. Following Circuit Judge Clark (and Frankfurter's accompanying dissent), Black said that numerous episodes throughout the trial demonstrated Medina's "distrust" and "hostility" to the lawyers. No lawyers who had been called "liar," "brazen," or "mealy-mouth"—Medina's words—should be tried before a judge who had so publicly attacked their honor and integrity. Black furthermore argued for reversal because of the summary nature of conviction and sentence. He deplored the appellate court's refusal to read the whole record and its reliance on Medina's certificate. Black apparently recognized that the majority found compelling Tom Clark's "guilt by representation" thesis.[20]

In a separate dissent Frankfurter went far beyond the limited concerns he had expressed to Jackson a few months earlier. His opinion, including a 47-page appendix of excerpts of trial exchanges between Medina and the lawyers, neatly merged his usual procedural concerns with substantive issues. In time, Frankfurter's statements proved to be the real challenge to Medina's neo-folk idol status and to the prevailing climate of fear and paralysis that infected much of the legal profession.

Although Frankfurter asserted at the outset that the case involved "procedural regularity"—that is, whether Medina was the proper judge of the contempt—he offered a lengthy analysis of the substance of the charges. For this purpose, he refused to be bound by the altogether "too brief" excerpts in Medina's certificate and instead appended further exchanges for what he labeled a "much more balanced perspective." With the additional materials, Frankfurter came to the heart of the matter: "Not only were the contempts directed against the trial judge. The conduct of the lawyers had its reflex in the judge." In short, Medina's concern for his health, his personal animosity toward the lawyers, their cause, and their politics pervaded the record and colored his judgment of contempt.

Frankfurter lectured Medina with an elementary lesson in judicial decorum, and laid out a bill of particulars against his conduct. Medina had engaged, Frankfurter charged, in "dialectic, in repartee and banter, in talk so copious as inevitably to arrest the momentum of the trial" and weaken his own authority; he failed to exercise "moral authority"; he indulged the lawyers, "sometimes resignedly, sometimes playfully, in lengthy speeches"; and the wrangles "were punctuated by occasional minatory intimations from the Bench." In sum,

Medina was the wrong man to deal with the alleged contempt; his action, Frankfurter insisted, did violence to "a belief that punishment is a vindication of impersonal law."[21]

Despite the spirited battle within the Supreme Court, the convicted lawyers had nothing but some eloquent dissents to show for their two and one half years of challenge to Medina's judgment. While the Circuit Court had dropped a few of the lesser specifications, the sentences and the onus of conviction remained intact. Furthermore, in executing the sentences, government officials proved to be less than gracious winners.

All the lawyers surrendered in New York City on April 24, 1952. The government refused Gladstein's request that he be allowed to put himself in custody in San Francisco, and Gladstein paid his own travel expenses to New York. The California attorney also expressed a desire to serve his sentence on McNeil Island in Washington, a place nearer to his family and friends. Instead, he was sent to Texarkana, Texas, hardly one of the "country club" institutions. Nor did he travel first-class; he was driven cross-country for nearly seven weeks, manacled and in leg irons. He was held incommunicado in seven jails en route to Texas and deprived of normal prisoner privileges.[22]

Sacher, who had asked to remain in the East near his family, went to Ashland, Kentucky, along with Crockett, who had asked not to be put in any southern jail. McCabe had only thirty days to serve and was held in the New York Federal House of Detention for the entire period. Isserman originally was held in New York, but he suffered badly from asthma during his confinement. A sympathetic doctor arranged his transfer to Danbury, Connecticut, a more comfortable place with better medical treatment.[23]

iv

The contempt convictions, the appeals (for their clients as well as themselves), and the hardship of imprisonment constituted a bitter ordeal for the lawyers. The process was lengthy, costly, and, ultimately, humiliating. But at the same time, the lawyers simultaneously confronted threats that imperiled their professional existence. On the heels of Medina's pronouncement in October 1949, various bar groups—with the cooperation of government officers and agencies—started actions to disbar the various lawyers. Bar associations and judges in New York, New Jersey, Michigan, California, and Hawaii, on their own initiative or at the prompting of public officials, came forth to offer their special supplement to the public punishment.

The activities of these "private governments" again cost the beleaguered lawyers enormous amounts of time, energy, and money. Bar association hearings and court appeals almost entirely consumed their professional lives—in Isserman's case, for over a decade. Added to this was the frustration of different, overlapping, and continual threats from bar groups in different jurisdictions. Even a decisive, forthright opinion by the Supreme Court rejecting disbarment of Sacher, who stood under the most counts of contempt, failed to stem the harassment. Throughout, the lawyers faced a peculiar form of double jeopardy, but one for which there was no constitutional, and very little legal, protection. Tom Clark's "legal woodshed" resembled more a chamber of horrors where professional torture, not admonition, was the norm.

Events in New York shortly after the contempt sentences demonstrated the symbiotic relationship between the bar and the government. Following a conference in early December 1949 between Chief Judge John Knox of the Southern District of New York and Robert Patterson, president of the Association of the Bar of the City of New York, Frank Adams was appointed to gather information for consideration in disciplinary proceedings against Sacher and Isserman. Adams, then in private practice, had formerly served in the U.S. Attorney's office in New York. He immediately consulted newly appointed U.S. Attorney Irving Saypol, as well as Frank Gordon and Irving Shapiro, special assistants to the Attorney General, and the FBI's New York field office agents.

Adams told the FBI that the bar was "extremely anxious to take action" against Sacher and Isserman. The rules for disciplinary proceedings in the federal district required a hearing before a judge. Adams decided not to call Judge Medina or prosecutor John McGohey (who had just been named to the federal bench) as witnesses. But he expressed interest in using others who had been at the prosecuting counsel table, including Gordon and Shapiro, and two FBI agents. The FBI's reaction to the request offered a revealing sidelight to the affair. J. Edgar Hoover immediately rejected the idea. Taking the cue, the New York office told Adams that it was not "within the province" of the Bureau to testify at a hearing "which would undoubtedly receive publicity," adding that such activity might be construed as "persecution."[24] Given its long-term surveillance of the lawyers, including their private, professional conferences during the trial, the Bureau's concern for probity was ironic. Yet if Adams had insisted, he could have subpoenaed the agents. Of course, he was not about to defy Hoover.

In April 1950, Adams filed a petition in federal court on behalf of the New York City bar ordering Sacher and Isserman to show cause why they should not be disbarred. Chief Judge Knox referred the matter to Judge Henry Goddard, who had just concluded presiding over Alger Hiss's second trial. The petition included a lengthy affidavit chronicling the contempt specifications and numerous trial comments by Sacher and Isserman—all labeled as improper, insolent, unprofessional, and provocative. In July, Goddard transferred the case to Carroll Hincks, a visiting federal judge from Connecticut. After numerous postponements, Hincks held a hearing in December 1950. Briefs were not filed for another six months, and Hincks did not announce his decision until January 1952.[25] Coincidentally or not, Hincks's opinion came down just as the Supreme Court heard arguments in the contempt appeal.

Hincks ordered Sacher permanently disbarred and Isserman suspended from practice in the federal district bar for two years. Quantitative and qualitative standards dictated the different judgments. Isserman's misconduct, Hincks contended, was not so frequent or so grave as to require permanent exclusion. Furthermore, Hincks had hopes that the "experience of discipline" would rehabilitate Isserman and restrain his future courtroom behavior. Sacher was another matter. Hincks found no "venality or lack of fidelity" to his client's interests. Sacher's problem was his "temperament," which so favored an "excessive zeal" on behalf of his clients that it obscured a recognition of his responsibilities as an officer of the court. Finally, Hincks offered some career counseling: the very qualities that made Sacher unfit as a lawyer, he said, "might well be unobjectionable in commercial fields where competitive effort is not subject to the restraints required" of a lawyer. Hincks's remarks betrayed the thinly veiled anti-Semitism that animated much of the disciplinary effort.

The bar association had prepared its own list of contempt findings against Sacher and Isserman, supplementing Medina's with some the examining attorneys found even more culpable. Judge Hincks agreed. For example, the judge focused on a particularly sharp exchange between Sacher and prosecutor McGohey while arguing a motion near the end of the case:

> MR. SACHER: They [the early Christians] did so many things, more than this evidence disclosed, that if Mr. McGohey were a contemporary of Jesus he would have had Jesus in the dock.
> MR. McGOHEY: Your Honor, I resent that.
> THE COURT: I don't blame you.
> MR. McGOHEY: That is the most unconscionable thing I have ever heard, your Honor. I have been born and raised in this city. It is well known that I am a member of the Catholic Church. I firmly, with all my heart, believe that Jesus Christ is divine, that he is the Son of God, and to have it said in this courtroom, where I am a member of the bar, that I would have persecuted my God is an insult that I can't resist interrupting for.
> THE COURT: Please refrain from any such reference again, Mr. Sacher. That was quite improper, and I don't blame Mr. McGohey at all for resenting it; anyone would.
> MR. SACHER: I say to your Honor—
> THE COURT: It is a terrible thing to say.
> MR. SACHER: I say to your Honor that the resort to so-called secrecy—
> THE COURT: You don't even apologize for it.
> MR. SACHER: I am proceeding with my argument, your Honor. I have no apologies to make.

In oral arguments before Hincks, Sacher explained that he had refused to apologize because he believed his "historical allegation" had been misunderstood and made to appear as a personal attack on McGohey. Upon reflection, however, Sacher was willing to qualify his remarks. But it was too late, for Hincks found such conduct was "provocative in the extreme," as well as "intentionally provocative." Finally, the incident offered "crowning proof," Hincks said, that Sacher was a master in the art of inflammation and so accustomed to the practice that it was not "safe" to have him as a member of the bar. It was curious that of all the incidents that occurred during the trial, Hincks emphasized a charge that even Medina had not found contemptuous.[26]

Six months earlier, Isserman had been suspended by the New Jersey Supreme Court pending disbarment proceedings. Anticipating a lengthy battle there which would take at least two years, Isserman chose not to appeal Hincks's decision. With Telford Taylor as his counsel, Sacher pursued his appeal, which indeed lasted two years.

In July 1953, in the Second Circuit Court, Augustus Hand again rendered judgment against Sacher, this time with Judge Harrie Chase concurring. In general, Hand found that Hincks's recital of instances of misconduct amply supported the disbarment order and he agreed with Hincks that Sacher's misbehavior during the trial justified anticipating future misconduct. Finally, Hand noted that disbarment is not meant to punish an attorney, but to protect the court and "relieve the public" of an unfit lawyer.[27]

Judge Charles Clark again dissented, and treated Hincks's opinion almost casually, noting Hincks's difficulty as a visiting judge, called upon to weigh the actions of a fellow jurist. Clark found Hincks's ruling anomalous, to say the least, in that he disbarred Sacher while complimenting him. He also believed that Hincks violated the fundamental principle that disbarment should be invoked only as a last resort.[28]

Clark concentrated on the original setting of the contempt actions. He returned to his own earlier questions of Medina's behavior and, more importantly, invoked the critical perspective that had developed in the intervening three and one half years. The contempt conviction, Clark said, "raised the insistent question whether the judge's [Medina's] action did not appear more of a vindictive than a judicial nature." Aware that he was touching on a sensitive and painful subject, Clark nevertheless forthrightly discussed Medina's behavior. Referring to the Supreme Court dissents of a year earlier, Clark cited criticism of Medina "in the highest circles." Medina, he said, had himself engaged in altercations "and even to a certain extent promoted them." Given that behavior, it would be only fair then to accept "some reciprocal lack of restraint" by the lawyers. The time for retribution had passed; the courts, Clark concluded, had nothing to gain from "vindictive harshness" and mercy would enhance their reputation for toler-ance, human understanding, and strength.[29]

When Sacher's discipline case first came before the Supreme Court in Novem-ber 1953, it appeared that, at best, the justices were closely divided. Reed, Burton, and Minton at that point may have been for affirming the lower court, while Frankfurter, Black, and Douglas remained sympathetic to the appellants. (Clark recused himself again.) But this time, Jackson clearly was disturbed by the severity of the punishment. Sacher's six months' jail sentence was for Jackson "almost the ultimate in humiliation," and he saw no need for further action. Yet sensing an even division of the Court, which would have meant affirming the disbarment order, he was reluctant to speak out. "I have the gravest doubts," he told Frankfurter, "whether the slightest good can come of bringing up this case." Jackson preferred a simple denial of review as the lesser evil. He also was hesitant in joining the three colleagues who were on record as denying or downgrading the contempt. Once again, Frankfurter pressed Jackson to speak out and "not to underrate the importance of a dissent."[30]

Dissent for Jackson, however, proved unnecessary. The key was the new Chief Justice, Earl Warren. In November neither Frankfurter nor Jackson had the vaguest idea of Warren's views. But Warren voted to grant certiorari, and the case was argued in March 1954, followed by a decision three weeks later. The unsigned opinion revealed Jackson's hand, for it was confined to the simple issue of severity. The Court's statement noted that Hincks's disbarment order came before the final affirmance of the contempt sentences, thus implying the trial judge might have decided otherwise. This statement provoked a spirited dissent from Justice Reed, who accused the Court of acting as a trial court. In any event, Sacher's disbarment was overturned on the ground that it was "unnecessarily severe."[31]

Sacher died in 1963, having passed his remaining days in relative obscurity and with a diminished practice. He had an encounter with HUAC in the late 1950s and successfully appealed a contempt citation from the committee. At least he was spared further professional harassment after the Supreme Court overturned the New York disbarment order.

Not so for Isserman. Ranking at best third in the defense hierarchy during the Foley Square trial, and only fourth in contempt specifications by Medina, Isser-man nevertheless paid the heaviest price of any of the lawyers. Why? A different jurisdiction, the timing of his appeals, and perhaps a personal vendetta against him by one of the most prominent American jurists contributed to his special ordeal.

Isserman originally had been admitted to the bar in New Jersey as an attorney in 1923 and as a counselor in 1926. The New Jersey bar wasted no time instituting disciplinary proceedings against Isserman after the Foley Square trial. Less than two weeks after Medina's action, the Ethics Committee of the Essex County Bar summoned Isserman to a hearing on November 3, 1949. The attorney elected to remain in New York, preparing various post-trial motions, but he was represented by counsel in New Jersey for what resulted in a rather perfunctory hearing. Four days later the committee formally presented a request to the New Jersey Supreme Court for disciplinary proceedings. The sole evidence was Isserman's contempt conviction.

The contempt appeals delayed the state court's action until 1952. Chief Justice Arthur Vanderbilt, speaking for a unanimous court, recounted the various judicial statements from three courts that had judged the lawyers' actions as contemptuous. He thereupon ruled that Isserman had violated his New Jersey oath and numerous canons of professional ethics as well. Vanderbilt rejected every argument Isserman presented in his behalf. Most revealing was his reaction to what amounted to a plea for mercy. Isserman suggested that New Jersey should not exceed the two-year suspension laid down by the federal court. Vanderbilt, however, insisted that he must be judged "by the standards of practice prevalent" in the state, for New Jersey was primarily responsible for his conduct. "[W]e cannot permit a lawyer admitted to practice in New Jersey," he said, "to do in the courtroom of another jurisdiction what he would never have been allowed to do here." And in one final swipe, Vanderbilt mentioned that Isserman had been convicted of statutory rape in 1925 and subsequently was suspended for six months—without acknowledging that Isserman had received a full and unconditional pardon in 1933. The verdict was absolute and Isserman's name was stricken from the rolls. A month later, the court rejected a motion for a rehearing based on the lack of notice of Isserman's pardon.[32]

Time and personalities were not in Isserman's favor. A year after the New Jersey action, the Supreme Court refused to review the decision. Justices Black and Douglas published a brief dissent, arguing that Isserman never had an opportunity to confront his accusers. On the same day the Court denied certiorari, it also handed down an order disbarring Isserman from practice before that tribunal.[33] But the holding revealed that the Court's division was closer than appeared in the denial of certiorari.

The prevailing Supreme Court rule required disbarment of a lawyer similarly disbarred by any state unless he could show good cause to the contrary. The justices divided evenly in Isserman's case. Vinson, Reed, Burton, and Minton held that he must be disbarred, while Black, Frankfurter, Douglas, and Jackson disagreed. Under the rules, Isserman lost for want of a majority.

Vinson's opinion ordering disbarment relied heavily on the contempt conviction and on a state's right to judge its own practitioners. Like Vanderbilt, Vinson dismissed any consideration for leniency. To Isserman's argument that the suspension in New York offered an appropriate form of punishment, Vinson coldly replied that the federal court might reconsider its judgment in the light of New Jersey's action.[34]

Justice Jackson's dissenting opinion united some very divergent forces within the Court. Unlike Black, Frankfurter, and Douglas, Jackson had no doubts as to the merits of the contempt conviction. Nor, apparently, was he troubled by the procedural aspects of the New Jersey action. But Jackson was disturbed by the harshness of both the state's and his own court's actions. There were no precedents where contempt had led to disbarment; with his conviction, sentence, and suspension, Jackson believed, Isserman already had paid a heavy price and had fulfilled the principle of deterrence—a heavy price, he noted, that was for no more than "several unplanned contumacious outbursts during a long and bitter trial." The permanent disbarment, Jackson concluded, was a "severity" which served no useful purpose.[35]

Changed circumstances quickly worked to Isserman's benefit. After the order disbarring Isserman in the Supreme Court came down, and after the death of Vinson in September, the high court changed its rule. In April 1954, the Court announced that, effective in July, it would require a majority of judges participating to disbar. Isserman's case apparently precipitated the change. On October 14, a 4–3 majority reversed the previous order and found no grounds for disbarment.[36] Thus Isserman found himself in three contradictory positions: disbarred in New Jersey, suspended in the New York federal courts, and eligible to practice before the highest court in the land.

The New York bar, however, was not quite through with Isserman. After the New Jersey disbarment in 1952, Frank Adams brought proceedings to invoke the district court rule disbarring an attorney similarly punished in any other court. Chief Judge Knox conducted hearings and filed a memorandum for disbarment. But apparently Sacher's appellate victory persuaded Knox to drop the matter. The New York bar, however, was not similarly deterred and continued its action. Hearings were reopened and, on January 27, 1958, Chief Judge John Clancy set down an order for disbarment. The Second Circuit Court of Appeals finally concluded the persecution in September 1959. Speaking for a 2–1 majority, Charles Clark, now Chief Judge, reversed Clancy and found even the two-year suspension "severe" for a man whose "derelictions seem comparatively mild." Clark noted the reality that Isserman had been under practical suspension since the end of the Foley Square trial. Enough "discriminatorily severe" punishment, he contended, had been inflicted on Isserman.[37] The decision was extraordinary since appellate courts generally concurred with lower courts' attempts to maintain discipline. Here, however, harassment was too apparent for the higher court to overlook.

Although he was permitted to practice before five federal district courts and the U.S. Supreme Court, Isserman had not done so since New Jersey's disbarment. Isserman's full rehabilitation required a change in the state court's finding. So long as Arthur Vanderbilt dominated the state's supreme court, there would be no change. But by 1961, none of the judges from the 1952 tribunal remained. And then a unanimous opinion sharply reversed Isserman's fortunes.

The New Jersey court admitted that petitions seeking reappraisal of a disbarment rarely succeeded, but added that "a showing of impressive circumstances" unknown to the judges who had rendered the verdict could alter matters. This case hardly lacked curious, not to say striking, features. The U.S. Supreme Court's overturning of Sacher's disbarment, its refusal to disbar Isserman, and the Circuit Court's reversal of Isserman's New York disbarment offered two indisputable incongruities: no other court had disbarred Isserman despite New Jersey's action, and Isserman, certainly one of the lesser offenders, was the only attorney who suffered "the extreme disciplinary sanction."[38]

The 1961 state court judges, unlike their predecessors, chose to consider the merits of the contempt conviction. They noted Medina's statement that he would have overlooked the individual incidents during the trial save for his belief that a conspiracy was involved. But since the conspiracy count had been discarded in the first court of appeal, Isserman's contempt alone did not warrant disbarment. Isserman had carried that stigma for nine years, and that, the court concluded, was "more than enough."[39]

Isserman's reinstatement by the state supreme court was not as simple and straightforward as it appeared on the surface. After Isserman filed a petition for modification of the disbarment order in May 1960, the state court referred the matter for a hearing by the Essex County Ethics Committee. The secretary of the committee was Frederick Vonhof, an old friend of Vanderbilt's, who had initiated the committee's original action in 1949. After more than a decade, he had not undergone any change of heart. Isserman's FBI file in fact indicates that Vonhof went to extraordinary lengths to find damaging information on Isserman.

In July 1960, J. Edgar Hoover received a letter in which the writer expressed great appreciation if further assistance could be given to the Ethics Committee. A few weeks later, the Newark field office reported to the Director that FBI agents had conferred with the person who had made the inquiry about Isserman. The Newark agent also informed Hoover that the same person had visited HUAC for information. Finally, Hoover's correspondent had approached the FBI "in hope of obtaining 'just that little extra' which will be of aid [words blacked out] in deciding the matter concerning Isserman." No one but Vonhof could have had such interest in Isserman at the time.[40]

The Ethics Committee held a two-day hearing in September 1960, with Isserman present. Whether the committee received "just that little extra" or not from the FBI is unknown, but it refused to alter its view of Isserman since the first inquiry in 1949. The committee's final recommendation was brief, harsh, and unyielding. It rejected Isserman's contention that disbarment was severe and pronounced his proofs of subsequent good behavior and community activity "very meager." The facts and circumstances, the committee concluded in a 6–1 vote, did not justify Isserman's reinstatement.[41]

The state supreme court nevertheless ignored the findings of the Ethics Committee and simply noted that the committee failed to find any present evidence of Isserman's unfitness. Overriding the bar's recommendation, coupled with a willingness to examine the record of the contempt conviction, represented remarkable changes from the uncritical, grinding processes a decade earlier. The charges finally ended Isserman's long ordeal and left him with the dubious distinction of being probably the first American lawyer ever disbarred for forensic conduct. A quarter century after the trial even Judge Medina was surprised by Isserman's suffering. "I did not contemplate the disciplinary proceedings," he told Isserman. But J. Edgar Hoover apparently regarded Isserman as a continuing menace, for he kept the lawyer on the Security Index List into the 1970s.[42]

V

In Michigan and California, the other lawyers' fates differed sharply from Sacher's and Isserman's. Yet their pain, costs, and turmoil were every bit as torturous. After the trial, George Crockett and Richard Gladstein returned home to resume their careers after nearly a year's absence. Their lives, like Sacher's and Isserman's, would never be the same.

Upon his return to Detroit, Crockett found some old acquaintances wary of him. But they were outnumbered by the black lawyers, substantial members of the white legal community, and prominent local labor leaders who supported him. With such allies, Crockett hastily formed the Crockett Defense Committee to raise funds for his contempt appeal, to publicize the factual background of the case, and, perhaps most important, to head off possible disbarment proceedings. As early as January 1950—three months after the contempt judgment—the committee published a defense of Crockett prepared jointly by the local National Lawyers Guild chapter and the black Wolverine Bar Association.

The pamphlet was distributed to judges and lawyers throughout the state. The bulk of it analyzed the various contempt specifications against Crockett and enlarged the context of each count by adding lengthy selections from the transcript that Medina had omitted. The report concluded that Medina had acted improperly under Rule 42, that the specifications against Crockett were relatively minor given the context of each issue and of an extremely controversial mass trial, and finally that his punishment was unduly severe.[43]

The efforts of the Michigan lawyers, of course, did not save Crockett from serving his sentence. But the early massing of support and the counterattack against Medina probably helped deflect extreme disciplinary proceedings. Following Crockett's release from prison, the Michigan State Bar Grievance Committee filed charges of unprofessional conduct against him. A hearing was held in Detroit and a deal was struck between Crockett's lawyers and the state bar prosecutors. Crockett would return to New York, apologize in open court to Medina, and in exchange would not be disbarred or suspended. At that point, Crockett believed all proceedings against him would be dropped.

Crockett traveled to New York, accompanied by his attorney and a representative of the Michigan bar. Before Medina, Crockett chose his words very carefully. He offered his "apologies" for the conduct that Medina had held contemptuous. "It was never my intention," Crockett continued, "during the course of that trial or any other time to be disrespectful or discourteous to your Honor or to the Court." He told Medina that his professional conduct always had been above criticism and that he intended to keep it so. "It is in evidence of that intention," Crockett concluded, "that I am back here today to tender my apologies to your Honor." Medina simply nodded, said that he accepted the apology, and abruptly ended the proceeding.

Much to Crockett's surprise, instead of dismissing the proceedings against him, the State Bar Grievance Committee found him guilty of professional misconduct and recommended a public reprimand. Disgusted and exhausted by this unexpected turn of events, Crockett decided to give up the fight and accept the reprimand. But he always remained convinced that the state bar had reneged on its agreement.

The bar's complaint was brought before a three-judge tribunal of the Circuit Court for Wayne County (Detroit) on November 12, 1954. Crockett filed an answer and, in an oral presentation, offered what he regarded as a plea of nolo contendere. Presiding Judge Herman Dehnke, speaking also for his colleagues, made it clear that the court was not entirely satisfied with Crockett's sincerity and repentance. The judges were particularly annoyed with Crockett's contention that the special nature of the Foley Square trial, rather than his own misconduct, was responsible for his difficulties. Nevertheless, they decided that Crockett's prior record, punishment, and subsequent apology to Medina weighted any doubts in his favor. Accordingly, the judges accepted the grievance committee's recommendations that Crockett be found guilty of professional misconduct and be publicly reprimanded. Their procedure and the tone of their remarks, however, indicate that they entertained the thought of a stiffer penalty.

Responding to Dehnke's remarks, Crockett refused to admit he was guilty of criminal contempt and again insisted that his conduct had to be judged within the context of the charged atmosphere of the trial and the public mood at the time. Recent judicial decisions, he noted, offered indications of sober second thoughts regarding harassment of lawyers. He pointed to the recent Supreme

Court rulings in favor of Sacher and Isserman, and he particularly noted the Court's action just that week in reversing a contempt citation against a District of Columbia lawyer. Finally, Crockett returned to the familiar theme that the punishment of lawyers had chilling, intimidating effects. He claimed he was literally swamped with clients who were defendants in actions linking them to Communist activities and who were unable to secure counsel. Lawyers refused to handle such cases, he said, for fear they would be associated with their clients' beliefs. And all this, he concluded, jeopardized the professional canon that no lawyer should refuse a case because of personal considerations.

Virtually ignoring Crockett's remarks, the judges proceeded to their "public reprimand"—which they likened to a loving parental rebuke. They offered a somewhat patronizing acknowledgment that Crockett, as a black man, faced special obstacles, but nevertheless asked him to "disabuse" his mind of its "mistaken and erroneous notions." Finally, they told Crockett he was able and young enough "to reach distinguished heights"; little did they realize that they were addressing a future judge and congressman.[44]

Gladstein, like Crockett, returned home to a mixed reception. But more than the other lawyers, Gladstein had a wide range of friends and admirers, particularly in the San Francisco legal community. Although essentially identified as a "labor lawyer," Gladstein had cultivated friendships that reached through all shadings of political opinion and varied practice among his colleagues. By 1949 Gladstein was perhaps the pre-eminent labor–civil liberties lawyer in the Bay Area, and he commanded the respect and admiration of judges and adversaries as well. The diversity and breadth of Gladstein's friendships were exploited in his behalf, as they similarly had been for Crockett. Sacher and Isserman largely relied on a narrow, largely like-minded circle of supporters, which proved ineffective. Gladstein's and Crockett's allies, more broadly based groups, were more helpful in their local communities in combating professional inquisitions.

Indicative of such support was the spontaneous praise Gladstein received early in 1950, shortly after his return to San Francisco, from Chief Judge Michael J. Roche of the federal district court. Gladstein was then trying a suit in Roche's courtroom when at one point during the proceedings Roche interrupted to comment on Gladstein's contempt conviction. The "misfortune in New York" was a shock to him. Gladstein, Roche observed, had always been "of extreme help to the court, courteous [and] dignified." He was at a loss to understand how any judge could send Gladstein to jail.

There was no public mention of Roche's remarks, but FBI agents in San Francisco, New York, and Washington took notice. As the news filtered through FBI channels—on its way, of course, to the Director—someone appended summaries of previous investigations of Roche. There was little to report, outside of the usual background checks, but it was noted that Roche had on several occasions expressed admiration for Hoover and the Bureau. The final recommendation was that no further inquiry be made for fear of impairing the Bureau's "present friendly relations" with Roche. Hoover knew his man and promptly agreed.[45] Roche generally was regarded as the most pro-government judge in his district; furthermore, he had recently presided over the treason trial of "Tokyo Rose." Given the FBI's special interest in that proceeding, Hoover undoubtedly held him in high regard.

Roche's statement was encouraging to Gladstein, yet there were still dangers for him to confront. While he was in prison, several efforts were launched to have him disbarred. Conservative elements within the California bar, encouraged and aided by outside groups such as the American Legion, began preparations to file charges in the fall of 1952. The most immediate danger, however, arose in Hawaii, where Gladstein had agreed to serve as defense counsel for another Smith Act case.

More than the other attorneys, Gladstein had left the New York trial disillusioned, bitter, and regretful. The nature of the defense strategy, the lack of structure and order among the lawyers, and his inability to control his clients made his future participation in such cases unlikely. The contempt penalty weighed heavily on his mind. But a number of the Hawaiian Smith Act defendants were prominent in the Longshoremen's Union and Gladstein had worked closely with them for years. "They were different people from those in New York," Gladstein later recalled, "as different as day from night." Nor were they "a little bunch of Stalinists," added Mrs. Gladstein, herself a longtime political activist.[46]

The Hawaii trial, like the one in New York, promised to be difficult. This time, however, Gladstein headed the defense team and he looked forward to the challenge. But before the trial commenced, he found himself assaulted from an unexpected quarter. J. Frank McLaughlin, one of the territory's federal judges, filed an order to show cause why Gladstein should not be disbarred in Hawaii. Although McLaughlin was not scheduled to try the Smith Act case, for reasons apparently all his own he began the action against Gladstein. McLaughlin was a militant anti-Communist with close ties to the islands' sugar and shipping interests.

McLaughlin filed his complaint on September 10, 1952, but he granted a continuance for nine months so Gladstein could proceed with the Smith Act trial. (Gladstein received notice of McLaughlin's order while in Texas serving the last days of his sentence.) The judge had asked the local bar association to initiate the proceedings, but the executive board unanimously refused on the grounds that Gladstein was not a member and that no action had been taken against him in California, New York, or the U.S. Supreme Court. The president of the bar association informed Gladstein and his lawyers that McLaughlin had little support in either the legal or the business community.[47]

On June 19, 1953, two hours after the conviction of the Hawaiian Smith Act defendants, McLaughlin called Gladstein before him and announced his determination to revive his original order. In open court the next day, he declared that Gladstein "had been living on borrowed time." By then, the state bar in California had begun an investigation to consider disciplinary proceedings against Gladstein. Two days earlier, Gladstein's lawyers tried to persuade McLaughlin to hold his action pending the outcome of events in California. McLaughlin, however, insisted that because he had acted first, the state bar should give way to his jurisdiction. He expressed annoyance, furthermore, that the California bar had refused to give him any information relative to its investigation and findings. "I can understand the secrecy," McLaughlin said, "but certainly it should not extend to a request by a court." He added rather angrily that there was something wrong with a state bar that could not trust a court. Perhaps because of his own drives in this case or because of his unpleasant dealings with the state bar, McLaughlin flatly stated he had "no confidence" in what the California bar would do.[48]

Gladstein's lawyers conferred with McLaughlin shortly after the U.S. Supreme Court had disbarred Isserman. McLaughlin believed that ruling gave him ample precedent, and he declared that any proceeding before him would be pro forma. But Isserman had petitioned for rehearing, and since the Supreme Court had not yet responded, McLaughlin was compelled to stay his own action. McLaughlin certainly stretched the Isserman analogy, for the Supreme Court had acted on the basis of New Jersey's disbarment of Isserman. No such order had been entered against Gladstein.

On June 20, after stating that Gladstein had been living "on borrowed time," McLaughlin issued a *sua sponte* order suspending the lawyer until further orders. The judge's bias and hostility were all too evident. When Gladstein's lawyers complained that there was no hearing on the merits and McLaughlin's actions could have damaging effects elsewhere, the judge snapped: "Isn't it late for him to be thinking about it now? The consequence might have been reflected on earlier by Mr. Gladstein. When he was performing in New York." McLaughlin then offered a continuance pending the outcome of Isserman's Supreme Court petition for rehearing. The delays in Isserman's case continued for sixteen months because of the changes in the Court's personnel and the backstage maneuverings for a reversal. And so matters drifted in Hawaii until October 1954. By then the Supreme Court had restored Isserman's name to its rolls and it had reversed Sacher's disbarment.

Notwithstanding the Supreme Court's decisions, McLaughlin stubbornly decided to proceed. Shortly after the Isserman decision, he suggested to Gladstein's lawyers that they might file jurisdictional objections based on Isserman's case. But Gladstein and his lawyers did more, and in November 1954 they presented an affidavit of personal bias and prejudice against McLaughlin. The affidavit complained that McLaughlin had combined the functions of complaining witness, prosecutor, judge, and jury. Furthermore, in his conferences with the lawyers and in his comments in open court, he consistently displayed hostility, bias, and prejudgment of the matter.[49]

McLaughlin, of course, refused to disqualify himself. But Gladstein's affidavit became the prime exhibit in a subsequent petition to the Court of Appeals for the Ninth Circuit, where Gladstein appealed for a writ of mandamus against McLaughlin, ordering him to refrain from further proceedings. On January 31, 1955, the Circuit Court ordered McLaughlin to "desist and refrain" and to vacate his suspension. The circuit panel, however, allowed McLaughlin an oral appearance to show cause why he should not disqualify himself. Finally, in April, the Circuit Court formally granted Gladstein's petition in an extraordinary ruling against another sitting judge.[50]

Nearly six years had passed since the turmoil of the Foley Square trial. The popular approval that accompanied Medina's contempt judgment had abated, Senator Joseph McCarthy had been censured by his colleagues, and the passions and enthusiasms for witch-hunting had cooled. The Supreme Court's reversal of Sacher's New York disbarment and its own action in restoring Isserman's right to practice in Washington offered clear signals that most believed the lawyers had suffered long enough. The Ninth Circuit judges agreed.

At the outset of Chief Judge Denman's opinion, he flatly stated that Gladstein's affidavit was "clearly sufficient" to disqualify McLaughlin. He saw no purpose in allowing McLaughlin to proceed, for the judge's prejudice was all too apparent and any hearing would "cast unjust reflection" on Gladstein and prove harmful to his future career. Any further proceedings in McLaughlin's court, Denman held, could cause Gladstein irreparable damage to his property (that is, his practice) and to his reputation.[51]

Gladstein was not the only "winner" and McLaughlin was not the only "loser" in this case. For now, nearly three years after the Supreme Court had sustained the contempt convictions, Judge Denman suggested that the matter of the lawyers' guilt in the 1949 trial was not so clear. Taking note of Justice Frankfurter's dissent and lengthy appendix in the contempt case, Denman said that "an unprejudiced judge," considering Medina's "provocative language," could hold that Gladstein should not be suspended at all.[52] The direct criticism toward Medina and the oblique questioning of the Supreme Court's approval of Medina certainly demonstrated dramatic changes in the national political climate.

The McLaughlin imbroglio, serious in itself, was played out against the far more threatening attempt to disbar Gladstein in California. Shortly before his release from prison in August 1952, Gladstein told his partner that he was anxious to resume his work. But very powerful enemies were determined to prevent him from doing so. A San Francisco American Legion post passed a resolution during the summer calling for Gladstein's disbarment. One of the San Francisco municipal judges reported that during the August meeting of the American Bar Association, she and other California judges and lawyers were criticized for their "laxity" toward Gladstein. Specifically, they were pressed as to why they had not disciplined Gladstein as New York and New Jersey had Sacher and Isserman. The judge and others insisted that Gladstein always had been respectful in their courts and believed there was no justification for bringing charges.[53]

In October, however, the Board of Governors of the State Bar of California notified Gladstein of a preliminary investigation of his conduct. Gladstein and his lawyers never determined who had brought the complaint, despite repeated attempts to find out. As it turned out, they rightly suspected that New York bar leaders influenced the California decision.[54]

Early in 1953 the state bar appointed a three-man special investigating committee to hear formal charges. James H. Farraher, a well-known Catholic, conservative corporate lawyer, headed the group. The committee first appointed Paul Dana to prepare the evidence against Gladstein. Dana, a senior partner in a San Francisco insurance defense firm, reviewed the New York transcript, and after mulling it over, rejected the assignment. According to Gladstein, Dana told him that he did not believe prosecution was warranted. In a letter to Gladstein's partner, Dana said that he had acted for reasons of his own "conscience," adding that the "independence and spirit" of the bar was our most precious possession next to the Bill of Rights.[55]

The committee then turned to another San Francisco attorney, Reginald G. Hearn. With Hearn as "prosecutor," the committee conducted a formal hearing on the charges. Hearn called no witnesses, relying instead chiefly on Medina's contempt certificate. Gladstein's defense was headed by I. M. Peckham, like Farraher a Catholic, conservative Republican San Francisco attorney. The bulk of the hearing work was handled, however, by James E. Burns, also a well-known Catholic lawyer. Backing them up for the research and preparation of briefs were Benjamin Dreyfus and Norman Leonard, one of Gladstein's partners. Hearn was outgunned. "We had the bright lawyers, we had the right approach, and we had the merits," Dreyfus later recalled. They also filed depositions in Gladstein's behalf by ten San Francisco trial judges and an amicus brief signed by 164 local lawyers, covering a wide spectrum of practices and political opinions.

Gladstein was the primary witness. Hearn took him through each of Medina's charges. Sometimes Gladstein would respond that he did not remember the particular incident; sometimes he would admit that he might have been wrong;

but usually he vigorously defended his conduct in New York without hesitating to charge Medina with provocation. It was an impressive performance and it evoked particular sympathy from Chairman Farraher.[56]

In June 1954, well over a year after his appointment, and nearly a year after the hearings concluded, Hearn completed his examination of the record and recommended that formal charges be brought to a hearing committee. In his report to Farraher, Hearn noted that the State Business and Professional Code, as well as the Canons of Ethics of the State Bar, provided for disbarment or suspension of any lawyer who disobeyed a court order. In short, the contempt conviction offered sufficient justification for further proceedings. Yet Hearn did not stop at that point, yielding instead to a desire to link Gladstein with a larger Communist conspiracy.

Hearn noted that Communist tactics operated on the maxim of divide, confuse, and conquer. The bar, he asserted, had a special duty to prevent these tactics in the courts. Gladstein was an experienced, skillful practitioner who had often represented Communists and undoubtedly was familiar with their methods. An "unbiased reader" of the New York trial transcript would find, Hearn concluded, that Gladstein's mannerisms "might be classed as having a certain parallel to the strategy of the accused." While Gladstein's behavior may have been conditioned by "several unfortunate remarks" by Medina, that excuse could not apply throughout the trial.

Hearn's statement did not respond at all to Gladstein's briefs or to the formal testimony. He offered instead the remarkable statement that the facts of the case were sufficient to warrant a decision "without the imposition thereon of legal principles." The case was a "novel" one, he claimed, and called for "some pioneering in thought" by the investigating committee. What apparently made it novel was the matter of Communist tactics, allegedly embraced by Gladstein.

Hearn hardly was original. His linkage of lawyers and Communist tactics directly descended from Tom Clark's dictum of five years earlier. Lawyers "who act like Communists and carry out Communist missions in offensives against the dignity and order of our courts," Clark wrote, "should be scrutinized by grievance committees of the bar and the courts."[57] For Hearn, both the parallel and the mandate were clear.

Gladstein's lawyers filed a bristling reply to Hearn's recommendation. What particularly upset them was Hearn's assumption that the investigation was merely what he had called a "casual and pedestrian function," designed to prepare the stage for a formal hearing body. They insisted that the investigating committee had the serious obligation to determine whether the evidence they heard could justify any charges. Hearn's failure to discuss that evidence, they maintained, was tantamount to a concession that the facts did not justify further proceedings. The lawyers then hammered at Hearn's description of the case as a "novel" one, calling for "pioneering" in thought by the committee. Hearn, they contended, had sought to establish "a new test of guilt by representation to support a disciplinary proceeding." In effect, this required lawyers to abandon representation of unpopular clients.

Returning to the evidence, Gladstein's lawyers pointed out that he had admitted his contempt in a few instances, and readily conceded that some of his statements should never have been made. But they argued that misconduct in open court did not mean that Gladstein was guilty of unprofessional conduct. No evidence demonstrated that improper motives, venality, or moral turpitude prompted Gladstein's behavior. (They cited the Supreme Court's reversal of Sacher's disbarment, dismissing both charges of conspiracy and moral turpitude.) Finally, Gladstein's lawyers noted his jail sentence and the nearly five years of uncertainty and strain since his contempt conviction as punishment enough.[58]

The uncertainty drifted on for another two years, however. In September 1956, the Board of Governors of the State Bar finally acknowledged a report from the investigating committee, ordered it filed, and resolved not to initiate further proceedings. Joyfully, Gladstein called Chairman Farraher to tell him of the outcome and thank him for his fairness. Farraher responded that he was delighted with the result and believed "that justice had prevailed."[59] After nearly seven years of ordeal, including appeals, prison, McLaughlin's summary proceeding, and charges by the bar, Gladstein's long professional siege was over.

vi

The contempt convictions and the subsequent disciplinary proceedings against the Foley Square lawyers were the leading example of repression of the legal profession during the 1950s. The incident illustrated the potential of Attorney General Tom Clark's 1946 call for action against Communist or fellow-traveling lawyers. And the long affair had ripple effects of its own.

Publications of the National Lawyers Guild, to be sure, maintained a steady drumbeat of criticism against the various overt and subtle forms of repression. But more "respectable" voices flourished in the climate of the times. The dean of the University of Michigan Law School in 1951 urged procedural "reforms" to enable the state bar association to act more effectively against subversive members of the bar. He suggested that the Code of Professional Responsibility be amended to include an obligation of loyalty to the government, that the state police be allowed to collect information on alleged subversives for disbarment proceedings, and that the state bar make use of confidential police files. The dean emphasized that he was concerned with acts of disloyalty and not with impeding free expression. But in those times, such disclaimers were meaningless. The procedural changes merely masked the obvious substantive goal of "eliminating the unfit from professional practice."[60]

Throughout this period, the American Bar Association regularly passed resolutions impugning the purpose and conduct of lawyers who represented Communists and strongly urged local disciplinary action. In 1951 the ABA recommended that local groups disbar all Communists. The next year, it instructed its Special Committee to Study Communist Tactics, Strategy, and Objectives to work with state and local groups and bring disciplinary proceedings against lawyers who had Communist affiliations or who had claimed the Fifth Amendment before investigating committees.[61]

State and local actions against such lawyers multiplied across the nation. Two Michigan attorneys were questioned by the state bar's Committee on Professional Ethics for distributing comments critical of the Rosenberg trial. Disbarment proceedings were brought against a white Mississippi lawyer who represented blacks and received fees from the Civil Rights Congress. The New Mexico bar refused an examination to an individual who had belonged to the Communist Party in the 1930s, while a California applicant was excluded because he refused to answer questions about past Party membership. A Pennsylvania lawyer was cited for contempt during a trial by the presiding judge for his refusal to answer whether he was a Communist. The contempt charge was reversed, but at the same time a local bar association disbarred the attorney. That action took ten years to reverse. One of Richard Gladstein's associates in the Hawaiian Smith Act trial publicly criticized the proceedings and the local bar subsequently suspended her for one year. A Florida attorney was disbarred for invoking the Fifth Amendment when questioned about his alleged Communist Party membership.[62]

The disciplinary hand of the bar was not always direct. In some cases, lawyers who represented Communists were punished, but not so clearly for their political beliefs or their courtroom conduct in cases involving leftist defendants. Vincent Hallinan, one of Harry Bridges' lawyers and a participant in the California Smith Act trial, was convicted of tax fraud and briefly suspended from practice. His crime, of course, could not be condoned and perhaps merited professional punishment, but it is revealing that three other California attorneys similarly found guilty were not suspended. A North Carolina lawyer who had defended local Communists was disbarred for irregularities in two divorce cases. Once again, the penalty was disproportionate to the crime.[63] The net effect nevertheless threatened, and perhaps intimidated, lawyers who represented politically suspect clients.

Following the Foley Square trial, the Justice Department resorted to an extensive use of the Smith Act and secured 126 indictments against other Party officials in the next few years. In a series of trials spread throughout the country, juries acquitted only ten of those charged. The convictions were devastating for the Communist Party, and they certainly are crucial to any explanation for the Party's virtual demise in the 1950s.

Defendants at first encountered enormous difficulties in securing counsel. For a second New York trial, over two hundred lawyers refused requests from the accused. Pennsylvania CP leader Steve Nelson defended himself after more than one hundred attorneys turned him away. By 1953, however, an ABA committee began to reverse its earlier policy and declared that all defendants, "however unpopular," were entitled to representation and recognized that such lawyers need not necessarily agree with their clients. The chairman of the Philadelphia bar's Civil Rights Committee volunteered his services for local defendants. Two years later, the county bar in Cleveland assembled a top-flight team of defense lawyers, and the jury in that trial returned the first acquittals, breaking a streak of convictions that stretched over eleven other trials. Following the Cleveland verdict, a disappointed U.S. Assistant Attorney General promptly labeled the lawyers as "communist dupes."[64]

Defending Communists and fulfilling the dictates of the legal system still involved risks—risks that had been perpetrated and magnified by the profession. The bar had been a witting and sometimes eager accomplice legitimating the government's policy of destroying organized Communist activity in the United States. That role conflicted with the profession's cherished canons, including the right to representation and a lawyer's responsibility to conduct a zealous defense of a client's interests. Such political collaboration did violence to the bar's own values and impaired some of the integrity and vitality of the legal system it served and revered.

As the nation confronted the political dissent and turmoil evoked by the civil rights struggles and the Vietnam War a decade later, there was abundant evidence that the political climate still could intimidate lawyers. Civil rights activists and blacks in the South often had to rely on northern lawyers to defend them. The divisiveness over the draft and the war in Southeast Asia resulted in numerous cases, and again fears of ostracism pervaded the legal profession. Yet something had been learned from the sordid experiences of the 1940s and 1950s: "It is always difficult to obtain counsel to defend an unpopular cause . . ."[65] So noted Circuit Judge Harold R. Medina in 1966.

7

POLITICIZING PERJURY
The Ordeal of Owen Lattimore

I think [Lattimore] is the top Soviet spy.
—SENATOR JOSEPH R. MCCARTHY

I am not and have never been a Communist, a
Soviet agent, a sympathizer, or any kind of pro-
moter of communism or Communist interests,
and all of these are nonsense.
—OWEN LATTIMORE

I hope every witness who comes here is put under
oath and his testimony is gone over with a fine-
tooth comb, and if we cannot convict some of
them for disloyal activities, perhaps we can convict them for perjury.
—SENATOR JOSEPH R. MCCARTHY

i

G REAT events often make bad history. The triumph of the Chinese Communists in 1949 generated enough outrageous interpretation to scar American society for several generations. The flow of ink in this country may have matched
the flow of blood in China. After Chiang Kai-shek was defeated, his partisans and
their American sympathizers continued the struggle on American soil. The effort
provoked a virtual civil war within the American political system, resulting in
profound political ramifications and numerous personal casualties. Sino-American
relations were frozen for over twenty years, while experts and policy makers were
sacrificed and exiled from the American government.

The persecution of Owen Lattimore was both an extension and a consequence
of the Chinese Revolution and, in some sense, the focus of the domestic strife
in the United States. Lattimore was a widely published scholar, sympathetic to
the emerging nationalist movements in East Asia. He was a sometime adviser to
the American government and to Chiang Kai-shek and a harsh critic of the

183

ineptitude and corruption of the Generalissimo's regime. Those were not enviable credentials in a time hostile to messengers of bad news.

Lattimore was much more than a messenger in the minds of some people; he was, they charged, the leading Soviet agent in the United States, who, more than anyone else, had been responsible for influencing a policy that undermined Chiang's government and promoted the interests of his Communist opponents. Senator Joseph McCarthy made that charge early in 1950. While he did not originate it, he gave it his peculiar twist. Indeed, after McCarthy suddenly divined Communist subversion in February 1950 and burst on the scene with his famous numbers game of Communist agents in the State Department, he typically offered to stake everything on his charge that Lattimore was the "top Soviet espionage agent." But Lattimore was no easy victim. He was tough, resourceful, courageous, and defended by superb legal counsel. His confrontation with McCarthy exposed the senator's shallowness, while Lattimore emerged a bit scarred but unbowed after his self-proclaimed "ordeal by slander." McCarthy continued his crusade (for a while, at least) as he cast about for other targets. McCarthy was, however, merely an expendable point man for Lattimore's embittered, vengeful, implacable enemies. More formidable adversaries eventually pursued and baited Lattimore. While they realized they could not legally prove that he was "a conscious articulate instrument" of a Soviet conspiracy, or punish him for that, they subjected him to an extensive inquisition designed to entrap him in perjury.

The renewed effort was directed largely by Senator Pat McCarran, a Nevada Democrat and a powerful baron in the Senate's feudal political structure. McCarran's contributions to the perversion of law, politics, and ideology in the period dwarf those of McCarthy. "McCarranism," not "McCarthyism," would be a more apt description for the times. Aided by formidable investigators, armed with the vast resources of Chiang's sympathizers who created the "China Lobby," McCarran commanded an insurrection against American policy makers. Like McCarthy, he too demanded Lattimore's head as his tribute. But McCarran's inquisition was far more damaging, and he was instrumental in bringing a perjury indictment against Lattimore, with ramifications that lingered long after McCarran's death. He intimidated and coerced the Department of Justice's prosecutorial staff to a point where it acted against the wishes of the President. Significantly, however, McCarran's crusade did not attract the wholehearted support of J. Edgar Hoover and the Federal Bureau of Investigation. And a few courageous federal judges ultimately denied McCarran his victim.

Lattimore's persecution nonetheless served the political purposes of willful men and women. For a generation, Lattimore and his views were repudiated and neutralized, along with those of other contemporary China experts, and the implacable hostility between the United States and the People's Republic of

China reflected that action. But Lattimore's ordeal had meaning beyond his fate or the larger issue of foreign policy, for his persecution struck at the very heart of the individual's rights to his beliefs, associations, and political expressions.

ii

Owen Lattimore was not exactly a household name when McCarthy leveled his charges against him in 1950. Over a year earlier, Congressman John F. Kennedy had criticized the pernicious advice of "the Lattimores and the [Professor John K.] Fairbanks," but the public must have been disappointed when McCarthy offered it nothing more than an obscure college professor. But for some, Lattimore was one of the most informed, perceptive Orientalists in the United States; for others, he was long suspected of being an undercover Soviet agent seeking to further Communist revolutions in Asia; and for some, such as the militantly anti-Communist columnist Joseph Alsop, he was one with "an unfortunate habit of being silly" about Asian politics.[1]

Lattimore was born in Washington, D.C., in 1900, but shortly afterward his parents took him to China, where his father worked in the Chinese education system. Lattimore did not return to the United States as a resident until 1937. When he was twelve he was sent to Switzerland and England for schooling. He returned to China in 1919 to work as a journalist and a businessman. He traveled widely, particularly to the Chinese frontier dependencies of Inner Asia, such as Manchuria, Mongolia, and Turkestan, areas that commanded his lifelong interest. He mastered the Mongol language, as well as Chinese and Russian, so as better to understand the influences at work in the region. Various fellowships enabled him to study in and write about the area throughout the 1930s. After the Japanese invasion of China in 1937, Lattimore returned to the United States and the next year assumed the directorship of the Walter Hines Page School of International Relations at Johns Hopkins University.

In July 1941, President Roosevelt recommended Lattimore to Chungking to serve as Chiang Kai-shek's "political adviser," but his duties were ill-defined. He vigorously supported Chiang, advocating an increase in American supplies to Chiang and a cutoff of war materials to Japan. Lattimore returned to China late in 1942 to work with the Office of War Information team in Chungking for a few months, and in the spring of 1944 he accompanied Vice-President Henry Wallace, who was sent by FDR to China to settle political differences with Chiang. The mission resulted in the recall of General Joseph Stilwell, although Lattimore apparently had no significant influence on the decision. His only other government service came in October 1945, when President Harry S. Truman appointed him as an adviser to the Pauley reparations mission to Japan.

Lattimore's writings in the 1930s combined his travel accounts with descriptions of the historical settings of the areas he visited and offered extensive analysis and commentary on current political conditions. For a specialized, politically sensitive audience, Lattimore regularly contributed articles to *Pacific Affairs*, which he edited from 1934 to 1941 and which was published by the Institute of Pacific Affairs (IPR). While his books such as *Desert Road to Turkestan* (1929), *Manchuria: Cradle of Conflict* (1932), *The Mongols of Manchuria* (1934), and *Inner Asian Frontiers* (1940) garnered good critical notices, they did not command a large audience. But some American diplomats respected his writings and expertise. In 1937 the American Embassy in China forwarded some of his writings to Washington, underlining his view that the Chinese Communists were nothing less than committed Marxists and that any notion they had deviated from their revolutionary goals was as foolish "as to suppose that the Soviet Union is on its way back to capitalism."[2]

Lattimore gained wider prominence with the publication of his *Solution in Asia* early in 1945. The work offered a trenchant commentary on Western imperialism and prophetically focused on the emerging nationalism throughout the Asian continent. Lattimore was an unabashed "Asia Firster," an irony totally lost on his later enemies who held similar views. "The time has come," he wrote, "to give Asiatic policy a top priority in America's relations with the world." He warned of the alluring appeal of the Soviet Union to subjugated peoples which the Soviets skillfully exploited and which matched their growing strength. Whatever our own views of Soviet "democracy," he noted, the United States had to recognize that some Asians saw it as democratic because they could "integrate themselves with it, instead of being subordinated to it as colonial subjects."

Lattimore highly praised Chiang, but he believed that the situation in China required that the United States acknowledge the legitimate aims, as well as the strength, of the Chinese Communists. Again, he had no illusions about the Communists, frankly recognizing their revolutionary aims. While he favored some coalition arrangement, he sharply, almost contemptuously, disputed the views of "China experts" and reporters who believed that Chiang was losing control. Despite his sympathetic understanding of nationalist forces and his antagonism to traditional imperialism, Lattimore offered a view of the American concept of the "open door" for China policy that would have warmed the bones of John Hay and J. P. Morgan. "We need political stability and economic prosperity in China," he wrote, "so that we can invest our capital there safely and sell our products in an expanding market."[3]

Four years later, on the eve of his public notoriety, Lattimore expanded some of his 1945 analysis which appeared remarkably prescient in the light of the revolutionary upheavals in China, Indochina, the Netherlands East Indies, Malaya, and other outposts of Western imperialism. In *The Situation in Asia*, Lattimore coolly analyzed the success of the Chinese Communists to be the result of a skillful blend of military tactics and popular political appeals. He also argued that the situation remained fluid enough so that the United States could cooperate with the emerging Chinese government in commerce and politics. The Communists, Lattimore believed, required stabilization, not continuing revolution, and the mutual interest of the American and Chinese people required the American government to cooperate in promoting stability. He dismissed as absurd the idea that Chiang's Formosa stronghold was "China."

Finally, Lattimore urged the United States to recognize nationalism as the bedrock of the Chinese political structure. If we respected that nationalism, he said, we would maintain enough influence to persuade the Chinese to incorporate features of "capitalism, private enterprise, and political democracy in their 'third country' architectural design." If we abandoned China's 450 million people to the Russians and the Communists, then, he warned, there would be more socialism in the Chinese political structure. Lattimore's advocacy of a "third force" of unaligned nations in fact was a leitmotif of the book and predictably provoked the editorial wrath and scorn of the *Daily Worker.*[4]

Lattimore's critics, however, viewed him neither as a detached observer nor as antagonistic to the Cominform. Max Eastman, a renegade Trotskyite, and John B. Powell, an American journalist who for nearly twenty-five years edited the *China Weekly Review,* a liberal magazine published in Shanghai, wrote an article in the *Reader's Digest* in June 1945 attacking Soviet sympathizers who believed that China could safely be left to Russian influence. They specifically charged that Lattimore was "perhaps the most subtle evangelist of this erroneous conception" and that his book *Solution in Asia* advocated a cheerful acceptance of "Soviet democracy" in Central Asia. More seriously, in 1946, a Washington *Times-Herald* article accused Lattimore of promoting Soviet policies and called him a longtime Stalin apologist. This attack contended that Lattimore's hostility to the Japanese imperial system and the Japanese business community, as well as his alleged criticisms of MacArthur's occupation policy, paralleled Soviet charges.[5]

More insidious and more dangerous to Lattimore was the "China Lobby," an amorphous network of Chinese and American supporters of Chiang. This group's financial angel and most outspoken publicist was Alfred Kohlberg, an importer of Chinese lace and self-proclaimed expert on Communist subversion. During a trip to China in 1934, Kohlberg became convinced of an IPR conspiracy to discredit Chiang. He developed important links to journalists such as Henry Luce and conservative columnist George E. Sokolsky and congressmen such as Representative Walter Judd of Minnesota, Senator William Knowland of California, and Joseph McCarthy. Kohlberg admitted later that he had supplied McCarthy with "documented" charges against Lattimore.

Kohlberg soon emerged as a founding member and dominant force in the

American China Policy Association, and within that group he increasingly denounced diplomats and scholars who criticized Chiang. He challenged the IPR to investigate pro-Communist influences in its ranks and on its Board of Trustees. When the latter refused to respond to his allegations, Kohlberg forced a referendum among the membership in 1947, but his proposal received only 66 votes out of over 1,200 cast. Kohlberg resigned from the IPR and continued his assault in public forums against those who had "betrayed" China and American interests.[6]

After the Red armies crossed the Yangtze and Chiang fled to Formosa in 1949, Kohlberg's appeal was increasingly attractive. Yet as the Communists consolidated their control of the mainland, American policy remained remarkably fluid and anticipated some inevitable compromise with the new rulers of China. In February 1949, General Albert C. Wedemeyer, who was Truman's liaison with Chiang and openly sympathetic to the Kuomintang regime, had recommended against further aid to Chiang's crumbling forces. Secretary of State Dean Acheson agreed and in March told his British counterpart that "the U.S. henceforth will pursue a more realistic policy respecting China." The State Department already had been preparing a "White Paper" documenting the ineptness and corruption of Chiang's government, and the inability of the American government to alter the course of events. Acheson finally persuaded Truman to release the statement in August 1949. That decision signaled an American determination to abandon Chiang, preparation for some accommodation with the Communists, and anticipation of criticism from partisan opponents and Chiang's domestic supporters.

Equally important, as early as February 1949, American policy attempted to prevent "Soviet domination of China for strategic ends." Buoyed by field reports of tensions between the Chinese Communist and Soviet leaders, the State Department hoped to encourage Mao to follow a Titoist course. Despite such provocations as the seizure of American consular and legation property, and Mao's July 1950 speech attacking the West and promising to "lean to the side" of the Soviet Union, Acheson and American policy makers persisted in seeking some means of accommodation. But Truman's reluctance to accept China's new rulers, domestic pressures, flawed communications, and the ambiguity of Chinese policy left matters in the air at the end of 1949.

Throughout the first months of 1950, Acheson continued to believe that recognition was inevitable and that it was possible to separate Peking from Moscow. He knew that Chiang was militarily finished and that Communist rule was secure. Acheson also realized that political realities dictated some drift and inertia in American policy at least until the November 1950 elections; accordingly, in January 1950, he publicly announced his willingness to "let the dust settle" before making any further formal moves.[7]

In his letter transmitting the "White Paper" to the President in the summer

of 1949, Acheson had flatly declared that the result of the civil war "was beyond
the control of the United States." Nothing the United States might have done
within its capabilities could have altered the result, and nothing it did contributed
to the outcome. The result was, he concluded, "the product of internal Chinese
forces, forces which this country tried to influence but could not."

Acheson's emphasis on the internal explanation for the Communist success
was an obvious response to early attempts to blame Communist influence and
subversion for the failure of American policy. But Acheson's public posture,
illustrated by his politically convenient statements to deflect, pre-empt, or appease potential critics, often contradicted his resolve. In the transmittal letter,
for example, Acheson charged that China's new rulers were "ideologically affiliated" with and subservient to the Soviet Union. Acheson and his colleagues
played that theme in a minor key until the Chinese intervention in the Korean
War in November 1950. The theme then emerged as the major chord the next
year when Assistant Secretary of State Dean Rusk called China a "Slavic Man-
chukuo." Acheson knew better. Within the privacy of government councils in
December 1949, he told the Joint Chiefs of Staff that "Mao was not a true
satellite in that he came to power by his own efforts and was not installed in office
by the Soviet Army."[8]

The transfer of power in China eventually revived long-standing congressional
suspicions concerning Communist subversion in the American government. Numerous congressional committees periodically charged that the government was
covering up Communist espionage and had failed effectively to prosecute the
Amerasia case of 1945. That case involved the publication of classified reports
in *Amerasia,* a left-wing periodical devoted to Far Eastern affairs. After the
appearance of a Canadian parliamentary report on Soviet espionage in North
America and the Communist coup in Czechoslovakia in early 1948, various
congressional committees in the Republican-controlled 80th Congress questioned the effectiveness of the State Department's loyalty program. Michigan
Republican Bartel J. Jonkman, who conducted a one-man investigation for the
Committee on Foreign Affairs, was satisfied that the Department had handled
the problem effectively. He assured the House that the State Department had
"swept out" all "known or reasonably suspected" subversives, Communists, and
fellow travelers. Jonkman's optimism, however, did not impress other congressmen conducting their own investigations.

In March 1948, a House subcommittee interrogated a number of administrators on the effectiveness and results of the State Department's loyalty program.
A few weeks earlier, investigators for a House Appropriations subcommittee
reported on their searches of departmental personnel files and provided the
subcommittee with dossiers of 108 alleged security risks. Chairman Karl Stefan
(Rep.-Neb.) charged that the State Department had retained too many persons

with links to Communist or liberal groups and publications. The Department's Director of the Office of Control responded that only 57—one of Senator McCarthy's later magic numbers—were still employed and that their cases had been thoroughly investigated. Stefan was not satisfied, however, and called for further action.[9]

The congressional investigations sustained an issue that would not die; yet events, rather than individuals, nurtured it. The Communist takeover of Czechoslovakia early in 1948, the Berlin blockade later in that year, the Communist triumph in China, and Soviet testing of an atomic weapon in 1949 only reinforced the growing belief that spies and subversives facilitated Communist successes. In early 1950, Alger Hiss's perjury conviction, Klaus Fuchs's espionage conviction in England, and Judith Coplon's in the United States further confirmed that belief. The search for scapegoats was an easy alternative to understanding the complexity of world events. Meanwhile, Chiang Kai-shek and his American supporters sought to influence American public opinion with their simple versions of conspiracy. Armed with the leftover dossiers of the House's 1948 investigation of the State Department, Senator Joseph McCarthy took simplicity to a new level.

McCarthy's sudden discovery of anti-Communism to bolster his political fortunes is an oft-told tale. He burst upon the national scene with a speech in Wheeling, West Virginia, to a group of Republican ladies on February 9, 1950. The Republican Party dispatched its luminaries to offer Lincoln Day speeches to the faithful; the strategists' choice of Wheeling for McCarthy perhaps was a measure of their esteem for him. McCarthy told his Wheeling audience that he had in hand "a list of 205" known Communist Party members working in the State Department. But the next day he hastily claimed he had been misquoted and now said that the 205 were "bad security risks." Moving west, backing and filling more, he said in Salt Lake City that only 57 of the 205 were "card-carrying members of the Communist Party."

After his return to Washington, McCarthy appeared on the Senate floor to elaborate his charges and offer the "evidence" demanded by some of his colleagues. On February 20, in the course of a six-hour harangue, he claimed that 81 Communist Party members had been in the State Department, although not all were still employed. When senators repeatedly challenged him for specifics, McCarthy relied on innuendo, vague associations, and long-disproven allegations, most of which came from the Stefan subcommittee hearings. When confronted with his conflicting totals, he shot back: "Let's stop this silly numbers game." Altogether, it was a scandalous performance that played havoc with the Senate's traditional stylized discourse. McCarthy proved and documented nothing, absolutely nothing. But he had his issue and his audience. His rambling, convoluted "speech," which required an artisan's patience and skill to dissect, was simply made to order for journalists who yearned for the quick, sensational headline. The senator and the reporters well provided for each other's needs.

The headlines laid the basis for McCarthy's greater triumph. On February 22 the Senate unanimously instructed its Foreign Relations Committee "to conduct a full and complete study and investigation as to whether persons who are disloyal to the United States are or have been employed by the State Department." The subject was not new; this time, however, the issue became the focus of national attention.[10]

The Senate inquiry was chaired by Millard Tydings of Maryland, chairman of the Armed Services Committee and a leader of the Democratic Party's conservative wing. Brien McMahon of Connecticut and Theodore Green of Rhode Island, party liberals who nevertheless managed to acquire significant influence in senatorial "club" politics, filled the other Democratic positions. Republicans Henry Cabot Lodge of Massachusetts and Bourke Hickenlooper of Iowa represented, respectively, their party's liberal and conservative factions. Within the committee, Lodge (when he appeared) and Hickenlooper generally deferred to McCarthy, although Lodge later filed a separate report concluding that his Wisconsin colleague's charges were unfounded. Unlike similar probes in which staff counsel and investigators dominated the proceedings, in this one the five senators participated actively and aggressively. Indeed, their own intramural conflicts and their examination of Senator McCarthy through the thirty-one days of testimony, running from March 8 to July 7, 1950, produced perhaps the most meaningful senatorial debate on McCarthy's role and purpose.

Senator McCarthy and the committee alike recognized the shopworn quality of his charges and "evidence." But rather than concede his bluff, the senator raised the stakes. In a floor speech early in March, McCarthy directed his charges to the more general proposition that the actions of American officials had led to Chiang's defeat. China, he said, had been betrayed by officials "more loyal to the ideals and designs of communism than to those of the free, God-fearing half of the world." Once again, McCarthy found a cause, but this time he joined one on the rise. He not only offered a working hypothesis for the committee, but he supplied them with an audacious formula for trapping the conspirators.

McCarthy reminded his colleagues that the government had never punished Al Capone for his well-known criminal activities, but rather had convicted him of income tax evasion. Similarly, McCarthy said, the Communists had been "too clever" and it was difficult to "get them" for their espionage activities. But the recent perjury convictions of Alger Hiss and William Remington offered a useful lesson. Accordingly, he urged that every witness's testimony be examined "with a fine-tooth comb, and if we cannot convict some of them for disloyal activities, perhaps we can convict them for perjury."[11] The Tydings committee members did not follow McCarthy's advice, but it was not lost on others.

McCarthy moved to his newfound China theme on the third day of his examination by the committee and then offered his most sensational disclosure to date. He charged that Owen Lattimore was the "principal architect" of Far Eastern policy. While he admitted Lattimore was not presently on the government's payroll, he added that Lattimore had his own desk in and "free access to the Department." McCarthy quoted selected passages from Lattimore's work, cited his associations with the IPR and the alleged Communist influences in that organization, and reiterated the Eastman-Powell and Washington *Times-Herald* charges of 1945–46. At this point, however, McCarthy largely confined himself to a "guilt by association" attack on Lattimore. Lattimore's "close collaboration and affiliation" with Communist organizations and his "friendship and close cooperation" with pro-Communists made him an "extremely bad security risk," the senator charged. But the conclusion was clear: Lattimore's "affinity for the Soviet cause" in the Far East already had done "incalculable and irreparable harm" to the nation.[12]

The following week the committee met with McCarthy in executive session. McCarthy was now convinced that his allegations against Lattimore were so substantial that the committee could not lightly dismiss them. He told his fellow senators that if they could "crack this case it will be the biggest espionage case in the history of this country." While McCarthy wrangled with his colleagues over his sources—assuring them they did not come from J. Edgar Hoover—he insisted that the FBI files would demonstrate that Lattimore was no disinterested theorist, but "definitely an espionage agent." He assured Tydings of his "sincerity" about the case, quickly adding that Lattimore was "the top of the whole ring of which Hiss was a part." "Top" was his operative word: "I think he is one of the top espionage agents." And again: "I think he is the top Russian spy." McCarthy's executive session revelations did not remain top secret for long. He himself tantalized reporters with claims that he knew the "top Russian espionage agent," and the day after his testimony, he told them, "I am willing to stand or fall on this one."

Lattimore's name inevitably leaked from the committee, and on March 26 columnist Drew Pearson broadcast a full account of McCarthy's charges. Afterward, McCarthy characteristically backed down from his more extreme remarks and retreated to his earlier position that Lattimore was "the principal architect" of Far Eastern policy and had an inordinate number of suspicious friends and activities.[13]

Owen Lattimore then was on the other side of the world in Afghanistan with a United Nations Technical Assistance Mission. After his name leaked to the press, he received a cable in Kabul from the Associated Press on March 25 asking for his reactions. "Pure moonshine," he shot back, adding that he was delighted that McCarthy had staked his whole case on him. He promised that the senator would "fall flat on his face." To another reporter, he expressed the hope that the publicity would help sales of his books.

Lattimore had no difficulty understanding the origin of McCarthy's charges, recognizing at once the hand of Alfred Kohlberg and other Kuomintang propagandists. He also realized that his independence and expertise made him an easy target of opportunity, but he confidently believed that the common sense of the American people would value just those qualities. Lattimore did not underestimate McCarthy's challenge. He acknowledged that the charges offered a "circumstantial picture of a man who might have existed." While he was not that man, Lattimore knew he had to refute the charges and he knew the trap: "People might think I was trying to defend myself against real charges."

In the meantime, in Washington, Lattimore's wife approached Abe Fortas, who with Thurman Arnold and Paul Porter had established one of the most respected and most formidable Washington law firms. Prominent subcabinet officials in the New Deal (Arnold also had been a circuit justice), these men created a successful practice, particularly representing corporate clients in their dealings with the federal government. But they also were alarmed at the climate of fear and hysteria infecting Washington and were ready to defend individuals on a *pro bono* basis. Owen Lattimore was one of their first beneficiaries.

Fortas eagerly accepted the case. After reviewing Lattimore's writings, and before his client returned to the United States, Fortas wrote to Tydings inviting committee investigators to examine Lattimore's writings and private files and allow him to respond to the charges. Arnold and Porter also signed the letter, lending their prestige to the request. A similar joint letter went to McCarthy, asking him to retract the charges and informing him of his liability for remarks made without senatorial immunity.[14]

Lattimore, accompanied by Fortas, appeared before the committee on April 6. Tydings treated the witness politely and with deference. (The senators called him "Dr. Lattimore," although he had no earned graduate degrees, and they offered him opportunities to rest during the reading of his prepared statement.) Lattimore opened with a lengthy defense of his career and a vigorous counterattack against McCarthy. He contended that the Wisconsin senator had harmed American foreign policy, instituted a reign of terror among government employees, used secret files indiscriminately, and failed to substantiate his charges. He pointed to McCarthy's inexperience in foreign policy matters and expressed amazement at how quickly the senator had become an expert on Far Eastern affairs. The professor sardonically suggested that his accuser was merely a mouthpiece for others: "the sound and fury come from the lips of McCarthy, but . . . there is an Edgar Bergen in the woodpile. And I fear that this Edgar Bergen is neither kindly nor disinterested." He later suggested that Alfred Kohlberg and Freda Utley, an ex-Communist journalist, had provided material to McCarthy and that the charges were largely a rehash of the 1947 IPR referendum issue.

Lattimore challenged McCarthy's offer to stand or fall on this case and to repeat his accusations off the Senate floor. He also suggested that McCarthy "lay his machine gun down," as he was "too reckless, careless, and irresponsible to have a license to use it." Lattimore's boldness reflected his perception of the friendly forum and his disdain for McCarthy's influence.

Turning to the larger question of Asian policy, Lattimore boldly reaffirmed his respect for the emerging nationalism on the continent. He told the senators that reconquering China and restoring Chiang to power was impossible. Instead, he urged the alternative of fostering relations with China to encourage its independence from the Soviet Union. When Senator Hickenlooper tried to pin him down as to whether he favored diplomatic relations with the Chinese, Lattimore replied that we should announce our intention to have friendly relations, and if the Chinese government refused, then they would bear the onus for conflict. He also lectured the Iowa Republican on the realities of Formosa, contending that Chiang had brutally imposed an alien government on a population that had little identity with China. Finally, Lattimore repeated one of the basic themes of his writings: Asia no longer could be controlled by foreign powers using surrogate, compliant native governments.[15]

Responding to Hickenlooper, Lattimore advocated a total withdrawal of American troops from South Korea. The professor admitted that would inevitably lead to a Communist takeover, but he thought it wise for the United States to disentangle itself from an inept and corrupt regime, just as it should have in China long before the Communist military victory. Hickenlooper did not pursue the point, apparently aware, as Tydings later pointed out, of the Republicans' vulnerability since they had overwhelmingly voted against American aid to the South Korean government a few months earlier. All this occurred two months before the North Korean invasion of the South.[16]

Lattimore's forthrightness on complex foreign policy questions impressed his audience. But national attention was riveted on the simpler problem of whether the professor was a Communist. On this issue he was equally forthright: "I was not a Communist then [1936]; I was not and have not been a Communist at any other time, and I am not a Communist now." He repeated the point on several occasions. Near the end of his testimony, Senator Tydings announced that four of the senators had talked to J. Edgar Hoover, who had shown them summaries of the FBI's files on Lattimore. They contained nothing, Tydings said, demonstrating that Lattimore was a Communist or had been engaged in espionage. "Up to this moment, at least," Tydings told Lattimore, he was completely "in the clear."[17]

When the committee resumed its public hearings two weeks later, however, new witnesses again aroused suspicion. Louis F. Budenz, the former editor of the

Daily Worker, already had established himself as a star witness against alleged Communists in a number of investigations and trials. When he appeared on April 20, the leading members of the Senate's right-wing Republican bloc, Homer Ferguson, William Knowland, Karl Mundt, Kenneth Wherry, along with McCarthy, attended the hearing. The FBI had already consumed hundreds of hours interviewing Budenz, yet he never offered any indication that Lattimore was a Communist or a spy. Now, much to the surprise of the Bureau, he offered some vague, yet sinister allegations.

Budenz's testimony centered on an alleged Communist cell within the IPR and Lattimore's participation in that group. But his contentions were all based on hearsay, such as the assertion of a Party leader who allegedly had told him to "consider" Lattimore a Communist. But finally Budenz was forced to admit: "Outside of what I was officially told by the Communist leaders, I do not know of Mr. Lattimore as a Communist." When confronted with Lattimore's opposition to Soviet policies, such as his support of Finland in 1940 and the Marshall Plan in 1947, Budenz lamely said that the Party regularly granted "exemptions" if one continued to mainly support its programs. He quickly added that he had no present knowledge of Lattimore's position.

A year prior to his testimony Budenz had published an article, "The Menace of Red China," in *Collier's.* Although he had discussed Communist influence on American policy toward China, he nowhere mentioned Lattimore's name. The committee learned that there had been a reference to Lattimore which had been deleted after discussions between Budenz and his editor. It was innocuous at best, saying simply that one pro-Communist member of the IPR had referred to Lattimore's writings "in the most complimentary manner." That incident, the hearsay character of Budenz's remarks, and the committee's discovery that Budenz had never told the FBI anything about Lattimore before McCarthy's charges, persuaded the senators that Budenz was unreliable and might have fabricated his testimony.[18]

On May 1, free-lance author and ex-Communist Freda Utley appeared to discuss her knowledge of Lattimore. Utley never accused him of being a Communist, but contended that his writing increasingly reflected Soviet policy after 1936. She called him an apologist for Stalin and said that Lattimore was a tool "in the Communist strategy for world conquest."

The committee allowed ample rebuttal of the Budenz and Utley testimony. Ex-Communist Bella Dodd, herself usually a very cooperative witness, totally dismissed Budenz's allegations, as did former Party leader Earl Browder. Finally, on May 2 and 3, Lattimore himself appeared to refute the new charges.[19]

Throughout the Tydings hearings, the FBI operated as an interested, though shadowy spectator. Hoover appeared in executive session to share his summaries of the Bureau's files on Lattimore, yet offered nothing to substantiate the charges.

Within his own domain, however, Hoover directed a massive investigative operation of Lattimore. Ever jealous of his prerogatives, Hoover reacted sharply to the McCarthy charges for fear of being pre-empted, as HUAC had done with Whittaker Chambers in 1948.

By March 1950 the Bureau had had Lattimore under investigation for over a year and, according to one internal estimate, it had devoted "approximately" 2,059 hours and 10 minutes (all of which, excepting 44 hours, was "overtime") preparing just one report to the Director. Lattimore had been followed and his phone tapped since March 1949. Hoover carefully audited the investigation at all times, sometimes chiding his agents for dilatoriness, and strongly urging that no pertinent information be withheld from the Justice Department.[20]

When Hoover summarized his files for the Tydings committee he apparently was satisfied that Lattimore was merely another left-liberal, naïve college professor. But Hoover clearly was shaken shortly afterward when McCarthy announced that Budenz would appear to testify against Lattimore. The FBI already had a substantial investment of more than 3,000 hours of interviews with Budenz. Yet Budenz had never given agents so much as a hint that Lattimore might be a Soviet espionage agent. Hoover told the Attorney General that as late as March 27, 1950, Budenz had never admitted that he personally knew the professor. Citing the Whittaker Chambers experience as a model, Hoover said that his agents had refreshed Budenz's memory by reference to specific events. Interrogators also suggested to Budenz that he had been "negligent" in not furnishing the FBI with whatever information he had. At this point, the Bureau's concern largely was defensive, fearing that it would appear incompetent if someone else—in this case, McCarthy's or Tydings' investigators—discovered information first.

In subsequent conversations with FBI agents, Budenz was contrite. He said that he had not mentioned Lattimore earlier because his information was "'flimsy' and 'not legal'" and that he had devoted most of his time to furnishing legal evidence." In the meantime, he promised he would provide the Bureau with any material before giving it to the Tydings committee. Thus, whatever the quality of the evidence, the FBI would retain its pre-eminence.

But some key FBI men raised serious doubts about Budenz's importance. L. B. Nichols, one of Hoover's closest aides, had little respect for Budenz's credibility: "It would appear that had he had information he would have volunteered it." At the same time, the New York agent in charge of refreshing Budenz's memory was not as impressed as Hoover with the results. He dismissed Budenz's explanations of his earlier failure to name Lattimore as merely "rationalization" and concluded that Budenz had failed to provide evidence "to prove the original purpose of this investigation, namely, espionage."[21] Such doubts in time spread throughout the Bureau and ultimately altered even Hoover's evaluation of the charges against Lattimore.

Early in April 1950, Hoover suddenly suggested to Attorney General J. Howard McGrath that a grand jury be convened to consider any possible espionage charges against Lattimore. Somewhat cryptically, he added that the names of the grand jury witnesses should be made public to create "a wholesome public response." In all probability, Hoover was anxious to dispel any public doubts that the FBI had failed in any way to consider the validity of the accusations against Lattimore. Nothing in the FBI files at this time suggests even the possibility that the charges were true. That fact was keenly appreciated by the Attorney General and his assistant, who promptly told Hoover his plan was "premature." They warned that a grand jury's failure to indict would be construed as a "whitewash," a political risk that the Administration wished to avoid.[22]

The Tydings committee's report on July 20, 1950—one month after the Korean War erupted and decisively altered Far Eastern policy—totally repudiated McCarthy's charges and vindicated Lattimore. Republican Senator Hickenlooper refused to sign the report, while Lodge, his fellow Republican, offered a separate statement that in no way weakened the committee's conclusions. The majority report contemptuously dismissed the Budenz and Utley testimony as hearsay and noted that the witnesses had no knowledge of Lattimore as a spy or as a Communist. Supported by remarks from former Secretaries of State Cordell Hull, James Byrnes, and George Marshall, as well as Acheson, the committee concluded that Lattimore had no role or influence in formulating Far Eastern policy, let alone having been the "principal architect" of such policy as McCarthy had contended. Indeed, the committee went to some lengths to praise Lattimore's expertise and profundity.

Finally, the report addressed the majority's primary concern—Senator McCarthy. This case, on which he had been willing to stake everything, the majority said, "vividly illustrates the danger of promiscuous and specious attacks upon private citizens and their views." In a rare departure from senatorial courtesy, the majority charged that McCarthy's "distortion" of facts had been "truly alarming."[23]

McCarthy was down but far from out. The Tydings report was virtually buried in the wake of the Korean conflict, which reinforced popular fears of a global Communist conspiracy. The aggressiveness of that design also reinforced the growing belief that American policy had been inept or, more darkly, shaped by subversive elements within the government. However discredited his original charges, McCarthy's influence increased after the spring of 1950. Congressmen found themselves increasingly vulnerable to charges that they were "soft on Communism," and many established politicians fell to the new shrill militancy. Even the veteran Tydings was defeated in the Maryland primary, after McCarthy campaigned in the state, charging that his colleague had conducted not an investigation but a "whitewash." Clearly, Tydings had been targeted, as the state was flooded with outside money and workers to defeat him. The tactics were dirty; on one occasion, the McCarthy people circulated a contrived picture of Tydings and Earl Browder seemingly engaged in intimate conversation.[24]

Owen Lattimore hastily published his memoir, *Ordeal by Slander*, recounting his encounter with McCarthy and giving a defense of his record and a sharp criticism of McCarthy's techniques. Lattimore deplored the senator's growing influence and was somewhat pessimistic about the future. Yet he thought that his "ordeal by slander" was over. In fact, it had only begun.

iii

The Korean War and the Chinese intervention in November 1950 decisively affected Sino-American relations—and Owen Lattimore. The growing hostility toward the People's Republic of China only magnified the question of who "lost" China. The relatively quiet, rational discussion of American policy that had characterized the Tydings hearings now gave way to a frantic clamor for scapegoats and a hardening of policy. Meanwhile, the Truman administration floundered amid partisan political assaults, and it alternately proved either impotent or accommodating in its responses. The primary impetus for documenting a conspiracy theory of subversion to explain the Communist takeover of China, however, came from Congress, aided and abetted by the China Lobby. In particular, Senator Pat McCarran's Internal Security Subcommittee, under the guise of investigating the Institute of Pacific Relations, gave focus to that congressional concern. The McCarran committee revived Lattimore's ordeal, and in a manner that made McCarthy's efforts appear amateurish.

McCarthy, even at his most influential moment, remained a Senate outsider. McCarran, on the other hand, epitomized the insider, with favored powerful committee positions and ideological alliances on both sides of the aisle. After his election as a Democrat in the New Deal sweep of 1932, McCarran quickly displayed two principles of action that characterized his career: a brilliant ability to manipulate the Senate's rules and unremitting opposition to the President and his own political party. When he died in 1954, the New York *Times* headline appropriately described McCarran as a "Foe of Roosevelt."

At the outset of his career, McCarran gained seats on the Appropriations and Judiciary committees, becoming chairman of Judiciary in 1951. McCarran's position as chairman of the Judiciary Committee best explains his special power in the Senate, for that committee received about 40 percent of all bills, ranging from immigration, jurisdiction, patent, and private claims to constitutional amendments and the appointments of judges, marshals, and federal attorneys. McCarran proudly noted that he was in a special position to quash any national divorce bill, a proposal at odds with his Catholic and Nevada loyalties. In the

1940s, McCarran created and ran the Senate Internal Security Subcommittee, which may have outstripped the better-known House Committee on Un-American Activities in everything but sensational headlines.

McCarran was an old hand at anti-Communist crusades. In 1946, as chairman of the Appropriations Subcommittee on the State Department, he attached the so-called McCarran Rider that gave the Department almost absolute discretion to discharge anyone suspected of disloyalty. Four years later he sponsored the Internal Security Act and secured its overwhelming passage over Truman's veto. In 1952 he co-sponsored an immigration and naturalization law which tightened quota and political requirements for new immigrants.[25]

McCarran's investigation of the IPR was authorized by Senate resolutions directing ongoing studies of the extent, nature, and effects of subversive activities in the United States. Committee investigators earlier had recovered IPR records from a Massachusetts barn, and these materials formed the basis for the hearing. As the subcommittee's investigation began on July 25, 1951, McCarran announced that it was particularly concerned with subversive influences on the nation's Far Eastern policy. In a sense, the verdict came first, as McCarran portrayed the IPR as ostensibly a respectable organization that had been infiltrated by Communists and fellow travelers. He also noted that the committee would rely heavily on the testimony of ex-Communists, who had "no illusions about the Communist Party and its purposes, and have developed antibodies against further infection."[26]

The hearings extended nearly a year, until June 1952, compiling a record of over 5,000 pages. The ideological balance of the Tydings investigation was nowhere evident in McCarran's committee, since the other three Democrats (Eastland, O'Connor, and Willis Smith) and the three Republicans (Ferguson, Jenner, and Watkins) represented the conservative wings of their parties.

In June 1951, the committee announced its intention to call Lattimore as a witness. But the summons did not come until late February 1952, when the hearings were nearly half completed. Lattimore in fact wrote to McCarran in November and December 1951 expressing his eagerness to testify and requesting a hearing date. After his appearance, beginning on February 26 and ending on March 14, Lattimore's eagerness must have worn thin, as his twelve days of testimony established a dubious record. The interrogation covered more than 800 pages, including exhibits. Once again, Abe Fortas, occasionally spelled by Thurman Arnold, accompanied the witness.

The contrast between this hearing and the Tydings investigation two years earlier is striking. The Tydings hearing was a hastily assembled affair to consider the sensational charges of one senator. The panel's attitude toward McCarthy and his charges bordered on contempt, and Lattimore was treated with courtesy and deference. In 1950, Lattimore quickly seized the initiative, counterattacked

McCarthy, and established himself as a credible, respectable, and knowledgeable authority on the Far East and American policy toward the area.

The McCarran committee's hostility erupted the moment Lattimore took the stand, and intense animosity marked the entire proceedings. On the first day Lattimore distributed a fifty-page statement to reporters. Indignant at Lattimore's attempt to steal publicity, the committee bitterly assailed him. With mock graciousness, however, the members consented to Lattimore's reading that statement—but on their terms. It took the witness three days to deliver his remarks, as he was repeatedly interrupted by cross-examination that minutely dissected his choice of words, his attitudes, and his conclusions. The committee was well prepared, having amassed documents covering events stretching back nearly twenty years. The effect was to put Lattimore on the defensive, further arousing his hostility and belligerence. Furthermore, the McCarran hearing was more carefully stage-managed by the senators, who were ably and actively assisted by their counselors, J. G. Sourwine and Robert Morris, and their research director, Benjamin Mandel, all of whom were well versed in the subject and experienced in harassing hostile witnesses. The whole affair resembled an American Inquisition.

Lattimore refused to offer passive answers to accommodate his tormentors. Instead, he unhesitantly joined the issues with barbed, angry responses that revealed his intellectual brilliance and, in McCarran's mind at least, contempt and arrogance. At one point he protested that the investigation of the IPR was designed "as a stick to beat me with." Sourwine then asked if Lattimore's ego compelled him to conclude that the committee was primarily interested in him. "Not my ego; my epidermis," Lattimore shot back. When asked whether it was a fact that Communism had made great advances in Asia following the departure of the State Department's more conservative policy makers, Lattimore agreed, but quickly added: "Of course, the advances of communism since the death of Julius Caesar have been even greater." When questioned what he meant by having "about three minutes" of conference with President Truman, Lattimore wryly said he didn't have a stopwatch with him at the time. He enraged the senators when he used a popular description of Knowland as the "Senator from Formosa." Curiously, the committee completely passed over Lattimore's tag of "the Wisconsin whimperer" for Joe McCarthy.[27]

Lattimore's interrogation was carefully planned and preceded by a number of witnesses who condemned his views and associations. A former Soviet intelligence officer claimed that he had been told by a superior in the 1930s that Lattimore was "our man" in the IPR; a prominent political scientist testified that Lattimore followed the "Communist Party line"; presidential aspirant Harold Stassen contended that Lattimore was shaping a China policy favorable to the Communists during World War II; and Karl Wittfogel, a University of Washington professor, a former Communist, and Lattimore's associate in the IPR, charged that Lattimore had published articles by a German Communist with the pseudonym of "Asiaticus," knowing they promoted Soviet views. Wittfogel also testified that Lattimore knew Chi Chao-ting, an IPR researcher, to be a Communist. Wittfogel's accusations particularly interested the committee, and they later proved to offer fruitful grounds for pursuing action against Lattimore despite his forceful denials of the allegations.[28]

The committee, however, chiefly relied on Louis Budenz's portrayal of Lattimore as an undercover Soviet agent, shaping an American policy that would assist a Communist takeover of China. When Budenz testified to the Tydings committee he was in the process of having his memory "restored" through FBI interviews, and the result was altogether unconvincing to the committee as well as the FBI. Now, in August 1951, he significantly expanded and embellished his earlier testimony to link Lattimore categorically to Communism.

Budenz described Communist infiltration of the IPR and the Soviet-line articles that appeared in its publication, *Pacific Affairs*, edited by Lattimore. Budenz again offered the comment of a highly placed Party leader "to consider [Lattimore] a Communist" when Lattimore accompanied Vice-President Wallace to China in 1944. From that, Budenz concluded that Lattimore, along with John Carter Vincent, a State Department Far East specialist, guided the Wallace mission to Communist objectives. Wallace's primary recommendation to Roosevelt involved the recall of General Stilwell, which had been demanded by Chiang. The powerful anti-Communist columnist Joseph Alsop, who had participated in that recommendation, patiently tried to explain to the committee that it had in no way served Communist purposes and that Lattimore had no part in it. But the committee found Budenz's hearsay evidence, and his gloss on it, more appealing and convincing despite Alsop's reputation and firsthand observations.[29]

The committee highly valued the testimony of ex-Communists, sinners who had found a new church. The senators were equally impressed and persuaded by professional informant Harvey Matusow. He told them that Lattimore's books were used as official Party guides on Asia. Matusow later became even more prominent when he admitted in 1955 that he was a professional liar. He then acknowledged that he had lied to the McCarran committee, and Matusow may not have underestimated his value: "My unfounded attacks on Lattimore just placed me in the role of expert of the experts. I had reached the top rung of the ladder."[30]

In time Matusow's numerous contradictory allegations aroused suspicions in the Justice Department and the FBI. Budenz, too, continued to raise doubts within the Bureau, just as he had when he first attacked Lattimore in 1950. In his McCarran testimony, Budenz stated that Lattimore "was specifically mentioned as a member of the Communist cell under instructions." Yet he never expressed such certainty throughout his numerous interviews with the FBI. When confronted by the Bureau with this discrepancy in October 1951, Budenz told agents that he considered himself free "to state what he knows to be a fact" when testifying before a congressional committee. But when furnishing information to the FBI, he felt obliged "to use more cautious language" and only to provide "information which in his opinion he can legally prove to be a fact." In other words, the committee offered immunity from any libel suits. Equally puzzling and unpersuasive was Budenz's contention that one could not be a member of a Communist cell unless he was a Party member. That presumption led him to conclude that Lattimore's pro-Soviet views in the IPR proved that he was part of the IPR's Communist cell and hence constituted "indisputable evidence" of his Party membership.[31]

Lattimore categorically refuted Budenz's testimony as nothing but lies, innuendos, and distortions. He flatly denied again that he had ever been a Communist. Repeatedly asked whether he ever received any orders, instructions, or suggestions from any Communist or pro-Communist sources, he answered: "Not that I considered to be Communist," except for his conversations with Chinese Communists for scholarly or official purposes. On being read a list of names by the committee, Lattimore denied he ever knew, or was told, that any were Communists. He denied that he ever published articles by Communists, except from Russian contributors, and that *Pacific Affairs* disseminated pro-Communist opinions. Acknowledging that some Communists may have penetrated the IPR, he nevertheless refused to admit that they had influenced the organization's policies.[32]

Lattimore's anger ultimately led him to an ironic trap. He flatly charged Budenz with perjury and demanded that the committee refer Budenz's testimony to the Justice Department. But Senator Homer Ferguson correctly pointed out that Lattimore thereby ran the risk of having his own statements scrutinized for possible perjury. That, of course, was a risk that Lattimore willingly assumed when he testified in 1952; in retrospect, it is clear that under the circumstances committee members and government prosecutors had little difficulty in deciding who had committed the perjury. Lattimore's interrogation is sprinkled with attempts to entrap him. Thurman Arnold claimed he had never seen anything "more vicious or contemptible" than the committee's treatment of Lattimore. "They are crookedly and dishonestly attempting to spring traps on him." Arnold also complained that McCarran was harassing and threatening both Fortas and himself.[33]

The McCarran committee's report in July 1952 offered few surprises. It concluded that the IPR had been controlled and exploited by the American Communist Party and the Soviet Union; furthermore, the Institute was a typical front group for Communist policies, utilizing "eminent individuals" to screen its activities. The committee named John Carter Vincent as the "principal fulcrum of IPR pressures and influences in the State Department," and charged that John Paton Davies, Jr., a longtime State Department China specialist, lied when he denied recommending that the CIA employ individuals with known Communist associations. But Owen Lattimore attracted the committee's chief concern. Since the 1930s, the report concluded, he had been "a conscious articulate instrument of the Soviet conspiracy" and, with Vincent, had influenced a policy favorable to the Chinese Communists. Further, the committee charged Lattimore with perjury on at least five separate, substantial matters relevant to the inquiry and recommended perjury indictments against Lattimore and Davies.[34]

Meanwhile, McCarran had laid other groundwork for Lattimore's indictment. Two months earlier, McCarran conducted public hearings on Truman's nomination of Federal Judge James P. McGranery as Attorney General. The senator and others repeatedly raised questions regarding rumors that McGranery intended to prevent grand jury proceedings against Lattimore. However premature, the reports of bringing charges obviously were well founded. McGranery deferentially denied any such intention, but McCarran believed that Justice Department officials were pushing McGranery to quash any action. When McCarran eventually cleared McGranery's nomination, the new Attorney General committed himself to seeking an indictment and to appoint Roy Cohn as a special assistant to handle the case. Several months later, President Truman told McGranery that he thought Lattimore had been "shamefully persecuted" and asked to be informed before any grand jury presentation. McGranery's commitment eventually proved more compelling than the President's misgivings.[35]

iv

McCarran's quest to convict Lattimore of perjury was a matter of long standing. FBI investigators and lawyers in the Department of Justice earlier had considered the possibility that Lattimore had committed perjury in his 1950 testimony before the Tydings committee. In September 1950, as part of its ongoing investigation into possible espionage by Lattimore, the FBI's Baltimore field office listed over one hundred of Lattimore's activities that merited further investigation. But its most promising lead was what the agents considered "clear evidence" that Lattimore had lied to the Tydings committee, and in April 1952 the Baltimore office urged that Hoover authorize a concerted effort to prove Lattimore's perjury. Several weeks later the Baltimore office recommended that Lattimore be put on the Security Index File, because reports that he was a Soviet agent were "accurate," although the evidence "presently" was insufficient.

Nearly a year later, however, the Bureau's analysts rejected the perjury allegations. Except that Lattimore may have lied when he denied knowing that Chinese political writer Chi Chao-ting was a Communist, a September 1951 memo completely dismissed the charges. Apparently Hoover was determined to find something, since seven months later the Baltimore office reported that it still was investigating Lattimore's associations with Chi. Finally, in May 1952, Hoover learned that twenty-seven investigative reports had failed to produce any corroborative evidence on the Lattimore-Chi connection.[36]

In June 1952, just as the McCarran committee was preparing its public report on the IPR hearings, Edward Hummer, a Justice Department lawyer and former FBI agent, prepared a lengthy memorandum analyzing the espionage and perjury allegations against Lattimore and others. Hummer dismissed all of them as insubstantial or grounded on insufficient evidence. A perjury indictment, he warned, would "invite a full acquittal and thus place Lattimore on a pedestal and make him a martyr, a role he would relish but does not deserve. It would give him the excuse to write a new book, no doubt entitled, 'Ordeal by Trial.' "

Hummer's memo subsequently developed an interesting history of its own, particularly because McCarran cited it to prove that the Justice Department was trying to protect Lattimore. Hummer's superiors consistently claimed that the memorandum involved only the Tydings hearings. But Hummer certainly was aware of the McCarran committee's pending charges, for he commented on that committee's citation of five alleged "untruths" and concluded that they "appear trivial and there is some doubt as to their materiality."[37]

Roy Cohn's appointment as a special assistant to the Attorney General early in 1952 counteracted any doubts about the Justice Department's enthusiasm for prosecuting Lattimore. Before he went on to greater notoriety with Senator McCarthy in 1954, Cohn had made a name for himself (and a reputation for ambition and aggressiveness) in 1952 when he accused the Justice Department of thwarting an investigation of Communist infiltration into the United Nations staff. Cohn then was in the U.S. Attorney's office in New York, and he claimed that his superiors in Washington discouraged his attempts to secure grand jury indictments. A congressional committee subsequently investigated his charges against his Justice Department superiors, and while the charges were not substantiated, the committee members praised Cohn for his "courageous" efforts.[38]

Cohn's first involvement with Lattimore came in May 1952, when he sought a grand jury investigation of his theory that Lattimore had been sent to Afghanistan in 1950 by pro-Soviet UN employees. The Justice Department, however, blocked Cohn. Probably McCarran knew of the incident and for that reason prevailed upon McGranery, the new Attorney General, to hire Cohn for the express purpose of drawing an indictment against Lattimore.

The FBI realized that Cohn was interested in "getting" Lattimore and knew that other Justice Department lawyers believed they had insufficient evidence to secure an indictment. Yet within two weeks the FBI learned that Hummer now had agreed that there might be two viable charges—namely, that Lattimore had lied when he denied knowing that Chi and "Asiaticus" (a pseudonym for another contributor to *Pacific Affairs*) were Communists. On September 19, Cohn submitted a 10-page memorandum to the Attorney General recommending a perjury prosecution. In the meantime, McCarran had let it be known that he would "get back at the [Justice] Department" for its delays in handling the case. The FBI reported that the senator had "blown his top" and had charged that Justice was attacking his committee's integrity. Apparently realizing the weakness of the government's case, and knowing McCarran's growing wrath, the FBI chose to maintain a low profile in the case. While Hoover certainly encouraged gathering evidence on Lattimore, he sensed the danger of fully committing himself and the Bureau to an unpromising battle.[39]

McCarran publicly pressured Attorney General McGranery in a letter released to the press on October 4, 1952, questioning the Department's delays and demanding prompt action against Lattimore. McCarran's statement merely put the finishing touches on his earlier pressure, for on October 6 Hummer offered his superiors a 56-page memorandum recommending prosecution. Yet Hummer and his superiors harbored some doubts and they offered what the FBI called "lawyer-like appraisals of the strength and weaknesses of the case." Departmental discussions continued through October and November. Charles B. Murray, head of the Criminal Division, later contended that his staff always agreed that the case should be presented to a grand jury but they recognized an obligation to appraise the jurors of the case's weaknesses.[40]

The FBI at this time was well aware of the case's shortcomings. D. M. Ladd, one of Hoover's top aides, in an analysis of the government's case, argued that six of the eight government charges of Lattimore's alleged perjury were very weak and not likely to produce either an indictment or a conviction. He rated two charges—Lattimore's knowledge of Chi and his denial that he had prepared a trip to visit Chinese Communist leaders in Yenan in 1937 (which he later admitted in testimony that he had "completely forgotten")—as "fairly good" for producing an indictment. Hoover noted that the Justice Department had not invited the Bureau's views. Yet when he received the formal announcement that the grand jury would meet on December 4, he circulated word that the Bureau should be "fully prepared."[41]

Assisted by Cohn, Hummer offered the government's case to the grand jury on December 4. Six days later the jurors unanimously voted for six counts and only one dissented on a seventh. At the last moment Cohn tried to insert an additional charge, alleging that Lattimore had lied to FBI agents. But the Bureau believed that the charge had little factual basis and furthermore feared exposure of its "technical installation"—that is, a telephone tap. Cohn was persuaded to drop the matter. Just prior to the indictment, Cohn sensed that his mission was over; he told Hummer that he would not continue with the case, as he had accepted a position with McCarran's Judiciary Committee. He actually left to work—and to achieve greater fame—with Senator McCarthy.[42]

The indictment against Lattimore descended from the general to the particular: Count 1 charged him with lying when he denied that he was sympathetic to Communists or their interests; Counts 2–7 concerned his denials that he knew certain persons were Communists, that he had published articles by known Communists, that he had met the Soviet Ambassador after July 1941, that he had handled mail for an FDR aide when he briefly had a desk in the Executive Office Building, and that he had made prior arrangements for his 1937 trip to Yenan.

In the waning days of the Truman administration, top officials in the Justice Department decided to let Eisenhower's incoming Attorney General select a prosecutor.[43] But McCarran sought to ensure that Hummer not prosecute the case. Despite departmental denials, McCarran knew that Hummer had criticized his committee's charges during the summer of 1952. Hoover characteristically ordered his aides to be "most circumspect" in their dealings with Hummer, who had been an FBI agent for ten years. Indeed, for the next few months, the record indicates that Hoover and the Bureau spent more energy on gaining distance from Hummer than in pursuing the case. Hummer eventually offered a sworn affidavit to Hoover refuting a McCarran aide's statement that Hummer had told him that the Bureau had closed its case on Lattimore.[44] But Hoover continued to distrust Hummer.

McCarran remained determined to discredit Hummer and prevent his selection as prosecutor. During the confirmation hearings in 1953 for Attorney General-designate Herbert Brownell, McCarran publicly accused Hummer of opposing the indictment and asked the nominee if such a person should prosecute the case. As if on cue, Brownell replied that he would find someone committed to "rigid enforcement" of the law, someone other than Hummer.[45]

Brownell eventually settled on a Justice Department veteran, Leo Rover. Apparently Rover was not impressed with the government's evidence when he took over in February 1953, for he repeatedly requested FBI help in developing further material. For example, he wanted FBI agents to testify regarding the Communist slant of Lattimore's writings. But Hoover aide Ladd recommended denying the request and the Director emphatically agreed. By March, with his court appearance only two months away, Rover admitted to the FBI that the lack of evidence for some charges was like having the cart before the horse. Hoover self-righteously told his staff that the Justice Department was at fault for failing to coordinate its case with the Bureau. More seriously, Hoover was concerned with the motions by Lattimore's counsel, Thurman Arnold, directing that the

FBI produce some of its reports which would have exposed the telephone taps. Meanwhile, rumors persisted that Rover had little confidence in the case.[46]

The hidden doubts within the government regarding the strength of the case were confirmed on May 2, 1953, when Federal District Judge Luther Youngdahl dismissed four of the charges and found the others so vague as to entitle the defendant to a bill of particulars. It was a stunning setback for the government.

Youngdahl had been active in the progressive wing of the Minnesota Republican Party since the 1930s. After serving six years as municipal judge in Minneapolis, he was elected county district judge in 1936. Six years later he was elected to the state supreme court. In 1946 he successfully ran for governor and he became the first to be elected to three terms. In October 1951, President Truman appointed him to the Federal District Court in the District of Columbia.[47]

Youngdahl, responding to a variety of motions by Lattimore's lawyers, Thurman Arnold and former Wyoming senator Joseph O'Mahoney, held the indictment defective because the committee's questions were not pertinent to their inquiry. First, he found that Count 1, charging Lattimore with lying when he denied that he was sympathetic to Communism, was "so nebulous and indefinite that a jury would have to indulge in speculation in order to arrive at a verdict." Juries, he said, should not decide issues on conjecture. The charge's vagueness violated the Sixth Amendment, since Lattimore could not adequately respond to questions whose nature was not clear. In addition, Youngdahl relied on First Amendment guarantees and held that the count restricted freedom of belief and expression. The charge contended that Lattimore concealed his sympathy to Communism, not that he had lied about his belief in Communism or membership in the Party. The judge found no relation to overt, potentially harmful action, and the charge effectively challenged the defendant's beliefs. As such, he said, it involved "merely a speculation into the uncertainties of the human mind."

Counts 3 and 4, involving "Asiaticus" and Lattimore's publication of articles by Communists, fell for similar reasons. Youngdahl found Count 7, regarding Lattimore's preparations for the Yenan journey, inconsistent and indefinite. Finally, he had "serious doubt" whether the remaining charges could pass the test of materiality, but held he would determine that during a trial. In the meantime, he granted the defense motion for a bill of particulars on three counts (2, 5, and 6), requiring the government to state the overt acts upon which it had based the charges.[48]

McCarran refused to comment on Youngdahl's action. But Senator Arthur V. Watkins (Rep.-Utah), a member of the subcommittee, called the judge's reasoning "faulty." Youngdahl's First Amendment concerns particularly annoyed Watkins, who thought the issue was simply whether Lattimore had lied. The Washington *Post*, meanwhile, approvingly noted Youngdahl's exposé of the case's "flimsiness" and urged the Justice Department to "think carefully" before proceeding.[49]

Following the decision, prosecutor Rover informed the FBI of his intention to appeal and urged the Bureau to "keep moving as if nothing had happened." Despite the continued study of Lattimore's writings, and comparison of them with Communist sources, Hoover recognized the difficulty of proving more than coincidence. He complained that Lattimore had a facility "for expressing a point of view without committing *himself* to the idea." It would require, Hoover observed, a politically mature judge and jury to recognize the affinity.[50] For much of the next year as the government prepared its appeal, Hoover watched his agents pursue "new" leads and evaluate reports. But aside from his continued vigilance against cooperating with Hummer, Hoover's enthusiasm and participation markedly declined.

In September 1953, Hummer circulated word that the government's appeal was a "cinch." He attempted to enlist the Bureau in gaining access to information from Chiang Kai-shek's files, but Hoover told his staff that the FBI should not "wet-nurse" Hummer. Furthermore, the Bureau had its own doubts as to the existence and reliability of such material. The FBI's effort at this time was at best desultory, and certainly it uncovered no valuable new evidence.[51]

In May 1954, Hummer relayed a rumor to the FBI that the Court of Appeals would reverse Youngdahl's opinion. He optimistically told the FBI he was preparing a trial brief and there were no further leads to investigate. His confidence was misplaced. In July the nine-man appellate court decisively affirmed Youngdahl's dismissal of Counts 1 and 7, with only one dissent. Five members of the panel, however, voted to reverse the lower court on Counts 3 and 4. Rover at first planned to appeal, but by August he decided to convene a grand jury to secure a new indictment on Count 1. Rover's enthusiasm was buoyed by a Justice Department content analysis of Lattimore's writings which claimed to demonstrate that he agreed with the Communist line 97 percent of the time. Hoover remained unimpressed, as he firmly rejected a lower-level Justice Department request that the FBI cooperate in presenting such information.[52]

In October 1954, a grand jury reindicted Lattimore on two counts of perjury. The first count charged him with lying when he told the McCarran committee he had not followed the Communist line. The indictment this time elaborated the materiality of the charge and the meaning of "follower of the Communist line" and listed Lattimore's writings and statements as proof of the charge. The second count alleged that Lattimore had promoted Communist interests and made a similar offering of materiality and proof. The new indictment, unlike the earlier one, made no mention of Lattimore's "sympathy" for Communist interests. Lattimore predictably attacked the new charges, contending that the government was anxious "to create the impression that I said a lot of things that I did not say." He pointed out that Presidents Roosevelt, Truman, and Eisenhower similarly would have been guilty of perjury if they said they never had followed the Communist line. Characteristically, he asserted his loyalty and independence. "I have never deliberately lent myself to the promotion or advancement of communism," he said, "and I have always followed the dictates of my own conscience and not the commands of any alien system." His lawyer, Thurman Arnold, described the indictment as a "ghastly absurdity."[53]

Rover dramatically tried to improve his chances for success when he filed an affidavit of prejudice with Judge Youngdahl on October 22, requesting the judge to disqualify himself. Hummer again confidently reported to the FBI that Rover had "lowered the boom" on Youngdahl and considered it "inconceivable" that the judge would remain in the case.[54] Hummer, a veritable Ministry of Misinformation, greatly underestimated Youngdahl's courage and determination.

Youngdahl ruled on Rover's motion the next day, barely masking his outrage. Rover had charged Youngdahl with "a fixed opinion" of Lattimore's innocence because of his previous ruling, but Youngdahl responded that eight of nine appellate judges had agreed with him in dismissing the vital first count and that the government had not appealed further. Following statutes and Supreme Court opinions, Youngdahl asserted that bias or prejudice must be based on something other than a judge's rulings. Since the government had offered no other proof, Youngdahl accused the government of subverting due process. He found the affidavit irresponsible, reckless, and "so patently and grossly insufficient" that he believed its purpose was to discredit or intimidate the courts, and he rejected the motion as "scandalous." Youngdahl's performance was impressive, but Hummer now predicted he would "bend over backwards" to ensure a fair trial. Rover himself was quite bitter, particularly after the Attorney General refused to allow an appeal from Youngdahl's ruling on the affidavit of prejudice.[55]

Perhaps Rover was even more bitter over his isolation. Senator McCarran, Lattimore's most determined persecutor, died on September 28, the same day that a Senate select committee voted to censure Senator McCarthy. While McCarran's death and McCarthy's disgrace did not diminish their aims, a great deal of their driving energy was never replaced. Successors such as Senators James Eastland and William Jenner, among others, offered relatively pale imitations. And with the anti-Communist issue somewhat on the wane, Youngdahl's refusal to disqualify himself caused no stir. In fact, Senator Thomas Hennings, a ranking Democratic member of the Judiciary Committee, called for an investigation of Rover's efforts. A few days later the Republican chairman of the committee, William Langer, agreed to hold hearings, though none was ever held.[56]

Defense counsel Thurman Arnold was outraged at the affidavit of prejudice. Arnold saw it as a deliberate attempt by the government to embarrass Youngdahl, and he thought that Attorney General Brownell wanted to force the judge into disqualifying himself. Arnold also saw a more devious purpose in Brownell's action. If Youngdahl refused to disqualify himself, Arnold reasoned, then the affidavit would be renewed before a higher court; but if he disqualified himself, the second judge would feel pressured not to follow the earlier ruling which allegedly had been biased. Finally, Arnold noted that the Attorney General had a subtle influence because he determined whether a judge would be promoted.[57]

As the trial neared in January 1955, Hoover occasionally ordered further investigations, but he continued to limit the FBI's cooperation. The Director's aides were reluctant to have FBI agents participate in the trial and possibly reveal some "rather delicate problems" (presumably illegal surveillance) in connection with the investigation. They also refused to prepare charts analyzing Lattimore's writings.[58] Throughout this period the Bureau's interest was minimal and it lacked any apparent confidence in the government's case.

Judge Youngdahl remained unimpressed, as he dismissed the new indictment on January 18, 1955. This time he relied only on the Sixth Amendment and the Federal Rules of Criminal Procedure, finding it unnecessary to raise First Amendment questions. Basically, Youngdahl contended that the phrase "follower of the Communist line" as used in the first count had no meaning "about which men of ordinary intellect could agree, nor one which could be used with mutual understanding by a questioner and answerer unless it were defined at the time it were sought and offered as testimony." Although the government had provided a definition in the indictment, it was not the definition given to Lattimore at the time of his testimony; furthermore, the issue was what the phrase meant to Lattimore, not to the government. Youngdahl thought that the differing views on the phrase offered an invitation for a jury to impose its own definition. When an element in an indictment was subject to such divergent interpretations, in effect the accused was not adequately informed as to the charges and able to provide for his defense. In addition, Youngdahl found that Count 2, charging promotion of Communist interests, was dependent upon Count 1, and accordingly invalid. Finally, he declared that to try the defendant on charges "so formless and obscure" would be "unprecedented" and would reduce the Sixth Amendment and the rules of criminal procedure to "a sham."[59]

Rover again was anxious to appeal Youngdahl's decision. But Justice Department opinion was divided; in particular, Solicitor General Simon Sobeloff was reportedly lukewarm to the idea. Rover remained determined to at least prosecute Lattimore on the five outstanding counts of the original indictment. The prosecutor, however, had other problems, as one of McCarran's important witnesses, Harvey Matusow, recanted his testimony. While Matusow had not appeared before the grand jury, his revelation that he had lied about Lattimore certainly lessened the credibility of the charges. Rover's superiors nevertheless authorized an appeal of Youngdahl's most recent ruling, but on June 14, 1955, the Circuit

Court of Appeals, in a 4–4 vote, affirmed Youngdahl's decision. The judges offered only a one-paragraph *per curiam* opinion.[60]

The Circuit Court opinion had a decisive effect on the Justice Department. Rover pushed hard for a Supreme Court review and for beginning a trial on the five earlier counts. But Solicitor General Sobeloff refused to appeal, and his opposition apparently convinced Attorney General Brownell. Several weeks later, the Justice Department decided not to appeal and to dismiss the remaining charges. Lattimore, though "surprised and happy," characteristically declared that the decision "should have been made a very long time ago."[61] However undramatic the conclusion, Owen Lattimore's ordeal was over.

                                    V

The techniques for repressing and punishing political enemies vary with the varieties of regimes. Although bound within a frame of a formal and customary rule of law, Henry VIII of England readily used treason charges to eliminate political foes. Since the king embodied the state, his prerogative courts regarded criticism of or opposition to the sovereign as treasonable. Joseph Stalin had the luxury of a totally arbitrary and capricious system that enabled him to dispatch his enemies to Siberia, where they simply vanished. Ironically, on the eve of Lattimore's ordeal, Stalin demonstrated that neither the persecution of old China Hands nor paranoia about Chinese policy was an exclusively American phenomenon. Just before Mao consolidated his control in 1949, Stalin exiled to Siberia the legendary Mikhail Borodin, who had failed to make the Chinese Revolution Stalin desired in the 1920s; Borodin died there two years later.

Democratic societies are not immune to political reprisals, however different the techniques. Owen Lattimore inspired a sophisticated effort to prove that he had perjured himself when he denied being sympathetic to Communist interests. Perjury, of course, had proven a useful weapon for the government to punish such alleged Soviet espionage agents as Alger Hiss and William Remington; but those prosecutions were designed to overcome statutory time limitations on substantive crimes. While there were occasional allegations that Lattimore was a Soviet espionage agent, his real crime in the minds of his accusers was that he had advocated views similar to those of the Soviet Union. Even worse, they believed that the sheer weight of his literary output proved that he had a decisive, pernicious influence on American policy makers and public opinion.[62] But even in those grim times, constitutional safeguards effectively protected a private citizen's right to express views on matters relevant to public policy.

In a typically cynical aside, Senator McCarthy offered the solution for coping with cases such as Lattimore's when he urged his colleagues to find contradictions that would justify a perjury prosecution. McCarthy had neither the power nor the stamina to press the issue in Lattimore's case. But Senator McCarran proved to be both more influential and more persistent, as his senatorial power base gave him special leverage to force the Justice Department to pursue the case. When McCarran suspected that the Department was not acting in good faith, he successfully applied enough pressure to ensure the indictment he demanded. While McCarran held their nominations hostage, two Attorneys General publicly assured him that they would vigorously prosecute the case. He forced an Attorney General to select Roy Cohn as a special assistant for the express purpose of preparing an indictment against Lattimore. Finally, he secured the removal of a prosecutor whose commitment he suspected and gained the appointment of one wholly devoted to the prosecution.

McCarran and his allies imposed a dubious case on a somewhat reluctant Justice Department hierarchy. Significantly, the senator's ideological ally, FBI Director Hoover, encountered pressures from within his bureaucracy dictating a cautious involvement in the case. While the Bureau committed enormous resources and energies to investigating Lattimore's alleged espionage and perjury, the results were meager. Hoover and his aides seemed to sense the dubiousness of the enterprise and their records reflected their unwillingness to become prominently identified with any prosecution of Lattimore.

The personal courage and the constitutional convictions of a politically independent judge largely determined Lattimore's fate. Judge Luther Youngdahl's dismissal of the indictment and his refusal to disqualify himself are eloquent testimonials to judicial independence amid the hysteria and conformity of the time. Youngdahl responded as executives and bureaucrats feared to do. Yet his very action underlined the fragility of constitutional liberty and the growing reliance upon courts to defend it. The Lattimore case all too sadly reflected that truth as other government agencies overlooked their obligations to defend basic constitutional guarantees.

Lattimore's eventual victory undoubtedly contributed to a waning of anti-Communist hysteria and the accompanying doctrine of guilt by association. Yet that victory harbored some sobering realities that tempered any celebration. Lattimore's intelligence, courage, and pugnaciousness undoubtedly made him a formidable adversary, but his defense also required expert and courageous legal counsel. Fortunately, Lattimore had the services of Abe Fortas and Thurman Arnold, who lent their services *pro bono;* otherwise Lattimore would have been reduced to the best civil liberty that money could buy. The costs of defending Lattimore have been conservatively estimated at $2.5 million—in 1950 dollars. Vigilance is not the only price of liberty.[63]

Lattimore never fully recovered his prestige and influence, and his talents were lost to future policy makers. Happily, he accepted an invitation to develop Chinese studies at the University of Leeds in England, a move which probably made both him and the architects of American Chinese and Southeast Asian policy more comfortable.

The perjury indictment vividly illustrated the ever-present potential for the abuse of governmental power, and it introduced a special dimension to the nature of loyalty. Substantive charges of espionage or even Communist Party membership were only alleged, but neither formally brought against Lattimore nor ever proven. His persecution really raised the question of punishing the nonconformist, the dissenter, and, more specifically, one whose views in any way paralleled those of Communist enemies.

"Fellow traveler" was the popular term for individuals sympathetic to Communist policies. The pejorative term implied that Communists monopolized or dominated certain ideas, which no loyal American could share. While the origins of the term are obscure, it accompanied the Popular Front activism of the 1930s when a broad spectrum of political groups, including Communists, coalesced on labor, civil rights, and foreign policy issues. The wartime alliance with the Soviet Union enlarged the potential for shared concerns. Defenders of the status quo reflexively responded with Red-baiting tactics, applying them indiscriminately to non-Communist and Communist alike.

Lattimore epitomized the fellow traveler to the McCarran committee, and this was the essence of their accusations against him. His muddled defense of Stalin's purges in the late 1930s, for example, made him vulnerable to the charge of being a Soviet agent or sympathizer. His criticisms of Western imperialism and his support for nationalist movements throughout Asia paralleled Soviet views. Of course, if one believed that such ideas could only serve Soviet aims, then Lattimore was indeed suspect. But those ideas also reflected American ideals of national self-determination, which in turn served American interests of "open door" international politics and economics. It is amusing now to find that Lattimore's typically American concern for fostering trade with China paralleled Communist Party leader Earl Browder's telling the Chinese Communists in 1945 that they must allow American businessmen to make a commercial profit.[64] To accuse Lattimore of sympathy with the Soviet Union because of such an opinion was analogous to indicting Franklin Roosevelt for supporting Lend-Lease to the Soviet Union and criticizing European colonialism in Asia, George Marshall for advocating a coalition government in China in 1946, and Republican congressmen for voting against aid to South Korea in January 1950.

Lattimore's views were those of a private citizen. Right or wrong, they were protected by traditional constitutional guarantees. He did not shout "Fire!" in a crowded theater and his writings hardly activated the Smith Act principles that prohibited teaching and advocating the overthrow of the government by force. Short of acts of treason, the American Constitution legitimated political discourse and opposition. But such protection must involve more than the freedom to advocate political views; it must include freedom from any governmental or official inquiry into their motivation and validity. If there is to be a marketplace for ideas, then free, totally unrestricted access and display are indispensable.

The official intimidation of Lattimore was pernicious. Its effect on the conduct and content of American foreign policy and, specifically, Sino-American relations was devastating. But the manner of that intimidation, resorting as it did to a disingenuous use of perjury charges, struck at the vitals of constitutional liberty and a free society. Owen Lattimore's ordeal was nothing less than a mockery of political freedom and constitutional liberty.

8

"THIS RENEGADE AMERICAN"
The Sedition Trial of John William Powell

> Proceeding in a vein which surpasses the savagery
> of Hitler Germany and Hirohito Japan in the last
> war, the American invaders, by a systematic
> spreading of smallpox, cholera, and plague germs
> over North Korea, have shocked and horrified the
> entire world.
> —JOHN WILLIAM POWELL, 1952

> All the phoney exhibits imaginable cannot give
> validity to a preposterous fraud.
> —STATE DEPARTMENT OFFICIAL, 1952

> "When I use a word," Humpty Dumpty said in
> a rather scornful tone, "it means just what I
> choose it to mean—neither more nor less."
> "The question is," said Alice, "whether you *can*
> make words mean so many different things."
> "The question is," said Humpty Dumpty,
> "which is to be master—that's all."
> —LEWIS CARROLL, *Through the Looking Glass*

i

IN May 1951, with the Korean War stalemated, the North Korean government dramatically demanded that American Generals Douglas MacArthur and Matthew Ridgway be tried as war criminals for using bacteriological warfare. Little more was heard about the subject until February 1952, when Peiping Radio (as it was then called) accused the United States of using germ warfare in North Korea. In March, the Chinese charged that American germ warfare operations had extended to Manchuria and reported the outbreak of serious epidemics. Two months later, North Korea claimed that several captured American pilots had confessed to dropping germ bombs. Inevitably, the Communists enlisted interna-

215

tional groups of lawyers, diplomats, and scientists to support their contentions.

The American government and media dismissed the reports as typical Communist propaganda ploys. The Army countered that the Chinese Communists sought to conceal their inability to cope with seasonal epidemics; the State Department said that the charges were made to divert attention from the deadlocked peace talks; and the New York *Times* reported that Chinese photographs offering proof of germ warfare were fakes. Most Americans readily discounted the charges.

Yet it was a delicate subject. The United States had never signed the Geneva Protocol of 1925 outlawing chemical and bacteriological warfare (CBW). The United States, moreover, was particularly sensitive to such charges because it had dropped the atomic bomb on Asians, thus fostering the belief in some quarters that its action had racist motives. The allegations of germ warfare in Korea and China aroused similar suspicions.

The American government boycotted the various international commissions investigating the charges, contending they were Communist fronts. But in its own way, the government sought exoneration. Following the war the government focused attention on Americans who had supported the Communist allegations. The military prepared court-martial proceedings against former prisoners of war who had confessed to germ warfare crimes, and in 1955, the House Committee on Un-American Activities threatened deportation proceedings against a naturalized citizen who had endorsed the Chinese charges.

The government's major effort, however, centered on an attempt to convict John William Powell, his wife, Sylvia, and an associate, Julian Schuman, for sedition and treason. Powell was an American journalist who owned, edited, and published the *China Monthly Review* in Shanghai. Powell had remained in China after the revolution for personal and business reasons before returning home in 1953. His magazine extensively covered the achievements of the Chinese regime, life in the New China, and the sins of Chiang Kai-shek's discredited and defeated government. Similar articles appeared throughout the Korean War, but the magazine devoted much attention to criticizing American military and diplomatic policies. From 1951 to 1953, Powell published a variety of stories detailing the Communists' germ warfare charges, including the Chinese and North Korean governments' documentation of those charges.

The American government went to extraordinary lengths to discredit Powell for his views. A congressional committee interrogated him and then lobbied hard for his prosecution. The State Department and some military officials, anxious to vindicate their refutation of the germ warfare charges, also eagerly sought to punish Powell. Powell was indicted in early 1956 for sedition, but the proceedings resulted in a mistrial nearly three years later. Despite repeated threats to retry him or indict him for treason, the government never renewed its efforts, and all charges against Powell, as well as his wife and Schuman, finally were dropped in 1961.

The government's efforts revealed two conflicting goals. Some officials demanded Powell's conviction to discredit his views of American foreign and military policies. Others sought to suppress or limit access to evidence that might have exposed policy secrets or substantiated Powell's charges. In effect, the government argued that the accused had committed sedition, but it would not allow him to defend himself by proving the truth of what he had said. The government would not produce material other than its contentions that what Powell said was untrue. Putting it another way, the government maintained that sedition consisted of repeating charges that the government denied. And beyond the particular fate of the Powells and Schuman, the government's efforts reflected a pervasive vindictiveness against anyone or any policy sympathetic to what it regarded as the outlaw regime in Peking.

ii

The character of the Cold War abruptly shifted when North Korean armies crossed the 38th parallel on June 25, 1950. The United States promptly labeled the invasion an act of naked aggression, designed and supported by the Soviet Union, while the Communist bloc insisted that it was a defensive act to thwart the bellicose designs of Syngman Rhee's South Korean government. President Harry S. Truman, responding to what he later recalled as his toughest decision, ordered General MacArthur to dispatch American troops from Japan to aid the South Koreans. Truman simultaneously called upon the United Nations to join in repelling the invasion. Taking advantage of a Soviet boycott of the Security Council, the UN supported the American request and technically assumed command, though the operation essentially was an American one.

The North Koreans swept down the peninsula in the summer of 1950, eventually pinning down American and South Korean forces in the Pusan perimeter. With a daring, brilliant counterattack, however, MacArthur launched an amphibious landing behind enemy lines at Inchon in September. Within two weeks, his armies had reclaimed Seoul and pushed the invaders back to the North. Despite Chinese warnings, the UN on October 7 authorized pursuit across the 38th parallel. At Wake Island a week later, MacArthur assured Truman that he saw little chance of Chinese intervention and predicted that North Korean resistance would end by Thanksgiving. On November 24, as MacArthur's forces reached the Yalu River that divided North Korea and Manchuria, he confidently announced a final drive to end the war. Two days later Chinese troops poured across the Yalu and sent UN forces reeling before battle lines were stabilized below the 38th parallel. After General Ridgway assumed command in the field in December, the UN forces regained the initiative and again by March were poised at the 38th parallel.[1]

The UN armies eventually recrossed the old boundary line, but largely to secure a more defensible border and to increase pressure on the North Koreans and Chinese to accept a truce. The war then settled into isolated contests for position as the peace negotiations tediously dragged on. It was in that context, in early spring 1952, that the Chinese and North Koreans charged that American forces had launched germ warfare.

The New York *Times* carried dispatches reciting the Communist charges, largely buried in accounts of the Panmunjom truce negotiations, labeling the accusations propaganda designed to improve the Reds' bargaining position. Before publishing a series of Chinese germ warfare photographs, the *Times* submitted them to the Pentagon for verification. Military authorities assured the newspaper that they were fakes and claimed that the photographs of alleged germ bombs were actually those of 500-pound leaflet bombs. The *Times* dutifully reported the denial. But the same day, the Army's Chief of the Chemical Corps told a House subcommittee that retaliatory bacteriological warfare did not require complicated weapons. "The means of delivering germs to enemy territory are simple," he said, and involved available, well-stocked equipment, "such as the containers used currently for dropping propaganda leaflets."

The Chinese meanwhile sought to mobilize international opinion by inviting delegations to view its exhibits and by releasing confessions of American pilots who had allegedly dropped germ bombs. In August, a Chinese delegation attending the International Red Cross conference in Toronto mounted an exhibit of what it called "irrefutable" evidence of photographs, photostats, and taped interviews with captured fliers. The *Times,* citing American military sources, again reported that the so-called germ bombs were nothing more than leaflet carriers and that the insect portraits were fakes. The State Department delegate to the conference refused to view the exhibit. "All the phoney exhibits imaginable cannot give validity to a preposterous fraud," he declared.[2]

The most extensive English-language airing of the charges appeared in the *China Monthly Review.* John William Powell's magazine was the successor to the *China Weekly Review,* which his father had edited since 1917 and owned after 1922. John Benjamin Powell established the *Review* in the style of the *New Republic.* He also edited an English-language daily in Shanghai and represented numerous American and British newspapers and magazines. The elder Powell actively promoted Sun Yat-sen's and Chiang Kai-shek's unification policies. By the 1930s he was an outspoken critic of Japanese militarism, and in December 1941, after the Japanese occupied Shanghai, they closed down his editorial offices and arrested him. Powell suffered terribly in prison and eventually lost both feet as a result of frostbite and gangrene. After he was repatriated in 1942, he strongly supported Chiang until his death in 1947. In a *Reader's Digest* article written with Max Eastman, Powell cited growing Soviet influence in Asia and warned that Owen Lattimore was a "subtle evangelist" of the "erroneous conception" that Soviet activities were benign.[3]

As Chiang desperately tried to impose his rule on China after the war, the *Review,* now operated by Powell's son, grew increasingly critical. John William Powell (Bill) was born in Shanghai in 1919 but was reared mainly in the United States. He spent a year in China in 1927 and again in 1941 when he worked for his father after attending journalism school at the University of Missouri. A physical deferment kept Bill from military service, but he joined the government, first with the Federal Communications Commission and then as a news editor with the Office of War Information, eventually serving in Chungking. When ill health prevented his father's return to China, Bill assumed control of the magazine. Bill also published a translation digest of the daily Chinese press.[4]

During the civil war years the *Review* featured articles on the internal struggle in China, the developing Cold War, domestic insurrections in Indochina and Malaya, and trade problems. Editorials and essays highlighted the inefficiency, cruelty, corruption, and press censorship of Chiang's Kuomintang government. Powell also harshly criticized MacArthur's Japanese occupation policies, particularly the "reverse course" which resulted in the restoration to power of conservative political and economic groups. Periodically, American activities were criticized, such as the investigations of the House Un-American Activities Committee, the affinity of some policy makers and politicians for Chiang, and the growing diplomatic intransigence of the United States vis-à-vis the Soviet Union. Nonetheless, the National City Bank, Pan American, Cal-Tex, Ford, and other American corporations regularly advertised in the magazine.

As Chiang's forces retreated, the *Review* published laudatory reports of conditions in Communist-held territories. Early in 1949, associate editor Julian Schuman ventured 120 miles from Shanghai to report that Communist rule was pleasant and efficient in contrast to the harshness of the Kuomintang. Yet late in 1948, the *Review* had editorially disparaged Communist claims that the United States was spying in their territory, and it criticized Communist press censorship in Peking. A few months earlier, it also condemned the Soviet Union for its obstruction of UN efforts to bring about a united Korea.

When the Red Army entered Shanghai in May 1949, the *Review* welcomed the new rulers with the hope that the change would "mark the beginning of a new era—an era in which the people of China can now begin to enjoy the benefits of good government." The terror of the Kuomintang's last days in Shanghai, it charged, had exposed its "essential rottenness."

In August, Powell acknowledged that subscriptions had declined significantly from their peak of 10,000 and that advertising revenue also was down dramatically. With the Kuomintang defeated and the major portion of the country liberated by the Communists, Powell believed there was less need for the *Review* and considered closing it. But encouraged by both Chinese and foreign friends, he decided to continue. He anticipated little difficulty publishing under the new regime. While he acknowledged the magazine's economic problems, he quickly added, "Politically, we're not the least bit indisposed."[5]

Powell's criticism of Chiang's Kuomintang and his sympathy for the Communist government did not go unnoticed in Washington. Ruth Shipley, the ever-vigilant Passport Office chief, refused to renew his passport in September 1949 on the grounds that Powell was a "known Red sympathizer" and that his magazine was "consistently pro-USSR and general[ly] pro-Chinese Communist." The following February, Shipley's office labeled Sylvia Powell a "Communist Propagandist" after she wrote an article for a Portland newspaper praising the new order in Shanghai and criticizing American support for the Nationalists' blockade of the harbor.

Meanwhile, State Department security officers filed critical reports on the Powells. The American Consulate in Shanghai complained that they were among a group of Americans who were "inclined to lean away from the principles and tenants [*sic*] of our Government's policies and rules" and consequently had caused the Consulate "embarrassment and considerable trouble." The reports complained that Bill Powell's editorials and articles were decidedly "Pink" and that "his arguments held a sincere tendency in that direction." One security officer thought the Powells had no further claim on American protection and suggested that the Department refuse to consider evacuating them from Shanghai.[6]

But the Powells were not about to come home. They occupied a unique, if not privileged position, as they continued to publish the *Review* long after other English-language publications suspended operations. In July 1950, Powell nevertheless decided to close his magazine because of declining revenues, which he blamed on the loss of advertising, blocked currency accounts, and the Nationalists' blockade of Shanghai. But a few weeks later he again changed his mind and announced that the *Review* would continue as a monthly. With the Korean War still raging, Powell considered it necessary to preserve the magazine as a forum to challenge the United States' "adventuristic policy" and "anti-China campaign."[7]

The revamped *Review* reflected the concerns of revolutionary China. Articles described the building of new sewer lines in Shanghai, the abolition of labor corruption, government assumption of YMCA activities, and the new relationships between foreigners and Chinese. Following the outbreak of the Korean War, and especially after the Chinese intervention in November 1950, the *Review* offered strident attacks on the American conduct of the war and its policy toward the People's Republic of China. Powell contended from the outset that the war largely had been provoked by the South Korean government's border raids.

In January 1951, Powell charged that American planes had carried out reconnaissance missions and had bombed and strafed targets in Manchuria. The following month he quoted such American sources as *Newsweek* and the Chicago *Daily News* to report that the United States was using Japanese troops in Korea. He described South Korean atrocities, in both parts of that unhappy land. The *Review* devoted much space to American prisoners of war, periodically publishing names and addresses in order to notify relatives, and in particular it noted those who had signed anti-war statements. Photo coverage portrayed American prisoners as happy, well fed, and well clothed, while contrasting pictures appeared of U.S. Marines guarding stripped North Koreans. Meanwhile, the *Review* increasingly reprinted articles from Communist sources such as the American and British editions of the *Daily Worker, Masses,* and *Mainstream.*[8]

Early in 1952, with the war stalemated and the armistice talks deadlocked, the *Review* extensively publicized the Chinese and North Korean charges of germ warfare. Labeling the American action a "crime against humanity," the *Review* called upon the American people to demand "an end to these acts of sickening barbarism which the Pentagon madmen are daily committing in their name." Among its detailed charges, the *Review* claimed that an American naval ship, masquerading as an epidemic-control ship off the east coast of North Korea, actually had an array of bacteriological installations and that the crew was testing germ weapons on Chinese and Korean prisoners.[9]

In the following months, the *Review* charged that the United States had spread smallpox in North Korea, had dropped containers of bacteria-carrying insects, and had launched artillery shells containing germ-laden flies and spiders. Accompanying photographs showed dead mice allegedly infected by rinsings from anthrax-coated feathers dropped over northeastern China. The information paralleled reports of the Chinese and North Korean governments and was supported by the findings of various international commissions and foreign reporters, some of whom worked for Communist publications. The *Review* also claimed that American POWs had been infected after U.S. planes dropped infested ants over their camp. Finally, the *Review* reported that a number of POWs had testified to their knowledge of the weapons, and an American sergeant had said that his men had been secretly inoculated against bacteriological weapons.[10]

By June 1953, the Powells finally decided they no longer could sustain their operation in the face of steady financial losses. They complained again that foreign restrictions had imposed an intolerable burden on their ability to fill overseas subscriptions. The Japanese government and British colonial authorities in Malaya had banned the magazine, while American postal officials periodically prohibited its mailing in the United States. In the farewell issue, the editors praised the achievements of the *"new* China," claiming that more progress had been made in the few years since liberation than had even been imagined during the previous thirty-two of the *Review's* existence. The four years of the new regime, they said, had been "one of the great periods of history and we feel particularly fortunate to have been able to witness it at such close range." The Powells and their two children departed Shanghai in August. Powell naïvely believed, as he later recalled, that he could market his China expertise in the United States.[11]

Powell's return inevitably aroused interest in Washington. The CIA reported that his departure from China indicated an "upcoming commie campaign based on his statements." The State Department advised the Tokyo embassy and various consulates that the Powells' passports were to be turned over to the ship's captain, who was then to deliver them to immigration authorities in San Francisco. The Department authorized steps to prevent the Powells from landing in Japan and meeting Japanese Communists. The next day, Ruth Shipley requested the owners of the *President Wilson,* on which the Powells had booked passage from Hong Kong, to direct their captain to hold the passports and prevent any landing in Japan.

The shipping executives were not so easily intimidated. They ordered the captain to take the passports only if they were turned over by American government representatives. Fearing possible legal action, they told the captain not to restrain or obstruct the Powells if they desired to land in Japan. Yet the owners understood the reach of official power, since they assumed that the Japanese would not grant landing permits. The company was spared the challenge as the American consul in Hong Kong delivered the passports to the ship's purser.[12]

On the trip home, Powell discovered an unexpected market for his expertise when the CIA pumped him for information and tried to recruit him for future work. After he landed in San Francisco, customs officials and FBI agents also pressed him for information on China. But most significantly, J. Edgar Hoover asked the FBI's Washington field office to prepare a summary report on Powell, and the Director provided his agents with an Army Intelligence memorandum on Powell.

The Army's report unequivocally labeled Powell a loyal Communist Party member. He was reported to have been in Moscow in September 1949, and upon his return to China, he was allegedly ordered to work closely with several Russians in Shanghai. Powell and the Russians supposedly had instigated a petition among American Shanghai residents urging diplomatic recognition of the Communists, and through coercion and deception, they reportedly had influenced many reporters to defame the Nationalists.

Hoover acknowledged that the Army's information had been supplied by a representative of Chiang Kai-shek's government. Although the Lattimore case had convinced the Bureau that such sources were unreliable, Hoover never questioned the charge of Powell's Communist affiliations despite evidence that discredited it. The Nationalists' information, for example, placed Powell in Japanese-occupied China throughout much of the war, where he allegedly worked for several newspapers. Powell actually had returned to China in 1942 with the Office of War Information staff in the Nationalists' Chungking capital. And according to Powell, he never visited Moscow in 1949 or at any other time.[13]

Bill Powell's lengthy absence from the United States made him oblivious to the hardened attitudes toward Communist China and the dangers of praising the Peking regime. The FBI tailed Powell as he visited friends and relatives around the country. A military or CIA agent in Hong Kong warned that Powell might become an effective propagandist for the Communist Chinese regime in view of his "superficial, plausible way of putting things." Meanwhile his baggage, including nearly two thousand books from the *Review* library, was held at the Customs Service office in San Francisco because the library contained publications and films of "a political nature."[14]

After Powell returned, he gave a lengthy interview to a Portland newspaper, favorably contrasting the life of the average Chinese under Communism with life under Chiang. Land reform, he argued, had worked, and farmers for the first time had earning power to afford such luxury goods as thermos bottles, flashlights, and bicycles. He contended that private businessmen in Shanghai supported the new government because it had overcome the ruinous inflation of the Kuomintang years. While they could not hire and fire workers at will, Powell said, they were not concerned "because they have more business than they can handle." As for American relations with Peking, Powell argued that the policy of isolating China simply had not worked. Industrialization and modernization were proceeding; meanwhile, other nations, such as England and France, had benefited from increased trade.[15]

Hoover apparently was satisfied that Powell's publications and statements warranted prosecution, and in early 1954 he recommended such action to the Justice Department's Criminal Division. Impatiently, the FBI chief prodded his superiors for a quick decision. Warren Olney, Assistant Attorney General for the Criminal Division, did not, however, reply until April. Olney's staff agreed that Powell's articles were "replete with half-truths, distortions and shadings of the truth, statements which are lifted out of context and adapted to the propaganda purposes of the Review, and others which are rank absurdities." But Olney also noted the heart of the problem: Powell's statements offered no basis for prosecution because of the impossibility of demonstrating their falsity. He admitted to Hoover that it was difficult to distinguish between facts and opinions in the articles.

Olney nevertheless authorized an investigation of Powell's statements that an alleged epidemic-control ship, commanded by General Crawford F. Sams, operating off the Korean coast, had been fitted with bacteriological installations to test germ warfare weapons on Chinese and Korean prisoners. Olney also requested the FBI to ascertain whether General Omar Bradley had testified to Congress in January 1952 that the United States had a "spectacular" plan to end the war, as Powell had reported some months later. With some prescience, Olney also asked Hoover whether any material on these subjects could be made public in the event of a trial.[16]

The FBI quickly gained access to the so-called "Sams Report" of March 1951, in which General Sams described how he had led a landing party in the Wonsan area of North Korea to check reports of bubonic plague among Chinese and Korean soldiers. FBI investigators were told that Sams probably could testify to this fact, but because his report contained "related intelligence information" and other facts about the operation, the Navy Department had to consider carefully whether he could testify in court. As for the Bradley statement, the FBI found no witnesses who could recall it.

Several weeks after the FBI learned of the "Sams Report," it encountered the difficulty of securing military cooperation for any criminal proceeding. The Navy Department briefing officer who divulged the report said that he could not testify without clearance from his superiors. Since Sams had acted as an army officer, army channels would also have to be checked.[17]

Nearly two years later, in 1956, the FBI encountered further military secrecy and resistance when it attempted to probe Powell's contention that Japanese bacteriological warfare units had conducted tests on American prisoners in Manchuria during World War II. In an April 1952 article in his magazine, Powell had charged that the United States had suppressed information that it was currently employing Japanese BW officers, who had been involved in the wartime experiments. A Defense Department official admitted to FBI agents in March 1956 that the experiments had occurred, but declared that the findings were not introduced in the Tokyo war crimes trials because they were irrelevant to the cases presented and because it was feared that public disclosure would seriously prejudice the occupying forces.[18]

Recently released documents, however, reveal that the information was not acknowledged because the United States had a "primary interest" in the Japanese officers. General Charles Willoughby, MacArthur's intelligence chief, had noted in 1947 numerous Russian attempts to question and try the Japanese officers, but American officials had been "warned not to let the Russians in on this." And in 1956, the Defense Department seemed to believe even more keenly in keeping the matter secret. The FBI investigators were told that the story involved "classified technical information" and was regarded as "highly sensitive." There was little hope that any of the data could be made public in a criminal trial.[19]

The government's interest in Powell developed an added dimension in September 1954, when he was summoned to testify before the Senate Internal Security Subcommittee, chaired by the Indiana Republican William Jenner. The subcommittee had long been the fiefdom of Senator Pat McCarran and just two years earlier it had completed a lengthy probe of American policy toward China during the civil war years. McCarran, it will be recalled, almost single-handedly forced the prosecution of Owen Lattimore. Jenner, like McCarran, had an affinity for the Chiang regime, and under his leadership the subcommittee conducted numerous investigations of alleged subversives. McCarran no doubt was pleased by the decision to interrogate Powell. But he was on a speaking tour on September 27 when Powell testified, and never had a chance to pursue the matter, for he died suddenly the next day.

Jenner's investigation operated under a broad mandate to expose what he called "interlocking subversion in government departments." He was not interested, he said, in scrutinizing participants in the "Communist world conspiracy" as individuals, maintaining rather that they were parts of a pattern that needed exposure. He acknowledged his predecessor's work in revealing the wartime conspiracy in Washington and China, a conspiracy, Jenner said, that included Owen Lattimore, John S. Service, John Paton Davies, Jr., John Carter Vincent, and John K. Fairbank. After the war, they were replaced, Jenner added, by those who formed "a little cluster in Shanghai," centered in the *China Weekly Review*, where they served and furthered Communist aims. Jenner was particularly interested in the *Review* and in those who had returned home to raise the "Red China banner at every opportunity."

All that pointed to an introduction of Powell. But first the committee arranged to hear witnesses who allegedly had been adversely affected by Powell or his articles. Mrs. Dolores Gill testified that Powell had written to her in January 1951 assuring her of her husband's good treatment as a prisoner of war. Powell had told her that the Chinese treated POWs "with the greatest leniency and fairness in order to win over their support." Mrs. Gill also reported that she had heard from various pro-Communist sources that her husband was well. Nearly two years after Powell's letter, however, she learned from her husband's fellow prisoners that he had died of malnutrition and dysentery; to Jenner's chagrin, she offered no evidence that her husband had died before Powell wrote his letter. The next witness was an army physician held captive for thirty-three months. He testified that the *Review* was extensively used for "forced indoctrination" and that his captors emphasized Powell's germ warfare articles. Other POWs had similar stories.[20]

Once called, Powell invoked the Fifth Amendment over fifty times, refusing to reveal whether he was a Communist, his knowledge of certain persons, or what articles he had written since his return. He acknowledged that his wife was employed but he refused to say in what capacity. He frankly discussed the finances of the *Review* while declining to acknowledge that he had fought efforts of the Post Office to bar the magazine from the mails. He refused to discuss his letter to Mrs. Gill but freely admitted publishing the names and addresses of American POWs. The committee raised no questions regarding either the content or the validity of Powell's writings that at the same time so concerned the Justice Department. The articles, however, were entered on the record, and several former POWs who followed Powell to the stand claimed they had been forced to read them.

The day after his appearance Powell appeared at the National Press Club. He flatly denied that he was or ever had been a Communist, but added that he would not tell that to the Jenner committee because the "whole hearing was an entrapment procedure." He also distributed a statement protesting the American embargo on trade with China, which he claimed the committee would not let him read at the hearing.

Jenner was outraged. In a prepared statement, he charged that Powell—"this renegade American"—was in the United States "to soften up the American people, as he tried to soften up our fighting men, so we will agree to trade with the Soviet bloc and keep quiet if Red China is admitted to the UN." Jenner thought it "time to end this folly" and announced that he had asked the Attorney General to press treason charges against Powell.[21]

The subcommittee revived its hearings in San Francisco in December, with Senator Herman Welker (Rep.-Idaho) conducting the proceedings. The purpose apparently was to give the committee another opportunity to expose Powell, who, Welker complained, had been spreading "vicious propaganda" around the country. Powell, technically still under subpoena, did not appear when Welker called him. Sylvia Powell testified, but after offering some background information on her life before she went to China, she invoked the Fifth Amendment to every other question. Finally, an exasperated Welker offered her an opportunity to "repent" for her "defection." Mrs. Powell declined the offer.

Welker then recalled Mrs. Gill, who repeated her agonizing account concerning her husband's imprisonment. Welker, of course, was interested in Powell's letter assuring her of Lieutenant Gill's good health, as well as the propaganda clippings she received from the *Review* and pro-Communist publications. Ex-POWs again testified that they were forced to read the *Review,* that they knew nothing of germ warfare, and that prison camp conditions, contrary to Powell's reports, were brutal. An army physician testified that he was with Lieutenant Gill at the time of Powell's letter and that Gill was starving and already had dysentery, which eventually caused his death. He angrily charged that Powell "was a maker of propaganda. He didn't just go along with it; he made it, he manufactured the stuff."

The San Francisco testimony buttressed the committee's foregone conclusions. Welker charged that Powell's articles were designed for indoctrination and had to be read by POWs on pain of punishment; they related false information on prison conditions, American atrocities, germ warfare, and casualties; they consistently supported North Korean and Chinese policies and opposed those of the American government; they promoted Communist-front organizations internationally and within the United States; and by publishing prisoner lists the *Review* encouraged Americans to consult Communist propaganda publications for news of loved ones—"a dastardly plot indeed," Welker noted.

Welker again urged the Justice Department to act against Powell. He complained that Powell was still free to lecture around the country and to criticize the government, while taking the Fifth Amendment before Congress. If such behavior were condoned by the Justice Department, the senator lamented, then "it is a dark, a sad day for our Republic and freedom-loving people everywhere."[22]

When Powell failed to appear at the San Francisco hearing, the committee accused him of hiding. But a few weeks later Powell showed up at a public forum in Palo Alto to advocate recognition of China and the resumption of trade. He also repeated his germ warfare charges, contending that he had seen some of the evidence examined by international commissions that supported the allegations. He claimed to have been in areas where plague, cholera, and smallpox had been eradicated but in which new cases had suddenly erupted. The committee was particularly annoyed when Powell made such statements because in his Washington press conference Powell had denied he had actually seen evidence of germ warfare. In its January 1955 report the committee concluded that Powell had propagated false information against the United States and that his magazine was controlled and supported by the Chinese government.[23]

Following the San Francisco testimony, Jenner submitted the transcript to the Justice Department and pressed harder for a treason prosecution. Assistant Attorney General William F. Tompkins informed Jenner that Powell had been under investigation for some time, but that the available evidence was insufficient to gain a treason indictment because of the strict evidentiary requirement providing for two witnesses to the same overt act. Tompkins nevertheless assured Jenner that the Department's ongoing investigation would seek to develop proof of treason or the violation of other federal statutes. A month later, Tompkins informed J. Edgar Hoover that Powell's magazine articles were under intensive study for possible violation of the sedition statutes.[24]

The investigation of Powell and his wife was now expanded to include their China associate, Julian Schuman. Schuman had been a free-lance journalist in

China from 1947 to 1953, providing dispatches to the Chicago *Sun-Times,* the
Denver *Post,* and the American Broadcasting Company, among others. For
much of the period, he worked closely with Powell, writing numerous articles and
serving as an associate editor of the *Review.* When he left China in December
1953, he was probably the last American reporter to depart.

Schuman's interest in China developed from his wartime participation in the
Army's language-training program. He studied Chinese language and civilization
at Harvard, but the Army used him to decipher code messages in English and
never sent him to China. Schuman later continued his studies at Yale under the
G.I. Bill. Failing to land a journalistic assignment, he left for China on his own
in 1947.

Schuman first worked for the *China Press* in Shanghai, an English-language
newspaper owned by one of Chiang Kai-shek's closest associates, H. A. Kung. A
rewrite man, he also wrote articles which he peddled to American sources. He
started working for Powell and the *Review* early in 1949 and stayed with the
magazine until it closed four years later. After he returned home in December
1953, two FBI agents questioned him at length and indicated to him he was
suspect for having remained in China. The FBI kept him under surveillance for
some time. When Schuman appeared before the Senate Subcommittee on Internal Security in March 1956, he discovered that his questioners had a detailed list
of the people and places he visited after his return. Schuman's congressional
testimony largely summarized his Chinese studies and his employment record in
China. Although he responded to most questions, he steadfastly refused to discuss
his political affiliations.[25]

In September 1955, Hoover complained that the Justice Department was
"delinquent" in its handling of the Powell matter. William Tompkins, head of
the Internal Security Division, replied to Hoover with a "top secret" memo
informing him that the Attorney General had been advised on August 11 that
there was insufficient evidence for a treason indictment and that "novel legal
questions" cast doubt on the feasibility of a sedition prosecution.

Tompkins spelled out the problems a few weeks later. The sedition statutes
applied only to activities carried out within the United States or its admiralty and
maritime jurisdiction. Accordingly, the government would have to proceed on the
theory that sending the magazine from China to the United States conveyed the
allegedly seditious statements within the meaning and limitation of the statute.
Tompkins requested Hoover's aid in identifying American subscribers and determining whether there was a U.S. distributor. Beyond that, the Justice Department still had to prove the falsity of Powell's writings.

Tompkins complained that the "noxious" articles were "couched in such
phraseology as to render them impervious to charges of falsity." The BW articles
he thought were the most vulnerable. For example, Tompkins cited statements

from Powell's April 1952 article, entitled "Germ Warfare: A Sign of U.S. Desperation in Korea":

> Since VJ Day, Japanese war criminals, turned into "experts," have been working for the Americans in developing bacteriological warfare. . . .
>
> Since January 28 [1952], the Americans have unleashed B-W on a scale much larger than any previous period in Korea. From that date, throughout February, and into March, US planes have regularly dropped special paper and cardboard containers filled with various types of flies, fleas, ticks, spiders, mosquitoes, ants and other bacteria-carrying insects. . . .
>
> On February 26, on the Imjin River front, northwest of Inchun, artillery of the US 3rd Division laid down a smokescreen and afterwards fired six shells carrying germ-laden insects—flies and spiders. . . .

Tompkins urged that the FBI determine what evidence would be available for use in a criminal trial to disprove such statements. Finally, Tompkins informed Hoover that current law only required the government to disprove the truth of Powell's writings and not that they actually affected American military operations or aided foreign enemies.[26]

iii

The history of sedition prosecutions in the United States reflects periods of social turmoil and demands for political conformity. The short and unhappy life of the Sedition Act of 1798 offered a classic response to potential foreign threats and domestic subversion as the possibility of war with France and the spread of revolutionary doctrines within the nation alarmed the ruling Federalists. The Sedition Act was ostensibly aimed at persons forming an unlawful conspiracy with an intent to oppose the lawful measures of government or who counseled insurrection, riot, or unlawful assembly. In fact, it was aimed at Jeffersonian editors and proscribed writing, printing, or uttering any false, scandalous, and malicious criticisms against the government, Congress, or the President with an intent to defame or bring them into disrepute. Conviction for violation of the law carried a maximum penalty of two thousand dollars' fine and two years' imprisonment.

The act expired on March 3, 1801. But during the three years of its existence, the government launched a series of prosecutions before sympathetic federal judges who defined intent in terms of a supposed "bad tendency." The Jeffersonian opposition denounced the measure as unconstitutional and, undoubtedly, popular indignation against the law contributed to the Federalists' defeat in 1800. Despite that election, despite the demise of the law, despite Jefferson's subsequent pardons of offenders, and despite congressional repayment of the fines levied, there was no decisive constitutional repudiation of sedition legislation. Perhaps most Americans disapproved of such repression, but that consensus flourished in a climate largely free from foreign threats and domestic discord.[27]

The Civil War inevitably provoked enactment of a new sedition law. The statute of July 31, 1861, was aimed at conspiracies within the states or territories designed to oppose by force lawful measures of government. This law remained on the books and was incorporated in the 1909 criminal code revision. One significant change extended jurisdiction to any place subject to the jurisdiction of the United States.[28]

Deep domestic divisions during World War I and fears of Bolshevism resulted in new sedition statutes. Encouraged by President Woodrow Wilson, Congress enacted a series of stern laws designed to prevent any threats to the successful prosecution of the war. In the Espionage Act of 1917, Congress made it unlawful to convey false reports that tended to interfere with military operations. The law also struck at persons willfully causing or attempting to cause insubordination, disloyalty, mutiny, or the refusal of military duty. Subsequent amendments in May 1918 enlarged the categories of seditious language to include any speech or publication intended to cause contempt, scorn, or disrepute of the form of government, the Constitution, the flag, or the military, and penalized any words or acts supporting an enemy cause or opposing the military cause of the United States. Conviction carried a fine of $10,000, a twenty-year prison term, or both.[29]

The Supreme Court lent its imprimatur to the constitutionality of sedition legislation. In a series of cases, the Justices invoked various doctrines, ranging from Oliver Wendell Holmes's presumably liberal test of "clear and present danger" to a more predominant view of "bad tendency," reminiscent of Federalist rulings in the 1790s. The net effect served to legitimate sedition prosecutions as part of the government's arsenal to combat dissent. After the war, some of the legislation was quietly repealed, but the basic laws of sedition remained intact.[30] New amendments were adopted in the 1940s and made applicable to national emergencies as well as to wartime. In its enlarged, updated form, the Espionage Act of 1917 became the less glamorously labeled Section 2388 of Title 18 of the United States Code.

The first prosecution for sedition during World War II involved a government financial analyst, Elmer Hartzel, who wrote a series of mimeographed tracts that scurrilously attacked the President, Jews, and our alliance with England. He called for abandoning the Allies and for a race war at home. Hartzel mailed his articles to high-ranking military officers and to various trade associations and service organizations which had persons registered under the Selective Service Act of 1940. Hartzel frankly contended that he hoped to divert white Americans from the war effort and unite them against internal racial enemies in the hope of combating Communism. By a narrow majority, the Supreme Court overturned

Hartzel's conviction, holding that his writings did not demonstrate a willful intent to cause insubordination, disloyalty, mutiny, or a refusal to serve in the armed forces. Furthermore, Hartzel's opinions, while "vicious and unreasonable," were not in themselves proof of an intent to violate the law.[31]

The sedition laws were applied in at least seven other reported cases during the 1940s. The most prominent involved the indictment and conviction of William Pelley, leader of the neo-Nazi Silver Shirts. Pelley was convicted for publishing articles which argued that Germany and Japan were powerful and their policies morally justifiable; that the United States and Great Britain were weak and morally corrupt; that President Roosevelt and Prime Minister Churchill were reprehensible; and that the United States was menaced by a conspiracy of Communist, Jewish plutocrats.[32]

iv

Despite the unrest and turmoil of the Cold War era, sedition prosecutions seemed out of fashion. But on April 25, 1956, a grand jury in San Francisco returned thirteen counts of sedition under Section 2388 against Powell, his wife, and Schuman. The indictment marked the first time the government invoked a 1953 statute terming the Korean "police action" a war.

The indictment charged the defendants with falsely accusing the United States of aggression in Asia, of having used germ warfare in Korea and China, of having stalled the truce negotiations, and of having underestimated American casualties. The articles were designed, the government maintained, to interfere with American military operations and to promote the success of American enemies. All this was tied to the government's contention that the accused had conspired to convey to the American public news of the war that they "knew was false and untrue." Ten counts applied to Powell alone, including the basic ones of publishing false reports on germ warfare, atrocities, casualties, the treatment of American POWs, and American peace efforts.

Besides the specific incidents of military news reported by the Powells and Schuman, the indictment cited articles in the *China Monthly Review* contending that the United States was corrupt, its policies reprehensible, its military policy aggressive, and that Chiang Kai-shek was an American pawn while the North Korean and Chinese people were "peace-loving, honest, and just." Such statements, the government contended, were designed to encourage military insubordination and obstruct military recruitment.

The indictment's clear implication was that the United States government could require an uncritical acceptance of its policies. True, the American media had regularly published enemy charges that the United States had initiated aggression, engaged in germ warfare, and obstructed the truce negotiations. But such claims were either buried or discredited—"balanced" might be the euphemism—by appropriate American government denials. Powell, however, published them as rendered, indicating his *opinion* that they were valid. To a large extent, the indictment challenged Powell's right to that opinion.

Finally, the indictment was so framed as to place trial jurors in a delicate position. The defendants' statements were either unfamiliar or implausible to most Americans. To acquit the Powells and Schuman required jurors to believe the accused and that the United States had actually engaged in germ warfare. Apparently the government was so sensitive on this issue that it produced General Sams as a witness before the grand jury to refute Powell's report that Sams had tested germ weapons on Korean and Chinese prisoners.[33]

The indictment was a culmination of the political assault on Powell the government had conducted since his return. He was depicted, as Senator Jenner had described him, as a "renegade American" who had sought to embarrass and discredit his government's policies. The catalogue of charges virtually paralleled those leveled in the Senate Internal Security Subcommittee's report of a year earlier. The indictment in effect legitimated what essentially was a political judgment.

The charges raised historical as well as emotional issues. The defense basically had three options: it could demonstrate the absence of evil intent; or it could demonstrate the absence of damage—that is, that the remarks in question presented no clear and present danger; or it could demonstrate the truth of the defendants' remarks. Given the context, the defendants chose to counter the indictment by seeking to prove the truth of Powell's words. Their quandary was, however, that the government controlled both the evidence and access to it. Paradoxically, that situation ultimately proved equally troublesome for the government.

From the outset the defendants maintained that they would have to obtain vital evidence from the People's Republics of China and North Korea. But the State Department had not issued passports valid for travel to China since May 1952 and for North Korea since October 1955. One month after they entered not guilty pleas in September 1956, the Powells and Schuman obtained a district court order for the taking of depositions in China. Shortly afterward, the Chinese government announced that fifty persons were prepared to testify in behalf of the defendants. The government, however, objected to taking the depositions in Peking on the ground that its counsel could not have access to the mainland. Federal Judge Louis Goodman then ordered that the depositions be taken in Hong Kong. A. L. Wirin, one of the Powells' lawyers, however, informed the court in late December that the Chinese witnesses could not travel to Hong Kong, a circumstance that would require him to visit the mainland.

There was the rub: the procedure entailed taking depositions in China, yet the

State Department refused to validate passports for travel. The Chinese well understood the stakes. Originally, they had said that Wirin could enter without a passport, but then reversed themselves, obviously forcing a dilemma on the American government. But in March 1957 Judge Goodman declared he had no jurisdiction to order the State Department to issue a passport. Five months later Wirin requested an order asking the Chinese government to furnish judicial assistance to determine the availability of prospective witnesses. The Chinese again used the opportunity to make a policy point when they responded that such a request could not be honored without a prior agreement between the American and Chinese governments. The U.S. Attorney in San Francisco complained that the Chinese move was a subterfuge "to embarrass the United States and force recognition." Finally, in October 1957, Wirin filed for a dismissal, contending that the government's refusal to validate his passport deprived the defendants of an adequate opportunity to prepare their defense.

Judge Goodman agreed that China and Korea were the most likely sources for evidence. He found impressive Wirin's list of more than one hundred prospective witnesses who could offer evidence to counter the specific charges that the defendants had falsely characterized the American war effort, truce negotiations, war casualties, and the use of germ warfare. He also agreed that these people could not be interviewed by a foreign representative and that a proper defense required a lawyer familiar with American procedures and rules of evidence.

Judge Goodman's dilemma was clear. He acknowledged that he neither could nor would question the wisdom of American policy on travel to China; yet could he allow that policy to inhibit the constitutional rights of the defendants? Whatever the dictates of foreign policy, Goodman ruled, they could not infringe the defendants' rights. The choice was the government's: if it adhered to its policy of forbidding travel, then it would have to discontinue the prosecution. Three weeks later the State Department reluctantly agreed to issue Wirin a passport for China and North Korea without restrictions. John Foster Dulles adamantly insisted that the decision in no way affected the general policy of forbidding travel to those countries.[34]

The judge's action in the case exasperated the Passport Office. Its restrictive policies denying passports for political reasons, already under increased judicial scrutiny, would be sharply restricted by the Supreme Court the following year. Even while contending that it merely was enforcing presidential and departmental policy on travel restrictions, the Passport Office staff repeatedly urged its superiors and the Justice Department to resist Goodman's orders. One high-ranking official went so far as to favor dropping the prosecution rather than establish "another precedent that any . . . Judge can countermand the decisions of the President . . . and the Secretary of State." But higher authorities in the State Department believed that it was more important to try the Powell case than to maintain passport purity for China. The Passport Office meanwhile enlisted FBI cooperation to investigate the possibility that Wirin had perjured himself when he denied present or past membership in the Communist Party.[35]

Wirin entered China on January 7, 1958, and left at the end of February. He interviewed fifty witnesses, some of whom claimed they saw American planes drop containers of insects, while others were prepared to testify that the insects carried fatal diseases. But Wirin reported that no witnesses would appear at a trial unless the United States and China negotiated a judicial assistance agreement. The State Department emphatically told Wirin that it would not discuss the matter with the Chinese. Just before the scheduled opening of the trial on July 14, 1958, Wirin appeared before Judge Goodman to move for dismissal on the grounds that the witnesses could not appear because of the hostility between the two nations. Goodman denied the motion, and the Circuit Court of Appeals for the Ninth Circuit refused to issue a writ of mandamus directing a dismissal.[36]

As part of the truth defense, Powell's lawyers secured subpoenas to the Departments of State and Defense, the CIA, the National Security Agency, and various congressional committees, as well as to Generals Omar Bradley, Matthew Ridgway, and Mark Clark. The orders directed that documents be produced relating to American aggression, germ warfare, and the conduct of truce negotiations. The Justice Department soon learned that most of these materials were highly classified and could not be released under any circumstances. Yet failure to produce them might lead to a dismissal of the charges.

The Justice Department's communications to the CIA illustrated the government's dilemma. When the defense requested CIA documents relating to its support of Nationalist Chinese troops in Burma during the Korean War, the CIA advised the Justice Department that such records were classified and could not be brought to court.

Justice Department officials decided to attack the subpoenas on grounds of relevancy. They advised the court that the government would not offer proof concerning the matters of aggression and of stalling the truce negotiations. They asked the court for a motion to quash those parts of the subpoena, but anticipated that the defense lawyers would oppose such a motion in order to force the government to assert broad claims of privilege and thereby invite dismissal of the indictment.

Government investigators and prosecutors eventually decided to focus on the bacteriological warfare charges. Again they encountered the problem of classified documents. The Army worried that testimony of its officers and possible cross-examination might lead into classified material. The Army informed the Justice Department that at one point in the Korean War the Commander in Chief in the Far East asked the Defense Department when biological warfare weapons would be available. Naturally, the Army refused to declassify this information and it feared the materials might be elicited during a trial. Military officials suggested that the government stipulate that the United States had the capability to conduct biological and chemical warfare, but that such weapons had never been sent to the Far East. Finally, the Justice Department expressed concern that the defense would call Chinese witnesses and demand that the classified "Sams Report" be produced.[37]

Army officers were in a bind. While top officials had acknowledged that the trial could have propaganda value to unfriendly nations, that consideration was outweighed by a more compelling need to "terminate these pernicious falsehoods . . . once and for all." Yet various sections of the Army were concerned about the necessity for maintaining secrecy on the Army's BW capability. They also worried that the defense would "confuse the true facts" and twist them for propaganda purposes, a conclusion apparently based on rumors that the Powells' lawyer was a Communist Party member and that the northern California Communist Party had contributed $12,000 to the defense. Just two months before the trial opened, Defense Department representatives believed that dropping the case would be preferable from a foreign policy standpoint. The State Department sharply disagreed.[38]

The question of how much, and exactly which, material relating to germ warfare could safely be revealed vexed military censors. The Army finally agreed to the stipulation that it had such capability, but that only "defensive" BW weapons had been sent to the Far East. General Omar Bradley was prepared to testify that BW would have been employed only for retaliatory reasons and at the President's specific direction.

The "Sams Report" was most troublesome. The available portions of the report reveal that Sams had planned forcibly to enter a North Korean hospital, inject morphine in an unwilling patient who allegedly suffered from bubonic plague, and kidnap him for a physical examination. No provisions were made for returning the patient or for his subsequent welfare. Although Sams apparently did not carry out his plan, the Army preferred not to disclose that he conspired to do so, for it constituted a violation of the Geneva Rules of Land Warfare. Quite simply, the United States had planned and encouraged what would have been a war crime and then had rewarded the instigator with a medal rather than punish him. The propaganda ramifications were obvious. Besides, Army censors argued, if the "Sams Report" was withheld, the government would not have to acknowledge publicly that such actions had in fact been contemplated or occurred. They recognized that the defense might draw certain inferences if the material was withheld, but without official acknowledgment, such interpretations would appear to be typical "propaganda slams of a Communist enemy" and the United States could appear to be the injured party. The Army tentatively agreed to a sanitized version of the "Sams Report," deleting the names of agents and the plans for abducting an enemy patient. The prosecutors, however, doubted that such a version would be acceptable to the court and made contingency plans to avoid invoking the Sams affair altogether.[39]

The attempt to suppress the "Sams Report" was ironic. Seven years earlier, shortly after the general's mission, the military eagerly publicized his exploits. After a calculated leak appeared in *Newsweek* in April 1951, *Collier's* published an article the following September bearing unmistakable signs of official sanction. It portrayed Sams as a courageous military doctor who conducted a daring commando raid to determine if bubonic plague had spread among the North Korean populace. If the account was accurate, it unintentionally depicted Sams as an incompetent doctor. He reportedly determined that the disease was hemorrhagic smallpox and therefore UN troops need not be inoculated—all this on the basis of secondhand information, since Sams allegedly never examined enemy soldiers or civilians. The story was released at the time to counter Communist claims that Sams and a navy "epidemic-control ship" lying off the North Korean coast were testing BW weapons. Sams received the Distinguished Service Cross; the citation praised him for obtaining "conclusive information of such significance as to affect the immediate conduct of the United Nations armed effort in Korea." The article and the citation, of course, were for public consumption; yet seven years later, the Army steadfastly refused to declassify the relevant documents. Sams's mission undoubtedly involved more than the military cared to reveal.

Irony aside, the affair highlighted the government's dubious attempt to punish Powell for opinions that deviated from the official line yet differed little from those of other journalists. Nearly a year before Powell discussed Sams's mission, *Newsweek* reported that a "Navy Epidemic Control Laboratory ship" actually was a cover for landing parties to "kidnap Chinese Reds" to test them for bubonic plague. The magazine obviously was satisfied with that version. Powell's sources, however, led him to the conclusion that the "masquerading" ship was used for "testing germ weapons" on North Korean and Chinese prisoners.[40] What, then, was at stake, sedition or the government's control of information?

v

Three years after the indictment was returned against the Powells and Schuman, and after several postponements, Judge Louis Goodman finally ordered the trial set for January 1959. It promised to be a lengthy affair, with the government prepared to offer witnesses and testimony that the defense was equally prepared to challenge on jurisdictional and procedural grounds. Similarly, the defense strategy was designed to force the government to reveal more than it desired. Each side, in short, hoped to demonstrate its own particular perception and concern for "truth."

Before the trial opened, the government carefully sought to limit the issues and evidence. On January 9 the government moved to dismiss the count charging Powell with having made false statements about the truce negotiations. The government also moved to quash subpoenas requesting evidence relating to the alleged American aggression in Korea and elsewhere in Asia, as well as the alleged American use of Japanese war criminals to develop bacteriological weapons. Assistant U.S. Attorney James B. Schnake informed the court that the government would offer no evidence on these issues. The government, he said, was seeking "simply to control the proof in this case and submit the case to the jury in a certain limited fashion—that is, controlling the evidence."

Schnake was particularly concerned with the subpoenas directed to the Defense Department regarding chemical and bacteriological warfare. He offered the court the Army's stipulation that it had the capability for CBW, but that except for tear gas no such weapons had been shipped to the Far East. Since none had been transported, no records existed of any such movement, Schnake said. The defense request for documents relating to the development, production, and manufacture of BW weapons was therefore no longer necessary. Schnake insisted that such documents were not relevant to the indictment which related to the use of such weapons in Korea. The defense demand amounted to a "fishing expedition" that threatened military security, Schnake charged. Defense lawyer Doris Walker heatedly responded that she was not willing to allow the government to define the boundaries of proof for the defense.

Judge Goodman agreed to quash the subpoenas. He expressed concern that the government would have to haul "freight cars" of documents that might not be at all relevant to the case and that he would have "to look through dozens of freight cars" to determine what was material. While he concluded that such an effort was unnecessary, he warned the government that he would order it to produce any documents relevant to the defendants' rights or material to the charges—and "if they don't produce [them] under those circumstances there is appropriate relief."[41]

The prospect of a sensational trial on the issue of germ warfare and procedural rulings was suddenly aborted when Goodman declared a mistrial after three days of testimony. The trial opened on January 26. Following U.S. Attorney Robert Schnacke's opening statement, Walker unsuccessfully moved to dismiss the indictment on the grounds that the United States was not technically at war and that the prosecutor had argued beyond the indictment. The next day, Charles Garry, substituting for Wirin, who had had a heart attack, told the jury that the defense planned to rest its case both on the truth of the defendants' writings and on First Amendment grounds. For the next day and a half, the government introduced witnesses who testified to Powell's special relationship with the Communist government in Shanghai and the mailing of his magazine's subscriptions to the United States.

On January 29, Schnacke read into the record numerous *Review* articles dealing with POW statements on germ warfare. He then called Private Page Baylor, a POW for thirty-three months. When Baylor was asked whether he ever saw the *Review* distributed in the camps, Walker objected because the question raised issues outside the scope of the sedition laws. Goodman dismissed the jury at that point to hear arguments on the objection. Despite a lengthy plea from Schnacke, the judge firmly held such testimony inadmissible because the sedition laws covered actions only within the jurisdiction of the United States.[42]

In an exchange with the judge, Schnacke mistakenly referred to the evidence as having established "actual guilt of treason." Judge Goodman picked up on the word "treason" and pointed out that Baylor's testimony probably would be valid under a treason indictment since treason law was not subject to jurisdictional limitations. And then, in an apparently innocent manner, Goodman noted that the "evidence so far presented in this case would be prima facie—I am not ruling on what a jury would do—would be prima facie sufficient to sustain a verdict of guilty under the treason statute." A few minutes later, Goodman repeated the substance of his statement, emphasizing that the evidence already introduced in the trial "would be prima facie sufficient to support and sustain" a guilty verdict under the treason law. The context of Goodman's remarks indicates that he raised the treason issue to demonstrate how the government's case was applicable under one statute and not another.[43]

The Oakland *Tribune*, an afternoon daily, promptly reported Goodman's remarks with a sensational headline: "Judge Says Powells, Aide Guilty of Treason." Another area newspaper headed its article with: "Powell Flayed by Trial Judge." The news reports, however, accurately quoted Goodman's remarks.

The next morning the defense lawyers promptly moved for a mistrial on the grounds of prejudicial publicity. Prosecutor Schnacke replied that in the interest of a fair trial he had no objection to the motion. Goodman, obviously furious, was anxious to establish that the newspaper statements, and not his own, were the basis for the motion. Walker circumspectly stated that her motion related only to the newspaper accounts. Goodman insisted that he had not passed any judgment on the defendants and declared it "inconceivable" that he had said the defendants were guilty of treason. If the court had, he continued, then it "must have been out of its mind at the time" or it was guilty of some "inadvertence" which would have required the judge himself to move the mistrial. But he went on to flay the newspapers, accusing them of doing "their best to thwart the just administration of justice."

In his chambers, Goodman lectured reporters on their responsibilities and again defended himself. He insisted that his discussion of treason was only "academic" and designed to explain the jurisdictional problems of the sedition indictment and to point out that Schnacke's reference to treason was inappropriate because the defendants were not charged with treason. Goodman further defended his action in a formal opinion a week later.[44]

The government, however, was not through with the Powells and Schuman. After Goodman declared a mistrial, Schnacke immediately filed a complaint of treason against the defendants and asked that they be held without bail, as treason was a capital offense. Garry quickly objected, contending that there had been no prima facie showing of treason and that the government had not offered two witnesses to any overt act. Goodman agreed, noting that the evidence in the case had long been known to the government, thus suggesting that if the government really had a treason case, it should have sought such an indictment earlier. He ordered the existing bail arrangements continued pending an indictment. Defense lawyer Doris Walker accused Schnacke "of one of the dirtiest tricks." The prosecutor for his part refused to answer reporters' questions as to why he had suddenly raised the treason charges after the mistrial.[45]

But there were no further indictments. When the government requested a continuance of the treason complaint in July 1959 in order to complete its investigation, the U.S. Commissioner denied the motion and dismissed the complaint. That dismissal, however, was not a final judgment on the merits and the government was free to pursue the case. Two years later, Attorney General Robert F. Kennedy reported that "because of existing conditions on the China mainland," it was impossible to obtain the requisite two witnesses to the overt act of treason. (He did not identify any act.) Kennedy also reviewed the outstanding sedition charges, but contended that the government's efforts were frustrated by the statutory exclusion of testimony by former POWs. An eight-year search for legal punishment for the defendants' unpopular opinions sputtered to an end when Kennedy ordered the sedition indictment dismissed and closed the investigation of treason charges.[46]

vi

The defendants had won their freedom, but the cost was enormous. The Powells and Schuman had spent over $40,000 from their own savings and from funds raised in their behalf. Fortunately, they received a good deal of gratis legal assistance. Jobs were hard to obtain, either because of political pressures or the demands of the proceedings. Schuman returned to China to work for a government publishing firm and later helped to launch an English-language newspaper. Powell eventually developed a new career renovating houses in San Francisco, but maintained his interest in China and germ warfare. Through the years, he persisted in securing classified documents in an attempt to prove the truth of what he had written in the early 1950s.[47]

The trial's odd, dramatic conclusion may have been ideal for the government.

Given the restraints of evidentiary requirements and trial procedures, a conviction might well have been difficult to secure. Yet the onus of accusation and official indignation remained. When Kennedy finally ordered all charges dropped in 1961, the announcement cleverly implied that legal technicalities, and not problems of evidence, allowed the defendants to escape prosecution.

The government all too readily acquiesced in the mistrial motion, sensing that it could not prove its case without such testimony as that of Private Baylor; moreover, the defense undoubtedly would have demanded documents and witnesses on other issues. However unexpected the incident creating the mistrial, the government must have welcomed it as a convenient escape from a potentially embarrassing dilemma. If the government had desired to proceed with the trial, the prosecutor might have asked the judge to interrogate the jurors regarding the effect, if any, of the newspaper article on their impartiality. His failure to do so indicates that reasons other than a concern for the defendants' rights prompted his support of the mistrial motion.

By 1961 the Korean War and germ warfare charges were distant memories, and Senator Jenner no longer was in Congress to exert pressure on the Justice Department. But there still were secrets to keep. Judge Goodman's sensitivity toward the defendants' procedural rights underlined the potential for exposure and alerted the government to the precariousness of its case. The risks of continuing the trial or renewing the charges were enormous for the government. Happily, the mistrial could be blamed on forces outside its control; technicalities could be said to have prevented further prosecution. Most important, the government's denial of the germ warfare charges remained intact. It was indeed an ideal situation.

The indictment against the Powells and Schuman represented an attempt to vindicate official history. The defendants in their articles had challenged that version and their charges rankled diverse elements within the government. The affair in a sense paralleled the post-World War II war crimes trials that in part reflected an attempt to prove the victors' view of history. But the historical issues in San Francisco were not as clear or as easily resolved as those in Nuremberg or Tokyo.

The defendants' articles had accused the United States of aggression in Korea, of having stalled the truce negotiations, and of having engaged in germ warfare. The truth of those charges was hard to determine. The origins of the Korean War were complex. The decision of American policy makers to pursue the North Korean invaders to the Yalu River, at the risk of Chinese intervention, clearly was open to question. And certainly in those years, the United States, together with the Chinese Nationalists, conducted numerous clandestine operations against mainland China and its neighbors.[48] Finally, no useful purpose could have been served by detailing the convoluted military and diplomatic considerations involved in the lengthy truce negotiations. The government's decision virtually to abandon those charges represented the wisest course of action.

The government's case finally narrowed down to the "preposterous fraud," the "preposterous hoax" of germ warfare. Among other items, the indictment charged Powell with having accused the United States of using Japanese BW experts for its own purposes. But after more than three decades of official denials, with the American government even refusing to acknowledge the Japanese use of bacteriological warfare in China during World War II, facts eventually emerged that sustained Powell's contention. Just as the United States and the Soviet Union had recruited German nuclear and rocket scientists for their own purposes, so both sides used captured Japanese BW experts. The American government refused to press BW charges in the Tokyo war crimes trials and later ridiculed the Soviet BW trial at Khabarovsk in 1949 as propaganda. But a generation later, following a Japanese television documentary in 1976, the Army finally acknowledged the Japanese BW program. The subsequent release of documents detailed the Japanese operation and the American government's subsequent use of Japanese personnel. But the Justice Department knew all this before the indictment against Powell was prepared.[49]

The charges regarding American use of bacteriological weapons during the Korean War remain unproved. The government went to extraordinary lengths to make an example of Powell for endorsing the Chinese and North Korean accusations; yet it also went to extraordinary lengths to limit any inquiry into those charges. To demonstrate that the United States did engage in germ warfare required the insuperable task of disproving a negative. What may well have been at work here was what CIA Director William Colby described in 1975 as the concept of "plausible denial," which the government periodically employed to cover diplomatic and intelligence activities. By that Colby meant that "if the United States could deny something and not be clearly demonstrated as having said something falsely, then the United States could do so."[50] Throughout the proceedings against Powell, the government carefully controlled the evidence, determined to suppress anything that might even imply, let alone prove, that it had engaged in germ warfare. The sanitizing of the "Sams Report" is a case in point.

The government could ill afford any prolonged inquiry into the BW program. Such investigation would have opened a veritable Pandora's box that might have exposed either bona fide military secrets or ones that would have proven so embarrassing as to cast doubt on the government's veracity. A quarter century later, for example, the American people learned that the CIA had contracted for BW weapons from the Army, that it had engaged in mind-control drug experiments on Americans, and that the Army had conducted BW experiments on unsuspecting American civilians, particularly in New York and San Francisco.

The Army also revealed in 1977 that the Korean War accelerated the development of BW retaliatory capability. However much a jury would have been inclined to disbelieve Communist charges of germ warfare in Korea and China, such revelations in 1959 might well have undermined the government's credibility.[51]

The whole truth undoubtedly lies buried in governmental archives in Washington and Peking. But the rapprochement between the two governments after 1971 makes it unlikely that either side will offer any startling revelations in the foreseeable future. Both nations, for their own and mutually supporting reasons, have an interest in suppressing what once was a bitter point of contention. For now, we must either accept the government's defense on faith or speculate in a most circumstantial manner that the charges indeed were true.

It is easier to speculate about the government's decision to persecute Powell. That choice was motivated by political and foreign policy considerations. Powell's "pernicious" charges rankled the diplomatic and military establishment, while some such as Senator Jenner saw him as a "renegade American," subservient to Communist manipulation. Either way, he was viewed as a menace who should be punished. Powell's writings challenged official orthodoxy, an orthodoxy that mobilized and sustained the nation's rationale for its international posture. To tolerate Powell's heresy would have constituted a tacit admission that he was correct. The State Department's persistent demands for Powell's trial, despite growing reluctance in other sectors of the government, particularly reflected that posture.[52]

The government was compelled by its own logic to persecute Powell. Its decision to pursue exoneration and vindication through the legal process, however, eventually trapped the government in its own Catch-22, and ultimately the government had to abandon its efforts lest it risk acknowledging its misdeeds. The government's action undoubtedly was prompted by deeply felt purposes of national policy; to have carried it through, however, would have been self-destructive and foolish.

EPILOGUE
Political Injustice and the Rule of Law

> The shepherd drives the wolf from the sheep's
> throat, for which the sheep thanks the shepherd
> as a *liberator*, while the wolf denounces him for
> the same act as the destroyer of liberty, especially
> as the sheep was a black one. Plainly, the sheep
> and the wolf are not agreed upon a definition of
> liberty.
>
> —ABRAHAM LINCOLN, 1864

i

THE Cold War years were grim, bleak times for American liberty as the threat of international Communism produced repression unprecedented in scale, intensity, and duration. The menace from abroad heightened concerns for potential domestic subversion. Even before the dream of peace was shattered in the late 1940's, the combination of external and internal forces had activated governmental repression. The depression years had increased the allure of extremist solutions (from both the left and the right), and the Nazi-Soviet Pact of 1939 heightened the worst fears of totalitarian threats to the United States. The rapprochement with Communism during World War II proved tenuous, of course. The Soviet spy revelations in Canada, the subjugation of Eastern Europe, the Czechoslovakian coup, and the Communist takeover in China reinforced long-standing convictions of Soviet aggressiveness and hostility. Beyond that, the sensational disclosures that the Soviets had recruited ostensibly loyal Americans as spies spurred political and popular demands for repression.

Anti-Communism long had been a staple of American political religion, at least since the Bolshevik Revolution. Periodically, anti-Communism took on the fervor of a crusade, ruthlessly trampling those who did not march in lockstep. After 1945, the government sanctioned that religion with official acts that included prosecuting the American Communist Party, imposing vague, capricious loyalty standards for government employees, conducting arbitrary, at times extralegal persecution of alleged subversives, compiling and loosely disseminating personnel files filled with spurious, dated allegations, and publicly castigating those who expressed views that deviated from officially sanctioned or politically popular versions of events.

There was some basis for the fears of the times, but the record of official reaction betrays a cavalier disregard for liberty and due process. The ready use of nameless, faceless informers, the promiscuous use of surveillance, the arbitrary standards of administration, and the challenges to private beliefs and associations cast a dark shadow over all attempts to maintain security. Anti-Communist ideology, to be sure, animated much of this behavior; but ideological drives were all too often colored by self-serving political ambitions and the whims of strategically placed power holders. Those choices reflected personal animus and aggrandizement, rather than committed ideological goals. J. Edgar Hoover, for one, certainly was a prominent, articulate anti-Communist. Yet that ideology generally was subservient to his personal, territorial concerns. Ideology, it appears, was for public consumption and after-the-fact justification.

We will never fully tally the incidence of official wrongdoing and attempts at repression. In employee loyalty proceedings, for example, there are thousands of cases which offer little more than ambiguous statistical evidence of action, and they include innumerable cases in which the government never was challenged or which never required action, as persons quietly resigned, rather than run a process which appeared rigged, potentially embarrassing, and certainly terribly expensive. Moreover, we will never fully explore and comprehend the hundreds of incidents in which persons were investigated and interrogated by federal and state legislative committees, the callous unrestrained deportations of undesirable aliens, the mischievous results of alleged counter-intelligence activities by the FBI and police agencies, the stifling of dissent in professions and unions, the chilling intimidation of critics of official policies, and even the use of extralegal tactics to aid and abet desired political aims. What we know, however, offers a distressing record of abuse and portrays a legal system that at times mocked its very purpose and being.

It is instructive to note that these terrible wrongs were done with a terrifying consent and encouragement of the society. Fear and intolerance pervaded the citizenry as well as officialdom, and official initiatives worked in tandem with social demands. The premium on unquestioning, uncritical loyalty, the search for scapegoats, and the pressure for conformity gathered momentum from below, as well as above. Unity was confused with uniformity. Curiously, only the more sober, more restrained spirit that is reflected in our institutions rather than in ourselves established limits and ended the American Inquisition.

ii

Law was subverted and repressed in the name of law. The ill-defined discretion inherent in large claims to act against subversion, as well as the multiplicity and dispersal of sources of authority, inevitably impaired the integrity and the sanctity of law. Whim and caprice often animated the exercise of discretion; inertia or conflict marked the determination of jurisdiction between competing authorities. The procedural results, consequently, abused the sanctity of personal liberties and rights and, at times, perverted legal norms. To a point, the legal system tolerated the accompanying distortion; yet the very autonomy of the law thwarted any total inversion of the system. There *were* limits to repression and abuse of the norms, as the guardians and executors of law ultimately found themselves bound to the Rule of Law.

The English historian E. P. Thompson, arbitrating the myopic claims of nationalistic celebrants of an ever-progressing society and legal system, and of those Marxists who see the legal system as an oppressive weapon in the hands of the ruling class, has argued that the law eventually develops autonomy. Law has its own ideology, within the context of which specific rules may stand in particular relationship to general social norms. "It may," Thompson contends, "be seen simply in terms of its own logic, rules, and procedures—that is, simply *as law.*" And, he reminds us, "it is not possible to conceive of any complex society without law."

Rulers make law, and among other things, that law legitimates their power and authority. But there is a two-way street here. Law reinforces the regime's will, but the rules are for rulers and ruled alike. The effectiveness of the law's ideology requires an impartial and just application of the law, otherwise "it will mask nothing, legitimize nothing, contribute nothing to any class's hegemony." Law, Thompson observes, must in some measure be independent from manipulation and seem to be just. Yet "it cannot seem to be so without upholding its own logic and criteria of equity; indeed, on occasion, by actually *being* just."[1] Power holders, in short, must to some extent respect the Rule of Law that they impose; if they do not, they are reduced to the exercise of arbitrary, extralegal power, which usually offers only momentary security and authority. If law is to maintain its hegemony and supremacy, then power holders sometimes have to risk losing their immediate goals. Law is not irrelevant; it is not, as Thompson rightly concludes, humbug.

But the reality is that power holders *do* sometimes subvert the law and cynically manipulate it to their own ends. Does this not then justify a certain contempt, a justification of rejection, for any notion of the Rule of Law? What "legitimacy" cloaked the endless, grinding persecution of Harry Bridges, the vengeful disbarment of Abraham Isserman, the cynical prosecution of Owen Lattimore, the vindictive indictment of John William Powell, or the petty harassment of Rockwell Kent?

Law was subverted, to be sure; yet *that* law also trumped its own excesses. The house of law has many mansions. Such division, unfortunately, occasionally threatens the vitality of the Rule of Law. If, however, the latter is to be enforced by the regime, and if the Rule of Law is to maintain its supremacy, then ultimately its autonomy and ideology must be allowed to prevail.

All is not entirely well that ends well, of course, as the pain and costs for the victims of injustice are indelible. But eventual justice and vindication are important, whether it be at the bar of law, as for Bridges, Isserman, Lattimore, Powell, or Kent, or ultimately at the bar of history, as for Iva d'Aquino or Beatrice Braude. For then we reinforce, reaffirm, and enrich the Rule of Law as we discover and acknowledge the law's manipulation—even when the victim can only receive an apology or a historical footnote. The "victories" over repression and the subversion of the law—however long in coming and however painful to the victims and society—reflect the power holders' submission to the Rule of Law. The Rule of Law must be judged by its mistakes, of course; but it also is entitled to be judged by its whole record. For the United States in the Cold War era, it was the worst of times; however redeemed, it sadly was not the best of times. There was a large cast of villains and victims; still it was not "Darkness at Noon." It was not a closed system. We have a society that permits the individual to resist under the Rule of Law and to use it to rectify the violations of the norms of that system.

In *ancien régime* France, Cardinal Richelieu argued that for reasons of state "urgent conjecture" must sometimes take the place of assured truth. But wherever law ends, tyranny begins, as John Locke wrote in his great apologia for constitutionalism. While we certainly have had our Richelieus, the Lockean faith in the Rule of Law has prevailed. It is indeed a fragile, precarious perch, yet the alternative is unthinkable. Plainly, to paraphrase Lincoln, a rapacious, partial government will not always respect liberty. The sheep and the wolf invariably will be at odds over the nature and extent of liberty. The Rule of Law is their only shepherd.

NOTES

CHAPTER 1

1. Clark Lee, *One Last Look Around* (New York, 1947), pp. 84–89; 118. *Record of Trial of Iva Ikuko Toguri d'Aquino, Testimony of Clark Lee*, 7:478–531, *passim*. Hereafter cited as *Record*. Transcript of Lee's notes of interview with d'Aquino, September 3, 1945, d'Aquino File, Department of Justice. Hereafter cited as D'AQUINO, DOJ. For comment on Lee's testimony, see San Francisco *Chronicle*, July 15, 1949. A copy of the aborted contract between d'Aquino and the correspondents, September 1, 1945, is in the d'Aquino File, Army Intelligence Command, Department of the Army, Fort George Meade, Maryland. Hereafter cited as D'AQUINO, DOA. Mrs. d'Aquino's first formal affidavit to military authorities, detailing her negotiations with Lee and Brundidge, was on December 21, 1945. Leslie Nakashima, a Japanese newspaperman, helped Lee and Brundidge find Radio Tokyo employees. For a statement that he did not find the "one and only 'Tokyo Rose,' " see his deposition in the Wayne Collins Papers, in possession of Wayne Collins, Jr., San Francisco. Hereafter cited as WCP. In Lee's trial testimony, he was uncertain whether Nakashima had told him he had found "a" or "the" Tokyo Rose. *Record, Lee*, 7:478–79. For wartime descriptions of "Tokyo Rose," see, e.g., *Time*, April 10, 1944; *Collier's*, January 8, 1944. Also see M. Duus, *Tokyo Rose* (Tokyo, 1979).

2. *Record, Martin Pray*, 43:4712; *ibid., Defendant*, 46:5182, 5206.

3. Memorandum, Special Agent 2260, September 10, 1945, Investigation Summary, March 14, 1946, Memorandum, Legal Section to Chief of Counter-Intelligence (CIC), April 17, 1946, D'AQUINO, DOA.

4. Statements: Charles Hughes Cousens, October 25, 28, November 10, 1945; Wallace E. Ince, January 8, 1946, *ibid.* For further description of d'Aquino's conflicts with the other Nisei, see *Record: Defendant*, 49.5484–85.

5. D'Aquino Affidavit, December 21, 1945; Counter-Intelligence Memorandum, January 10, 1946; Foreign Broadcast Intelligence Service, "Radio Report on the Far East"; Memorandum, Legal Section to CIC, April 17, 1946; *ibid.*, April 27, 29, 1946; Transmittal of Case Record, May 1, 1946, D'AQUINO, DOA.

6. Hoover to Tillman, October 11, 1945, *ibid.*

7. "Certificate of Identification," D'AQUINO, DOJ.

8. D'Aquino Statement to Tillman, April 30, 1946; State Department documents on Ikuko Toguri, *ibid.* American Consulate General documents, December 1, 1941, April 4, 1942, D'AQUINO, DOA. The FBI was fully aware of the suspect's attempts to leave Japan; see Report of Confidential National Defense Informant S-90 (n.d.), *ibid. Record*,

Defendant, 46:5122–69, offers Mrs. d'Aquino's formal trial testimony on the background of her story. For her explanation of her fears, see *ibid.,* 49:5502–5.

9. Eliff to Caudle, May 15, 1946, D'AQUINO, DOJ.

10. Caudle to Carter, August 27, 1946; *ibid.,* September 13, 1946; Carter to Attorney General Clark, September 13, 1946; Carter to Caudle, June 19, 1946, *ibid.*

11. Eliff to Caudle, September 19, 1946; Caudle to Eliff, n.d., *ibid.*

12. Caudle to Clark, September 24, 1946; Clark to Caudle, September 26, 1946, *ibid.*

13. Caudle to Hoover, October 4, 1946; General Headquarters, U.S. Army, Pacific, to Commandant, Sugamo Prison, October 23, 1946, *ibid.* New York *Times,* October 22, 1946.

14. Quinn to Secretary of State, October 24, 1947, D'AQUINO, DOJ. *National Legionnaire* (November 1947), p. 3; *ibid.* (May 1948), p. 2. Eldred L. Meyer to Tom Clark et al., November 13, 1947, D'AQUINO, DOJ.

15. Eldred L. Meyer to Quinn, December 22, 1947; Congressman Franklin J. Maloney to Clark, February 5, 1948; Ford to Maloney, February 20, 1948, *ibid.* Ford's statement that d'Aquino was the only American-born woman announcer on Radio Tokyo was wrong, of course. He knew better from the evidence; furthermore, Clark Lee's book, published some months earlier, severely criticized the broadcasts of Mrs. Genevieve Faville ("Mother") Topping, an American missionary then over eighty years old. Lee, *One Last Look Around,* p. 84.

16. Press Release, December 3, 1947, D'AQUINO, DOJ.

17. Undated clipping, c. November 1947, *ibid.*

18. Wayne Collins to Lyndon B. Johnson, November 4, 1968, WCP. This was a formal request for a presidential pardon. Brundidge claimed the announcement that d'Aquino would not be prosecuted made him "indignant" and he thereupon contacted Hoover offering to get the necessary evidence in Japan. But according to Brundidge's account, this was in December 1947; the announcement regarding the dropping of the investigation had been made by Carter over a year earlier. What obviously prompted his renewed interest was the passport application and/or the possibility that Winchell was getting mileage out of a story that Brundidge regarded as peculiarly his. Nashville *Tennessean,* May 2, 1948.

19. Carter to Clark, December 5, 1947, D'AQUINO, DOJ. Carter soon successfully prosecuted another Nisei treason case, involving brutality toward U.S. prisoners of war. *United States* v. *Kawakita,* 96 F. Supp. 824 (S.D. Calif. 1950). Kawakita's death sentence was commuted by Eisenhower and he was pardoned by Kennedy. Carter subsequently was appointed to the Ninth Circuit Court of Appeals.

20. D'Aquino to Winchell, April 14, 1948; Carroll to d'Aquino, April 20, 1948; Winchell to Carroll, May 14, 1948; Carroll to d'Aquino, May 27, 1948, WCP. Interestingly, in his May 27 letter, Carroll used the salutation "Dear Rose." Also see Carroll to Willoughby, April 20, 1948; G-2 Memorandum, May 4, 1948; Willoughby to Carroll, May 4 (?), 1948, D'AQUINO, DOA. Willoughby's disdain for the civilian case is expressed in a note to his aide. Willoughby to Bratton, March 3, 1949, *ibid.*

21. Quinn to Ford, December 12, 1947; *ibid.,* January 9, 1948; Ford to Quinn, n.d., D'AQUINO, DOJ.

22. Bratton to Willoughby, March 22, 1948; C.A.W. to Willoughby, April 8, 1948, D'AQUINO, DOA.

23. Hogan to Quinn, April 12, 1948; Quinn to Ford, April 13, 1948; Ford notation, April 15, 1948, D'AQUINO, DOJ. Bratton to Willoughby, April 1, 1948, D'AQUINO, DOA.

Nakashima Deposition, WCP. Nakashima had witnessed the September 1945 contract with Mrs. d'Aquino. In the trial, the defendant repeated her view of Lee's notes and Brundidge's story. *Record, Defendant,* 47:5219–20.

24. Hogan to Quinn, April 20, 1948; Quinn to Clark, April 26, 1948; Clark to Quinn, April 26, 1948; Quinn to Whearty, April 28, 1948, D'AQUINO, DOJ.

25. Nashville *Tennessean,* May 2, 1948. Quinn to Clark, May 21, 1948; Clark to Quinn, n.d.; Quinn to Clark, May 28, 1948; Quinn to Whearty, June 3, 1948; Ford to Whearty, n.d.; Hoover to Clark, June 11, 1948; Clark to Evans, June 3, 1948, D'AQUINO, DOJ. Brundidge's articles appeared in the *Tennessean* on May 2, 5, 9, 10, 12, 14, 19, 20, 21, 23, 1948.

26. DeWolfe to Whearty, May 25, 1948; Quinn to Clark, May 27, 1948; Clark to Quinn, May 28, 1948, D'AQUINO, DOJ. See *Chandler v. United States,* 171 F. 2d 921 (C.C.A. 1st 1948); *Best v. United States,* 184 F. 2d 131.

27. Wiener to Quinn, July 6, 1948, D'AQUINO, DOJ. On English law, see Foster, *Crown Law,* *216; see *Haupt v. United States,* 330 U.S. 631 (1947), and *Cramer v. United States,* 325 U.S. 1 (1945) for discussion of intent. The definitive study of the historical growth of treason law in England and the United States is in James Willard Hurst, *The Law of Treason in the United States: Selected Essays* (Westport, Conn., 1970).

28. DeWolfe to Quinn, July 26, 1948; DeWolfe to Whearty, August 23, 1948; De-Wolfe to Campbell, January 12, 1949, D'AQUINO, DOJ. Provoo was tried in New York in 1954 and convicted for treason as a result of aiding the enemy while a prisoner of war. The conviction later was reversed by the Circuit Court and the government dropped the case. *United States v. Provoo,* 124 F. Supp. 185 (S.D. N.Y. 1954); *Provoo v. United States,* 215 F. 2d 531 (C.C.A. 2d 1954). Hogan successfully argued that Ince's case not be joined with d'Aquino's. Hogan to Whearty, August 20, 1948, D'AQUINO, DOJ. When the American lawyer who, as a CIC investigator, had urged prosecution for the others protested the d'Aquino indictment, he received a patronizing reply from Justice. George S. Guysi to author, September 4, 1981.

29. "Receipt of Prisoner," September 25, 1948, signed by Tillman; Hogan to Quinn, July 27, 1948, D'AQUINO, DOJ.

30. Campbell to Royall, August 13, 1948; Campbell to Hogan, August 2, 1948, *ibid.* D'Aquino's lawyer and the ACLU, however, bitterly protested his inability to see his client during the FBI's initial interrogations in San Francisco. Collins to Tom Clark et al., September 27, 1948; Ernest Besig, Director, ACLU, to Clark, September 27, 1948; DeWolfe to Campbell, September 28, 1948, *ibid.*

31. Isaac Pacht to Clark, August 25, 1948; Ralph Reynolds to Clark, August 24, 1948; Campbell to Pacht, September 8, 1948, *ibid.*

32. DeWolfe to Whearty, November 12, 1948; DeWolfe to Campbell, November 12, 1948, *ibid.*

33. Campbell to Clark, December 2, 1948, *ibid.* FBI Report, San Francisco (Yagi), October 5, 1948. D'Aquino File, Federal Bureau of Investigation.

34. Campbell to Brundidge, December 14, 1948; Hogan to William Foley, December 24, 1948; Campbell to Clark, January 5, 1949, D'AQUINO, DOJ.

35. Hogan to Brundidge, April 20, 1949; Hogan to the Files, May 26, 1949, *ibid.* Lee, *One Last Look Around,* p. 85.

36. Story to Campbell, May 27, 1949, D'AQUINO, DOJ. The Civil Censorship Detachment of the Occupation Army monitored Tamba's and Felipe d'Aquino's phone calls to

Collins. Given Story's knowledge of Tamba's movements, possibly all of Tamba's calls were tapped. See Transcripts, December 15, 1948; June (?) 1949, D'AQUINO, DOA. Tillman to DeWolfe, May 20, 1949, D'AQUINO, DOJ, reports on the FBI agent's observations of Tamba.

37. Campbell to Clark, June 8, 1949, *ibid.* The U.S. Attorney in San Francisco apparently was unaware of the Washington decisions, as several weeks later he informed his superiors of his intention to interview Brundidge. He never did, of course. Frank Hennessy to Campbell, June 22, 1949; Hennessy to Campbell, September 2, 1949, *ibid.*

38. San Francisco *Chronicle*, July 3, 8, 1949.

39. *Record, Tillman*, 16:1597–99; Hennessy to Campbell, September 2, 1949, D'AQUINO, DOJ. In the concluding arguments, one of the defense lawyers raised the matter of bribery and delicately suggested Brundidge's involvement. The issue, however, necessarily was restrained by the boundaries of the trial testimony. *Record, Arguments*, 2:251–56.

40. San Francisco *Chronicle*, July 6, August 2, 1949.

41. *Record, Mitsushio*, 10:919, 11:971; *ibid.*, *Oki*, 9:672; *ibid.*, *Defendant*, 49:5434–36; 5513–15. The Chicago *Tribune* published an article on March 22, 1976, claiming that one of the chief accusers in the trial had admitted giving false testimony. Several months later, however, both Oki and Mitsushio refused to retract any of their testimony or to submit an affidavit in support of d'Aquino's pardon request. Yasuhiro Fujita (Tokyo lawyer) to Wayne Collins, Jr., October 14, 1976, WCP.

42. Mann Memoir, Collection of Antonio Montanari, Jr., San Francisco; San Francisco *Chronicle*, September 30, 1949. In 1976, Mann said he was surprised at the severity of the sentence. Furthermore, he stated he regarded Roche's final comments as virtually directing the verdict. Obviously remorseful, Mann added: "In my idea of justice, . . . the prosecution failed miserably to convict her." *Ibid.*, February 16, 1976.

43. *Ibid.*, October 7, 1949.

44. *D'Aquino v. United States*, 192 F. 2d 338 (C.C.A. 9th 1951); certiorari denied, 343 U.S. 935 (1952). Rehearings denied, 343 U.S. 958 (1952); 345 U.S. 931 (1953). The Circuit Court found at least twelve errors in the trial court, but excused them as nonprejudicial. The treason conviction carried a loss of citizenship rights, but being native-born, d'Aquino could not be deported. On the attempts to collect the fine, see J. Walter Yeagley to Edward Hanrahan, May 9, 1966, D'AQUINO, DOJ; Chicago *Tribune*, March 23, 1971. Clifford I. Uyeda, *A Final Report and Review* (Seattle, 1980), summarizes the Japanese American Citizens League's efforts to secure a pardon. Earlier, President Ford had revoked the infamous Executive Order 9066, ordering the evacuation of the Japanese-Americans in 1942.

45. D'Aquino to Winchell, April 14, 1948, WCP.

CHAPTER 2

1. Braude Affidavit, November 15, 1977, in PLAINTIFF'S MOTION FOR PARTIAL SUMMARY JUDGMENT, *Beatrice Braude v. United States* (U.S. Court of Claims, No. 451–77 [Filed: November 23, 1977]), 6–7, 11–12. Hereafter cited as PLAINTIFF'S MOTION. Interview, Beatrice Braude (December 27, 1979); Braude to author, January 14, 1980. I also am indebted for the cooperation rendered by Braude's attorney, Maxwell J. Mehlman of Arnold & Porter, Washington.

2. For basic historical surveys of loyalty problems, see Merle Curti, *The Roots of*

American Loyalty (New York, 1946); Henry Steele Commager, *Freedom, Loyalty, Dissent* (New York, 1954); and Harold M. Hyman, *To Try Men's Souls* (Berkeley, 1959).

3. The background is summarized in *The Report of the President's Temporary Commission on Employee Loyalty* (Washington, 1947). The House subcommittee report is in *Congressional Record,* 79 Cong., 2 Sess. (July 20, 1946), pp. 9601–4.

4. *Report of the President's Commission, passim.*

5. The basic studies of the loyalty program are Eleanor Bontecou, *The Federal Loyalty-Security Program* (Ithaca, N.Y., 1953) and Ralph S. Brown, Jr., *Loyalty and Security: Employment Tests in the United States* (New Haven, 1958). The political entanglements of the loyalty program are best analyzed in Alan D. Harper, *The Politics of Loyalty: The White House and the Communist Issue, 1946–1952* (Westport, Conn., 1969). Francis H. Thompson, *The Frustration of Politics: Truman, Congress, and the Loyalty Issue, 1945–1953* (Cranbury, N.J., 1979), covers much the same ground. The most skillful, detailed critical discussion of Truman's culpability is in David Caute, *The Great Fear: The Anti-Communist Purge under Truman and Eisenhower* (New York, 1978). Paul L. Murphy, *The Constitution in Crisis Times, 1918–1969* (New York, 1972), analyzes the constitutional question.

6. Bontecou, *Federal Loyalty-Security Program,* pp. 33–34.

7. Dwight D. Eisenhower, *The White House Years: Mandate for Change* (Signet ed., New York, 1965), pp. 375–377. Remark by Philip Young in Washington *Post,* November 5, 1954.

8. Adam Yarmolinsky, *Case Studies in Personnel Security* (Washington, D.C., 1955), documents the proceedings of some loyalty hearings.

9. *Peters* v. *Hobby,* 349 U.S. 331 (1955); *Cole* v. *Young,* 351 U.S. 536 (1956); *Service* v. *Dulles,* 354 U.S. 363 (1957). In 1959 the Court pointedly attacked the loyalty/security program in *Vitarelli* v. *Seaton,* 359 U.S. 535 (1959), and particularly in *Greene* v. *McElroy,* 360 U.S. 474 (1959). In the latter case, Chief Justice Earl Warren condemned the use of "faceless informers," unknown to the accused. "Certain principles have remained relatively immutable in our jurisprudence," Warren noted. "One of these is that where governmental action seriously injures an individual, and the reasonableness of the action depends on fact findings, the evidence used to prove the Government's case must be disclosed to the individual so that he has an opportunity to show that it is untrue." *Ibid.,* pp. 506–7, 496. But compare the Court's earlier, ambiguous support for the loyalty program in *Bailey* v. *Richardson,* 341 U.S. 918 (1951).

10. For somewhat sensationalized accounts of the Coplon case, see David J. Dallin, *Soviet Espionage* (New Haven, 1955), pp. 478–92; Sanche de Gramont, *The Secret War: The Story of International Espionage Since World War II* (New York, 1962), pp. 66–108. Earl Latham, *The Communist Controversy in Washington: From the New Deal to McCarthy* (Cambridge, Mass., 1966), offers a much more sober account of Soviet espionage activities and Communist subversion in the period.

11. The appellate cases are reported in *United States* v. *Coplon,* 185 F. 2d 629 (2d Cir. 1950), and *Coplon* v. *United States,* 191 F. 2d 749 (D.C. Cir. 1951). The Supreme Court denied certiorari in both cases in 342 U.S. 920 (1952) and 342 U.S. 926 (1952). Dallin (cited above), a onetime Menshevik, probably summed up prevailing popular opinion when the convictions were reversed: Coplon, he wrote, "went unpunished because of the strict adherence of a democracy to legal procedure and to observance of technicalities, which sometimes verges on the absurd." Dallin, *Soviet Espionage,* p. 492.

12. Streibert to Braude, December 31, 1953. Unless otherwise noted, all correspondence is from Braude's File, reproduced in PLAINTIFF'S MOTION.

13. Streibert to Braude, February 1, 1954; Streibert to Ives, January 25, 1954.

14. Braude Affidavit, pp. 15–16. Braude to U.S. Civil Service Commission, May 14, 1956.

15. "Report on the Action Taken in USIA on Employees Subject to the 'Personnel Rider' in P.L. 207," January 12, 1954. USIA Personnel Security Regulations. See PLAINTIFF'S MOTION.

16. Memorandum, USIA Office of Security, December 28, 1953; Charles M. Noone (USIA Security) to Mr. Beall (USIA Personnel), December 28, 1953.

17. J. Edgar Hoover to James E. Hatcher, April 6, 1948, May 17, 1951; FBI Reports on Loyalty Investigation of Beatrice Braude: February 13, 14, 17, 24, 27, 1948.

18. Hoover to Hatcher, June 21, August 7, 1951; FBI Reports on Loyalty Investigation of Beatrice Braude: May 11, 21, July 28, 1951.

19. Conrad E. Snow (Chairman, State Department Loyalty Security Board) to Braude, September 27, 1951, interrogatories attached.

20. Interrogatories for Beatrice Braude, Executed Copy of Answers, October 9, 1951. Braude Interview, December 27, 1979. According to one source, Civil Service Commission investigators during World War II were directed not to ask questions about the Washington Book Shop and organizations such as the ACLU, the Socialist Party, the National Lawyers Guild, etc. Caute, *The Great Fear*, p. 268.

21. Loyalty Security Board Memorandum (State Department), October 31, 1951; Snow to Braude, February 11, 1952; Civil Service Commission Personnel File Memorandum, January 5, 1952.

22. Braude Interview, December 27, 1979. Braude to Byron Scott, February 22, 1956; Mary G. McHale to Braude, October 2, 1956.

23. Braude Affidavit, pp. 23–24.

24. Andreé Orienter to Stuart J. Land, June 27, 1974.

25. Scott to Civil Service Commission, December 19, 1956. Scott served as counsel to a number of people with "security problems." See, e.g., Latham, *Communist Controversy in Washington*, p. 159 n.

26. L. V. Meloy to Scott, May 1, 1957.

27. Braude to Macy, November 26, 1963; Johnson to Braude, December 13, 1963.

28. Braude Interview, December 27, 1979. Caute, *The Great Fear*, p. 324.

29. Memorandum, Harris to Paul J. McNichol, June 8, 1965; Memorandum, Thomas E. Hoffman to McNichol, June 11, 1965.

30. Harris to Braude, June 20, 1965.

31. Lawrence Speiser to Macy, January 4, 1967.

32. McNichol to Hoffman, January 10, 13, 1967. Hoffman to McNichol, June 11, 1965, emphasis added.

33. Macy to Speiser, February 14, 1967, Civil Service Commission Staff Report attached.

34. Braude to Speiser, February 18, 1967. Braude to Bernice Bernstein, January 9, 1967.

35. David Bernstein to John Burns, December 15, 1966; Burns to Marvin Watson, December 23, 1966, both in DEFENDANT'S OPPOSITION TO PLAINTIFF'S MOTION FOR SUMMARY JUDGMENT, *Beatrice Braude* v. *United States* (U.S. Court of Claims, No. 451–77). Watson to Burns, February 6, 1967 in MEMORANDUM TO ACCOMPANY S. 546 (prepared by Arnold & Porter for Senate Judiciary Committee, May 2, 1979). Bernice Bernstein to Braude, May 10, 1968.

36. Braude Interview, December 27, 1979; Braude to author, January 14, 1980. MEMORANDUM TO ACCOMPANY S. 546 (note 38, *supra*), 18–19.

37. Complaint for Declaratory Judgment and Other Relief and Demand for Jury Trial, *Braude* v. *Keogh,* Civil Action No. 76-2275 (D.D.C., December 13, 1976); Answer, February 14, 1977; and Order Granting Defendant's Motion to Dismiss, August 17, 1977, in PLAINTIFF's MOTION, Exhibit 50.

38. PLAINTIFF's MOTION, pp. 34–36, 39–50.

39. DEFENDANT's OPPOSITION, pp. 7–23.

40. PLAINTIFF's MOTION, pp. 62–65.

41. *Beatrice Braude* v. *United States,* 585 F. 2d 1049, 1052–53 (Ct. of Claims 1978). Skelton had been appointed to the court in 1966 by President Johnson, and Kunzig by Nixon in 1971.

42. *Ibid.,* pp. 1053–57.

43. *Ibid.,* pp. 1058–60. Nichols had been appointed together with Skelton in 1966.

44. *Ibid.,* pp. 1064–67. "Developments in the Law—Statutes of Limitations," *Harvard Law Review* (1950), 63:1177, 1219. For a case analogous to Braude's, differing in that it involved a large defense contractor—and the result, see *General Aircraft Corp.* v. *United States* (Ct. of Claims, 544-77 [April 27, 1978]).

45. *Braude* v. *United States,* 585 F. 2d 1049, 1068–69 (Ct. of Claims 1978).

46. Associated Press dispatch, Madison *Capital Times,* October 19, 1978.

47. See Report (to accompany S. 546), Senate Committee on the Judiciary, 96 Cong., 1 Sess. (December 20, 1979); Transcript, H.R. Subcommittee on Administrative Law and Governmental Relations, 96 Cong., 2 Sess. (August 22, 1980), pp. 1–18. The Republican floor opposition was led by Robert Bauman, a lame duck and a well-known spokesman for the Moral Majority. Interview, Max Mehlman, September 21, 1981.

48. *Olmstead* v. *United States,* 277 U.S. 438, 485 (1928).

CHAPTER 3

1. Sam Hynes, "The Case of Ezra Pound," *Commonweal* (December 9, 1955), 63:251. For typical comments that Pound was unfairly incarcerated, see Louis Dudek (ed.), *Dk/'Some Letters of Ezra Pound* (Montreal, 1974), p. 106; Hayden Carruth, "The Poetry of Ezra Pound," *Perspectives* (1956), 16:158. Also see Harry M. Meacham, *The Caged Panther: Ezra Pound at St. Elizabeth's* (New York, 1967), p. 33.

2. The biographical literature on Pound is staggering. For background, see H. A. Sieber, "The Medical, Legal, Literary and Political Status of Ezra Weston [Loomis] Pound . . ." This is a Library of Congress report prepared for Congress in 1958. Besides the familiar biographical details, the Sieber report compiles a good deal of opinion favorable to Pound's cause. Among the more useful biographies, see Noel Stock, *The Life of Ezra Pound* (New York, 1970); C. David Heymann, *Ezra Pound: The Last Rower* (New York, 1976); Charles Norman, *Ezra Pound* (New York, 1960); Hugh Kenner, *The Pound Era* (Berkeley, 1971); Michael Reck, *Ezra Pound: A Close Up* (New York, 1967); Peter Ackroyd, *Ezra Pound and His World* (New York, 1980).

3. Pound's wartime broadcasts are compiled in Leonard W. Doob (ed.), *"Ezra Pound Speaking": Radio Speeches of World War II* (Westport, Conn., 1978). The quoted passage is from the February 19, 1942, speech.

4. Tim Redman, "The Repatriation of Pound, 1939–1942: A View from the Archives," *Paideuma* (1979), 8:447, 456. Additional documents from the Passport Division confirm that Pound did not request a passport to return to the United States. Memorandum, June

8, 1942; Frances Knight to John Edwards, November 1, 1955. Pound File, Passport Division, Department of State.

5. Mezzasoma (Minister of Popular Culture) to Minister of Finance, December 4, 1943, Pound File, Federal Bureau of Investigation. Hereafter cited as POUND, FBI. Also see Heymann, *Pound*, pp. 145–50 *passim.*

6. Pound to Biddle, August 4, 1943. Pound File, Department of State. Hereafter cited as POUND, DOS. The FBI investigation of Pound began in 1942. J. Edgar Hoover to Adolf A. Berle, Jr., December 12, 1942, *ibid.*

7. The Pound File, Department of the Army, Intelligence and Security Command, Fort George Meade, Maryland, contains directives authorizing Pound's arrest. Army Counter-Intelligence worked closely with the FBI. See Frank L. Anprin (FBI Agent, Rome) to Colonel Stephen J. Spingarn, April 27, 1945. The file also contains Pound's Genoa statement of May 7, 1945.

8. Michael King, "Ezra Pound at Pisa: An Interview with John L. Steele," *Texas Quarterly* (1978), 21:49–61; Homer Somers, 1946 Memoir, Somers File, Pound Archives, Beinecke Library, Yale University. Also see David P. Williams, "Ezra Pound in the Stockade," *Poetry,* January 1949.

9. Neuropsychiatric Examinations of Pound, June 14, 15, 1945; Steele Memorandum, July 19, 1945. Judge Advocate General Papers: War Crimes Branch, National Archives. Hereafter cited as JAG:WCB.

10. Gen. John M. Weir to Gen. Adam Richmond, July 3, 1945; Neuropsychiatric Examination of Pound, July 17, 1945, *ibid.*

11. Ezra Pound to Shakespear and Parkyn, October 5, 1945, copy in Archibald Mac-Leish Papers, Library of Congress. Hereafter cited as MACLEISH, LC.

12. Affidavit, P. V. Holder, November 20, 1945; Record of Trip, P. V. Holder, November 19, 1945, JAG:WCB.

13. Julien Cornell, *The Trial of Ezra Pound: A Documented Account of the Treason Case by the Defendant's Lawyer* (New York, 1966), pp. 13–15; T. S. Eliot to Archibald MacLeish, October 17, 1945, MACLEISH, LC. Pound himself originally considered hiring Lloyd Paul Stryker, his Hamilton College classmate and one of the most distinguished criminal trial lawyers in the country. But he realized the fee might be too high. Laughlin and Eliot thought it unwise to have "a very successful criminal lawyer." *Ibid.*

14. Indictment, in Ezra Pound File, St. Elizabeth's Hospital. Hereafter cited as POUND, ST. E. The government's case rested on evidence compiled by the FBI in Italy since 1943. See POUND, FBI. For the FBI's role beginning in 1943, see Gen. Adam Richmond to Gen. John M. Weir, June 18, 1945, JAG:WCB.

15. *National Cyclopedia of American Biography* (New York, 1970), 52:397–98.

16. Cornell, *Trial of Pound*, pp. 26–27.

17. *Ibid.*, pp. 35–36. The transcript of the trial is reprinted in *ibid.*, pp. 154–215. J. Edgar Hoover to William F. Tompkins, March 8, 1956, Pound File, Justice Department. Hereafter cited as POUND, DOJ.

18. King, "Psychiatric Examination of Ezra Pound," December 13, 1945, POUND, ST. E.

19. Gilbert, King, Muncie, and Overholser to Laws, December 14, 1945; King to Overholser, December 27, 1945, *ibid.* Many years later, Pound told Overholser that he thought King had "stuck his neck out possibly the furthest." Meacham, *The Caged Panther,* p. 116. The Justice Department eventually learned of King's report. Justice Department Memorandum, January 27, 1945, POUND, ST. E.

20. Clinical Record, December 21, 1945, *ibid.*

21. *Ibid.*, January 24, February 6, 1946.

22. *Ibid.*, January 28, 1946; Rorschach Summary, January 10, 1946, *ibid.*

23. Overholser to Matlack, January 18, 1946, *ibid.*

24. Cornell, *Trial of Pound*, p. 41.

25. *Ibid.*, p. 43. Cornell to Overholser, December 8, 1959; Overholser to Cornell, December 11, 1959, POUND, ST. E. Cornell revealed the incident in his book published in 1966, two years after Overholser's death.

26. Cornell, *Trial of Pound*, p. 43.

27. See *ibid.*, Transcript, pp. 154–215.

28. Gen. William C. Menninger to Theron L. Caudle, March 22, 1946; Caudle to Menninger, April 2, 1946, POUND, DOJ. Col. Sidney Rubenstein, Memorandum, March 11, 1946, JAG:WCB.

29. McInerney to Matlack, March 22, 1946; Matlack to McInerney, April 2, 1946, POUND, DOJ. Dr. Jerome Kavka Interview, April 1, 1981. Also see column by Albert Deutsch, *PM*, February 14, 1946.

30. Matlack to Files, October 20, 1947, POUND, DOJ. An internal Justice Department memo from this period neatly summed up Overholser's power: "I assume Overholser's word is final in the matter." W. E. Foley to R. W. Whearty, November 29 (1947?), *ibid.*

31. Overholser to Charles Norman, January 8, 1960; Pound to Overholser, November 13 (1955?), POUND, ST. E. Jerome Kavka Interview, April 1, 1981.

32. Overholser to Baxter, June 6, 1955; *ibid.*, February 23, 1956; Overholser to Norman, January 8, 1960, POUND, ST. E. The hospital file is filled with correspondence regarding the suitability of visitors. See pp. 37, 42, 54, 55, 412, 413, and 1059. At one point, Pound suggested that the hospital use a form letter in reply to requests for visitation. "As a general rule, Mr. Pound prefers that strangers should write to him, rather than to this office without informing him. This process permits him to judge whether their visit is likely to be useful; or entertaining; or restful." He was not entirely facetious. Pound note, c. February 1956, *ibid.* The fact is that the hospital cleared all requests with Pound. For Overholser's role in arranging recordings, see pp. 534 and 578 of the hospital files. On interviews, Pound's comment is in a note to Overholser, c. October 1955, *ibid.* The file is filled with refusals to allow interviews by the New York *Times, Newsweek,* and *Esquire*, among others. Cf. Carroll F. Terrell, "St. Elizabeth[']s," *Paideuma* (1974), 3:363.

33. Overholser to Cornell, March 21, 1946; Cornell to Overholser, April 2, 1946, POUND, ST. E. Pound's request to his lawyer is in Cornell, *Trial of Pound*, p. 81.

34. Tiffany Thayer to Overholser, October 1, 1946; Overholser to Thayer, October 4, 1946; William Carlos Williams to Overholser, October 24, 1947; Overholser to Williams, October 26, 1947, POUND, ST. E.

35. William Foley to Files, October 28, 1948; Alexander Campbell to Overholser, November 1, 1948, Overholser to Campbell, November 23, 1948, POUND, DOJ.

36. Williams to Overholser, October 24, 1947; Williams to Harry S. Truman, December 31, 1946 (copy to Overholser). Also see H. L. Mencken to Overholser, April 15, 1946, POUND, ST. E.

37. Clinical Record, February 7, 1946, *ibid.*

38. *Ibid.*, pp. 1397f–n, 1398a–b, 1399a–e, 1400, 1402a–b, 1403, 1406, 1408, 1410.

39. *Ibid.*, p. 1411 a–d. The diagnosis was in accord with the American Psychiatric Association's *Diagnostic and Statistical Manual: Mental Disorders* (Washington, D.C., 1952), p. 37.

40. Clinical Record, 1412, POUND, ST. E. Overholser to Krumbiegel, August 18, 1953, *ibid.*

41. William F. Tompkins (Justice Department) to Overholser, September 30, 1954; Overholser to Tompkins, October 13, 1954, *ibid.* Meacham, *Caged Panther*, pp. 115–16. Also see Overholser to Pound, August 29, 1959, Overholser File, Pound Archives, Beinecke Library, Yale University.

42. Dudek, *Some Letters,* pp. 105–7. Pound's extensive writing activities are discussed at length in Kenner, *Pound Era,* pp. 506–36, and Stock, *Life of Pound,* pp. 427 ff.

43. Clinical Record, October 12, 1954, POUND, ST. E.

44. *Ibid.,* May 31, 1955, with note of Overholser's secretary, dated June 17, 1955. Overholser to Frank Loveland, March 26, 1957; Dr. William Cushard to Overholser, March 26, 1957, *ibid.*

45. Dr. Merrill Moore to Overholser, July 18, 1955, *ibid.*

46. Cornell, *Trial of Pound,* pp. 58–67; Norman, *Pound,* p. 425. A copy of the petition is in the hospital files. Pound's daughter never understood why the habeas corpus petition was withdrawn. Mary de Rachewiltz, *Discretions* (Boston, 1971), p. 304. Hoover to Tompkins, March 8, 1956, POUND, DOJ. In his petition, Cornell used the 1945 army psychiatrists' reports that Pound was sane—the same ones he believed would have carried no weight during the sanity hearing. FBI Report, March 19, 1956, POUND, FBI.

47. Cornell, *Trial of Pound,* p. 103; Norman, *Pound,* p. 429, for Pound's admission in 1960 that the Rapallo words were his. James Laughlin to author, April 28, 1981. Used with permission. Hoover to Tompkins, March 6, 1956, POUND, DOJ.

48. Thurman Arnold, *Fair Fights and Foul* (New York, 1965), p. 237.

49. *Time,* December 13, 1954; *Life,* February 6, 1956. "Prometheus Bound," Vatican Radio pamphlet, 1954. The situation in Italy was summed up in a Rome embassy telegram to Dulles, January 20, 1956, POUND, DOS.

50. New York *Herald Tribune,* January 30, 1957.

51. MacLeish to Overholser, November 16, 1956; Overholser to MacLeish, November 21, 1956; MacLeish to Overholser, November 29, 1956; Overholser to MacLeish, December 4, 1956, POUND, ST. E.

52. MacLeish to Milton Eisenhower, January 11, 1957, MACLEISH, LC. U.S. UN Mission to State Department, December 30, 1955, POUND, DOS. *Time,* December 13, 1954.

53. Frost et al. to Brownell, January 14, 1957, POUND, DOJ.

54. Hoover to the Attorney General, April 9, 1957, *ibid.*

55. MacLeish to Overholser, November 26, 1957; Overholser to MacLeish, December 5, 1957; MacLeish to Overholser, December 13, 1957, POUND, ST. E. Laughlin to MacLeish, November 27, 1956; Eliot to MacLeish, July 2, 1956, MACLEISH, LC. Eliot indicated that Francis Biddle supported quashing the indictment. He also reported, secondhand, that Overholser said that Pound was "not insane at the present time and could leave the hospital . . . if he could be sure of a quiet place to live in." Pound's desire to return to Italy had an element of perverse humor: "As I always spoke as an american, FOR the constitution, etc. it wd/be a joke of jokes to get out ON CONDITION that I return to Italy." Meacham, *Caged Panther,* p. 52.

56. Green to Foley, May 10, 1956, POUND, DOJ.

57. Thomas Hall to Foley, July 2, 1956; Foley to Tompkins, July 30, 1956, *ibid.*

58. Overholser to MacLeish, December 5, 1957; Herter to MacLeish, March 5, 1958, MACLEISH, LC.

59. Washington *Post,* April 7, 1958; New York *Times,* April 2, 1958. The government obviously needed assurances that Pound would not embarrass the United States if he returned to Italy. In February 1958, his wife wrote to Overholser stating that Pound

planned to go to Europe if released. She assured the superintendent that her husband had no views on current Italian politics and it would take him at least ten years to develop any. Dorothy Pound to Overholser, February 1, 1958, POUND, ST. E. In all probability, Pound again was speaking through his wife and willingly gave the government what it needed. It cost him little.

60. The trial materials are in the hospital file. Washington *Post*, April 19, 1958; New York *Times*, July 10, 1958.

61. Overholser to Fritz Redlich, April 20, 1961, POUND, ST. E.

62. Overholser to William Rogers (Arnold, Fortas & Porter), February 10, 1959; Rogers to Overholser, February 13, 1959; Arnold to Pound, March 3, 1959, *ibid.*

63. Overholser to Charles Norman, January 8, 1960, *ibid.*

64. Frederic Wertham, "The Road to Rapallo," *American Journal of Psychotherapy* (1949) 3:585–600; Thomas S. Szasz, *Law, Liberty and Psychiatry* (New York, 1963), pp. 200–7. Thomas S. Szasz, *Ideology and Insanity* (New York, 1970), pp. 30, 111. Cf. Jerome Kavka, "Ezra Pound's Sanity: The Agony of Public Disclosure," *Paideuma* (1975), 4:527.

CHAPTER 4

1. Linus Pauling, "My Efforts to Obtain a Passport," *Bulletin of the Atomic Scientists* (1952), 8:253–55. Horace Freeland Judson, *The Eighth Day of Creation: Makers of the Revolution in Biology* (New York, 1979), pp. 70–75, 128, 132–34, discusses the passport denial and its implications for Pauling's role in the DNA experiments. James D. Watson, *The Double Helix: A Personal Account of the Discovery of the Structure of DNA* (New York, 1968), discusses the "race" between himself (with Francis Crick) and Pauling, a point which Judson finds somewhat exaggerated.

2. Dean G. Acheson, *Present at the Creation: My Years in the State Department* (Signet ed., New York, 1970), pp. 38–39.

3. *Congressional Record*, June 6, 1952, pp. 6990–95.

4. *Department of State Bulletin* (July 7, 1952), 27:40–42. Helen Worden Erskine, "You Don't Go If She Says *No*," *Collier's* (July 11, 1953), 132:62–65. Isaiah Berlin, while attached to the British Embassy in Washington during World War II, aptly described Shipley as "a veritable ogre of formality and rectitude, who is not only above reproach but beyond intimidation." H. G. Nicholas (ed.), *Weekly Despatches 1941–1945: Weekly Political Reports from the British Embassy* (Chicago, 1981), p. 359.

5. New York *Times*, February 25, 1955.

6. *New Republic* (April 11, 1955), 132:3–4.

7. Richard Rovere, *Senator Joe McCarthy* (Meridian ed., New York, 1959), pp. 32–33.

8. *New Republic* (April 11, 1955), 132:3–4.

9. New York *Times*, April 1, 6, 1955.

10. *Ibid.*, July 25, 1975.

11. T. F. T. Pluncknett, *Tazewell-Langmead's English Constitutional History* (11th ed., London, 1960), pp. 60–77 *passim.* Also see Faith Thompson, *Magna Carta: Its Role in the Making of the English Constitution* (London, 1948); Reginald Parker, "The Right to Go Abroad: To Have and to Hold a Passport," *Virginia Law Review* (1954), 40: 866–68. Blackstone, *Commentaries*, Book I, *134.

12. *Urtetiqui* v. *D'Arbel*, 9 Peters 692 (1835). Department of State, *The United States Passport: Past, Present, Future* (Washington, D.C., 1976); Department of State, *The Department of State of the United States: Its History and Functions* (Washington, D.C.,

1893); Gaillard Hunt, *The American Passport* (Washington, D.C., 1898). Many relevant documents are contained in *The Right to Travel, Hearing*, Subcommittee on Constitutional Rights, Committee on the Judiciary, U.S. Senate, 85 Cong., 1 Sess. (March 29, April 4, 1957). Useful contemporary surveys can be found in Charles E. Wyzanski, Jr., "Freedom to Travel," *Atlantic Monthly* (October 1952), 190:66–68; Dorothy Fosdick, "The Passport—and the Right to Travel," *The New York Times Magazine*, July 17, 1955. Wyzanski was a distinguished federal judge and Fosdick had worked in the State Department, 1942–53. Some of the problems are discussed in David Caute, *The Great Fear: The Anti-Communist Purge Under Truman and Eisenhower* (New York, 1978), pp. 245–51.

13. Leonard B. Boudin, "The Constitutional Right to Travel," *Columbia Law Review* (1956), 56:53–54.

14. *Bauer v. Acheson*, 106 F. Supp. 445, 451–52 (D.D.C. 1952).

15. Brief for the Respondent, *Kent & Briehl v. Dulles*, Supreme Court of the United States, October Term, 1957, 123–28.

16. 22 C.F.R., Sections 51.135–43, August 28, 1952; *Department of State Bulletin* (June 9, 1952), 26:919.

17. Boudin, "The Constitutional Right to Travel," p. 66. "Passport Refusals for Political Reasons: Constitutional Issues and Judicial Review," *Yale Law Journal* (1952), 61:174–81.

18. Boudin, "The Constitutional Right to Travel," pp. 67–68.

19. *Ibid.*, p. 66.

20. *Ibid.*, pp. 64–65.

21. *Perkins v. Elg*, 307 U.S. 325 (1939).

22. *Bauer v. Acheson*, 106 F. Supp. 445 (D.D.C. 1952).

23. *Dulles v. Nathan*, 225 F. 2d 29 (D.C. Cir. 1955).

24. *Schachtman v. Dulles*, 225 F. 2d 938, 943–44 (D.C. Cir. 1955).

25. *Boudin v. Dulles*, 136 F. Supp. 218 (D.D.C. 1955); *Boudin v. Dulles*, 235 F. 2d 532, 535, 536 (D.C. Cir. 1956).

26. *Robeson v. Dulles*, 235 F. 2d 810, 811 (D.C. Cir. 1956). Leonard Boudin also represented Robeson.

27. The information on Kent is compiled from his FBI File. Hereafter cited as KENT, FBI. See reports of October 13, 1951; January 19, October 29, 1953; May 26, 1955; and January 30, 1956. Also see, *It's Me O Lord: The Autobiography of Rockwell Kent* (New York, 1955). In an appearance before Senator McCarthy in July 1953, Kent took the Fifth Amendment. U.S. Senate, Permanent Subcommittee on Investigations . . . , "State Department Information Program Centers" (July 1, 1953), pp. 417–21.

28. New York *Times*, April 19, 20, 22, 1949.

29. Louis Spiegler to Shipley, February 27, 1950; Herman Phleger to Warren E. Burger, January 31, 1956; U.S. Embassy, Moscow, to Secretary of State, March 9, 1950; U.S. Embassy, Helsinki, to Secretary of State, March 14, 1950, Rockwell Kent File, Department of State. Hereafter cited as KENT, DOS. New York *Herald Tribune*, August 20, 1950.

30. U.S. Embassy, Stockholm, to Secretary of State, March 16, 20, 1950, KENT, DOS. New York *Times*, July 14, 1950.

31. Kent to Passport Office, July 21, 1950; Shipley Memorandum, July 19, 1950, KENT, DOS.

32. Shipley to Kent, August 1, 1950; Kent to Shipley, July 29, August 4, 1950, *ibid.*

33. Kent to Albert Kahn, August 7, 1950, Kent Papers, Archives of American Art, Smithsonian Institution. Hereafter cited as KENT, SMITHSONIAN. Willis H. Young to Kent, August 11, 1950, KENT, DOS.

34. New York *Herald Tribune*, August 20, 1950; New York *Times*, August 19, 1950; Young to Kent, August 30, 1950, KENT, DOS.

35. Kent to Shipley, February 27, March 13, 1951; Shipley to Kent, March 21, 1951, *ibid.*

36. Shipley to Olney, August 26, 1953; Olney to Lumbard, October 2, 1953; Olney to Dulles, October 2, 1953, *ibid.*

37. Lumbard to Olney, October 26, December 2, 1953, *ibid.*

38. Shipley to Olney, March 9, 1954, *ibid.*

39. Shipley to Olney, April 23, September 22, 1954; Dulles to American Embassy, Paris, August 31, 1954; American Embassy, Paris, to Passport Office, November 22, 1954, *ibid.*

40. Tompkins to Knight, October 27, 1955; Knight to Tompkins, November 11, 1955, *ibid.*

41. Jean Laffitte to Kent, May 20, 1955, *ibid.* See New York *Times*, June 23, 24, 25, 1955, for reports of the Helsinki Conference.

42. Kent to Passport Office, May 28, 1955; Kent to Eisenhower, June 24, 1955, KENT, DOS.

43. Knight to Kent, June 29, 1955, *ibid.*

44. Kent to Knight, July 4, 1955; unidentified clipping, *ibid.* New York *Times*, July 9, 1955.

45. Kent to Foreman, July 14, 1955; Foreman to Kent, July 19, 1955; Kent to Foreman, July 23, 1955; Foreman to Kent, July 28, 1955, KENT, SMITHSONIAN.

46. Knight to Kent, August 18, 1955; Kent to Boudin, August 30, 1955; Boudin to Passport Office, September 2, 12, 1955; Knight to Boudin, September 14, 1955; Boudin to Knight, September 20, 28, 1955; Knight to Boudin, September 29, 1955, KENT, DOS.

47. C. S. Thomas to Passport Office, September 14, 24, 1955; Knight to Thomas, October 3, 1955; Knight to Otto Otepka, October 3, 1955; Belva B. Starry, Memorandum for the File, October 25, 1955, *ibid.*

48. Boudin to McLeod, October 26, 1955; Trueworthy, Memorandum of Conversation, October 27, 1955; Boudin to McLeod, October 27, 1955, *ibid.*

49. New York *Times*, October 31, 1955.

50. Robert Cartwright to Boudin, November 1, 1955, KENT, DOS. Boudin to Kent, November 2, 1955, KENT, SMITHSONIAN.

51. New York *Times*, November 9, 1955. Knight to Kent, November 25, 1955; Warren E. Burger to Department of State, December 22, 1955, KENT, DOS.

52. Boudin to John W. Sipes, November 30, 1955; Yingling (Legal Office, European Section, State Department) to Sipes, December 2, 1955; Boudin to Dulles, December 5, 1955; Sipes to Boudin, December 12, 1955; Boudin to Sipes, December 20, 1955, *ibid.*

53. *Boudin* v. *Dulles*, 136 F. Supp. 218, 222 (D.D.C. 1955).

54. Phleger to Burger, January 30, 1956, KENT, DOS.

55. Phleger to Burger, January 31, 1956, *ibid.*

56. *Kent* v. *Dulles*, 248 F. 2d 561 (D.C. Cir. 1957).

57. *Department of State Bulletin* (June 3, 1957), 36:896.

58. *Kent* v. *Dulles*, 357 U.S. 116, 125–26 (1958).

59. *Ibid.*, p. 128.

60. *Ibid.*, pp. 128–29.

61. *Ibid.*, pp. 129–30. Justice Tom Clark wrote a dissenting opinion, joined by Justices Burton, Harlan, and Whittaker.

62. J. Walter Yeagley to John M. Raymond, June 24, 1958; Raymond to Yeagley, June 25, 1958. Paul Robeson File, Department of State. A. H. Belmont to Clyde Tolson, July 29, 1958, KENT, FBI.

63. Boudin to Knight, June 27, 1958; Kent passport application, stamp of issuance, July 1, 1958; C. H. Seeley to Passport Files, March 12, 1959; American Embassy, Moscow Dispatch, December 16, 1960; Kent to Maurice Rice, June 11, 1959; Temple Wanamaker to Passport Division, June 19, 1959, KENT, DOS. New York *Times*, May 25, 1960.

64. Knight to William Boswell, January 26, 1962; Kent to Knight, February 5, 1962; Legal Division Review Sheet, February 20, 1962; Knight to Boudin, February 27, 1962; Kent application, January 10, 1962. Boudin confirmed the affidavit. Boudin to Knight, February 6, 1962, KENT, DOS. Paul Robeson signed a similar disclaimer.

65. "Legalizing Treason?" *U.S. News & World Report* (July 18, 1958), 45:100.

66. *Department of State Bulletin* (July 21, 1958), 39:110; *ibid.* (August 11, 1958), 39:250.

67. *Ibid.*, 39:250–54.

68. New York *Times*, July 23, 1958. Shortly after the decision, the Association of the Bar of the City of New York published its long-pending study of passport practice. Largely critical of prevailing practice, the report was relied on by congressional supporters of a liberal policy. See *Freedom to Travel* (New York, 1958).

69. *Department of State Bulletin* (December 1, 1958), 39:880–85; *ibid.* (April 13, 1959), 40:517–24; *ibid.* (May 18, 1959), 40:723–26; *ibid.* (August 31, 1959), 41:319–25.

70. *Communist Party* v. *Subversive Activities Control Board*, 367 U.S. 1 (1961). New York *Times*, April 19, 1963. Despite the passport given to Flynn, others were withheld because of political associations or beliefs. But in 1964 the Court reaffirmed the Kent case assumption of a constitutional right to travel and held the statute unconstitutional, as it swept "too widely and too indiscriminately across the liberty guaranteed in the Fifth Amendment" (*Aptheker* v. *Secretary of State*, 378 U.S. 500, 514 [1964]). But the next year the Court upheld a travel ban to Cuba which it construed as involving foreign policy considerations affecting all citizens, and not confined to class restrictions as in the Kent case (*Zemel* v. *Rusk*, 318 U.S. 1, 8 [1965]). The Court, however, said nothing about criminal sanctions for such a policy until two years later. In 1967 it reverted to the Kent doctrine and found that the Passport Act of 1926 did not provide for criminal sanctions (*United States* v. *Laub*, 385 U.S. 475 [1967]). The State Department then turned again to administrative sanctions, such as threatening revocation and non-renewal of passports, but the Circuit Court held the practice invalid in *Lynd* v. *Rusk* (389 F. 2d 940 [D.C. Cir. 1967]). Finally, in 1968, the State Department eliminated all sanctions for violations of the area restrictions. Thus the Kent and Zemel cases remain largely controlling: passports may not be denied on the basis of political beliefs or associations; yet travel for all persons may be restricted to certain geographical areas, provided that such restrictions are based on valid reasons of national security. In 1981, however, the Court limited the First Amendment protections regarding possession of a passport when it ruled that a citizen's conduct inimical to the national interest while abroad justified revocation of a passport. *Haig, Secretary of State*, v. *Agee* (June 29, 1981).

71. New York *Times*, February 24, 1975; May 29, 1977.

CHAPTER 5

1. Charles P. Larrowe, *Harry Bridges: The Rise and Fall of Radical Labor in the U.S.* (New York, 1972), offers the most complete account of Bridges' background and career. Larrowe chiefly is concerned with the effects of the government's persecution of Bridges and his union. My understanding of the San Francisco waterfront and the labor situation is based on Miriam Feingold's unpublished dissertation, "The King-Ramsay-Connor Case: Labor, Radicalism, and the Law in California, 1936–1941 (University of Wisconsin, 1976), Chapter 1, and works cited therein. Feingold's work includes an interview with Bridges. The government's initial understanding of Bridges' background is contained in a report from Inspector T. V. Donoghue to District Director Edward Haff, San Francisco Office, January 22, 1935. Harry Bridges File, Immigration and Naturalization Service, San Francisco. Hereafter cited as INS.

2. See Larrowe and Feingold, n. 1, *supra.* Also see *In the Matter of Harry R. Bridges: Findings and Conclusions of the Trial Examiner* (Washington, D.C., 1939), *passim.* This is the report of James M. Landis, following Bridges' 1939 deportation hearing. Hereafter cited as LANDIS. Charles A. Madison, *American Labor Leaders* (New York, 1962), has a chapter on Bridges' career. Other useful accounts are Arthur M. Schlesinger, Jr., *The Coming of the New Deal* (Boston, 1959), pp. 389–93; Frances Perkins, *The Roosevelt I Knew* (New York, 1946), pp. 315–19; George Martin, *Madam Secretary: Frances Perkins* (Boston, 1976), pp. 315–22, 406–18. San Francisco *Chronicle,* July 5, 1934, reported the responses of shippers and businessmen. For the Communist Party's role in 1934, see House Special Committee on Un-American Activities, 73 Cong., 2 Sess., Report, p. 270.

3. San Francisco *Commercial News,* May 31, 1934. Telephone Memo to Commissioner Shaughnessy, May 22, 1934, INS. The activities of the employers' groups are detailed in a report by the La Follette Subcommittee on Free Speech and Rights of Labor, 78 Cong., 1 Sess., Sen. Rep. No. 398, Part 3 (December 21, 1943), pp. 1029–1127.

4. Donoghue to Haff, June 13, 1934, January 22, 1935; Haff to Commissioner Daniel W. McCormack, February 2, 1935, INS.

5. Patrick J. Farrelly to Haff, April 12, 1935, *ibid.*

6. Perkins, *Roosevelt,* pp. 313–15; *Complete Press Conferences of Franklin D. Roosevelt* (New York, 1972), 4:45–46.

7. McCormack to F. P. Dickson, September 28, 1935; McCormack to F. V. Wyle, September 24, 1936, INS. FDR to Perkins, August 29, September 18, 1935. Harry Bridges File, O.F. 1750, Franklin D. Roosevelt Library. Hereafter cited as FDR Library.

8. Knowles to McCormack, December 18, 1935; W. W. Brown Memorandum to McCormack, April 20, 1936, citing Knowles's various letters; Reilly to McCormack, April 28, 1936; Perkins to McCormack, April 20, 1936; Brown et al. to McCormack, c. August 1936, INS. The Bridges file in the FDR Library contains numerous petitions and demands for deportation.

9. Shaughnessy to Perkins, January 13, 1937, INS; Perkins, *Roosevelt,* p. 318.

10. New York *Times,* October 6, 23, 1937; January 6, 1938; February 4, 5, 7, 8, 1938.

11. *Hearings,* Senate Committee on Commerce and Senate Committee on Education and Labor, 75 Cong., 3 Sess. (February 9, 1938), pp. 964–86, 1063–1102, *passim;* (February 10, 1938), pp. 1137–45; (January 25, 1938), p. 738. New York *Times,* February 10, 11, 1938.

12. For an example of internal pressure to prosecute, see Roy Norene (Portland Office)

to Reilly, December 18, 1937, INS. Houghteling to Bonham, January 4, 1938, *ibid.*, described the decision to pursue a hearing. John R. Steelman to Perkins, September 8, 1937, quoted in Donald A. Ritchie, *James A. Landis: Dean of the Regulators* (Cambridge, Mass., 1980), p. 94. Bridges also found himself under assault from the California courts in early 1938. Following a Superior Court injunction in a dispute between rival longshoremen's factions, Bridges sent a telegram to Perkins threatening a West Coast strike if the injunction was enforced. The telegram was reprinted in the newspapers, and Bridges was convicted of contempt on the grounds that the telegram had a tendency to interfere with the impartial application of justice. A bitterly divided Supreme Court overturned the conviction in December 1941. *Bridges* v. *California*, 314 U.S. 252 (1941). Also see *Bridges* v. *Superior Court*, 14 Calif. 2d 464, 94 P. 2d 983 (1939).

13. 40 Stat. 1012 (October 16, 1918); 41 Stat. 1008 (June 5, 1920).

14. Houghteling to Bonham, March 16, 1938; Bonham to Shoemaker, March 29, 1938; Bonham to Houghteling, April 18, 1938; Knowles to Cahill, March 28, 1938; Houghteling to Knowles, April 13, 1938; Aubrey Grossman to Cahill, March 31, 1938, INS.

15. *Strecker* v. *Kessler*, 95 F. 2d 976–80 (5th C.C.A. 1938).

16. T. B. Shoemaker Memorandum, April 28, 1938; Houghteling to Cahill, April 21, 1938; Houghteling to Perkins; Houghteling to Cahill; Houghteling to Bonham, April 15, 1938, INS.

17. Bonham to Houghteling, April 19, 1938; Houghteling to Bonham, April 20, 1938, *ibid.*

18. *Kessler* v. *Strecker*, 307 U.S. 22, 30–32, 33 (1939).

19. Bonham to Houghteling, April 21, 1938; Houghteling to Bonham, April 23, 1938; Bonham to Houghteling, May 9, 1938; Houghteling to Bonham, May 11, 1938, INS. Commissioner Houghteling and his legal counsel, T. B. Shoemaker, visited Senator Copeland on April 28 to explain the Strecker case and the decision to postpone action against Bridges. Copeland apparently was satisfied with their judgment and he praised the Service for its "realistic facing of the issues for the best interests of sound Americanism." Shoemaker Memorandum, April 21, 1938; Houghteling to Knowles, May 2, 1938, *ibid.* Much to the chagrin of Knowles, Copeland called off any further hearings. Knowles to Houghteling, April 26, 1938, *ibid.*

20. Knowles to Houghteling, April 26, 1938; Houghteling to Knowles, May 2, 1938, *ibid.*

21. Knowles to Houghteling, May 2, 1938; Houghteling to Knowles, May 28, 1938; Knowles to Houghteling, June 7, 1938; Harold L. Putnam (President, California Society, Sons of the American Revolution) to Houghteling, May 13, 1938; Houghteling to Putnam, May 17, 1938; Union of California Citizens to Bureau of Immigration and Naturalization, June 13, 1938, *ibid.* The Union flatly accused the INS of protecting Bridges because he was Pacific Coast Director of the CIO. Labor rival Joseph Ryan predicted in May that Bridges would not be deported. He complained that the Labor Department had "suppressed" evidence which Senator Copeland had tried to secure. New York *Times*, May 23, 1938. The reference probably was to Bonham's report, including affidavits attesting to Bridges' Communist Party membership.

22. *Ibid*, August 14, 15, 17, 31, September 1, 1938. For Frey's testimony, see *Hearings*, House Subcommittee of the Special Committee to Investigate Un-American Activities, 75 Cong., 3 Sess. (August 13, 1938), pp. 92–107. Jackson's letter is in *ibid.* (November 4, 1938), pp. 2075–83. Also see *ibid.* (December 7, 1938), pp. 2909–19; *ibid.* (August 13, 1938), pp. 2944–61. The committee's report is in 76 Cong., 1 Sess. (January 3, 1939).

23. House Committee on the Judiciary, 76 Cong., 1 Sess., No. 311 (March 24, 1939),

pp. 1–10. Martin, *Madam Secretary*, pp. 411–16. Committee Chairman Hatton M. Summers (Dem.-Tex.) insisted that the hearings be closed. Throughout, he ran the proceedings tightly and generally indicated his distaste for the affair.

24. Ritchie, *Landis*, p. 234 n. Allen Weinstein, *Perjury: The Hiss-Chambers Case* (New York, 1978), pp. 220–23, draws some sinister, but not very persuasive implications from Perkins' consideration of Donald Hiss as hearing examiner.

25. LANDIS, pp. 134, 6–7, *et passim.*

26. *Ibid.*, pp. 6 n, 51–52.

27. *Ibid.*, pp. 28–29, 56–76, 133.

28. *Ibid.*, pp. 67, 73. For complaints about Knowles and Keegan, see Ivan Cox to Perkins, September 9, 1938; Reilly to Cox, September 16, 1938; Reilly to Houghteling, n.d.; Houghteling to Arthur J. Phelan, October 10, 1938, INS. Interior Secretary Ickes thought that Perkins might overrule Landis, for she was "pretty jittery . . . about communism and I suspect that she is now in a cold sweat." Ickes, *The Secret Diary of Harold L. Ickes* (New York, 1954), 3:103.

29. New York *Times*, December 30, 31, 1939; San Francisco *Chronicle*, December 31, 1939, January 2, 1940.

30. H.R. Report No. 2269, 76 Cong., 3 Sess.; *History of the Immigration and Naturalization Service, Report* for House Committee on the Judiciary, 96 Cong., 2 Sess., p. 47; *Congressional Record*, 76 Cong., 3 Sess. (May 27, 1940), pp. 6916–18; (May 31, 1940), pp. 7199–7202, 7259–90. Gerard Reilly Interview, October 22, 1965, Department of Labor Archives.

31. *Congressional Record*, 76 Cong., 3 Sess. (June 13, 1940), pp. 12380–407. Most of the Democratic leadership voted for the bill, as did a young Texas congressman whom Bridges supported for the presidency in 1964.

32. Robert Jackson, "Oral History" (Columbia Oral History Program), pp. 304–7 (transcript provided by Professor Philip B. Kurland). 54 Stat. 673 (June 23, 1940). H.R. Report No. 994, 76 Cong., 1 Sess. Jackson wrongly recalled the sequence of events. Section 23 had not yet passed the Senate when he struck the deal. Memorandum, James Rowe, Jr., to FDR, August 13, 1970, reflects the Administration's concerns. FDR Library.

33. Hoover to INS, August 27, 1940; Department of Justice Announcement, February 12, 1941, Bridges File, Federal Bureau of Investigation. Hereafter cited as BRIDGES, FBI.

34. Hoover to Jackson, November 26, 30, December 2, 6, 9, 18, 1940, January 30, 1941; Department of Justice Announcement, February 12, 1941, *ibid.* For an example of Hoover's well-practiced technique of leaking his information to friendly congressmen, see the remarks of Representative C. Arthur Anderson, *Congressional Record*, 76 Cong., 3 Sess. (October 7, 1940), Appendix 6181.

35. Jackson, "Oral History," p. 307. New York *Times*, March 7, 1941.

36. Ritchie, *Landis*, p. 98, Jackson, "Oral History," pp. 315–16. Francis Biddle, Jackson's successor, claimed that Jackson disliked continuing the action because "his liberal friends" regarded it as political persecution. Biddle, *In Brief Authority* (New York, 1962), p. 297. Bridges, incidentally, condemned a 1940 ILA strike as sabotaging national defense —a position quite contrary to CP policy during the Nazi-Soviet alliance. Bridges to FDR, September 12, 1940, FDR Library.

37. *In the Matter of Harry Renton Bridges: Memorandum of Decision* (September 26, 1941), pp. 104–7.

38. *Ibid.*, pp. 107–17.

39. *Ibid.*, pp. 168–70.

40. Biddle, *In Brief Authority*, pp. 297–98. *In re Harry Renton Bridges, Before the*

Board of Immigration Appeals (January 3, 1942), pp. 8–11, 45–52, 80–95, 52–79, INS.

41. Lemuel Schofield, *Memorandum for the Attorney General, In re Harry Renton Bridges* (February 14, 1942), *ibid.*

42. *In re Harry Renton Bridges: Before the Attorney General in Deportation Proceedings* (May 28, 1942), *ibid.*

43. Biddle, *In Brief Authority*, pp. 302–3. FDR to Eleanor Roosevelt, June 12, 16, 1942, FDR Library.

44. *Business Week*, June 21, 1941, p. 53. John B. Hughes, "Can We Afford to Deport Harry Bridges?," *Liberty*, September 19, 1942, pp. 18–21, summarizes the sentiment of West Coast businessmen. Jackson, "Oral History," pp. 310–11. The ILWU Library in San Francisco has an extensive file of petitions sent to the White House and the Justice Department. The FDR Library has a similar file.

45. Minutes, CIO Board Meeting, n.d., pp. 7, 14, ILWU Library. Jackson, "Oral History," p. 311.

46. *Ex parte Bridges*, 49 F. Supp. 292 (N.D. Calif. 1943).

47. *Bridges* v. *Wixon*, 144 F. 2d 927, 939–43 (9th C.C.A. 1944).

48. *Bridges* v. *Wixon*, 326 U.S. 120, 154 (1945).

49. *Ibid.*, pp. 143–45.

50. *Ibid.*, pp. 157, 159, 159–65. Biddle, *In Brief Authority*, p. 307. Douglas' opinion went through several drafts, with each successive one narrowing the grounds for decision and diluting some of his stronger language regarding official behavior. See Box 106, William O. Douglas MS, Library of Congress. Murphy's conference notes reveal attitudes of various justices, particularly noting that Frankfurter believed Biddle was a "damn fool." Frank Murphy MS, Michigan Historical Collections, Bentley Historical Library.

51. *Bridges* v. *Wixon*, 326 U.S. 120, 166, 173–74, 178 (1945).

52. Carusi to Clark, August 27, 1945; INS Memorandum, August 27, 1945, INS.

53. Agnes Bridges, "Affidavit," September 11, 1945, and Sworn Statement, September 14, 1945; Wixon Telegram, September 13, 1945; L. H. Garner to H. J. Hart, September 17, 1945; Wixon to Carusi, September 18, 1945; Gladstein to Wixon, September 29, 1945; Wixon to Carusi, October 3, 1945; Montaquila Memorandum, October 26, 1945; Savoretti to Wixon, November 2, 1945, *ibid.* Also see San Francisco *Chronicle*, September 18, 1945.

54. Larrowe, *Harry Bridges*, p. 295.

55. Boyd to William Carmichael, February 24, 1948; Boyd to Hoover, July 20, 1948; John H. McGowan to Boyd, October 13, 1948; Barber to Boyd, September 21, 1948; Barber to Boyd, March 7, 1949; Barber to Boyd, October 18, 1948, INS. For Rathborne's CIO connections, and his awareness of the new anti-Communist mood, see Barber to Boyd, October 26, 1948, *ibid.*

56. Barber to Boyd, December 24, 1948; Barber to Boyd, March 7, 1949; Boyd to Peyton Ford, March 10, 1949; Boyd to Peyton Ford, June 16, 1949; Hitchcock to Clark, October 9, 1948, *ibid.* The Act of June 25, 1948, altered the statute of limitations from five to three years. 62 Stat. 862.

57. *United States* v. *Bridges*, 86 F. Supp. 922 (N.D. S.D. Calif. 1949), for denial of dismissal. For factual background, see *Bridges* v. *United States*, 346 U.S. 209, 212–14 (1953). Paul Jacobs, *The State of the Unions* (New York, 1963), p. 96; Vern Countryman, *Un-American Activities in the State of Washington* (Ithaca, N.Y., 1951), pp. 160–61. Bridges' 1949 trial was delayed because his chief lawyer, Richard Gladstein, was one of the defense lawyers in the then current Smith Act trial of leading Communists in New York. Gladstein subsequently was convicted for contempt in that trial. (See Chapter 6.)

Ironically, his replacement, Vincent Hallinan, similarly was convicted of contempt in the Bridges trial. Hallinan's version of events is in his memoir, *A Lion in Court* (New York, 1963), pp. 227–77.

58. Milwaukee *Journal*, June 27, 1949. Larrowe, *Bridges*, pp. 300 ff.

59. "Oral Opinion of Judge George B. Harris Revoking Bail . . . of Harry Bridges," August 5, 1950, typescript, ILWU Library. *Bridges* v. *United States*, 9th C.C.A., No. 12,597 (bail restored). *Ibid.*, 199 F. 2d 254 (9th C.C.A. 1952) (appeal denied).

60. *Ibid.*, 346 U.S. 209, 215–24, 209, 227–28. Reed's dissent disputed the majority's interpretation of the Wartime Suspension of Limitations Act. Burton to Black, Douglas, and Frankfurter, n.d., Hugo L. Black MS, Library of Congress. Burton's papers indicate he worked strenuously to keep the case in narrow bounds. Douglas, for example, would have overturned the decision on grounds of *res judicata.* See Memorandum, June 15, 1953; Burton to Black, Douglas, and Frankfurter, June 4, 1953, Harold H. Burton MS, *ibid.* A year later, Congress changed the limitations law back to five years.

61. I.. Paul Winings (General Counsel) to A. R. Mackey (Deputy Commissioner, INS), April 21, 1950, INS. *United States* v. *Bridges et al.*, 86 F. Supp. 931 (N.D. S.D. Calif. 1949); *ibid.*, 90 F. Supp. 973 (N.D. S.D. Calif. 1950); *Bridges* v. *United States*, 345 U.S. 979 (1953) (reversal of revocation of citizenship). General Counsel, INS, to Assistant Attorney General, Criminal Division, July 17, 1953, INS.

62. Taylor, "Opening Statement for the Respondent," typescript, ILWU Library. *United States* v. *Bridges*, No. 28876 (D.C. N.D. Calif.) July 29, 1955, typescript, *ibid.* Bridges' longtime lawyer, Richard Gladstein, recently had served a jail sentence for contempt in the New York Smith Act trial. He did, however, participate in the 1955 trial. Taylor, at the time, was James Landis' law partner.

63. Bridges Cases Files, ILWU Library. New York *Times*, March 19, 1958. *Proceedings of the 14th Biennial Convention of the ILWU (1961)*, pp. 15–19. Shortly before the Supreme Court's 1945 decision, the Harry Bridges Victory Committee received a notice from the IRS that it would have to file returns. Norman D. Cann (IRS) to George Wilson, February 2, 1945, Bridges Cases Files, ILWU Library.

64. For information on fees, see, for example, Gladstein to George Wilson, April 30, 1943, *ibid.* The Attorney General included Bridges' various defense committees on the list of subversive organizations. Again, considerable efforts and sums were expended to challenge that action. Norman Leonard to Louis Goldblatt, October 8, 1953; William Glazier to Jeff Kibre, January 7, 1955, *ibid.*

65. Jacobs, *State of the Unions*, p. 95; Bert Cochran, *Labor and Communism: The Conflict That Shaped American Unions* (Princeton, 1977), p. 89 n.; Joseph R. Starobin, *American Communism in Crisis, 1943–1957* (Cambridge, Mass., 1972), p. 258 n.

CHAPTER 6

1. The background of the Smith Act and the decision to try the leaders of the Communist Party is thoroughly discussed in Michal Belknap, *Cold War Political Justice: The Smith Act, the Communist Party, and American Civil Liberties* (Westport, Conn., 1977), pp. 9–76. For an "inside" view reflecting the Party's response to the prosecution, see Joseph R. Starobin, *American Communism in Crisis, 1943–1957* (Cambridge, Mass., 1972).

2. Tom C. Clark, "Civil Rights: The Boundless Responsibility of Lawyers," *American Bar Association Journal* (1946), 32:453–57.

3. Tom C. Clark, "Why the Reds Won't Scare Us" *Look*, August 30, 1949, pp. 50–53; *American Bar Association Journal* (1951) 37:312–13. Jerold S. Auerbach, *Unequal Justice* (New York, 1976), Chapter 8, is excellent on the political pressures confronting lawyers in this period. By late 1951, the White House apparently had decided that Clark's message may have been taken too literally. In a letter to an official of the American Bar Association, President Truman noted that lawyers traditionally had "risked the obloquy of the uninformed to protect the rights of the most degraded. Unless they continue to do so in the future, an important part of our rights will be gone." Truman to Arthur J. Freund, September 1, 1951, Felix Frankfurter Papers, Harvard Law School. Hereafter cited as FRANKFURTER, HLS.

4. James Willard Hurst, *The Growth of American Law: The Law Makers* (Boston, 1950), p. 255. William O. Douglas, "The Black Silence of Fear," *The New York Times Magazine*, January 13, 1952, pp. 37–38.

5. For contemporary biographies of Medina, see Daniel Hawthorne, *Judge Medina: A Biography* (New York, 1952); Irwin Ross, "Harold Medina—Judge Extraordinary," *Reader's Digest* (February 1950), 66:87–88. Medina's description of his judicial behavior in a patent trial a year earlier was astonishingly frank: "I bedeviled the witnesses with all kinds of absurd questions and I imagine the lawyers felt each day as though they were going into a torture chamber." Medina, "A New Judge Tries His First Patent Case," *Cornell Law Quarterly* (Winter 1948), 34:220, 223. Medina allegedly told Circuit Court Justice Augustus Hand that he couldn't think unless he was talking. Hand suggested that he talked too much. Medina replied, "Yes, but I can't help it." C. C. Burlingham to Felix Frankfurter, January 17, 1951. Felix Frankfurter Papers, Library of Congress. Hereafter cited as FRANKFURTER, LC.

6. The background information about the defense lawyers is from personal interviews with George Crockett, April 27, 1979; Richard Gladstein, August 19, 1978; and Abraham J. Isserman, June 11, 1978. Also see "George W. Crockett: The Opener," *Black Law Journal* (Winter 1971), 1:247–59. An FBI report in October 1949 emphasized the personal characteristics of the lawyers, demonstrating the Bureau's often picayune, if bizarre, concerns. Crockett was described as follows: "Dresses neatly; air of confidence; tendency to assume poses." Gladstein also dressed neatly and had an "oratorical" voice. Isserman was "neat" in dress, but had a "slight tendency to stammer." McCabe also was "neat," wore a Phi Beta Kappa key, and had "a very slight tendency to stutter." Sacher "dresses neatly," the report concluded. Abraham J. Isserman File, Federal Bureau of Investigation. Hereafter cited as ISSERMAN, FBI. Isserman's file contains numerous documents demonstrating the FBI's knowledge of defense strategy and division.

7. *United States* v. *Foster et al.*, Transcript 16:113–47. The contempt certificate is reported in *United States* v. *Sacher et al.*, 9 F.R.D. 394 (1949). Also see Norman Dorsen and Leon Friedman, *Disorder in the Court* (New York, 1973), pp. 49–56, for some of the exchanges between Medina and the lawyers.

8. Letters regarding the trial are scattered in Medina's personal correspondence and in a special collection (Box 5) of letters received after the verdict. Harold Medina Papers, Princeton University. The papers are temporarily stored at Johns Hopkins University and were made available to me through the kind cooperation of Professor J. Woodford Howard. The McGrath letter is from October 25, 1949, J. Howard McGrath Papers, Harry S. Truman Library.

9. 182 F. 2d 416, 419–23 (2d C.C.A. 1950).

10. *Ibid.*, pp. 453–56.

11. 9 F.R.D. 394, 395 (S.D. N.Y. 1949).

12. 182 F. 2d 416, 464–65. Clark differed sharply with his colleagues on Medina's failure to impose summary punishment at the time of each incident. Such punishment, Clark said, was "an extraordinary exception to due process of law, justified only by the urgent needs of the moment. When the need for this drastic action passes, the power so to act also passes." *Ibid.*, p. 465.

13. Clark to Black, March 15, 1952, Hugo L. Black Papers, Library of Congress.

14. 341 U.S. 952 (1951).

15. Frankfurter Memorandum for the Conference, February 27, 1951; Frankfurter to Jackson, October 4, 8, 1951; Frankfurter Docket Sheet, *Sacher* v. *United States;* Frankfurter Memorandum, October 8, 1951, FRANKFURTER, LC.

16. Jackson Memorandum, *Sacher* v. *United States,* October 9, 1951, *ibid.*

17. Frankfurter to Burton, October 15, 1951, *ibid.*

18. *Sacher et al.* v. *United States,* 343 U.S. 1, 5, 7, 11 (1952).

19. *Ibid.*, pp. 12–14.

20. *Ibid.*, pp. 14–20. Speaking for himself and Justice Douglas, Black reiterated his long-standing concern for summary contempt punishments and argued that the petitioners were entitled to a jury trial. *Ibid.*, pp. 20–23.

21. *Ibid.*, pp. 25–37. Frankfurter's appendix is in *ibid.*, pp. 42–89. The Court denied a rehearing on April 21, 1952. 343 U.S. 931. Frankfurter simply disliked Medina. Recalling Medina from a 1945 appearance before the Court, Frankfurter described him as "the most insufferable egotist by long odds who had appeared before us." In 1951, Frankfurter was unhappy about Medina's impending promotion to the Circuit Court of Appeals, describing him then as a "Messianic" character and a "super-egotist." Frankfurter to Learned Hand, April 24, 1951; Frankfurter to C. C. Burlingham, April 25, 1951, FRANKFURTER, LC. The Sacher decision has not had much value as a precedent. *Offutt* v. *United States,* in effect, amounted to a *sub silentio* overruling of Sacher. 348 U.S. 11 (1954). Also see *Mayberry* v. *Pennsylvania,* 400 U.S. 455 (1971), and *United States* v. *Meyer,* 462 F. 2d 827 (D.C. Cir. 1972).

22. Gladstein to George R. Andersen, June 24, 1952; Andersen to Board of Parole, July 1, 1952; Ewing Sibbett to Lawrence Sperber, August 4, 1952, Gladstein Office Files, Leonard & Patsey, San Francisco. Hereafter cited as GLADSTEIN OF. Isserman Interview, June 11, 1978; Crockett Interview, April 27, 1979; Gladstein Interview, April 19, 1978.

23. New York FBI Field Office Report to Washington, June 23, 1950, ISSERMAN, FBI; Isserman Interview, June 11, 1978.

24. Edward Scheidt to Hoover, December 9, 15, 1949; Hoover to Scheidt, December 19, 1949, ISSERMAN, FBI.

25. *In re Sacher and Isserman,* Order to Show Cause, U.S.D.C. (S.D. N.Y.), April 14, 1950. Docket entries, U.S.D.C. (S.D. N.Y.). Hincks's delay was even more mysterious since the Supreme Court had upheld the convictions of the Foley Square defendants in June 1951.

26. The opinion is unreported, although there is a mimeographed "Memorandum of Opinion." See pp. 3–4, 13, 14–15, 16, 18. The lawyers gained a Pyrrhic victory when Hincks rejected Medina's conspiracy finding. But the lack of a proven conspiracy, Hincks held, did not exonerate the lawyers from their own "proven misconduct."

27. *Association of the Bar of the City of New York* v. *Sacher,* 206 F. 2d 358, 359–61 (1953).

28. *Ibid.*, pp. 362–63. Cf. *In re Doe,* 95 F. 2d 386 (1938): "Disbarment is fitting only when the attorney has been guilty of corrupt conduct; of some attempt to suborn a witness; or to bribe a juror, or to forge a document, or to embezzle clients' property, or other things

abhorrent to honest and fair dealing." Augustus Hand was one of the judges participating in the Doe ruling.

29. 206 F. 2d 358, pp. 363, 365.

30. Frankfurter to Jackson, November 13, 1953, FRANKFURTER, LC; Jackson to Frankfurter, November 23, 1953, FRANKFURTER, HLS.

31. *Association of the Bar of the City of New York* v. *Sacher*, 347 U.S. 388, 389, 394 (1954). When the Court discussed the contempt issues in 1951, Frankfurter noted that Reed vigorously defended Medina in private, calling him "probably the outstanding judge of the lower courts for his courageous course" in the Foley Square case. Undated memo, 1951, FRANKFURTER, HLS. Justice Burton voted to affirm the lower court finding, but he did not join Reed's dissent.

32. *In re Isserman*, 9 N.J. 269, 275–77, 278–79 (1952). *In re Isserman*, 9 N.J. 316 (1952), rehearing denied. Isserman traced Vanderbilt's hostility toward him from the 1930s when defendants in a state sedition case dismissed Vanderbilt and accepted Isserman as their counsel. Isserman Interview, June 11, 1978.

33. *Isserman* v. *Ethics Committee of the Essex County Bar Association*, 345 U.S. 927 (1953). *In re Isserman*, 345 U.S. 286 (1953).

34. *Ibid.*, pp. 289–90.

35. *Ibid.*, pp. 292, 294.

36. *In re Isserman*, 348 U.S. 1 (1954). Burton, Reed, and Minton dissented, citing Vinson's opinion of a year earlier. Earl Warren probably cast the decisive vote for the rule change. The order in favor of Isserman was announced five days after Jackson's death.

37. *Association of the Bar of the City of New York* v. *Isserman*, 271 F. 2d 784, 785–86 (2nd C.C.A. 1959). Docket entries, U.S.D.C. (S.D. N.Y.). The bar association's files amply demonstrate that disciplinary proceedings would continue despite the Supreme Court's various rulings. The zest for witch-hunting still existed. After the district court disbarred Isserman in 1958, the New York *Daily News* declared: "Better late than never, of course; but in this case action comes pretty damned late." It then called for disbarring all attorneys who "clam up on Communism under the Fifth Amendment." January 31, 1958.

38. *In re Isserman*, 35 N.J. 198, 200–3 (1961).

39. *Ibid.*, p. 204.

40. New York Field Office to Hoover, July 22, 1960; New York Field Office to Hoover, July 29, 1960, ISSERMAN, FBI.

41. "Presentment of the Essex County Ethics Committee," *In re Isserman*, Supreme Court of New Jersey, No. D-12, September term, 1959.

42. Medina to Isserman, August 25, 1976; Isserman to Medina, July 7, August 31, 1976, Abraham J. Isserman Personal Papers. See reports of New York Field Office, February 4, 1965, March 11, 1971, April 6, 1972, ISSERMAN, FBI. The FBI had maintained surveillance on Isserman for approximately thirty years.

43. Crockett Interview, May 24, 1979; "Report of Investigation of Summary Contempt Citation against George W. Crockett, Jr." (Detroit, 1950); Crockett to Medina, March 8, 1954, Medina Papers, Princeton University.

44. Crockett Interview, May 24, 1979; *In the Matter of George W. Crockett, Jr.*, Misc. 80579, Michigan Circuit Court, Wayne County, November 12, 1954. Crockett later was elected to the Recorder's Court and gained national notoriety when he granted bail to those arrested in a 1969 Detroit riot. Following the riot, the New York *Times* observed that Crockett was "considered the finest expert on the Constitution on the Detroit bench." Curiously, the newspaper ignored Crockett's Foley Square experience. But Crockett remembered it well. After granting bail to the rioters, Crockett commented: "I know

. . . what it means when a judge says one year, two years, three years. I don't want to wish it on any of my associates, but I think it would do them some good if they would spend some time in jail." New York *Times*, April 1, 1969. Crockett was elected to Congress in 1980.

45. A. H. Belmont to D. M. Ladd, March 20, 1950; Hoover to New York and San Francisco Field Offices, March 20, 1950, ISSERMAN, FBI.

46. Gladstein Interview, August 19, 1978.

47. *In the Matter of Richard Gladstein*, Order to Show Cause, U.S.D.C. (Hawaii). M. C. Symonds to Benjamin Dreyfus, October 7, 8, 16, 1952, GLADSTEIN OF. Symonds was Gladstein's local counsel for the McLaughlin proceedings; Dreyfus was Gladstein's counsel for the state bar disciplinary investigation.

48. Symonds Memorandum of Conference with McLaughlin, June 18, 1953, *ibid.* Affidavit of Richard Gladstein of Personal Bias and Prejudice (November 1, 1954). Honolulu *Advertiser*, June 20, 1953. The presiding judge in the Smith Act trial, incidentally, praised Gladstein's conduct.

49. Symonds to Gladstein, October 22, 27, 1954, GLADSTEIN OF.

50. *Gladstein* v. *McLaughlin* (9th C.C.A.), Order, January 31, 1955; *Gladstein* v. *McLaughlin*, 230 F. 2d 762 (9th C.C.A. 1955).

51. *Ibid.*, p. 763.

52. *Ibid.*

53. Andersen to Gladstein, August 15, 1952; Gladstein to Andersen, August 22, 1952; State Supreme Court Justice Jesse W. Carter to Herbert Resner, October 24, 1951; Gladstein Memorandum, September 30, 1952, GLADSTEIN OF.

54. Frank Gordon to State Bar of California, October 27, 1949, Isserman File, Association of the Bar of the City of New York. Gordon periodically corresponded with bar groups in California, Michigan, and Pennsylvania regarding disciplinary proceedings against the Foley Square trial lawyers. Gordon had assisted in the prosecution of the Smith Act case. He later took over direction of the disciplinary actions against Sacher and Isserman. Benjamin Dreyfus Interview, December 28, 1978. Dreyfus to Jerrold Weil (Secretary, California State Bar), October 20, 1952; Weil to Dreyfus, October 23, 1952; Dreyfus to Weil, October 23, 1952; Weil to Dreyfus, November 19, 1952, GLADSTEIN OF.

55. Dreyfus Interview, December 28, 1978. Dana to Andersen, August 3, 1953, GLADSTEIN OF.

56. Dreyfus Interview, December 28, 1978; Gladstein Interview, August 19, 1978. Reply Brief on Behalf of Gladstein, July 7, 1954; Amicus Curiae Brief (In Behalf of Gladstein), GLADSTEIN OF.

57. Hearn to Farraher, June 23, 1954, *ibid.* Clark, "Why the Reds Won't Scare Us," *Look*, August 30, 1949, p. 52.

58. Reply Brief, July 7, 1954. Gladstein to Dreyfus, n.d., GLADSTEIN OF.

59. State Bar of California to Gladstein, October 23, 1956; Gladstein to I. M. Peckham, October 25, 1956, *ibid.*

60. E. Blythe Statson, "Disciplining Subversive Members of the Bar," *Michigan State Bar Journal* (1951), 30:16.

61. The contemporary literature by Guild members and the ABA actions are well treated in Alexander Milnor, "The Right to Counsel for the Politically Unpopular," *Law in Transition* (Spring 1962), 22:19–45. Also see Auerbach, *Unequal Justice*, pp. 237–40; Belknap, *Cold War Political Justice*, pp. 219–22. Government persecution remained a fact of life in the 1950s, as witnessed by a nearly decade-old attempt by the Justice Department to formally list the Guild as subversive.

62. "The Independence of the Bar," *Lawyers Guild Review* (1953), 13:158, 161;

Schware v. *Board of Bar Examiners,* 353 U.S. 232 (1957); *Konigsberg* v. *State Bar of California,* 353 U.S. 252 (1957); *Konigsberg* v. *State Bar of California,* 366 U.S. 36 (1961); *Schlesinger* v. *Musmanno,* 367 Pa. 476 (1957); *In re Schlesinger,* 404 Pa. 584 (1961); *In re Sawyer,* 360 U.S. 622 (1959); *Scheiner* v. *State,* 80 So. 2d 657 (Fla. 1955).

63. *In re Hallinan,* 43 Cal. 2d 343 (1954); *In re Gilliland,* 248 N.C. 517 (1958).

64. Belknap, *Cold War Political Justice,* pp. 152–84, 220–31; Charles Alan Wright, "Right to Counsel and Counsels' Rights," *The Nation* (November 21, 1953), 177:426–28. Arthur Freund, chairman of the ABA's Section of Criminal Law, acknowledged the widespread sentiment "that no lawyer of standing" could afford to represent Communist defendants "because of the damage which would be done to his reputation." Arthur J. Freund to William T. Gossett, November 26, 1952, FRANKFURTER, HLS.

65. The case was *United States* v. *Mitchell,* 354 F. 2d 767, 769 (1966), one of the first draft-resistance trials of the Vietnam War. Also see Eugene V. Rostow, "The Lawyer and His Client," *American Bar Association Journal* (1962), 48:146, and particularly Auerbach, *Unequal Justice,* Chapter 9, for more ominous developments.

CHAPTER 7

1. Robert Griffith, *The Politics of Fear: Joseph R. McCarthy and the Senate* (Lexington, Ky., 1970), p. 76 n.; Joseph Alsop, "The Strange Case of Louis Budenz," *Atlantic Monthly* (April 1952), 189:30. For a China Lobby view of Lattimore, see John T. Flynn, *The Lattimore Story* (New York, 1953). Irving Kristol, "Ordeal by Mendacity," *The Twentieth Century* (October 1952), 152:315–23, epitomizes the "liberal anti-Communist" view of the period.

2. *Current Biography,* December 1945, pp. 29–31. The diplomatic dispatch is quoted in Warren I. Cohen, *America's Response to China: An Interpretative History of Sino-American Relations* (New York, 1971), p. 170.

3. Owen Lattimore, *Solution in Asia* (Boston, 1945), pp. 207, 23–24, 69, 199, 92, 109, 120–22, 191.

4. Owen Lattimore, *The Situation in Asia* (Boston, 1949), pp. 141–43, 177–81. David Caute, *The Great Fear* (New York, 1978), p. 318.

5. Max Eastman and J. B. Powell, "The Fate of the World Is at Stake in China," *Reader's Digest* (June 1945), 46:13–22; Washington *Times-Herald,* June 6, 1946. Lattimore's criticism of the traditional Japanese political and social system exposed him to attack as Japan increasingly became attached to American geopolitical strategy.

6. Warren I. Cohen, "The China Lobby," in Alexander DeConde (ed.), *Encyclopedia of American Foreign Policy* (New York, 1978), 1:104–10; Charles Wertenbaker, "The World of Alfred Kohlberg," *The Reporter* (April 29, 1952), 6:19–22.

7. A persuasive account of the American reaction to the new Chinese Communist regime is by Warren I. Cohen, "Acheson, His Advisers, and China, 1949–1950," in Dorothy Borg and Waldo Heinrichs (eds.), *Uncertain Years: Chinese-American Relations, 1947–1950.* Ronald Steel's qualifications of Cohen's thesis is in *ibid.,* pp. 54–55. For a more critical account of the Truman administration's political ineptitude, see Thomas G. Patterson, "If Europe, Why Not China? The Containment Doctrine, 1947–49," *Prologue* (Spring 1981), 13:19–38.

8. Acheson's transmittal letter is reprinted in *State Department Loyalty Investigation, Report* of the Committee on Foreign Relations, U.S. Senate, 81 Cong., 2 Sess. (July 20, 1950), pp. 241–48. Hereafter cited as *Tydings Report.* Warren I. Cohen, *Dean Rusk* (Totowa, N.J., 1980), p. 66, contends that Rusk used his remarks to "shame" the Chinese

Communists into behaving as nationalists. Acheson's response to the military is cited in Allen S. Whiting, "China, America, and the Korean War," *Reviews in American History* (December 1981), 9:551. For a discussion of the ambiguities in the transmittal letter and Acheson's role, see Robert P. Newman, "Truman's Self-Inflicted Wound: The China White Paper of 1949," *Prologue* (Fall 1982).

9. For the history of the *Amerasia* case, see *State Department Loyalty Investigation, Hearings* of the Committee on Foreign Relations, U.S. Senate, 81 Cong., 2 Sess., pp. 923–1453. Hereafter cited as *Tydings Hearings.* John S. Service, *The Amerasia Papers: Some Problems in the History of U.S.-China Relations* (Berkeley, 1971), offers an account of the case by one of the accused and some of the "China Hands" who eventually were dismissed from the State Department. The Senate Internal Security Subcommittee prepared its own analysis of the case: *The Amerasia Papers: A Clue to the Catastrophe of China*, 2 vols., 91 Cong., 1 Sess. (Washington, D.C., 1970). For Jonkman's remarks, see *Congressional Record*, 80 Cong., 2 Sess. (August 2, 1948), pp. 9643–44. *Hearings,* Subcommittee on the Committee on Expenditures in the Executive Departments, 80 Cong., 2 Sess. (March 10 and 12, 1948), pp. 1–120, *passim. Hearings,* Subcommittee of the House Committee on Appropriations, 80 Cong., 2 Sess. (January 28, 29, 1948), pp. 169–210. Also see *Report* of *ibid.* (February 27, 1948), pp. 3–4.

10. *Tydings Report,* pp. 2–4. Griffith, *Politics of Fear,* pp. 45–57; Richard Rovere, *Senator Joe McCarthy* (Meridian ed., New York, 1960), pp. 125–40.

11. Griffith, *Politics of Fear,* p. 75. *Tydings Hearings* (March 8, 1950), p. 14.

12. *Ibid.* (March 13, 1950), pp. 92, 104.

13. *Ibid.* (March 21, 1950), pp. 278–85. Griffith, *Politics of Fear,* pp. 77–78.

14. Owen Lattimore, *Ordeal by Slander* (Boston, 1950), pp. 3–28.

15. *Tydings Hearings* (April 6, 1950), pp. 418–20, 424–30, 465–66.

16. *Ibid.,* pp. 463, 467–68, 485. Three years later an exasperated President Eisenhower found South Korean President Rhee "an unsatisfactory ally" and said he would have abandoned Rhee if it would not have left Japan so badly exposed. Robert H. Ferrell (ed.), *The Eisenhower Diaries* (New York, 1981), p. 248.

17. *Tydings Hearings,* pp. 424, 484.

18. *Ibid.* (April 20, 1950), pp. 487–557. Louis F. Budenz, "The Menace of Red China," *Collier's* (March 19, 1949), 123:23. For a critical account of Budenz as a professional informant and witness, see Herbert L. Packer, *Ex-Communist Witnesses* (Stanford, 1962), pp. 121–77. Also see Louis Francis Budenz, *This Is My Story* (New York, 1947); Louis F. Budenz, *Men Without Faces: The Communist Conspiracy in the U.S.A.* (New York, 1950).

19. *Tydings Hearings,* pp. 737–96 (Utley), 631–59 (Dodd), 799–921 (Lattimore).

20. A. H. Belmont to D. M. Ladd, March 28, 1950; H. H. Clegg to Clyde Tolson, April 6, 1950; Ladd to Hoover, April 10, 1950, December 30, 1952, Owen Lattimore File, Federal Bureau of Investigation. Used by permission of Owen Lattimore. Hereafter cited as LATTIMORE, FBI. There had been a brief FBI investigation of Lattimore in 1941. Charles Murray to Attorney General, January 27, 1953, Owen Lattimore File, Department of Justice. Hereafter cited as LATTIMORE, DOJ.

21. Hoover to Attorney General, April 11, 1950; Belmont to Ladd, April 11, 1950; L. C. Nulty to Belmont, April 17, 1950; Nichols to Tolson, April 11, 1950; Special Agent in Charge Whelan to Belmont, April 11, 1950, LATTIMORE, FBI. The White House at the time had access to a 1947 State Department investigation in which Budenz would not identify Lattimore as a Communist. Memorandum for Donald Dawson, Truman Papers, Official File, HST Library.

22. Hoover to Attorney General, April 11, 1950; Peyton Ford to Hoover, April 11, 1950, LATTIMORE, FBI.

23. *Tydings Report*, pp. 52–74.

24. Griffith, *Politics of Fear*, pp. 86–87, 125–31.

25. Gilman C. Ostrander, *Nevada: The Great Rotten Borough, 1859–1964* (New York, 1966), pp. 188–96; New York *Times*, September 29, 1954. Also see Alfred Steinberg, "McCarran: Lone Wolf of the Senate," *Harper's* (November 1950), 201:89–95.

26. *Institute of Pacific Relations, Hearings* of the Internal Security Subcommittee of the Committee on the Judiciary, U.S. Senate, 82 Cong., 1 Sess. (July 25, 1951), pp. 1–5. Hereafter cited as *McCarran Hearings*.

27. *Ibid.*, pp. 2898 ff., 2988, 3009, 3088, 3039–40, 3096. Lattimore's memoranda to Truman regarding China and Japan are in the Owen Lattimore File, Harry S. Truman Library. Hereafter cited as LATTIMORE, HST.

28. *McCarran Hearings*, pp. 181–222 (Alexander Barmine), 905–35 (Professor Kenneth Colegrove), 1035–75 (Harold Stassen), 3145–47, 276–88 (Karl Wittfogel). Also see pp. 3128–30, 3140.

29. *Ibid.*, pp. 1077–1110. Packer, *Ex-Communist Witnesses*, p. 171.

30. Harvey Matusow, *False Witness* (New York, 1955), pp. 104, 106.

31. Special Agent in Charge, New York, to Hoover, October 24, 1951, LATTIMORE, FBI.

32. *McCarran Hearings*, pp. 2947, 3123–29, 2953–55.

33. *Ibid.*, pp. 2953–63, 3382–3400, 3465, 3469–70. Packer, *Ex-Communist Witnesses*, pp. 121–77. Thurman Arnold, *Fair Fights and Foul* (New York, 1961), p. 216. Gene M. Gressley (ed.), *Voltaire and the Cowboy: The Letters of Thurman Arnold* (Boulder, 1977), p. 399. For the ordeal of another China expert before the McCarran committee, see Gary May, *China Scapegoat: The Ordeal of John Carter Vincent* (Washington, D.C., 1979), pp. 212 ff.

34. *Institute of Pacific Relations, Report* of the Internal Security Subcommittee, 82 Cong., 2 Sess. (July 2, 1952), pp. 223–26 *et passim*. Hereafter cited as *McCarran Report*. With some truth, the Washington *Post* charged that the McCarran committee had produced "a revision of history, a revision compounded out of McCarthian bigotry, McCarranesque spleen and MacArthurian legend. It is an attempt to perpetuate another fraud and hoax on the American people." July 4, 1952. No charges were brought against Davies.

35. *Nomination of James P. McGranery, Hearings*, Senate Committee on the Judiciary, 82 Cong., 2 Sess. (May 5, 6, 7, 8, 1952), pp. 8 ff., 25. Arnold, *Fair Fights and Foul*, p. 217. Truman to McGranery, July 5, 1982; McGranery to Truman, July 16, 1952, LATTIMORE, HST.

36. Special Agent in Charge, Baltimore, to Hoover, September 29, October 11, 1950; M. A. Jones to Nichols, September 6, 1951; Special Agent in Charge, Baltimore, to Hoover, April 24, 1952; Ladd to Hoover, May 6, 1952, LATTIMORE, FBI.

37. The Hummer memorandum is in the form of a letter from William Foley (Internal Security Section, DOJ) to James M. McInerney (Criminal Division), June 17, 1952, LATTIMORE, DOJ. Also see Charles Murray to Attorney General, January 27, 1953, for a later explanation of Hummer's memo, *ibid.* A partial copy of the McCarran staff analysis of Hummer's memo, January 23, 1953, is in the FBI file. Hummer has a modest reputation as the man who leaked FBI files on Alger Hiss to Father John Cronin, who, in turn, briefed Richard Nixon on Hiss. Fawn Brodie, *Richard Nixon* (New York, 1981), p. 201.

38. *Hearings*, H.R. Special Subcommittee to Investigate the Department of Justice, 80

Cong., 2 Sess. (December 29–31, 1952), pp. 1579–1812; *Time* (March 22, 1954), 63:23; Richard H. Rovere, "The Adventures of Cohn and Schine," *The Reporter* (July 21, 1953), 9:9–16; Howard Rushmore, "Young Mr. Cohn," *The American Mercury* (February 1953), 76:67–74.

39. Laughlin to Belmont, May 2, 1952; W. A. Branigan to Belmont, September 4, 18, 1952; Belmont to Ladd, September 19, 1952; Boardman to Hoover, September 22, 1952; Belmont to Ladd, October 1, 1952, LATTIMORE, FBI.

40. New York *Times*, October 4, 1952. Murray to Attorney General, January 27, 1953, LATTIMORE, DOJ. Cleveland to Belmont, November 28, 1952, LATTIMORE, FBI. Hummer's October memo has not been released.

41. Ladd to Hoover, December 1, 1952, *ibid.*

42. Murray to Attorney General, January 27, 1953, LATTIMORE, DOJ. Branigan to Belmont, December 4, 1952; Belmont to Ladd, December 10, 11, 1952; Branigan to Belmont, December 8, 1952, LATTIMORE, FBI.

43. Foley to Murray, December 23, 1952; Murray to Foley and Whearty, December 29, 1952, LATTIMORE, DOJ.

44. Murray to Foley, January 19, 1953, *ibid.* Nichols to Tolson, January 19, 1953; Branigan to Belmont, January 30, 1953; Nichols to Tolson, January 26, 1953; Branigan to Belmont, January 26, 1953; Ladd to Hoover, January 30, 1953; Belmont to Ladd, February 2, 1953; Nichols to Tolson, February 2, 1953; Hoover to Attorney General, February 4, 1953, LATTIMORE, FBI.

45. *Hearings* (Brownell Nomination), Senate Committee on the Judiciary, 83 Cong., 1 Sess. (January 19, 1953), p. 4.

46. Ladd to Hoover, February 24, 1953; C. E. Hennrich to Belmont, March 6, 1953; Belmont to Ladd, March 10, 1953; Hennrich to Belmont, March 13, 1953; Nichols to Tolson, March 17, 1953, LATTIMORE, FBI.

47. New York *Times*, July 6, 8, 9, August 22, 1951. *National Encyclopedia of American Biography* (New York, 1960), 1:405–6.

48. *United States* v. *Lattimore*, 112 F. Supp. 507, 515–19, 519–20 (1953).

49. New York *Times*, May 3, 1953; Washington *Post*, May 4, 1953.

50. Belmont to Ladd, May 6, 1953; Hoover to Special Agent in Charge, Baltimore, August 25, 1953, LATTIMORE, FBI.

51. J. F. Wacks to Branigan, September 18, 1953; Belmont to Ladd, December 31, 1953; Branigan to Belmont, January 7, 1954; Wacks to Branigan, April 5, 1954; Special Agent in Charge, New York, to Hoover, June 9, 1953, *ibid.* For a fuller explanation of Hoover's caution, see Robert P. Newman, "Bureaucrats as Heroes: The FBI in the Age of McCarthy," *Pitt* (February 1982).

52. Wacks to Branigan, May 11, 1954, LATTIMORE, FBI. *United States* v. *Lattimore*, 215 F. 2d 847 (D.C. Cir. 1954). Hoover to Special Agents in Charge, July 9, 1954; R. R. Raoch to Belmont, July 14, 1954; Wacks to Branigan, July 15, 1954, LATTIMORE, FBI. Rover to Simon Sobeloff (Solicitor General), July 16, 1954, LATTIMORE, DOJ. Branigan to Belmont, August 18, 1954, LATTIMORE, FBI.

53. New York *Times*, October 8, 1954. Arnold, *Fair Fights and Foul*, pp. 222–24.

54. Branigan to Belmont, October 22, 1954, LATTIMORE, FBI.

55. *United States* v. *Lattimore*, 125 F. Supp. 295 (1954). Branigan to Belmont, October 27, November 15, 1954, LATTIMORE, FBI.

56. New York *Times*, September 29, October 30, November 3, 21, 24, 1954. Branigan to Belmont, November 10, 23, 1954; Nichols to Tolson, November 23, 1954; Branigan to Belmont, November 24, 1954, LATTIMORE, FBI.

57. Arnold, *Fair Fights and Foul*, pp. 224–26; Gressley, *Voltaire and the Cowboy*, pp. 411–12. The Washington *Post* assailed Rover for having "demeaned his office." October 14, 1954.

58. Hoover to Special Agent in Charge, Washington, January 7, 1955; Hennrich to Belmont, January 15, 1955; Belmont to Boardman, January 17, 1955; Hoover to Tompkins, January 18, 1955, LATTIMORE, FBI.

59. *United States* v. *Lattimore*, 127 F. Supp. 405 410, 409–12, 413 (1955).

60. Belmont to Boardman, January 18, 1955; Branigan to Belmont, January 20, 1955; Belmont to Boardman, February 3, 1955; Hoover to Tompkins, February 7, 1955; Hennrich to Belmont, February 4, 1955, LATTIMORE, FBI. *United States* v. *Lattimore*, 232 F. 2d 334 (1955).

61. Branigan to Belmont, June 28, 1955, LATTIMORE, FBI. New York *Times*, June 29, 1955. It was not a good year for perjury charges against alleged Communists. The government lost three such cases during 1954–55. *Annual Report of the Attorney General* (1955), pp. 49–50.

62. *McCarran Report*, p. 215.

63. Professor Robert Newman, who has worked extensively with the Lattimore materials, has estimated the costs. Newman to author, December 26, 1981. As of 1982, the Arnold & Porter firm still represented Lattimore *pro bono* in his efforts to gain access to his various case files.

64. Philip J. Jaffe, *The Rise and Fall of American Communism* (New York, 1975), p. 57. Jaffe was active in the IPR and pleaded guilty after he was indicted in the *Amerasia* case. His book offers some interesting insights into the nature of leftist politics in the 1930s and 1940s. The Lattimore affair provoked an interesting sideshow among liberals on the issue of fellow travelers. After the *New Republic* published a lengthy critique of McCarran's influence and the indictment, Sol Stein replied on behalf of the American Committee for Cultural Freedom—later revealed to have been subsidized by the CIA. Stein defended the indictment and the McCarran committee's conclusions. Stein's letter prompted the resignation of prominent liberals from the Committee for Cultural Freedom. See Brian Gilbert (pseud.), "New Light on the Lattimore Case," *New Republic* (December 27, 1954), 131:7; "A Communication," *ibid.* (February 14, 1955), 132:20; "Correspondence," *ibid.* (February 28, 1955), 132:20. For another critical liberal view, see *The New Leader*'s March 1952 supplement on Lattimore and the IPR that paralleled the McCarran hearings.

CHAPTER 8

1. Harry S. Truman, *Memoirs* (New York, 1956), 2:316–464; Douglas MacArthur, *Reminiscences* (New York, 1964), pp. 334–96; Allen S. Whiting, *China Crosses the Yalu* (New York, 1960), pp. 116–72; William W. Strueck, Jr., *The Road to Confrontation: American Policy Toward China and Korea, 1947–1950* (Chapel Hill, N.C., 1981). For the basic criticism of official accounts of the origin of the war, see I. F. Stone, *The Hidden History of the Korean War* (New York, 1952, 1969). Stephen E. Ambrose, *Rise to Globalism* (Penguin Books, Baltimore, 1976), pp. 195–97, well summarizes the complex events.

2. New York *Times*, February 25, March 2, 4, 5, 25, April 3, 4, May 5, 6, 14, June 8, 21, July 1, August 5, 1952. John Cookson and Judith Nottingham, *A Survey of Chemical and Biological Warfare* (London, 1969), p. 63. Support for the Chinese charges came in

the *Report of the International Scientific Commission for the Investigation of the Facts Concerning Bacterial Warfare in Korea and China* (Peking, 1952). For a pro-Communist journalistic effort, see Wilfred G. Burchett, *This Monstrous War* (Melbourne, 1953), pp. 306–26. John C. Clews, *Communist Propaganda Techniques* (London, 1964), pp. 179–268, vigorously argues that the germ warfare charges were nothing more than a propaganda contrivance.

3. John B. Powell, *My Twenty-five Years in China* (New York, 1945); Irving Dilliard, "John Benjamin Powell," *Dictionary of American Biography* (Supplement, 1946–50), 4:678–80; J. B. Powell, "I Was a Prisoner of the Japanese," *Reader's Digest* (November 1942), 4:63–66; Max Eastman and J. B. Powell, "The Fate of the World Is at Stake in China," *ibid.* (June 1945), 46:13–22.

4. John W. Powell Interview, July 27, 1981.

5. *China Weekly Review* (August 6, 1949), 114:182. Hereafter cited as *CWR*. Powell Interview, July 27, 1981.

6. Passport Refusal, September 28, 1949; J. R. Geele to Travis Fletcher, March 13, 1950; William J. Supple to Spencer S. Beman, March 27, 1950; Robert C. Coudray to Robert V. Haig, August 25, 1950, Powell File, Passport Division, Department of State. Hereafter cited as POWELL, PD.

7. *CWR* (August 5, 1950), 118:164.

8. *Ibid.* (July 8, 1950), 118:94–95; *China Monthly Review* (January 1951), 119:3; (February 1951), 119:79; (May 1951), 119:219; (September 1951), 120:115; (December 1951), 120:276–77. Hereafter cited as *CMR*. Alf E. Bergesen, Memoranda of Conversations with John W. Powell, August 31, 1953, Powell File, Department of State. Hereafter cited as POWELL, DOS.

9. *CMR* (March 1952), 122:229–30, 226.

10. *Ibid.* (April 1952), 122:328; (June 1952), 122:562–63; (May 1952), 122:424, 426; (August 1952), 123:195–96.

11. *Ibid.* (June 1953), 124:2–3, 117; (July 1953), 124:10, 132. Powell Interview, July 27, 1981.

12. Memo to Director, CIA, June 25, 1953, Powell File, CIA. Dulles to Tokyo Embassy, July 21, 1953; Shipley to Glenn F. Weymuller, July 22, 1953, POWELL, PD. George Gillion to Captain J. D. Cox, July 31, 1953, Powell File, Army Intelligence Command, Fort George Meade, Maryland. Hereafter cited as POWELL, ARMY. McKillop to Dulles, August 10, 1953, POWELL, PD.

13. Stephen C. Worster (Rome Embassy) to Department of State, August 28, 1953; Frederick W. Hinke to Ruth B. Shipley, September 24, 1953, POWELL, DOS. Hoover to Special Agent in Charge, Washington, July 8, 1953, Powell File, Federal Bureau of Investigation. Hereafter cited as POWELL, FBI. Powell Interview, July 27, 1981.

14. FBI summaries of October 16 and 23, 1953, in Flinn to Shipley, February 4, 1954, POWELL, DOS.

15. Portland *Oregonian*, September 9, 1953. Powell Interview, July 27, 1981.

16. Olney to Hoover, April 13, 1954, POWELL, FBI. Olney suggested another avenue for prosecution. Powell reportedly had been contacting West Coast businessmen about the possibility of trade with China. If he had done so at the request or direction of persons outside the United States, his activities might constitute a violation of the Foreign Agents Registration Act.

17. Special Agent in Charge, Washington, Report, June 25, 1954; Special Agent in

Charge, Washington, to Hoover, July 15, 1954; W. A. Branigan to A. H. Belmont, July 27, 1954, POWELL, FBI. "Special Operations in North Korea," March 17, 1951, Report No. TB-1005-51, Department of Defense. Hereafter cited as "Sams Report."

18. Special Agent in Charge, Washington, to Hoover, March 13, 1956, POWELL, FBI.

19. John W. Powell, "A Hidden Chapter in History," *Bulletin of the Atomic Scientists* (October 1981), 37:44; John W. Powell, "Japan's Germ Warfare: The U.S. Cover-up of a War Crime," *Bulletin of Concerned Asian Scholars* (October–December 1980), 12:16. Special Agent in Charge, Washington, to Hoover, March 13, 1956; Hoover to Tompkins, March 21, 1956, POWELL, FBI. Philip R. Piccigallo, *The Japanese on Trial* (Austin, 1979), pp. 143–57, typically dismisses the Soviet trials of the Japanese BW units as nothing more than a propaganda exercise.

20. *Hearings,* Senate Committee on the Judiciary, Internal Security Subcommittee, 83 Cong., 2 Sess. (September 27, 1954), pp. 1822–30, 1830–48.

21. *Ibid.,* pp. 1848–1904, 1904–77, 2018. New York *Times,* September 29, 1954. The committee counsel, Alva C. Carpenter, had played a significant role in suppressing the evidence of Japanese complicity in BW during the Tokyo war crimes trials in 1946. Powell, "Japan's Germ Warfare," pp. 8, 17.

22. *Hearings,* Internal Security Subcommittee (December 13, 1954), pp. 2162–95, 2246–47, 2241–42.

23. *Administration of the Internal Security Laws, Report,* U.S. Senate Committee on the Judiciary, Internal Security Subcommittee, 83 Cong., 2 Sess. (January 3, 1955), pp. 50–71.

24. Tompkins to Jenner, December 15, 1954; Tompkins to Hoover, January 14, 1955, Powell File, Department of Justice. Hereafter cited as POWELL, DOJ.

25. Julian Schuman, *China: An Uncensored Look* (Sagaponack, N.Y., 1979), pp. 1–15. *Hearings,* Internal Security Subcommittee, 84 Cong., 2 Sess. (March 21, 1956), pp. 515–49.

26. Tompkins to Hoover, September 7, 29, December 18, 1955, POWELL, FBI. *United States* v. *Pelley,* 132 F. 2d 170 (1942).

27. 1 Stat. 596. Zechariah Chafee, Jr., *Free Speech in the United States* (Cambridge, Mass., 1948), pp. 27–30; Leonard W. Levy, *Legacy of Suppression* (Torchbook ed., New York, 1963), pp. xvii–xix, 249–309 *passim.*

28. 12 Stat. 284. 35 Stat. 1089, ch. 321, Sec. 6 (now 18 U.S.C. Section 2384).

29. 40 Stat. 219; 40 Stat. 553.

30. Paul L. Murphy, *The Meaning of Freedom of Speech* (Westport, Conn., 1972), pp. 59–100; Paul L. Murphy, *World War I and the Origin of Civil Liberties in the United States* (New York, 1979); William Preston, Jr., *Aliens and Dissenters: Federal Suppression of Radicals, 1903–1933* (Cambridge, Mass., 1963), pp. 181–276. Among the most important Supreme Court cases setting forth doctrine in this period are *Schenck* v. *United States,* 249 U.S. 47 (1919); *Abrams* v. *United States,* 250 U.S. 616 (1919); *Pierce* v. *United States,* 252 U.S. 239 (1920). For the repeal, see 41 Stat. 1359.

31. *Hartzel* v. *United States,* 322 U.S. 680 (1944).

32. *United States* v. *Pelley,* 132 F. 2d 170 (1942); 318 U.S. 764 (1942) (certiorari denied). Also see *United States* v. *Bell,* 48 F. Supp. 986 (D.C. S.D. Calif. 1943); 159 F. 2d 247 (9th C.C.A. 1946); *Fiedler* v. *Shuttleworth,* 57 F. Supp. 591 (D.C. W.D. Pa. 1944) (habeas corpus); *United States* v. *Gordon,* 138 F. 2d 174 (7th C.C.A. 1943); *Butler* v. *United States,* 138 F. 2d 977 (7th C.C.A. 1943); *Couchois* v. *United States,* 142 F. 2d 1 (5th C.C.A. 1944); *United States* v. *Guido,* 161 F. 2d 492 (3rd C.C.A. 1947).

33. Indictment, *United States* v. *Powell.* San Francisco *Chronicle,* April 26, 1956; Gene

Marine, "Sedition or Press Freedom?" *The Nation* (February 10, 1957), 124:136–38.

34. *United States* v. *Powell,* 156 F. Supp. 526 (1957). Wirin's original requests are in letters to Frances Knight, November 8 and December 8, 1956; Robert D. Johnson to File, January 6, 1958, A. L. Wirin File, Passport Division, Department of State. Hereafter cited as WIRIN, PD. William J. Sebald to William Tompkins, January 31, 1957; Loftus E. Becker to Dulles, December 10, 1957, POWELL, DOS, summarize the State Department's perception of Chinese motivations. Dulles to Hong Kong Consul, January 18, 1958, *ibid.*

35. Ashley J. Nicholas to John M. Raymond, January 17, 1957; Frances G. Knight to William Tompkins, January 24, 1957; Willis H. Young to Scott McLeod, January 29, 1957; Tompkins to Knight, February 3, 1957, WIRIN, PD. Loftus E. Becker to Tompkins, September 27, 1957; Walter S. Robertson to Tompkins, November 21, 1957, POWELL, DOS, reflect the State Department's desire to pursue the prosecution.

36. *In re Petition of John W. Powell et al.,* 260 F. 2d 159 (9th C.C.A. 1958). J. Walter Yeagley (Internal Security Division) to Lawrence E. Walsh (Deputy Attorney General), November 5, 1958, POWELL, DOJ. Wirin summarized the evidence he secured in China in a memorandum to Judge Goodman, undated, POWELL, DOS. Memorandum of Conversation with Wirin, April 1, 1958; Walter Robertson to William Knowland, April 8, 1958, *ibid.*

37. Yeagley to Walsh, November 5, 1958, POWELL, DOJ, summarizes the government's problems and responses. Allen S. Whiting, "What Nixon Must Do to Make Friends in Peking," *New York Review of Books* (October 7, 1971), 17:10–15, discusses American support for espionage, sabotage, and guerrilla activities on the mainland.

38. Memo for Record, Maj. Francis A. Tenore (Censorship Section), November 3, 1958; Central Records Facility Summary, September 9, 1958; "Discussion of Legal and Policy Implications," c. October 1958, POWELL, ARMY. Memorandum of Conversation, December 2, 1958 (representatives of State, Defense, and Justice Departments), POWELL, DOS.

39. "Sams Report." Hoover to Tompkins, December 4, 1958, POWELL, FBI. Col. C. E. Straight to Chief of Staff, November 26, 1958; Maj. Francis Tenore, "Sanitization of the Sams Report," n.d.; "Classification of the Sams Reports," n.d., POWELL, ARMY. The Tenore summary noted the following deletion from the "Sams Report": "We had already made plans that if detailed interrogation of these agents who had seen the cases did not clarify the diagnosis, then the party would proceed to the nearest hospital at Chilbro-ri. If the agent had found any cases in these hospitals which were accessible . . . then one or more of the cases would be knocked out by an intravenous morphine injection and the necessary examination made outside of the hospital and the laboratory materials obtained." The State Department offered no objections to releasing the report. John M. Raymond to Robert Dachert, December 23, 1958, POWELL, DOS.

40. *Newsweek,* April 9, 1951; Peter Kalischer, "Doctor Commando," *Collier's,* September 22, 1951, pp. 28, 60–61. Powell's discussion of the Sams mission for which he was indicted on several counts appeared in *CMR* (March 1952), 122:226.

41. Transcript, *United States* v. *Powell et al.* (January 9, 1959), pp. 1–45. Also see *Memorandum in Support of Motions to Quash and Modify, ibid.*

42. Transcript, *ibid.,* pp. 1–180, 341–49.

43. *Ibid.,* pp. 350–63.

44. *Ibid.,* pp. 464–70. San Francisco *Chronicle,* January 31, 1959. *United States* v. *Powell et al.,* 171 F. Supp. 202 (1959).

45. Transcript, *United States* v. *Powell et al.,* pp. 470–73; Oakland *Tribune,* January 31, 1959.

46. *Report of the Attorney General,* 1959, p. 249; *ibid.,* 1961, pp. 256–57.

47. Powell Interview, July 27, 1981. Powell, "A Hidden Chapter"; Powell, "Japan's Germ Warfare."

48. See, for example, Whiting, "What Nixon Must Do," *passim.* After Nixon's trip to China, he acknowledged that some Americans held captive in China actually were CIA agents. New York *Times,* February 1, 1973.

49. Special Agent in Charge, Washington, to Hoover, March 13, 1956, POWELL, FBI, mentioned the Japanese activities. Formal acknowledgment came in "Biological Testing Involving Human Subjects by the Department of Defense," *Hearings,* Senate Subcommittee on Health and Scientific Research, 95 Cong., 1 Sess. (March 8, 1977), p. 10. Powell, "A Hidden Chapter," *passim.* Shortly after Powell published his findings of experiments on American POWs, amply supported by documentary evidence, the Army's CBW unit vehemently denied the charges. *People,* January 11, 1982, p. 108. At the same time, the Reagan administration was contemplating significant expansion of American CBW capability. See, for example, David H. Morrissey, "The Return of Chemical Warfare," *The Progressive* (February 1982), pp. 25–28.

50. *Hearings,* Senate Select Committee on Intelligence Activities, 94 Cong., 1 Sess. (September 16, 1975), p. 24. Memorandum of Conversation, December 2, 1958, POWELL, DOS.

51. *Hearings,* "Biological Testing," pp. 10 ff., 36–39, 141 ff., 264 ff. *Final Report,* Senate Select Committee on Intelligence Activities, 94 Cong., 2 Sess. (April 26, 1976), pp. 385–422. New York *Times,* June 11, July 19, September 9, 1975; July 16, 1977.

52. Justice Department documents, finally released in May 1982, confirm that throughout 1959–60 the State Department pressed for a retrial on the sedition charges or bringing the case to court on treason indictments.

EPILOGUE

1. E. P. Thompson, *Whigs and Hunters: The Origin of the Black Act* (New York, 1975), pp. 260, 263.

INDEX